Sustainable Development Goals Series

The **Sustainable Development Goals Series** is Springer Nature's inaugural cross-imprint book series that addresses and supports the United Nations' seventeen Sustainable Development Goals. The series fosters comprehensive research focused on these global targets and endeavours to address some of society's greatest grand challenges. The SDGs are inherently multidisciplinary, and they bring people working across different fields together and working towards a common goal. In this spirit, the Sustainable Development Goals series is the first at Springer Nature to publish books under both the Springer and Palgrave Macmillan imprints, bringing the strengths of our imprints together.

The Sustainable Development Goals Series is organized into eighteen subseries: one subseries based around each of the seventeen respective Sustainable Development Goals, and an eighteenth subseries, "Connecting the Goals", which serves as a home for volumes addressing multiple goals or studying the SDGs as a whole. Each subseries is guided by an expert Subseries Advisor with years or decades of experience studying and addressing core components of their respective Goal.

The SDG Series has a remit as broad as the SDGs themselves, and contributions are welcome from scientists, academics, policymakers, and researchers working in fields related to any of the seventeen goals. If you are interested in contributing a monograph or curated volume to the series, please contact the Publishers: Zachary Romano [Springer; zachary.romano@springer.com] and Rachael Ballard [Palgrave Macmillan; rachael.ballard@palgrave.com].

Ibrahim Nandom Yakubu
Editor

Banking on Inclusion

Overcoming Financial Exclusion in Africa through FinTech Innovations

palgrave
macmillan

Editor
Ibrahim Nandom Yakubu
School of Business
University for Development Studies
Tamale, Ghana

ISSN 2523-3084 ISSN 2523-3092 (electronic)
Sustainable Development Goals Series
ISBN 978-3-031-96715-3 ISBN 978-3-031-96716-0 (eBook)
https://doi.org/10.1007/978-3-031-96716-0

Cover illustration: Nicolay Pandev gettyimages

This Palgrave Macmillan imprint is published by the registered company Springer Nature Switzerland AG
The registered company address is: Gewerbestrasse 11, 6330 Cham, Switzerland

Introduction

Banking on Inclusion: Overcoming Financial Exclusion in Africa through FinTech Innovations explores one of the most urgent development challenges facing the African continent—financial exclusion—and how digital financial technologies (FinTech) are reshaping the pathways to inclusion. The COVID-19 pandemic acted as a pivotal turning point, accelerating the adoption of digital finance and exposing deep-seated vulnerabilities in traditional banking systems. This book responds to that global shock and the subsequent digital transformation by presenting a broad and integrative analysis of how technology, innovation, and policy are converging to expand financial access and build more inclusive financial ecosystems across Africa.

Financial exclusion in Africa is complex and multidimensional. While mobile money, digital wallets, and app-based services have extended access, millions of Africans—particularly women, rural populations, and informal workers—remain underserved. The book opens with a foundational examination of these challenges in Chapter 1, which sets the stage by exploring the causes, contours, and consequences of exclusion. It then moves through a series of sectoral and technological analyses, covering mobile money (Chapter 3), digital banking (Chapter 4), innovative lending models (Chapter 5), blockchain and decentralized finance (Chapter 6), and InsurTech (Chapter 7).

Chapters 2 and 8 frame the evolution of FinTech ecosystems in Africa, highlighting how digital platforms have empowered traditionally excluded groups and reshaped the savings and investment landscape. The chapters provide both a historical context and forward-looking perspectives, showing how entrepreneurship, mobile penetration, and digital innovation are enabling more inclusive financial systems. Across these discussions, FinTech is portrayed not as a silver bullet, but as a powerful tool whose effectiveness depends on enabling policies, consumer trust, infrastructure, and digital literacy.

The book also delves into critical enablers of inclusion beyond access—such as financial education (Chapter 9), cybersecurity and data protection (Chapter 10), and ethical finance through Islamic FinTech (Chapter 11). These chapters unpack the often-overlooked institutional and behavioral conditions necessary to sustain financial inclusion and build public confidence in digital tools.

Regulation and policy frameworks form another core strand. Chapters 12 and 13 examine the regulatory challenges of FinTech and the potential of public–private collaboration to extend inclusion. Regulatory innovation, harmonization, and capacity building are emphasized as essential for navigating rapid FinTech evolution without compromising consumer protection or systemic stability.

Finally, Chapter 14 draws the book to a close with a strategic vision for the future. It highlights the policy and institutional reforms necessary to bridge persistent gaps and ensure that digital financial innovations translate into meaningful economic empowerment. It advocates for a reimagined inclusion agenda—one that centers users, reflects diverse needs, and harnesses FinTech to build more equitable financial ecosystems.

Together, the chapters in this volume offer a comprehensive, multidisciplinary, and policy-relevant contribution to understanding and advancing financial inclusion in Africa. They provide a nuanced view of the opportunities and limitations of FinTech in addressing structural exclusion, especially in post-pandemic recovery and resilience. For scholars, policymakers, development practitioners, and FinTech innovators, this book serves as both a resource and a call to action: to move beyond access and toward impactful, secure, and sustainable inclusion.

Contents

Notes on Contributors

Mubarik Abdul Mumin is a Ph.D. candidate at the School of Business, University for Development Studies, Ghana. He holds an M.Phil. in Logistics and Supply Chain Management from Kwame Nkrumah University of Science and Technology, Ghana. Mubarik has published in renowned journals, including the Journal of Money and Business, Technological Sustainability, Cureus Journal of Business and Economics, and the Journal of Innovative Digital Transformation.

Abdallah Abdul-Salam is the Results, Learning, and Business Development Manager at the Centre for Active Learning and Integrated Development (CALID). He is currently a Ph.D. candidate at the University for Development Studies, Ghana. He holds an M.B.A. in Management Information Systems from SD Dombo University of Business and Integrated Development Studies, and a Bachelor of Commerce degree with a specialization in Accounting from the University for Development Studies. His research interests include Information Systems and Information and Communication Technology for Development (ICT4D), with a particular focus on e-government, platform governance, and digital transformation.

Abdul-Hamid Abdul-Wahab is a lecturer of Finance in the Department of Finance at the University for Development Studies' (UDS) School of Business. He is also the Head of Department (HOD) of Business Analytics and MIS in the same university. He holds a Ph.D. in Business Administration (finance), a Master of Science in finance and Bachelor of Business Administration (finance), all from the International Islamic University Malaysia (IIUM). Dr. Abdul-Wahab has over 10 years' work experience through his current role and previous roles at IIUM, Society for Worldwide Interbank Financial Telecommunication (SWIFT), and the Islamic Financial Services Board (IFSB) at the Central Bank of Malaysia. At the IFSB, for instance, he was involved in various projects collaborating with stakeholders from international financial institutions such as the World Bank, IMF, and Islamic Development Bank (IsDB). Specifically, he was involved in projects such as the Islamic Financial Services Industry (IFSI) Stability Reports, development of Islamic banking and capital markets regulation standards and case studies for Facilitating the Implementation of IFSB Standards (FIS) Workshops. He also participated in workshops on Core Principles for Islamic Finance Regulation (Banking Sector); Revised Capital Adequacy Standard for Institutions Offering Islamic Financial Services (IIFS); and Guidance Note on Quantitative Measures for Liquidity Risk Management. His research interests cover a wide range of aspects of sustainable finance and Islamic finance within the context of the Middle East and Africa. He is a member of the International Council of Islamic Finance Educators (ICIFE).

Joshua Yindenaba Abor is a Financial Economist, qualified Accountant, and Professor of Finance with expertise in development finance. A former Dean of the University of Ghana Business School, he holds a Ph.D. from Stellenbosch University and completed Ph.D. coursework at Harvard. He consults for Afreximbank and has held roles with IMF, ECOWAS Bank, and AERC. His research spans banking, monetary policy, FinTech, and trade. He is widely published, serves on multiple boards, and is a member of the Bank of Ghana's Monetary Policy Committee.

Ibrahim Osman Adam is Dean of the School of Business and Professor of Management Information Systems at the University for Development Studies. His research interests center on digital technologies within business and innovation. He focuses specifically on e-commerce, e-government, social media, and broader digital transformations and dedicates a significant portion of his research to understanding the intricate connections within the ICT4D (Information and Communication Technology for Development) value chain. Adam examines ICT readiness, access, use, and impact across diverse business and societal contexts. His academic credentials include a Ph.D. in Information Systems from the University of Ghana Business School, and dual master's degrees from the

London School of Economics and Political Science (LSE) and Henley Business School, University of Reading. Furthermore, he is a Chartered Accountant with the Institute of Chartered Accountants, Ghana.

Farihan Alhassan is a seasoned financial specialist with 20 years of experience in banking. He previously led the Business & Commercial Clients Unit at Stanbic Bank Ghana and was once the youngest regional manager at Barclays Bank. Known for his strategic leadership and people-centered approach, he has excelled in retail and business banking, operational management, and business transformation. Recently appointed to GCB Bank as the CEO, Farihan is committed to strengthening its leadership and advancing Ghana's banking sector through innovation and performance-driven solutions.

Simplice A. Asongu holds a Ph.D. from Oxford Brookes University and is the Lead Economist and Director of the African Governance and Development Institute in Cameroon. He is also an Adjunct Professor at the University of Cape Town and affiliated with several institutions across Africa and the UK as a supervisor and research associate. He serves as Associate Editor for key journals and specializes in inclusive economic development, ICTs, education, poverty reduction, and innovation policy, with extensive expertise in economic and social policy.

Eric Kofi Boadi is a Senior Lecturer and Head of the Accountancy Department at the Faculty of Business and Management Studies, Koforidua Technical University, Ghana. He holds a Ph.D. and is a member of the Institute of Chartered Accountants (ICA). His research interests focus on economic development and foreign capital flows, contributing to academic discourse and policy-oriented finance studies. He also mentors' students and supports institutional growth through his leadership and academic expertise

Alhassan Bunyaminu is currently a Senior lecturer at the University of Professional Studies, Accra and he was the Faculty Research Officer (Head of Research) for the Faculty of Accounting and Finance. He previously taught at the West End University College, Kasoa, Ghana, University of Applied Management (A German University, Ghana Campus) and City of Bristol College, Bristol, UK. He has over 30 publications in Star rated Journals. Bunyaminu holds a Ph.D. in Finance (Specialization in Financial Analytics) from the University of Central Nicaragua, European Programmes, Austria, and he is a Chartered Global Investment Analyst

(CGIA) from the Chartered Global Investment Institute, USA. He has Masters in Statistics and Management Science from University of the West of England, UK, and Bachelors of Science Degree (Hons) in Statistics from the Open University, UK. Bunyaminu is a local governance expert and offers consultancy and research services to Metropolitan, Municipal and District Assemblies (MMDAs) across Ghana and Sierra Leone. Bunyaminu is also a capacity building and training provider for public and private organizations in management and finance. He is also a motivational speaker and inspires the youth in secular and religious matters. Bunyaminu has published extensively in star-rated journals and serves as a reviewer of journals published by Emerald, Taylor & Francis, SAGE, and Springer and continues to mentor up and coming lecturers to attain greater heights in teaching and research.

Richard Stephens Cromwell is a researcher with a strong academic background and diverse expertise. He holds an M.Phil. in Finance, a B.Sc. in Banking and Finance, and is currently a Ph.D. candidate of petroleum and energy studies at the University of Cape Coast (UCC), Ghana. His research interests encompass banking, finance, economics, and petroleum and energy studies, reflecting a multidisciplinary approach to addressing complex economic and financial issues. Beyond academia, Kwame serves as a consultant in business and research, providing analytical support and strategic guidance to organizations and individuals across various sectors.

Gifty Ewurama Enchill is a Ph.D. Candidate at the University of Stellenbosch Business School. She has been part and also conducted a number of research projects including; 'Incentive/Reward Scheme for Literacy facilitators' (NFED/World Bank Research Project), 'The Stock Exchange in Ghana' (University of Leicester M.B.A. Research), 'Corporate Governance, Gender Diversity and Firm Performance' (University of Ghana M.Phil. Thesis research), and 'Women on Boards in Ghana' (University of Ghana Business School and International Finance Corporation Research Project). She has also co-authored a number of academic publications.

Stephanie Giamporcaro is a Full Professor of Sustainable Finance at KEDGE Business School with a Ph.D. from the University of Paris Cité. Her research blends sociology, organizational theory, and financial market studies, focusing on sustainable finance and its societal impacts. She has published in top journals and serves as section editor for the Journal of Business Ethics. Stéphanie actively shares her work through media and forums and has supervised over 50 theses on ESG, SRI, Impact Investing, and Responsible FinTech.

Felix Owusu Gyebi is a Lecturer at the Accountancy Department, Koforidua Technical University, Ghana. He holds a Ph.D. in Finance from SDD-UBIDS and an M.Phil. in Finance from the University of Professional Studies, Accra. A member of the Institute of Chartered Accountants, as well as chartered in economics and taxation, his research focuses on economic development and foreign capital flows. He contributes to academic and policy discourse on finance and development through teaching and scholarly work.

Muazu Ibrahim is an economist at the World Bank. He holds a Ph.D. in Economics and Finance from the University of the Witwatersrand, an M.Sc. in Development Economics from SOAS, University of London, and a B.A. in Economics (First Class) from KNUST, Ghana. His research focuses on macroeconomic policy, financial sector development, and economic growth. He has published extensively in top-tier journals and serves as a reviewer for leading publications in finance and economics. His work is policy-driven and addresses key contemporary economic issues.

Khadijah Iddrisu is a lecturer at the Islamic University College, Ghana, with over five years of teaching and professional experience. She also serves as a part-time lecturer at SDD-UBIDS and works as a consultant for the African Export-Import Bank. She holds a Ph.D. and M.Phil. in Finance, an Executive Mini M.B.A. in Corporate Governance and Financial Reporting, and a B.Sc. in Accounting. Her research interests span finance, economics, sustainability, inclusiveness, foreign capital, and economic development, bridging academic rigor with practical impact.

Issah Iddrisu is a Senior Lecturer and Head of the Department of Human Resource and Development at the School of Business, University for Development Studies (UDS), Tamale, Ghana. He specializes in areas such as public management, organizational culture, employee trust, and workplace behavior. Dr. Iddrisu earned his Ph.D. in Management Science from the University of Science and Technology in China, where he studied from 2015 to 2018. Prior to that, he completed a Master's degree in Business Administration at the Beijing Institute of Technology and a Bachelor's degree in Development Studies at the University for Development Studies. His research contributions are notable, with over 25 publications to his credit.

Fuseini Inusah holds a Ph.D. in Computer Science from the Kwame Nkrumah University of Science and Technology in Ghana. He lectures at the University for Development Studies, Tamale, Ghana, with his research focused on Intelligent Systems with applications.

Osman Issah is a Senior Lecturer and Head of the Accounting Department at the University for Development Studies, Ghana. He holds a B.A. in Economics, an M.Sc. in Economics and Finance, and is a member of ACCA. His research interests span business administration, accounting scholarship, and financial economics. With a strong academic and professional background, he contributes to advancing financial education and research, playing a key role in developing future professionals in accounting and finance in Ghana.

Richard Mbayo is a Ph.D. student at Northern Arizona University, Flagstaff, USA. He holds a Master of Arts in Political Science (Chinese Politics) from Renmin University of China, Beijing, PRC, and a Bachelor of Development Studies from Kyambogo University, Kampala, Uganda.

Umar Mohammed is an independent researcher and holds Ph.D. in economics from Ankara Yildirim Beyazit University. His research focuses on migration and international economics, green energy, finance, and development. Dr. Umar's research works have appeared in various international journals, and he has presented his research findings at international and national conferences. He also serves as an ad hoc reviewer for some journals published by Emerald Publishing, Wiley, and Taylor and Francis.

Abdul-Latif Mohammed holds a Ph.D. in Management from the University of Newcastle, Australia, where his research explores the intersection of social entrepreneurship, institutional logics, and sustainability transitions. With a strong background in organizational studies, he adopts qualitative methodologies to examine how hybrid organizations navigate complex social and economic goals. Dr. Mohammed has contributed to international research collaborations and academic publishing. His work reflects a commitment to scholarly impact, real-world problem-solving, and inclusive development, particularly in emerging economies and the global South. His international academic background enables a cross-cultural and interdisciplinary approach to research and teaching.

Randolph Nsor-Ambala is an experienced development finance expert with a strong executive background across leading firms like Coca-Cola, MTN, and Diageo. For over 15 years, he has led donor-funded initiatives across sectors to empower the private sector, promote gender equity, and address climate change. As DBG's CEO, he is driving strategic growth through impact investing, ESG alignment, and MSME financing. His leadership strengthens DBG's mission to catalyze inclusive, sustainable transformation by expanding access to long-term finance and fostering private sector resilience.

James Atta Peprah is an economist and finance professor at the University of Cape Coast, Ghana, where he serves as Dean of the School of Economics. He holds a Ph.D. and M.Phil. in Economics, and a bilingual M.B.A. in Banking and Finance. His research focuses on development economics, financial markets, SMEs, and microfinance. He is the principal editor of a Palgrave Macmillan book on Ghana's financial sector and has extensive teaching, publication, and consultancy experience across Africa.

Wynn Gemini Rajula is a Ph.D. student at the School of Management, University of Electronic Science and Technology of China (UESTC), Chengdu, Sichuan, China. She holds an M.B.A. from East China University of Science and Technology, Shanghai, China, and a Bachelor of Accounting and Finance from Daystar University, Athi River, Kenya.

Mohammed Ridwan Saani is currently a Lecturer in the Department of Economics at the University for Development Studies, Tamale, Ghana. He earned his M.Phil. in Economics from the University of Ghana, Legon, and is currently pursuing a Ph.D. in Economics at the University of Cape Coast, Ghana. His research interests include financial economics, development economics, and labor economics.

Rashad Saani is a Chartered Accountant and Chartered Management Accountant. He holds an M.Sc. in Accounting and Finance from the Kwame Nkrumah University of Science and Technology, Ghana, and is currently pursuing a Ph.D. in Business Administration (Finance) at the University for Development Studies, Ghana. His research interests include corporate governance and finance, public sector financial management, and development finance.

Mubarik Salifu is a Senior Lecturer in the Department of Economics at the University for Development Studies, Ghana. He serves as the

Deputy Director in charge of the Third Trimester Field Practical Program (TTFPP) and Community-Based Education and Service (COBES) within the Directorate of Community Relations and Outreach Programmes (DCROP). Dr. Salifu holds a Ph.D. in Economics and a B.A. in Economics from the University of Cape Coast, Ghana, as well as an M.Phil. in Economics from the University of Ghana, Legon. Throughout his academic career, he has contributed to research projects as a team member and has published peer-reviewed articles in esteemed journals. Dr. Salifu has actively participated in numerous international conferences, workshops, and training sessions across Africa, serving as a panelist, presenter, or discussant. His research interests include Financial and Monetary Economics, Development Economics, Health Economics, and Poverty Studies, with a specific focus on developing and transitioning economies. He possesses strong communication and teamwork skills and is known for his diligence and ability to work effectively under pressure in multicultural environments. Dr. Salifu is proficient in statistical software packages such as STATA, EViews, and SPSS.

Yazidu Ustarz holds M.Phil. in Finance from the University of Ghana and a Ph.D. in Development Finance from the University of Stellenbosch Business School, South Africa. He is a Senior Lecturer and head, Department of Finance at the University for Development Studies in Tamale, Ghana. Dr. Ustarz research interests cover financial development, foreign capital inflows, sectoral growth, international trade among others. Dr. Ustarz has published in a number of reputable journals including The Journal of International Trade and Economic Development, Cogent Economics and Finance, African Journal of Economic and Management Studies, and Agricultural and Food Economics, among others.

Ibrahim Nandom Yakubu is a Lecturer at the UDS School of Business. He holds a Ph.D. in Banking and Finance and is a highly motivated and accomplished researcher with expertise in inclusive finance, financial markets, corporate governance, and sustainability. He is a recipient of the 2022 Emerald Literati Awards in the Outstanding Paper category. He is also a member of the African Accounting and Finance Association (AAFA) and serves as an associate editor for the Review of Business Management (RBGN) and the Cureus Journal of Business and Economics. With a strong quantitative background, Dr. Ibrahim Nandom has published several book chapters and research articles addressing critical issues in sustainability.

List of Figures

List of Tables

CHAPTER 1

Understanding Financial Exclusion in Africa: Challenges and Impacts

Ibrahim Nandom Yakubu, Rashad Saani, and Gifty Ewurama Enchill

Introduction

Financial exclusion remains one of the most pressing and multidimensional barriers to equitable development across the African continent (Bashiru et al., 2023; Devi, 2023). It refers to the condition in which individuals or segments of the population are unable to access or use essential financial services that are affordable, convenient, and secure. These services include savings and transaction accounts, credit, insurance, and payment platforms, all of which are foundational for day-to-day financial management, investment in productive assets, and resilience against economic shocks. In Sub-Saharan Africa, financial exclusion has long been intertwined with historical underdevelopment, fragmented infrastructure,

I. N. Yakubu (✉)
School of Business, University for Development Studies, Tamale, Ghana
e-mail: ibrahim.yakubu@uds.edu.gh

R. Saani · G. E. Enchill
Stellenbosch University, Stellenbosch, South Africa

I. N. Yakubu (ed.), *Banking on Inclusion*, Sustainable Development Goals Series, https://doi.org/10.1007/978-3-031-96716-0_1

gender inequality, and a predominance of informal economic systems (Dissaux, 2023; Nkwede et al., 2021).

Over the past decade, the landscape of financial services in Africa has undergone a transformation, particularly with the rise of mobile money and other forms of digital financial innovation (Ba, 2023; Onyango, 2025; Osabutey & Jackson, 2024; Simione & Muehlschlegel, 2023). These technologies have enabled millions to leapfrog traditional banking infrastructure, extending financial access to previously underserved and remote communities. Nonetheless, while access has increased, financial inclusion remains uneven.[1] Figure 1.1 illustrates the upward trajectory of account ownership in Sub-Saharan Africa, rising from a mere 23% of adults in 2011 to 55% in 2021. Although this represents significant progress, the region still falls far below the global average of 76% and the developing economy average of 71%. Moreover, account ownership does not always translate into usage or financial empowerment. A substantial portion of those with accounts remain passive users, often due to lack of financial literacy, poor digital skills, high transaction costs, or mistrust in formal institutions.

The persistence of financial exclusion in Africa has far-reaching implications. It restricts the ability of individuals and households to save securely, access credit for entrepreneurial ventures, insure against risks,

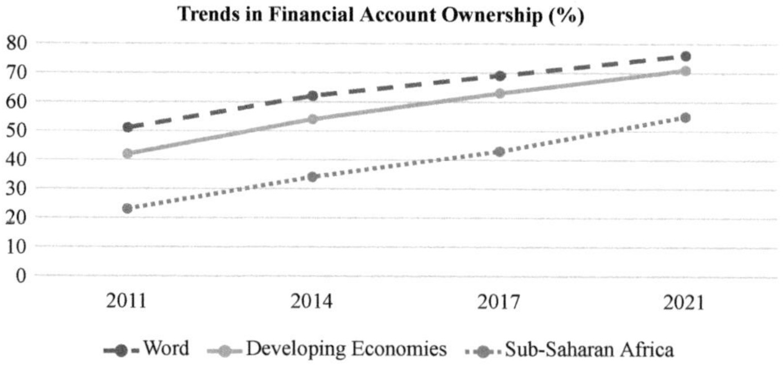

Fig. 1.1 Trends in Financial Account Ownership (%) (*Source* World Bank Global Findex Database [2021])

[1] https://www.worldbank.org/en/publication/globalfindex/brief/financial-inclusion-in-sub-saharan-africa-overview.

and participate in broader economic systems (Pearce, 2024). For women, young people, smallholder farmers, informal sector workers, and forcibly displaced persons, exclusion from the formal financial system reinforces cycles of poverty and dependence. At a macroeconomic level, widespread exclusion limits the growth potential of domestic financial markets, weakens monetary transmission mechanisms, and reduces the scope for tax revenue mobilization and social protection (Boel & Zimmerman, 2022; Tufail et al., 2025).

Understanding the contours of financial exclusion in Africa thus requires a comprehensive exploration of its structural, institutional, and behavioral dimensions. As the continent contends with both the challenges and opportunities of the digital age, the urgency of closing the financial inclusion gap has never been more pronounced. With accelerating adoption of mobile financial services, emerging fintech ecosystems, and regional policy efforts such as the African Continental Free Trade Area (AfCFTA), there is a unique window of opportunity to foster more inclusive financial systems. This chapter provides a foundational overview of financial exclusion in Africa, highlighting its key dimensions, the barriers to inclusion, and the consequences of being financially excluded.

Dimensions of Financial Exclusion

Financial exclusion occurs across multiple, overlapping dimensions that collectively determine whether individuals are meaningfully and sustainably connected to formal financial systems. In the African context, exclusion is often driven not only by the absence of bank accounts but also by deeper challenges related to usage, affordability, service quality, and product relevance.[2] Table 1.1 provides a structured overview of the three core dimensions of financial exclusion. Each dimension highlights a specific barrier that limits access to or engagement with financial services, offering a more comprehensive framework for analysis and intervention.

[2] https://blogs.worldbank.org/en/developmenttalk/financial-inclusion-in-africa--progress--challenges--and-the-roa0.

Table 1.1 Key dimensions of financial exclusion in Africa

Dimension	*description*	*Key challenges*	*Implications*
Access	The physical, digital, and procedural ability to reach and open financial services	Lack of bank branches, automated teller machines, mobile money agents, mobile phone ownership, national identification, internet access, or electricity	Prevents individuals from entering the formal financial system altogether
Usage	The frequency and manner in which financial services are actively utilized over time	Dormant accounts, lack of trust, limited financial literacy, poor product fit, and absence of practical use cases	Leads to superficial inclusion without meaningful engagement or impact
Quality	The effectiveness, safety, and responsiveness of financial services in meeting user needs	Non-transparent pricing, unreliable customer service, long delays, limited redress mechanisms, and poor user experience	Undermines trust and reduces the likelihood of continued usage

Source Authors' compilation based on insights from Demirgüç-Kunt et al. (2022) and Alliance for Financial Inclusion (2019)

Drivers of Financial Exclusion in Africa

Financial exclusion in Africa stems from the interplay of economic, institutional, and socio-cultural barriers. These barriers do not operate in isolation; rather, they reinforce one another and produce a compounded experience of exclusion, particularly for women, rural residents, informal workers, and other vulnerable groups (Khera et al., 2022; Okunade et al., 2023). Drawing on insights from the Global Findex Database, this section outlines the key drivers of exclusion.

Lack of Money

Among the most frequently cited reasons for not owning a financial account is the inability to afford one. In environments where the majority live on irregular or subsistence-level incomes, setting aside money for savings, transaction fees, or account maintenance can be unrealistic (Dorman, 2024). According to the Global Findex Database, majority of the unbanked population in Africa cited this as the most common

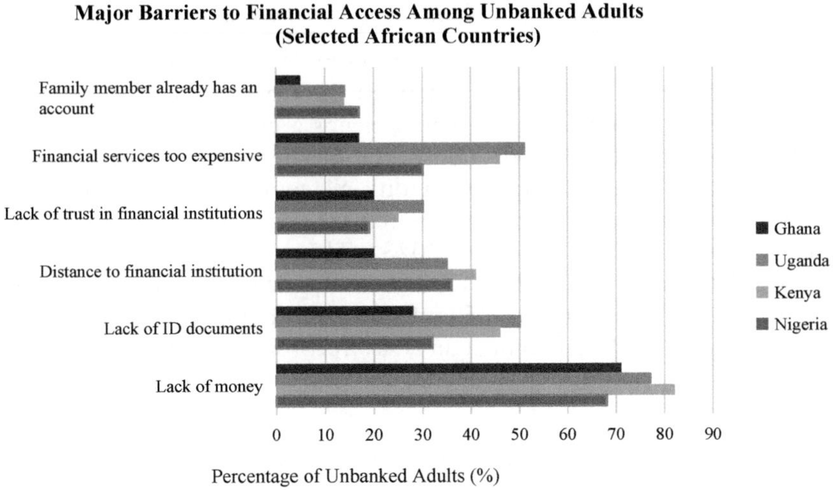

Fig. 1.2 Major Barriers to Financial Access Among Unbanked Adults (Selected African Countries) (*Source* World Bank Global Findex Database [2021])

barrier. For instance, 68% of unbanked adults in Nigeria and over 70% in Uganda and Ghana (as shown in Fig. 1.2) stated that they do not have enough money to open or maintain an account. This reveals a fundamental paradox: those who stand to benefit the most from financial services are often too poor to access them. Financial products that do not consider this economic constraint will continue to miss large portions of the population.

Lack of Identification Documents

A major institutional barrier to inclusion is the absence of identification. Know Your Customer (KYC) regulations require valid IDs to open financial accounts, yet many adults in Africa, especially women, displaced persons, and rural residents, do not possess formal identification (Hanmer et al., 2021). In Nigeria, 32% of unbanked adults cite this barrier; in Ghana, 28%; in Uganda, 50%; and in Kenya, 46% (see Fig. 1.2). These figures reflect not only the weakness of civil registration systems but also the bureaucratic and logistical challenges involved in acquiring formal documentation.

Distance to Financial Institutions

Geographic Inaccessibility further compounds exclusion. While mobile money and agent banking have extended the reach of financial services, physical distance from service points remains a constraint in many parts of Sub-Saharan Africa. Poor transportation networks, limited mobile coverage, and unreliable agent liquidity all contribute to a geography of exclusion, where financial services remain concentrated in urban and semi-urban areas (DigiPay Guru, 2023). This is particularly concerning for populations that depend on remittances, agricultural inputs, or credit for productivity. In Uganda, 35% of unbanked adults cite distance as a critical barrier, while different figures are recorded in Kenya and Ghana (see Fig. 1.2).

Cost of Financial Services

Affordability extends beyond the problem of insufficient income. Many financial services come with charges that are prohibitively high for low-income users. Transaction fees, withdrawal charges, SMS alerts, and mobile data costs make formal financial services unaffordable for daily or small-value transactions. As seen in Fig. 1.2, 46% of unbanked adults in Kenya, 30% in Nigeria, 51% in Uganda, and 17% in Ghana perceive financial services as unaffordable. These costs are especially burdensome for informal workers who depend on frequent, low-value transactions. Without appropriate pricing models, formal financial tools remain out of reach for many.

Lack of Trust in Financial Institutions

Trust plays a critical role in the adoption and continued use of financial services. In contexts where consumers have experienced fraud, hidden charges, or unresponsive customer service, mistrust becomes a barrier in itself. In developing countries, many unbanked individuals do not trust financial institutions, which significantly deters them from engaging with formal systems (Obiora & Ozili, 2024). This lack of trust is often exacerbated by limited financial literacy and weak consumer protection frameworks. For many, informal mechanisms, although riskier, are perceived as more accessible and responsive.

Gender-Based Barriers

Gender remains a pervasive axis of financial exclusion. Women across Africa face intersecting barriers such as limited control over household finances, lower literacy levels, fewer opportunities for paid employment, and cultural norms that restrict their agency (UN Aouinti, 2025; UN Women, 2021). Women are also less likely to own mobile phones, possess formal identification, or travel independently to service points. Despite targeted efforts through digital financial literacy and outreach programs (see Box 1.1), structural gender inequality continues to prevent many women from being meaningfully included in the financial system (Morsy, 2020).

Box 1.1: Gender-Based Digital Financial Literacy and Inclusion Initiatives in Africa

Digital financial literacy initiatives across Africa have played a vital role in narrowing the gender gap in financial inclusion, especially within marginalized and rural communities. In Kenya, programs like the M-Shwari 52 Week Challenge have motivated women to build savings through mobile platforms, with more than 270,000 participants collectively saving 4.5 billion Kenyan shillings. In Ethiopia, gender-focused campaigns are helping women gain confidence and skills to use digital financial services effectively. Mobile money providers such as M-Pesa and Airtel Money have incorporated educational tools, including SMS-based lessons, on financial topics such as savings, credit, and budgeting. Initiatives like Viamo's "Hey Sister!" offer localized financial education in various African languages, empowering women through culturally relevant content. At the national level, projects such as Malawi's Digital Financial Literacy Project extend outreach through mobile messaging and radio broadcasts targeting rural women. Together, these efforts aim to close gender gaps by providing women with the digital skills and confidence to navigate formal financial systems.

Source Kass-Hanna et al. (2022) and CNBC Africa (2023)

Digital Access and Literacy

The growing reliance on mobile and digital channels for financial services introduces new barriers related to technology access and competence. Mobile phone ownership remains uneven, especially among women, elderly adults, and the poor (GSMA, 2025). Moreover, the use of financial apps, mobile wallets, and even USSD codes assumes a level of digital and financial literacy that many in low-income or low-education settings do not possess (Ussif, 2024). As digital infrastructure expands, there is a risk of creating a new form of exclusion, known as digital exclusion, which may reproduce existing inequalities in new formats.

Global and Regional Comparisons of Financial Exclusion

Over the last decade, the global financial inclusion landscape has experienced substantial gains. However, the pace and magnitude of progress have varied widely across regions, and Sub-Saharan Africa continues to lag behind most of the world despite notable improvements. As shown in Fig. 1.3, global account ownership increased from 51% in 2011 to 76% in 2021, representing a 25-percentage-point gain over a decade. This upward trend reflects growing investments in digital financial infrastructure, national financial inclusion strategies, and innovations in mobile and online banking (Ermut, 2022; Macquarie, 2025; Sagadyn, 2024).

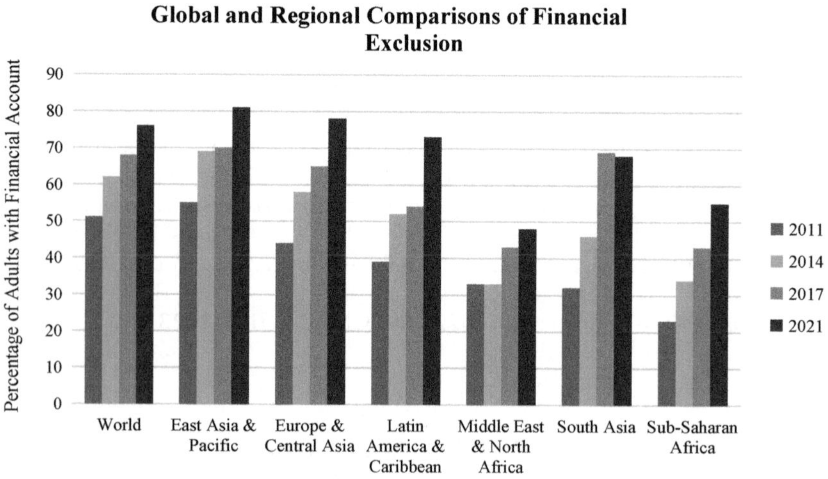

Fig. 1.3 Global and Regional Comparisons of Financial Exclusion (*Source* World Bank Global Findex Database [2021])

East Asia and the Pacific saw a significant leap, rising from 55% in 2011 to 81% in 2021. Much of this growth is attributed to large-scale initiatives in countries like China and Indonesia, which expanded digital payment ecosystems and connected vast rural populations to low-cost financial services (Heeks et al., 2024; Verma, 2024). Similarly, Europe and Central Asia registered a 34-percentage-point increase over the same period, reaching 78% in 2021, driven by strong legacy banking infrastructure and integration of digital finance in both public and private sectors.

Latin America and the Caribbean made striking progress in the past five years. After modest growth between 2011 and 2017 (from 39 to 54%), the region surged to 73% by 2021. This reflects the acceleration of digital wallet usage, expansion of agent banking, and increased social protection payments during the COVID-19 pandemic that brought millions into the financial system.

In contrast, South Asia experienced a more erratic trajectory. After jumping from 32% in 2011 to 69% in 2017, progress stalled, with account ownership slightly declining to 68% in 2021. This reflects saturation in countries like India, which drove earlier gains through initiatives such as the Pradhan Mantri Jan Dhan Yojana, and challenges in reaching the last-mile populations without sustained ecosystem investments (Prasad et al., 2024; Rai & Burman, 2023).

The Middle East and North Africa (MENA) region remains one of the least financially included globally, improving only modestly from 33% in 2011 to 48% in 2021. Structural constraints such as political instability, regulatory limitations on mobile money, and persistent gender inequality have hindered inclusion efforts across the region (Alhassan et al., 2021; Chehayeb & Taher, 2024).

Sub-Saharan Africa has made commendable progress, from 23% in 2011 to 55% 2021, largely driven by mobile money innovations, especially in East Africa. While this represents the fastest growth rate globally (a 32-percentage-point increase), the region still falls short of the global average by over 20 percentage points. Moreover, disparities within the region remain stark, with countries like Kenya, Ghana, and Rwanda far outperforming peers in Central Africa, where financial ecosystems remain underdeveloped (Macdonald, 2024).

These trends demonstrate that while Africa is moving in the right direction, its growth in financial access has not kept pace with most other regions. The comparative data underline a key message: technological innovation is necessary but not sufficient. Regions that made the most progress also invested in digital public infrastructure, inclusive policy frameworks, and robust consumer education.

Consequences and Implications of Financial Exclusion

The persistence of financial exclusion in Africa has far-reaching consequences that extend well beyond the inability to open a bank account or access a mobile wallet. At its core, financial exclusion denies individuals the tools and services needed to manage risks, invest in livelihoods, build resilience, and fully participate in economic life (Ifrim, 2022). Its effects manifest at multiple levels: individual, household, community, and national. This dynamic perpetuates a cycle of poverty, inequality, and underdevelopment.

Household and Individual Vulnerability

At the micro level, the inability to access and use financial services deepens vulnerability to shocks. Individuals without access to secure savings mechanisms rely on informal and often unreliable forms of financial management, such as hiding money at home, borrowing from family or loan sharks, or using rotating savings groups that lack regulatory protection (Phil-Ugochukwu, 2024). This makes it difficult to cope with emergencies such as illness, crop failure, or job loss, pushing many into deeper poverty when unexpected events occur (Goronja, 2025).

Lack of access to formal credit constrains the ability of low-income households to invest in productive assets such as farming tools, educational expenses, or microenterprise equipment (Mpofu & Sibindi, 2022). Informal lending channels, while flexible, are frequently more expensive and less reliable, trapping borrowers in cycles of high-interest debt or dependence on exploitative arrangements (Kumar & Sumalatha, 2024). In such contexts, financial exclusion directly limits the accumulation of human and economic capital, reducing long-term prospects for social mobility.

Moreover, exclusion disproportionately affects women, young people, and the rural poor. These are groups already facing intersecting forms of marginalization. For women, in particular, financial exclusion limits autonomy and the ability to make independent economic decisions. Without access to personal savings or credit, women are less able to respond to crises, invest in businesses, or challenge restrictive gender norms (Women's World Banking, 2024). This exclusion undermines gender equality and limits the broader development potential of families and communities.

Informality and Low Enterprise Productivity

Financial exclusion is both a cause and consequence of informality. In Africa, where informal employment dominates labor markets, most micro and small enterprises operate outside the regulatory and financial systems (Abdulkarim et al., 2022). These businesses typically lack access to working capital, credit history, insurance, or digital payment tools. These limitations reduce their growth, resilience, and ability to formalize.

Without access to finance, entrepreneurs are often forced to reinvest limited daily profits to sustain operations, reducing opportunities for expansion or innovation (Kumar & Antonioli, 2024). This perpetuates low productivity, low wages, and poor working conditions. It also deters integration into formal value chains, where financial transparency and access to digital payment systems are prerequisites for business partnerships.

As African countries seek to harness entrepreneurship for inclusive growth, the persistence of financial exclusion in the informal sector remains a major barrier. Financial tools such as microinsurance, pay-as-you-go financing, and digital credit scoring can help unlock the productivity potential of informal enterprises, but only if systems are inclusive and accessible.

Constraints on Human Capital Development

The link between financial access and human capital development is increasingly evident. Financial inclusion supports educational investment by enabling families to save securely, access educational loans, and participate in government scholarship or conditional cash transfer programs (Bryant, 2024). Excluded households, by contrast, may delay or forgo education for their children due to liquidity constraints, especially during seasonal income fluctuations.

Similarly, in health, financial exclusion limits access to insurance and pre-payment systems that can reduce the burden of out-of-pocket payments (Al-Hanawi et al., 2020). This results in late or forgone medical care, higher health-related debts, and lower resilience to health shocks. In turn, poor health and limited education reinforce intergenerational poverty and reduce the productivity of the future labor force.

Macroeconomic and Fiscal Implications

At a macroeconomic level, widespread financial exclusion limits savings mobilization and weakens the domestic resource base, constraining economic growth (Sirtaine, 2023). Financial systems depend on deposits to channel funds toward productive investment, yet in many African countries, savings rates remain low due to exclusion from formal accounts. This reduces the capacity of financial institutions to finance infrastructure, housing, agriculture, and small business development, which are sectors critical to inclusive growth.

Financial exclusion also has implications for fiscal policy. Governments seeking to broaden their tax base face difficulties in taxing the informal sector, where most transactions occur in cash and outside formal records (Yinusa et al., 2022). Digital financial systems, such as mobile money and merchant payment platforms, offer tools for improving tax compliance and broadening fiscal reach. However, their utility is limited when a large share of the population remains excluded.

From a financial stability perspective, exclusion can also lead to concentration risks. When formal finance serves only a small segment of the population, such as salaried and urban consumers, financial systems become less diversified and more vulnerable to sector-specific shocks (Naceur et al., 2024). Inclusive finance, by contrast, deepens the market, reduces systemic risk, and supports counter-cyclical resilience during downturns.

Implications for Inclusive Development and SDGs

Financial exclusion undermines progress on several Sustainable Development Goals (SDGs), including poverty eradication (SDG 1), gender equality (SDG 5), decent work and economic growth (SDG 8), and reduced inequalities (SDG 10). The inability to access financial tools limits individuals' capacity to participate in economic life, restricts voice and agency, and entrenches patterns of inequality (Women's World Banking, 2023; Yap et al., 2023). Financial exclusion is not just an economic constraint; it is a form of social exclusion that signals a deeper structural disconnect between individuals and the institutions meant to serve them. Inclusive finance, therefore, is more than an instrument of economic growth; it is a foundation for dignity, equity, and participatory citizenship.

Conclusion

Financial exclusion in Africa remains one of the most persistent and structurally entrenched barriers to inclusive development. Despite notable advances, particularly through mobile money and digital financial innovation, a significant portion of the population continues to be disconnected from formal financial systems. This chapter has explored financial exclusion through a multidimensional lens, examining its root causes and assessing its consequences.

From the analysis, it is clear that exclusion is not simply about the absence of a financial account. It also encompasses limited access, constrained usage, unaffordability, poor service quality, and a mismatch between the financial products available and the real-world needs of users. Each of these dimensions presents unique and overlapping challenges. When combined with broader socioeconomic factors such as poverty, gender inequality, and geographic isolation, they form complex and reinforcing systems of exclusion that cannot be resolved by digital solutions alone.

The evidence further shows that financial exclusion is not evenly distributed across the population. Women, young people, rural residents, displaced populations, and informal sector workers are disproportionately affected. In addition, regional disparities persist. On the global scale, Sub-Saharan Africa still lags most other regions in account ownership, highlighting the urgent need to move beyond fragmented access initiatives and toward the development of inclusive, integrated financial ecosystems.

The consequences of financial exclusion are far-reaching. At the household level, exclusion increases vulnerability to economic shocks, limits opportunities to save or invest, and reinforces intergenerational poverty. For small and informal enterprises, exclusion restricts productivity, reduces access to capital, and impedes integration into formal markets and value chains. At the macroeconomic level, exclusion weakens financial system depth, narrows the tax base, and undermines the effectiveness of fiscal and monetary policy. Socially, exclusion perpetuates inequality and slows progress toward achieving the Sustainable Development Goals.

To overcome these challenges, a comprehensive and intersectional approach is required. Expanding physical and digital infrastructure remains vital, but it must be complemented by efforts to address foundational barriers such as access to identification, affordability, trust in financial institutions, and basic financial and digital literacy. Policymakers must develop and enforce inclusive regulatory frameworks that not only support innovation but also protect consumers. Financial service providers must extend their focus beyond affluent urban populations, offering products that are context-specific, culturally appropriate, gender-sensitive, and compatible with irregular income flows. At the same time, donors and development partners must continue to fund innovation, facilitate knowledge exchange, and support capacity building across the financial ecosystem.

Above all, financial inclusion efforts must center the people they aim to serve. The success of any financial system depends not on the sophistication of its technology but on its responsiveness to the lived realities, aspirations, and constraints of excluded populations. Achieving this will require meaningful engagement with users, disaggregated data to track equity, and policies designed with intentionality. Without these, even the most advanced digital solutions will struggle to close the financial inclusion gap in a sustainable and equitable way.

References

Abdulkarim, A., Alter, A., Arzoumanian, S., Badr, K., Balima, H., Belgacem, A., Cardarelli, R., Maggi, C., Gaertner, M., Bizimana, O., Harb, M., El Hamiani Khatat, M., Priscilla Muthoora, S., & Vacher, J. (2022). *Informality, development, and the business cycle in North Africa*. Departmental Paper, International Monetary Fund.

Al-Hanawi, M. K., Chirwa, G. C., Kamninga, T. M., & Manja, L. P. (2020). Effects of financial inclusion on access to emergency funds for healthcare in the Kingdom of Saudi Arabia. *Journal of Multidisciplinary Healthcare*, 1157–1167.

Alhassan, A., Li, L., Reddy, K., & Duppati, G. (2021). The relationship between political instability and financial inclusion: Evidence from Middle East and North Africa. *International Journal of Finance & Economics, 26*(1), 353–374.

Alliance for Financial Inclusion. (2019). *Alliance for financial inclusion policy model: AFI core set of financial inclusion indicators*. https://www.afi-global.org/sites/default/files/publications/2019-12/AFI_PM_Core%20Set_FINAL_digital.pdf

Aouinti, N. (2025). *Accelerating action to bridge the financial inclusion gap*. https://www.africanenda.org/en/blog/2025/accelerating-action-to-bridge-the-financial-inclusion-gap

Ba, K. (2023). *The illusion of inclusion: The landscape of digital banking in Africa*. https://mitsloan.mit.edu/centers-initiatives/cde/illusion-inclusion-landscape-digital-banking-africa

Bashiru, S., Bunyaminu, A., Yakubu, I. N., & Al-Faryan, M. A. S. (2023). Drivers of financial inclusion: Insights from Sub-Saharan Africa. *Economies, 11*(5), 146.

Boel, P., & Zimmerman, P. (2022). Why Worry about Financial Exclusion? *Economic Commentary*, Federal Reserve Bank of Cleveland. https://www.clevelandfed.org/publications/economic-commentary/2022/ec-202209-why-worry-about-financial-exclusion

Bryant, J. H. (2024). *Inclusion in US financial services is at an all-time high—And tech can take us further*. https://www.weforum.org/stories/2024/04/financial-services-technology/

Chehayeb, R. J., & Taher, H. (2024). Mapping the current state of financial inclusion and its impact on economic growth in the MENA region. *Nurture, 18*(4), 911–923.

CNBC Africa. (2023). *Why it's time to ramp up financial literacy education across Africa*. https://www.cnbcafrica.com/2023/why-its-time-to-ramp-up-financial-literacy-education-across-africa/

Demirgüç-Kunt, A., Klapper, L., Singer, D., & Ansar, S. (2022). *The Global Findex Database 2021: Financial inclusion, digital payments, and resilience in the age of COVID-19*. World Bank Publications.

Devi, A. (2023). What is financial exclusion? A review. *Review on Islamic Accounting, 3*(2), 1–9.

DigiPay Guru. (2023). *Challenges, opportunities, and solutions of financial inclusion in developing nations in Africa*. https://www.digipay.guru/blog/challenges-and-solutions-of-financial-inclusion-in-africa/

Dissaux, T. (2023). Geographies of monetary exclusion in Kenyan slums: Financial inclusion in question. *Development and Change, 54*(1), 87–116.

Dorman, A. (2024). *Poverty Speaks 2023: Making tough choices*. https://www.communitysolutions.com/resources/poverty-speaks-making-tough-choices-2023

Ermut, A. (2022). *How new technologies create a pathway to financial inclusion*. https://www.weforum.org/stories/2022/05/new-technologies-improve-financial-inclusion/

Goronja, N. (2025). *The role of access to finance in reducing vulnerabilities*. https://www.centerforfinancialinclusion.org/the-role-of-access-to-finance-in-reducing-vulnerabilities/

GSMA. (2025). *The State of the Industry Report on Mobile Money 2025*. https://www.gsma.com/sotir/wp-content/uploads/2025/04/The-State-of-the-Industry-Report-2025_English.pdf

Hanmer, L., Esquivel-Korsiak, V., & Pande, R. (2021). *Understanding the gender gap in ID: Key research findings and policy lessons from Nigeria*. World Bank.

Heeks, R., Ospina, A. V., Foster, C., Gao, P., Han, X., Jepson, N., Schindler, S., & Zhou, Q. (2024). China's digital expansion in the Global South: Systematic literature review and future research agenda. *The Information Society, 40*(2), 69–95.

Ifrim, O. (2022). *The many faces of financial exclusion in the developed markets & who is at risk*. https://thepaypers.com/expert-opinion/the-many-faces-of-financial-exclusion-in-the-developed-markets-and-who-is-at-risk--1257545

Kass-Hanna, J., Lyons, A. C., & Liu, F. (2022). Building financial resilience through financial and digital literacy in South Asia and Sub-Saharan Africa. *Emerging Markets Review, 51*, Article 100846.

Khera, P., Ng, S., Ogawa, S., & Sahay, R. (2022). Measuring digital financial inclusion in emerging market and developing economies: A new index. *Asian Economic Policy Review, 17*(2), 213–230.

Kumar, B. P., & Sumalatha, B. S. (2024). Repercussions of Reliance on informal sources of finance: A study of tribal communities in Kerala. *The International Journal of Community and Social Development, 6*(1), 56–76.

Kumar, M., & Antonioli. (2024). *Small businesses matter: Increasing small business access to capital in the digital age*. https://bipartisanpolicy.org/report/small-businesses-matter-capital-access/

Macdonald, A. (2024). *Central Africa needs traction on financial inclusion to advance economic growth*. https://www.biometricupdate.com/202412/central-africa-needs-traction-on-financial-inclusion-to-advance-economic-growth

Macquarie. (2025). *How digital infrastructure investment could support economic prosperity*. https://www.macquarie.com/us/en/insights/how-digital-infrastructure-investment-could-support-economic-prosperity.html

Morsy, H. (2020). *Access to finance: Why aren't women leaning in?* https://www.imf.org/en/Publications/fandd/issues/2020/03/africa-gender-gap-access-to-finance-morsy

Mpofu, O., & Sibindi, A. B. (2022). Informal finance: A boon or bane for African SMEs? *Journal of Risk and Financial Management, 15*(6), 270.

Naceur, S. B., Candelon, B., & Mugrabi, F. (2024). *Systemic implications of financial inclusion*. Working Paper, International Monetary Fund.

Nkwede, F. E., Nkwede, J. O., & Nkwagu, L. C. (2021). Dilemma of financial exclusion and inclusion in Africa: Can Nigeria, South Africa and Ghana be compared? *African Journal of Social Issues, 4*(1), 105–122.

Obiora, K. I., & Ozili, P. K. (2024). Comparative analysis of financial inclusion in Nigeria, sub-Saharan Africa, and the World. *Perspectives on Global Development and Technology, 22*(3–4), 217–238.

Okunade, S. O., Olawumi, A. T., Adeyemi, O. J., & Amosun, O. O. (2023). Socio-economic and security effects of financial exclusion in Africa: An experts' View. *Annals of Social Sciences & Management Studies, 9*(2), 1–3.

Onyango, A. O. (2025). *Mobile money is transforming financial inclusion in Sub-Saharan Africa.* https://www.techforgood.net/thoughtleadership/mobile-money-is-transforming-financial-inclusion-in-sub-saharan-africa

Osabutey, E. L., & Jackson, T. (2024). Mobile money and financial inclusion in Africa: Emerging themes, challenges and policy implications. *Technological Forecasting and Social Change, 202*, Article 123339.

Pearce, B. (2024). *Opinion: Moving beyond access in financial inclusion to real impact.* https://www.finmark.org.za/knowledge-hub/articles/opinion-moving-beyond-access-in-financial-inclusion-to-real-impact?entity=news

Phil-Ugochukwu, A. I. (2024). Informal financial savings practices to facilitate formal financial inclusion. *World Journal of Advanced Research and Reviews, 24*(03), 1970–1979.

Prasad, L., Joseph, K. J., & Kakarlapudi, K. K. (2024). Towards inclusive finance in India: A comparative analysis of achievements, disparities, and implications. *Economic and Political Weekly (Engage), 59*(48), 1–20.

Rai, S., & Burman, A. (2023). *financial inclusion and digital transformation in India: Understanding Indian cities.* https://carnegieendowment.org/india/ideas-and-institutions/financial-inclusion-and-digital-transformation-in-india-or-understanding-indian-cities?lang=en

Sagadyn, G. (2024). *Innovations in mobile banking application development: What's new for 2025 and beyond?* https://speednetsoftware.com/innovations-in-mobile-banking-application-development-whats-new-for-2024-and-beyond/

Simione, F. F., & Muehlschlegel, T. S. (2023). *Mobile money, perception about cash, and financial inclusion: Learning from Uganda's micro-level data.* IMF Working Paper, International Monetary Fund.

Sirtaine, S. (2023). *Financial inclusion 2.0.—Creating more inclusive, resilient, and green futures.* https://www.cgap.org/blog/future-of-financial-inclusion

The basis to reaching all SDGs and the African Union Agenda 2063. https://africa.unwomen.org/sites/default/files/2024-12/un_women_africa_strategy_2022_-2025_0.pdf

Tufail, S., Aljarallah, R., Munir, M., Alvi, S., & Ul Hassan, M. (2025). Financial inclusion, financial depth, and macroeconomic fluctuations. *Economics, 19*(1), 20250135.

UN Women. (2021). Achieving gender equality and the empowerment of women in Africa is the basis to reaching all SDGs and the African Union Agenda 2063. https://africa.unwomen.org/sites/default/files/2024-12/un_women_africa_strategy_2022_-2025_0.pdf

Ussif, R. (2024). Financial inclusion in Ghana: Financial technology improving access to finance for mobile money enterprises. *Open Journal of Business and Management, 13*(1), 49–70.

Verma, S. (2024). *Indonesia Digital Payments Market Outlook to 2028.* https://www.kenresearch.com/industry-reports/indonesia-digital-payments-market

Women's World Banking. (2023). *From exclusion to empowerment: The meaning of financial inclusion.* https://www.womensworldbanking.org/insights/from-exclusion-to-empowerment-the-meaning-of-financial-inclusion/

Women's World Banking. (2024). *A vital response to climate change: Financial inclusion for women.* https://www.womensworldbanking.org/insights/a-vital-response-to-climate-change-financial-inclusion-for-women/

Yap, S., Shan Lee, H., & Xin Liew, P. (2023). The role of financial inclusion in achieving finance related sustainable development goals (SDGs): A cross-country analysis. *Economic Research-Ekonomska istraživanja, 36*(3), 1–22.

Yinusa, O. G., Ogede, J. S., & Tiamiyu, H. (2022). Does financial inclusion impact tax revenue in Sub-Saharan African countries? A panel data analysis. *African Journal of Management Research, 29*(1), 80–95.

CHAPTER 2

The Rise of FinTech in Africa: Empowering the Underserved and Unbanked

Khadijah Iddrisu, Farihan Alhassan, Stephanie Giamporcaro, and Joshua Yindenaba Abor

Introduction

Financial inclusion has been recognized as an essential tool for reducing poverty, contributing significantly to the achievement of Sustainable Development Goal (SDG) 1 (Iddrisu et al., 2022). Despite the persistent challenges of low financial inclusion and limited access to financial resources and services in Africa, the advent of technology has significantly improved the provision of these services. This advancement is commonly referred to as Financial Technology (FinTech). Since 2007, many financial

K. Iddrisu (✉)
Department of Banking and Finance, Islamic University College, Accra, Ghana
e-mail: khadijahiddris@iug.edu.gh

F. Alhassan
GCB Bank PLC, Accra, Ghana
e-mail: farihan@gcb.com.gh

S. Giamporcaro
Kedge Business School, Paris, France
e-mail: stephanie.giamporcaro@kedgebs.com

I. N. Yakubu (ed.), *Banking on Inclusion*, Sustainable Development Goals Series, https://doi.org/10.1007/978-3-031-96716-0_2

sectors across Africa have progressively incorporated FinTech into their service delivery. While there are various forms of FinTech services and innovations, Africa has been identified as the world leader of digital and mobile banking (World Economic Forum, 2023). In Kenya, for instance, M-PESA has enabled a large portion of the population to use mobile phones for various financial transactions, including bill payments and money transfers, among other services (Jack & Suri, 2011; Mbiti & Weil, 2011; Morawczynski & Pickens, 2009). Additionally, in Africa, a larger share of adults holds mobile money accounts, as opposed to accounts with banks or other financial institutions (Demirgüç-Kunt et al., 2022).

Also, the emergence of coronavirus disease 2019 (COVID-19) has increased the level of FinTech in Africa. In Sub-Saharan Africa (SSA) alone, 53% of global active mobile money accounts are concentrated, while South Asia contributes around 20%, and East Asia and the Pacific account for roughly 19% in 2022 (Awanis et al., 2022). SSA led in the growth of new mobile money accounts, surpassing Europe and Central Asia (2%), the Middle East and North Africa (MENA) (4%), South Asia (5%), and East Asia & Pacific (12%) (Awanis et al., 2022). At the country level, FinTech has also facilitated the provision of financial services to approximately 18.4 million people in Ghana by the end of October 2021, solely through mobile money platforms.[1] On average, mobile money transactions in Ghana amount to a value of GH¢18,979.35 million (Kulu & Bondzie, 2024). As FinTech is increasing in Africa, it is imperative to discuss how it has empowered and underserved and unbanked communities. Therefore, this chapter is dedicated to the discussion of the rise of FinTech and how it has empowered the underserved and unbanked communities in Africa.

The rest of chapter is structured as: section "Overview of the FinTech Sector" provides the overview of the FinTech sector, we discuss the historical perspective of FinTech in Africa in section "Historical Perspective of FinTech in Africa". The key drivers of FinTech growth in Africa was as

J. Y. Abor
Department of Finance, University of Ghana Business School, Legon, Ghana
e-mail: joshabor@ug.edu.gh

[1] Read more here: https://www.bog.gov.gh/wp-content/uploads/2022/03/The-Evolution-of-Bank-of-Ghana-Policies-on-the-Ghanaian-Payment-System.pdf Accessed January 7, 2025.

well discussed in section "Key Drivers of FinTech Growth in Africa". In section "Start-ups and Entrepreneurship", we looked at how FinTech start-ups and entrepreneurship has helped to drive FinTech innovation. Section "Government and Policy Responses" also discussed government and policy responses that led to FinTech boom in Africa. Concluding remarks were provided in section "Conclusion".

Overview of the FinTech Sector

FinTech, typically centered around the two key elements of finance and technology is defined in various ways. However, most definitions consistently revolve around the integration of these two core components. For instance, Mckinsey & Company (2024) recognizes FinTech as a real-world organization that relies on innovation and cloud management to provide financial assistance to customers. Financial Stability Board (2023) defines FinTech as technology-based innovation in financial services that can lead to new business models, applications, processes, and products, and has a significant impact on the delivery of financial services. A joint study by World Bank and the International Monetary Fund (IMF) identified that FinTech is a technological advancements with the potential to revolutionize financial services, driving the creation of innovative business models, applications, processes, and products (World Bank, 2022). Batunanggar (2019) also believes that FinTech is the development of information technology, including the internet, smartphones, and big data analytics, that helps deliver financial services more efficiently and cost-effectively. FinTech can also be defined as innovative financial services processes and products that result from advances in digital technology (Navaretti et al., 2018). In the view of Dorfleitner et al. (2017), FinTech is where businesses use innovative technologies to provide financial services.

Hence, it can be said that FinTech is the industry that uses technology to deliver innovative financial services or solutions. It is also made up of companies, technologies, and platforms that use digital tools to improve and transform traditional financial services such as banking, payments, lending, investing and insurance.

Features of FinTech Sector

The following are the key features in this sector:

1. **Technology-Driven Financial Service and Innovation**

This sector is mostly seen as providing financial services and solution which is precisely based on technology (Iddrisu et al., 2022). Some of these innovative technologies include platforms, artificial intelligence (AI), blockchain, big data, cloud computing, and Internet of Things (IoT).[2]

Also, the financial services are delivered through various means such as

a. Digital payment and transfer: The digital payment utilizes systems to facilitate the payment of goods and services (Tut, 2023). Some of digital payment innovations include mobile money, Google wallet, and Apple Pay, among others. This service has created a lot of convenience and fast transactions, among others. The digital transfer, in contrast, involves the movement of funds or data between accounts, eliminating the need for physical cash or cheques.
b. Digital borrowing and lending: These are FinTech services that focuses on allowing lending and borrowing through digital means. These services have facilitated transactions between surplus and deficit units, enabling them to conduct business efficiently. Due to this service, Small and Medium Enterprises (SMEs) can easily access credit without necessarily providing collateral and other official documents.
c. Digital insurance: This is a way of providing insurance services through technology which is Insurance Technology (InsurTech). This approach is more efficient as AI-driven claims assessments are used (Toukabri & Ettis, 2021).
d. Digital financial security and regulation: These are measures and frameworks in place to protect financial transactions, data, and systems in the digital landscape while ensuring compliance with legal and regulatory standards. Some of these services are sandbox, a common digital regulation tool. These services have improved

[2] Read more here: https://www2.deloitte.com/th/en/pages/technology/articles/5-key-technologies-in-FinTech.html Accessed January 17, 2025.

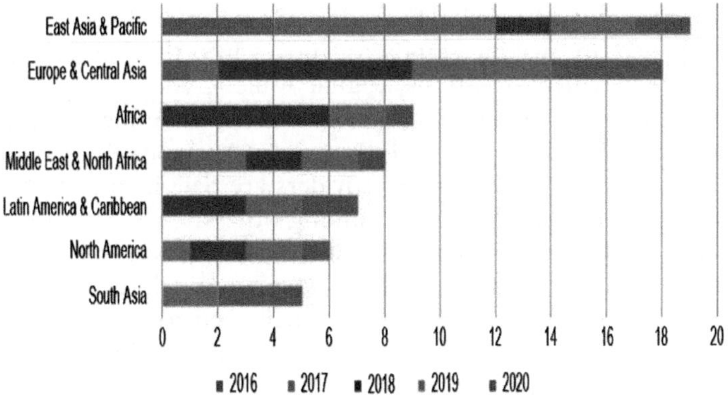

Fig. 2.1 Global Sandbox Adoption, 2016–2020, by region (*Source* World Bank [2020])

upon regulation of the financial services as they have presented a lot innovative ways of providing regulation. These services have been employed by a lot of countries as shown in Fig. 2.1.

e. Other services: There are other services such as personal financial management, budgeting tools, and financial planning resources which are provided to support efficient money management. Customers can access assistance for transactions and inquiries via chatbots, email, or phone. Credit score monitoring tools offer insights and recommendations for enhancing credit health. Moreover, features for recurring and scheduled bill payments help ensure payments are made on time.

2. **There Are Numerous Players that Exist in This Sector and These Include the Following**

a. **Start-ups**: These companies are the driving force of innovation in the FinTech sector, often specializing in niche areas such as payments, lending, and (InsurTech), among others. In Africa, some examples of these players include Nubank, Zeepay, Moove, and MNT-Halan among others.

b. **Technology and Service Providers Companies**: Major technology companies are making significant moves into the FinTech space by offering payment solutions, digital wallets, and financial services. Example of technology companies include Apple (Apple Pay), Google (Google Pay), and Amazon (Amazon Pay, lending to SMEs). Some of the service providers are Safaricom, MTN, Togo, Airtel, Telecel, and Vodafone, among others.
c. **Banks and other Financial Institutions**: Banks and other traditional financial institutions have increasingly integrated FinTech solutions into their operations to enhance customer experience and improve operational efficiency. Many are partnering with FinTech start-ups or creating their own digital platforms and services. For example, in Ghana, nearly all banks have integrated mobile money into their operations, while others have developed mobile applications to facilitate business transactions and provide a range of financial services.[3]
d. **FinTech Investors**: There are various entities and individuals who invest in FinTech. These include angel investors, venture capitalist, philanthropist, some financial institutions, crowd funders, and non-governemntal organisations (NGOs). For instance, Chimera Abu Dhabi invested US$200 million in MNT-Halan which represent more than 20% equity[4]
e. **Multilateral Development Banks (MDBs)**: Most MDBs have been allocating a lot of funds into FinTech sector. For example, in 2021, the International Finance Corporation (IFC) invested US$100 million in a bond issued by Liquid Telecommunications, a telecom and technology solutions provider, to enhance digital infrastructure across Africa, including Nigeria, aiming to boost broadband penetration (Khalifa, 2024).
f. **Governments and Regulators**: Governments and regulatory bodies play a critical role in shaping the FinTech landscape by establishing guidelines and frameworks for the industry's growth. They ensure compliance with financial regulations, promote innovation,

[3] Read more here: https://bog.gov.gh/wp-content/uploads/2019/08/Impact-of-Mobile-Money-on-the-Payment-Systems-in-Ghana.pdf Accessed January 19, 2025.

[4] For more information: https://afrikanheroes.com/2023/02/01/egyptian-FinTech-mnt-halan-raises-400m-in-new-funding-round-becomes-africas-latest-unicorn/ Accessed January 19, 2025.

and enhance consumer protection. In Africa, central banks have played a key role in providing regulatory services to the FinTech sector. For example, the Central Bank of Sudan provided licenses to mobile money operators to provide mobile payment services and manage customer's mobile wallets.[5]

g. **End-Users**: End-users, including companies such as Universities, utility companies, SMEs and individuals are crucial players, as they drive demand for innovative, accessible, and efficient financial products and services.

3. **Disruptive and Transformative**

FinTech is transforming the traditional financial services industry by leveraging cutting-edge technologies to offer faster, more cost-effective, and highly personalized financial products. These innovations streamline financial processes, reduce transaction costs, and enhance user experiences, making financial services more accessible and efficient for consumers and businesses alike. This has led to a wave of innovation within the financial industry, fostering the development of new solutions such as digital banking, mobile payments, and peer-to-peer lending platforms. For instance, Quickteller Paypoint, an agency banking platform in Nigeria introduced by Interswitch, an IFC partner, is enabling individuals and small businesses to access essential financial services (Khalifa, 2024).

4. **Global Reach**

Unlike earlier times where FinTech were identified in some few countries, now FinTech has gained attention globally. For example, FinTech was certainly understood in the United States, where official FinTech products, such as the Diner Club card, began. Today, almost every nation has an element of FinTech services and innovations. Some of the challenges facing the world, such as climate change, COVID-19, and the graves of the Ukraine-Russia war, have led to the appreciation of FinTech.

[5] Read more here: https://migrantmoney.uncdf.org/wp-content/uploads/2023/05/Sudan-Infrastructure-Assessment-Report-ENG.pdf Accessed January 19, 2025.

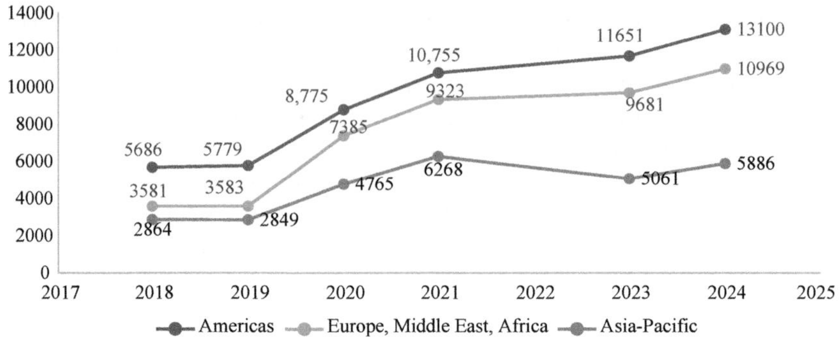

Fig. 2.2 Number of FinTech Globally, 2018 to 2024, by region (*Source* Authors' Computation based on Data[6] from Statista)

Data from Statista reveals that almost every region in the world has some FinTech services and innovations (see Fig. 2.2).

Importance of FinTech Sector

This sector has provided the global, regional and national economy with a lot of benefits. These are some of the benefits. The importance is but not limited to the following, financial inclusion, employment, enhance the performance of other sectors in an economy, attract more foreign direct investment.

1. **Provision of Alternative form of Financial Services and Enhancing Financial Inclusion**

The FinTech sector has significantly expanded access to alternative forms of finance, offering innovative solutions to a wide range of individuals and businesses, especially those who have been underserved by traditional financial institutions. FinTech companies use digital platforms to provide access to other financial products, such as microfinance, peer-to-peer lending, crowdfunding, and digital wallets. These alternatives are more accessible, faster, and more flexible than traditional banking services. As a result, FinTech plays a critical role in increasing financial inclusion, especially in developing regions where traditional banking

[6] The data can be accessed from here: https://www.statista.com/statistics/893954/number-FinTech-startups-by-region/ Accessed January 17, 2025.

access is limited. FinTech helps individuals and small businesses manage their finances, access credit, and participate in the formal economy, contributing to overall economic growth and poverty reduction. For instance, in Malawi, FinTech has reduced the unbanked population by 30%.[7] Also, the World Bank has reported that financial inclusion has increased in some African countries through the introduction of FinTech products (see Box 2.1).

Box 2.1 FinTech Sector Has Promoted Financial Inclusion in Some African Countries

The World Bank (2024) found that the FinTech sector, through products such as mobile money, has played a significant role in increasing financial inclusion across Africa, particularly in sub-Saharan Africa, and particularly in East Africa, where it was pioneered. By 2022, sub-Saharan Africa had the highest number of economies with more adults having a mobile account than a traditional bank account. On average, by 2022, 28 percent of adults in the region had a mobile account, and 20 of the 36 economies surveyed had more than 30 percent of mobile money users. While adoption rates remain low in some economies, mobile money has grown significantly in countries such as Tanzania, where mobile money account ownership rose from 32 percent in 2014 to 45% in 2021. This growth is becoming a common trend across the region. Mobile money has enabled increased access to accounts in both middle- and low-income economies. In countries such as Cameroon, mobile money has contributed significantly to account ownership, rising from just 12% in 2014 to 52% in 2021. Similarly, low-income countries such as Malawi and Togo have seen rapid growth in mobile money use between 2014 and 2017, rising from 18 to 43% and 50% respectively. As mobile money continues to spread, it is benefiting new users and, in some cases, leading to significant increases in account ownership. Several economies saw mobile money adoption grow by 20% or more between 2017 and 2021. In some countries, mobile money has replaced traditional bank accounts while bank account ownership has stagnated or declined.

Source World Bank (2024)

[7] For more information: https://ntchito.com/malawis-mobile-money-revolution-exploring-job-opportunities-and-FinTech-innovations/?srsltid=AfmBOoq3xXIhlzqrrr4zw_oql5bkZB3Y2mXaLFl_FWlcdM8a4O4F0960 Accessed January 19 2025.

2. **Creation of Employment**

FinTech sector has significantly contributed to job creation in Africa by fostering the growth of start-ups, tech hubs, and digital financial services. The rise of FinTech start-ups has created jobs in areas such as software development, business operations, marketing, and customer service. Additionally, the expansion of mobile payments, digital banking, and lending services has led to the hiring of agents and field representatives to support local communities. Moreover, FinTech has spurred growth in supporting industries like cybersecurity and regulatory compliance, while empowering small businesses to create new jobs. Through these avenues, FinTech has become a powerful driver of employment and economic growth across the continent. For example, in Malawi, the FinTech sector has employed over 80,000 individuals solely as mobile money agents. Additionally, the sector has created jobs in customer service, as well as opportunities for IT and FinTech professionals, among other roles. In 2021, the FinTech sector in Ghana directly provided employment to over 10,000 individuals.[8]

3. **Enhance the Performance of Other Sectors**

The FinTech sector has greatly improved the efficiency of various industries. For instance, mobile money enables farmers to receive payments for their produce, pay suppliers, and access credit. Similarly, many schools now accept tuition fees and application forms via mobile money and engage in other related services. In the healthcare sector, some hospitals allow patients to pay their medical bills through mobile money. Utility companies, such as water and electricity providers, have adopted mobile money and other FinTech platforms for bill payments. In Ghana, regulations require users to link their mobile money accounts to utility applications for seamless payment of utility bills.[9] These efforts from

[8] Read more here: https://www.stanbicbank.co.zw/gh/personal/about-us/news/the-impact-of-FinTech-on-ghanas-economic-growth#:~:text=Job%20Creation%3A%20The%20FinTech%20sector,employment%20effects%20benefiting%20many%20more. Accessed January 19, 2025.

[9] Read more here: https://www.gsma.com/sotir/wp-content/uploads/2024/03/GSMA-SOTIR-2024_Report.pdf Accessed January 19, 2025.

the FinTech sector have reduce corruption in the other sectors, enhance efficiency in service delivery and promote revenue collections.

4. **Attraction of Foreign Direct Investment**

The FinTech sector attracts Foreign Direct Investment (FDI) in Africa by showcasing strong growth potential, innovation, and vast market opportunities. The sector's rapid expansion, driven by mobile money, digital payments, and financial inclusion initiatives, presents attractive opportunities for international investors looking to tap into Africa's underserved financial markets. Additionally, FinTech fosters the development of digital infrastructure and technology ecosystems, which appeals to global investors seeking to capitalize on emerging market trends. FinTech's ability to bridge the gap between the formal and informal sectors also enhances economic stability and creates a more conducive environment for FDI. By increasing access to financial services, it helps stimulate entrepreneurship and business development, making Africa an attractive destination for foreign investment. Furthermore, favorable regulatory reforms in many African countries to support digital finance and innovation contribute to investor confidence, further boosting FDI inflows into the FinTech space.

5. **Global Connectivity**

FinTech promotes cross-border transactions by enabling businesses and individuals to engage in global trade more efficiently and cost-effectively, without relying on traditional financial intermediaries like banks. This allows for faster payments, lower transaction fees, and increased access to international markets. As a result, FinTech facilitates Africa's integration into the global economy, fostering greater economic collaboration, attracting foreign investments, and empowering local businesses to compete on a global scale. FinTech has made remittance easily due to its global connectivity. Now wonder remittance inflow has been increasing in Africa.

Challenges in the FinTech Sector

While FinTech offers significant benefits to both nations and the global economy, it also faces numerous challenges. Unlike more developed markets such as the United States, where FinTech has matured, Africa's FinTech industry is still emerging, which increases its exposure to a range of challenges and risks. Some of these challenges are as follows:

1. **Regulatory Challenges**

Though, policymakers in Africa are making a lot of efforts to enhance this sector, there is a regulation gap which hinders the potentials of this sector. One of these gaps are too much levies and charges which sometimes deter users to fully utilize such services. For example, in Ghana, the government imposes electronic-levy on all electronic financial transfer that end up reducing mobile money transfers (see Box 2.2).

Box 2.2: Electronic Levy Reduces Mobile Money Usage in Ghana
The Electronic Transfer Levy Act, 2033 (Act 1075) and Electronic Transfer Levy (Amendment) Act 2022 (Act 1089) impose a levy of 1% on all electronic financial transactions, such as mobile money transfers and online banking transactions in May 2022. Just after implementation, the number of transactions below GH¢100 decreased by 19%, the number of transactions between GH¢100 and GH¢200 decreased by 28%, and the number of transactions above GH¢200 decreased by 48%. Furthermore, the effect is still more than 20% lower than the pre-tax level even after 9 months. Similarly, the transaction value and mobile money revenue decreased by up to 35% compared to the same period last year, and after 9 months, revenue is still 20% lower than the pre-tax level. Meanwhile, fee-free cash withdrawal transactions have increased in value and volume since the introduction of the tax, with volume increasing by 25% and value increasing by 61% year-on-year, indicating a return to cash-based transactions. As a result of the reduced demand for tax revenue, the government's planned tax revenue was much lower than expected. Moreover, taking into account the loss of revenue from the tax cut on mobile money revenues and the negative impact on GDP growth due to the reduced availability of mobile money, the net tax revenue to the government is estimated to be negative almost GH¢1.4 billion per year.

Source Penteriani (2023)

Also, many African countries have intricate and time-consuming licensing processes that deter FinTech start-ups from entering the market. For instance, Kenya's M-Pesa initially encountered regulatory challenges, but the Central Bank of Kenya acknowledged the necessity for regulations specifically designed for mobile money services.[10] Some FinTech firms also face restrictions and limitations that hinder their ability to operate effectively. For example, Nigeria's cryptocurrency industry was disrupted in 2021 due to restrictions imposed by the Central Bank of Nigeria, which hindered innovation and growth in the financial services sector[10].

2. **Poor ICT Infrastructure**

Weak ICT infrastructure is a significant challenge for the FinTech sector in Africa. Many countries still struggle with limited access to reliable internet connectivity, slow network speeds, and frequent service disruptions. According to data from the International Telecommunication Union (ITU), poor ICT infrastructure in Africa limits internet access, with only a small portion of the population able to use it. In 2024, internet usage in the region reached a maximum of 37.5%, while other regions have seen internet access reach as high as 90% of their populations (see Fig. 2.3). This can impede the efficiency and scalability of FinTech solutions. Inadequate digital infrastructure makes it difficult for businesses to reach underserved populations, slowing down financial inclusion efforts.

3. **Cybersecurity Risks**

The growth of digital financial services heightens the risk of cyberattacks, data breaches, and fraud. Unlike other economies, Africa lacks the necessary resources to effectively track and address fraudulent activities within this sector. For example, in Nigeria, the first quarter of 2024 saw a 77.62% reduction in financial fraud losses within the banking sector compared to the fourth quarter of 2023. Despite this decline,

[10] Read more here: Regulatory Challenges in the African Finance Sector and its Impact on FinTech - Pierrine Consulting.

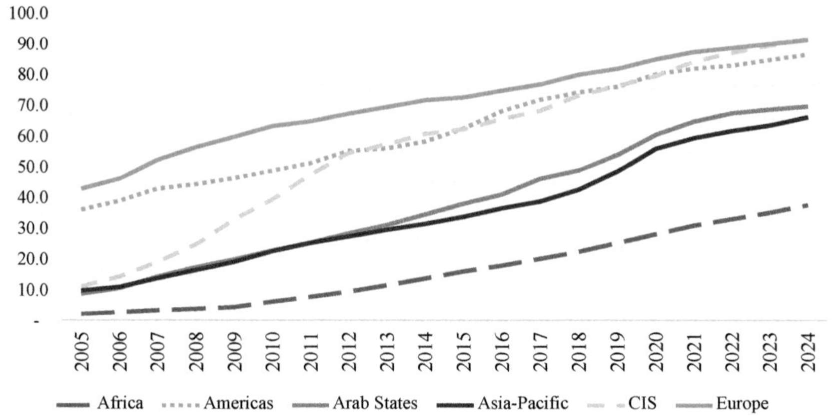

Fig. 2.3 Individual Using Internet (2005–2024), By Region (*Source* Authors' Computation based on Data[11] from International Telecommunication Union)

common fraud techniques, including computer fraud, mobile fraud, and POS-related fraud, continued to be widespread.[12]

4. **Customer Trust and Less Competition Among Other Forms of FinTech**

In Africa, a significant portion of the population especially the rural areas places greater trust in mobile money operators compared to other forms of FinTech services. This high level of confidence in mobile money platforms may inadvertently reduce competition within the sector, as consumers tend to rely more heavily on these operators for financial transactions. The lack of competition could lead to market inefficiencies, such as higher transaction costs, limited innovation, and reduced quality of service, as mobile money providers may feel less pressure to improve their offerings or lower their fees. For a healthy and dynamic

[11] The data can be accessed from here: https://www.itu.int/en/ITU-D/Statistics/Pages/facts/default.aspx Accessed January 17, 2025.

[12] Read this for more information: https://thepaypers.com/digital-identity-security-online-fraud/nigerian-FinTech-loses-nearly-usd-317200-previously-retrieved-from-fraudsters--1269874 Accessed January 17, 2025.

FinTech ecosystem to thrive, it is essential to foster a competitive environment where diverse players, including banks, FinTech start-ups, and other financial service providers, can innovate and offer consumers a range of choices.

Historical Perspective of FinTech in Africa

Historically, the African financial sector has been characterized by traditional banking, with limited access to formal financial services in certain communities, especially rural areas. Before the 2000s, traditional brick-and-mortar banks primarily served urban populations and low-risk customers. As a result, SMEs and low-income individuals faced limited or minimal access to essential financial services. At that time, the financial sector, especially the banking sector, was measured by the number of bank branches. An African country like Morocco was one of the traditionally high performers, with an average of 50 bank openings per year (Laghmari, 2020).

Until the introduction of M-PESA in 2007, African FinTech was centered on ATMs, also known as Autobank which was introduced in South Africa by Standard Bank[13] in 1981 and later adopted in other countries such as Ghana, Nigeria, and others (Rouse & Verhoef, 2016). ATMs used cards such as debit which is issued by the bank to conduct financial transactions such as withdrawal and checking balance. However, this FinTech product was mostly used by the elite and urban centers, leaving most Africans without access to financial services. Despite its widespread adoption in African countries, customers still visit banks to make financial transactions. As shown in Fig. 2.4, ATMs are on the rise in Africa, with South Africa and East Africa leading the way in ATM usage although, only few people patronize it. For example, 10.3% of every 100,000 people use ATMs, the highest usage in Southern and Eastern Africa in 2019 (see Fig. 2.2). The highest ATM usage in SSA was 6.7% per 100,000 adults in 2021 as shown in Fig. 2.2. South Africa leads the in-country ATM usage, with ATM usage increasing from 29.71% per

[13] It is worth noting that there is also a claim that United Building Society (later United Bank, now part of Absa) introduced the first ATM in Africa, particularly in South Africa in 1977. However, this is not well documented, so we will stick with Standard Bank as the first bank to introduce the first ATM in Africa.

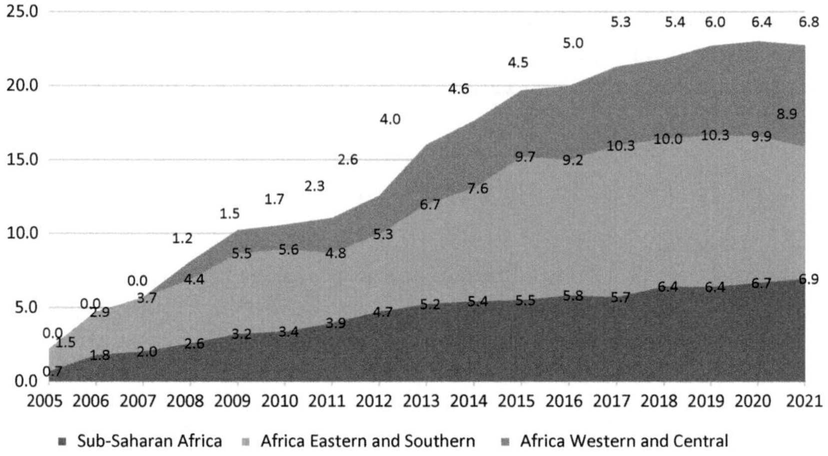

Fig. 2.4 Automated Teller Machines per 100,000 adults in Africa, by Subregion (*Source* Authors' Computation based on Data[15] from the World Bank)

100,000 adults in 2005 to 69.29% in 2015, and Nigeria from 0.68% in 2005 to 16.8% to 2015.[14]

Among other challenges, ATMs were not used to transfer money, South African Reserve Bank introduced another form of FinTech, Electronic Funds Transfer (EFT) in the late 1980s and late 1994. EFT modernizes banking processes and improves the efficiency, convenience, and security of financial transactions. Banks in South Africa such as the Standard Bank was pivotal in the implementation of EFT. Like ATMs, most African countries have introduced EFT and their banks are involved in its implementation. For example, in Uganda, the United Bank for Africa (UBA) is implementing provisions for EFT services.[16] To ensure effective use of ATMs, a variety of infrastructures have been introduced, including point-of-sale (POS), 24-hour ATMs, payment processing,

[14] For more details: https://ghana.inlaks.com/the-story-of-the-atm-and-its-role-in-financial-inclusion/ Accessed January 17, 2025.

[15] The data can be accessed from here: https://databank.worldbank.org/source/world-development-indicators# Accessed January 17, 2024.

[16] Read more from here: https://www.ubauganda.com/electronic-funds-transfer-eft/?utm_source=chatgpt.com Accessed January 18, 2025.

money transfers, and mobile transactions (Sanga & Aziakpono, 2022). These modern features have enhanced ATMs for additional functions such as bill payments, money transfers, and accepting deposits. The introduction of POS has led to the creation of human ATMs in some African countries like Nigeria, which aim to reduce queues by using decentralized cash dispensing agents and merchants. Most organizations use POS as a form of accepting payment for purchased goods and services.

The introduction of EFT led to the creation of electronic banking. This form of FinTech began to gain momentum in Africa in the early 2000s. E-banking is a banking method that allows customers to conduct financial transactions electronically.[17] Examples of such transactions include checking account balances, paying bills, transferring money, and applying for loans through an online platform or mobile application. This FinTech was first introduced in South Africa in the 1996 through Absa, which provided e-banking services to its customers. Some South African banks, such as Nedbank, First National Bank (FNB) and Standard Bank, followed suit and integrated this form of banking into their operations.[18] These four banks including Absa, Nedbank, FNB, and Standard Bank are now seen as the driver of the e-banking in South Africa (Maniraj Singh, 2004). In the early 2000s, some West African countries, such as Nigeria, Kenya, and Ghana, introduced this product through some banks including Ecobank and First Bank of Nigeria, which provided such services. The main features of this FinTech were focused on online balance inquiries, payments and funds transfer. However, this has evolved to integrate modern technology such as AI, instant transfer, mobile money, personal financial management, and new account opening, among others (Jibril et al., 2024).

While e-banking is a key FinTech product and has been a major driver of financial inclusion in Africa, it was still inaccessible to marginalized and rural communities due to the need to have a bank account. Due to the limited banking infrastructure to meet rural needs, many marginalized communities were unable to open bank account. To overcome this barrier, another FinTech product, mobile money (also known as mobile banking), has been introduced, which is among the most popular and

[17] Read more from here: https://businessjargons.com/e-banking.html?form=MG0AV3 Accessed January 18, 2025.

[18] https://www.itweb.co.za/article/banking-reinvented/JOlx4z7ko9Q756km Accessed January 18, 2025.

widely used FinTech products in Africa. This product was initiated by mobile operators, unlike other FinTech products initiated by banks in Africa. It was introduced in Africa in 2007 by Safaricom, a Vodafone subsidiary in Kenya (Laghmari, 2020). The product was originally called M-PESA in Kenya, where M stands for mobile phone and PESA means money in Swahili. Since then, almost all successful mobile operators have been modeled after M-PESA. M-PESA uses mobile phones to transfer money and make financial transactions. Users can also deposit money into an account stored on their mobile phones. The account holder can then use Short Message Service (SMS) to send money to their accounts. Also, mobile money uses the network of agent as intermediaries for money transfers and withdrawals. After the launch of M-PESA in Kenya, some countries started the adoption of this model. For example, Vodacom launched M-PESA in Tanzania in April 2008, MTN also adopted this model in some countries such as Ghana (March 2009), Uganda (March 2009), Rwanda (February 2010).[19] Thereafter, mobile money received a wide spread in Africa where almost every mobile operator has integrated this service into its business model. In 2020–2022, Kenya (69%), Rwanda (61%), Ghana (60%), Tanzania (45%), and Malawi were identified as countries with high mobile money usage (see Fig. 2.5).

Mobile money just like e-banking has evolved to capture diverse financial services through partnership with other institutions and sectors (Iddrisu et al., 2022). For example, these mobile operators partner with banks, insurance companies, utilities, schools, etc. to provide financial services. In Ghana, MTN partners with Ecobank to provide loans to consumers, while Miway Insurance partners with MTN to provide insurance services to consumers. Mobile money product has ranked Africa as leading mobile banking in the world. To enhance its efficiency, there has been integration of other technologies such as regulation and interoperability, among others (Rattel, 2024).

Although banks have, to some extent, integrated mobile money into their business operations or included it in their e-banking products, to remain competitive, some African banks introduced agent banking services, which allow customers in rural or underserved areas to access basic banking services through a third-party agent. The idea was adopted in Brazil and later adapted in Africa where South African legacy banks

[19] For more details: https://www.uncdf.org/article/7904/where-in-the-world-is-mobile-money-prominent Accessed January 18, 2025.

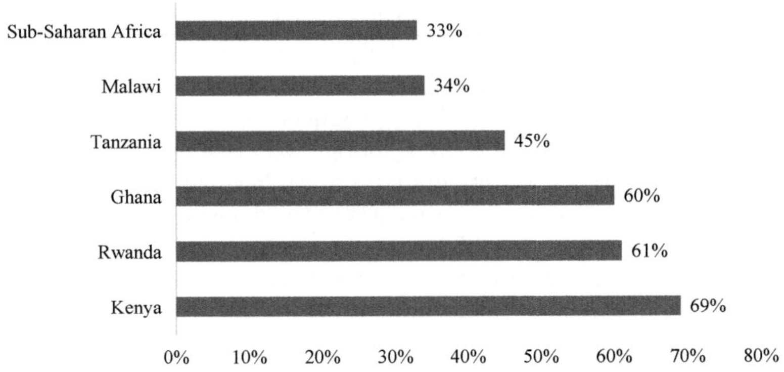

Fig. 2.5 Top Five Countries with High Mobile Money Adoption, 2020–2022 (*Source* Authors' Computation based on Data[20] from GSMA's Report)

[20] The data can be accessed from here: https://www.gsma.com/solutions-and-impact/connectivity-for-good/mobile-for-development/wp-content/uploads/2024/01/The-impact-of-mobile-interoperability.pdf Accessed January 17, 2024.

such as Standard Bank, Nedbank, Absa Bank, and FNB began offering cash deposits and withdrawals through post offices and retail outlets.[21] This FinTech later expanded to other countries. Unlike mobile money, which is regulated solely by mobile operators, agent banking is regulated by banks. For example, in Ghana, GCB, Cal Bank, and Fidelity Bank have agent banks, where agents transact banking business on behalf of these banks. Other examples include Paga in Nigeria, Fauri in Egypt, and First Bank of Nigeria's mobile payments.

After mobile money, other FinTech products have emerged in Africa that use mobile money, some of which use mobile wallets. For example, mobile money has enabled remittances, so there are other applications such as Kyshi, Wise, LemFi, Nala, Send by Flutterwave, Afriex, Chipper Cash, Eversend, Sendwave, etc.[22] which also facilitate remittance. While

[21] Follow this link for more information: https://paystack.com/blog/operations/agency-banking-africa#:~:text=This%20gap%20has%20driven%20the,of%20Latin%20America%20and%20Africa. Accessed January 18, 2024.

[22] For more information: https://techlabari.com/10-top-mobile-apps-for-remittances-to-africa/?form=MG0AV3 Accessed January 18, 2024.

PayPal was introduced globally in 1998 (Soni, 2022), Africa introduced this online payment platform in 2010, first introduced in South Africa by FNB Africa[8]. Since its adoption in Africa, other countries have also embraced it. Unlike other FinTech products that have been integrated into Africa after their global rollout, mobile wallets such as Google Wallet and Apple Pay were already integrated into Android and Apple phones, so they were integrated as at when they were introduced. Another important FinTech product is Bitcoin which started gaining traction in Africa around 2014 with early adopters in countries like Nigeria and Kenya.

From this historical perspective, it can be seen that South Africa has played a very important role in promoting FinTech in Africa. Moreover, despite the variety of FinTech products, mobile money or mobile banking is the most commonly used in Africa suggesting how mobile money has been successful in Africa. Furthermore, each FinTech product in Africa has evolved to capture the trending technology. Finally, almost all FinTech products in Africa are specifically integrated with mobile money. Currently, ATMs in Africa accept mobile money, POS accepts mobile money services, e-banking services accept mobile money services, PayPal (Kenya) accepts mobile money services, and some platforms such as Binance allow users in African countries to buy Bitcoin using their mobile money.

Key Drivers of FinTech Growth in Africa

There are a lot of drivers that has sustained and enhanced the growth of FinTech in Africa. We discussed the key drivers which include unbanked population and small-scale businesses, high mobile penetration, regulations and interventions, the emergence of COVID-19, global attention and support from development partners, emerging market for FinTech sector.

Large Unbanked Population and Small-Scale Businesses

Africa is one of the regions with the highest unbanked population and SMEs. The high unbanked population is due to the lack of sufficient formal documentation and information by most people to access financial services (Léon & Zins, 2020). At the same time, small businesses are also subject to information asymmetry, which makes them perceived as high-risk customers and has set as a barrier for them to access financial services especially loan (Ayyagari et al., 2017). Traditional banking or most commercial banks require formal documents to open an account or get a loan, as these are lacking, leaving most people unbanked or underserved, with only a few people having access to banking services. Other factors include geographical complexity, limited financial infrastructure to meet the needs of the growing population, and gender disparities, which are contributing to the growing unbanked population. Data from the World Bank suggest that financial inclusion in Africa especially SSA is very minimal as few people hold formal account (see Fig. 2.6).

In the same way, only few people in SSA have secured financial assistance from formal financial institutions as compared to other region (see Fig. 2.7). These situations have opened up opportunities for FinTech companies to offer alternative financial services such as mobile money, micro-loans, and digital wallets (Iddrisu et al., 2022).

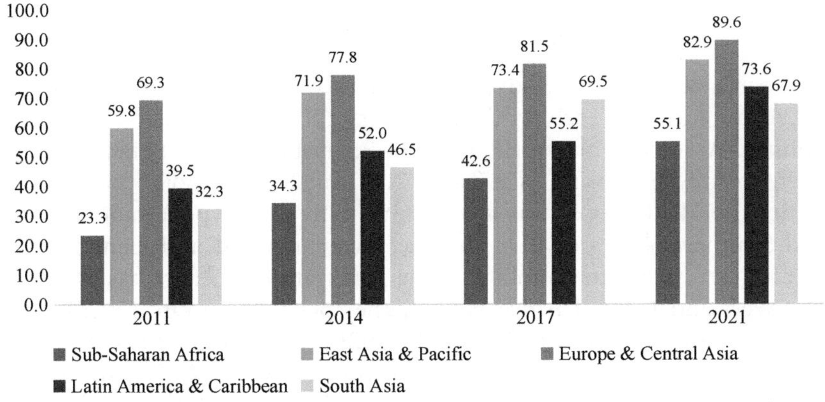

Fig. 2.6 Global Account Holding (% age 15+), 2011–2021, by region (*Source* Authors' Computation based on Data[23] from Global Findex Report, World Bank)

[23] The data can be accessed from here: https://databank.worldbank.org/source/global-financial-inclusion# Accessed January 17, 2024.

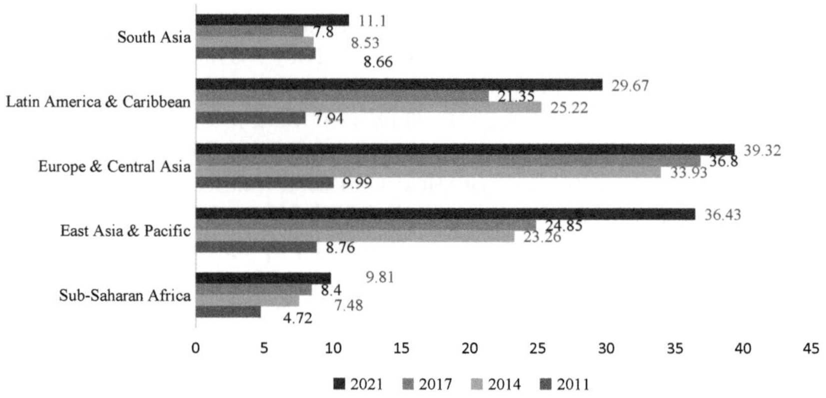

Fig. 2.7 Borrowed from a formal financial institution (% age 15+), 2011–2021, by region (*Source* Authors' Computation based on Data[24] from Global Findex Report, World Bank)

High Mobile Phone Penetration

FinTech's success is the high penetration of mobile phones in Africa. This is because most FinTech products are easy and widely available on mobile phones. According to World Bank data, mobile phone penetration has been steadily increasing (see Table 2.1). In 2000, mobile phone penetration per 100 people was around 3%, with higher penetration in East and Southern Africa (2.5%), and the lowest in West and Central Africa (0.5%). Ten years later, mobile phone penetration in Africa has increased, but West and Central Africa has a higher penetration rate (52.3%) than East and Southern Africa (38.5%). In 2020, mobile phone penetration in West and Central Africa has increased from 52.3% to 96.7%, and in East and Southern Africa from 38.5% to 70.3%. By 2022–2023, mobile phone penetration in West and Central Africa has increased again to over 100%.

The leading FinTech products in Africa which is mobile money require a mobile phone for its effective usage. Since, mobile penetration keeps increasing then it is an opportunity for FinTech firms to also produce more alternative financial services. No wonder in 2022, 53% of global active mobile money accounts were identified in SSA (Awanis et al.,

[24] The data can be accessed from here: https://databank.worldbank.org/source/global-financial-inclusion# Accessed January 17, 2024.

Table 2.1 Mobile cellular subscribers per 100 people in Africa, 2000–2023

Years	*Eastern and Southern Africa*	*Western and Central Africa*	*Sub-Saharan Africa*
2000	2.5	0.5	1.7
2001	3.5	1.0	2.5
2002	4.6	2.1	3.6
2003	6.1	3.3	5.0
2004	8.0	6.5	7.4
2005	12.6	11.1	12.0
2006	16.9	18.8	17.7
2007	21.7	25.0	23.1
2008	28.1	36.9	31.7
2009	32.6	44.3	37.4
2010	38.5	52.3	44.1
2011	48.0	58.2	52.2
2012	52.8	67.1	58.6
2013	57.7	75.0	64.7
2014	61.9	80.3	69.4
2015	66.5	83.3	73.3
2016	63.6	82.9	71.5
2017	63.5	81.4	70.8
2018	65.2	87.8	74.4
2019	67.9	91.3	77.4
2020	70.3	96.7	81
2021	74.7	95	82.9
2022	77.7	102.1	87.6
2023	81.3	100.8	89.2

Source Authors' Computation based on Data[25] from World Development Indicators, World Bank

2022), which almost correspond to the number of mobile phone penetration as in the same year out of 100 people, 87.6% were mobile cellular subscribers (see Table 2.1).

Policies, Regulations, and Interventions

FinTech in Africa has also increased due to intervention and most policymakers have identified it as a way to increase financial inclusion in

[25] The data can be accessed from here: https://databank.worldbank.org/source/world-development-indicators# Accessed January 17, 2024.

the continent. Since the inception of FinTech, various governments and other policymakers be it regional or global has implemented various policies to promote the growth of FinTech. For example, at the global level various policies including inclusive green finance, Consumer Empowerment and Market conduct (CEMC), National Financial Inclusion Strategy (NFI), Gender Inclusive Finance (GIF), and others by the AFI has largely promoted the growth of FinTech in some African countries (see Box 2.3).

Box 2.3: Alliance for Financial Inclusion Policies Have Promoted FinTech Growth in Africa

The Financial Inclusion Alliance (AFI) is a member-led global policy leadership organization focused on advancing financial inclusion. It works with central banks, financial regulators, international organizations, and the private sector. AFI promotes practical solutions and policy change through peer-to-peer learning, knowledge exchange, and peer-to-peer transfer. Established to provide a global knowledge-sharing platform, AFI has significantly expanded its financial inclusion policy agenda. With the support of donors and partners, the network has achieved tangible results in addressing financial exclusion. Supported by the International Climate Initiative (IKI) and the Federal Ministry of Economy and Climate, AFI brings together 90 central banks and financial regulators. Since 2019, AFI has implemented 89 projects in sub-Saharan Africa (46%), followed by the Middle East and North Africa (14%), Asia (13%), and other regions. Projects are focused on digital financial services (19%), accessible green finance (18.1%), national financial inclusion strategies (16.4%), consumer empowerment (15.5%), and other areas to support financial inclusion. AFI has also implemented a framework policy called the supervision of FinTech in the African region to facilitate in-country financial inclusion policy implementation across AFI network. The African countries who are members of AFI include Algeria, Angola, Central African States, Comoros, Congo, Cote d'Ivoire, Eswatini, Ghana, Guinea, Kenya, Lesotho, Liberia, Madagascar, Malawi, Mauritius, Mozambique, Namibia, Niger, Nigeria, Rwanda, Sao Tome and Principe, Senegal, Seychelles, Sierra Leone, Somalia, South Africa, Tanzania, The Gambia, Togo, Uganda, West African States, Zambia, and Zimbabwe.

Source AFI (2024)

At the regional level, African Union (AU) and its various sub-regional unions have implemented policies that seek to promote FinTech. Some of these policies and intervention include the Aspiration 2.2 of Africa's

Agenda 2063 which include the access to internet services and promotion of ICT diffusion in Africa.[26] In terms of sub-regions in Africa, the Economic Community of West African States (ECOWAS) Commission has launched the Western African Regional Digital Integration Program (WARDIP) aimed at increasing broadband access and use and advancing digital markets in Western Africa (see Box 2.4).

At the national level, most governments of African countries have implemented various policies and intervention which served as one of the key drivers to FinTech growth in Africa (see Table 2.2). Some of these policies have favored digitalization and internet connectivity. For example, the Moroccan government's Digital 2020 policy has paved the way for the expansion of internet connectivity and other digital infrastructure. Other interventions also provided an enabling environment for FinTech firms. For example, as some countries such as Ghana, Malawi, and Kenya, among others, integrated mobile money operators to the national switch platforms, it created a unified and efficient payment that facilitates seamless transactions across all network. Therefore, customers can freely transfer or receive fund from another person who uses different network. Also, this approach has enhanced remittance flow to Africa as users of FinTech in Africa can receive remittances from another region across the world. As more interventions increases, a lot of FinTech firms will also be attracted to the FinTech market and will introduce more innovations to meet growing needs.

Box 2.4: ECOWAS Commission Implement a Policy to Promote Digital Infrastructure

ECOWAS Commission pursue the implementation of the Digital Transformation for Africa/ Western African Regional Digital Integration Program (DTfA/WARDIP). The program aims to expand broadband access, promote competition, improve infrastructure, and make internet services more affordable and accessible in West Africa. It aims to reach 1.3 million citizens, including 50 percent women and people with disabilities, by creating employment opportunities and increasing access to services. The ECOWAS Commission, together with other regional partners, will support the creation of a single regional digital market with a grant of US$10.5

[26] Read more here https://au.int/en/agenda2063/aspirations Accessed January 18, 2025.

Table 2.2 FinTech policies and intervention in some Africa countries

Year	*Country*	*Policy/intervention*	*Aims/objective*
2002	South Africa	Financial Advisory and Intermediary Service Act (FAIS)	This act regulates the rendering of certain advisory and intermediary services to client in South Africa
2012	Nigeria	National Financial Inclusion Strategy	To ensure that a greater proportion of population in Nigeria have access to financial services
2014	Kenya	Regulation requirement to use interoperability systems	To enhance payment to payment (P2P) in the mobile money market
2014	Tanzania	Market-led bilateral agreement for P2P between Airtel, Tigo, and Zantel. In 2016, Vodacom join this agreement	To promote ensure transfer of funds between operators
2015	Ghana	Ghana established the Ghana Interbank Payment and Settlement Systems Limited (GhiPSS) Instant Payment (GIP)	To promote a fast, secure and efficient payment system between financial intuitions and individuals
2015	Rwanda	Central bank authorized interoperability	To enhance the efficiency, security, and accessibility of digital payment methods
2016	Malawi	P2P interoperability and connection to national switch	To create a seamless and efficient payment system among all the mobile money operators
2018	Egypt	Central Bank of Egypt FinTech and Innovation Strategy	To become the leader in financial services for MENA and Africa region
2018	Ghana	Mobile money interoperability incorporated into GIP	It allows direct and real-time transfer of funds between mobile money wallet, bank account, and e-zwich card across all network
2018	Kenya	Market-led interoperability went live through bilateral agreements	Enhance different payment service providers to connect and transact with each other
2018	Malawi	National switch platform launched for mobile money providers	To create a unified and efficient payment that facilitates seamless transactions across all network

(continued)

Table 2.2 (continued)

Year	*Country*	*Policy/intervention*	*Aims/objective*
2018	Rwanda	Approval of industry blueprint for interoperability	To promote a unified and efficient digital payment ecosystem
2019	Ghana	Regulation for interoperate among service providers	To enhance a seamless, efficient, and inclusive digital financial ecosystem
2020	Malawi	Connection of operators to the NatSwitch	To promote the country's financial ecosystem
2020	Morocco	Digital 2020	To create a favorable environment for digital transformation, with FinTech as a key focus area
2020	Tunisia	Regulatory sandbox	To enable FinTech firms to test innovative financial products and services in a controlled environment
2021	Algeria	Executive Decree No.21–44	The goal is to ensure a structured and regulated environment for electronic communication
2021	Rwanda	All service providers to connect to the national switch	The goal is to provide an organized and regulated environment for electronic communication
2022	Angola	Laboratório de Inovação do Sistema de Pagamentos de Angola	Aim to promote innovation in the FinTech sector through training and mentorship to start-ups
2022	Kenya	Launched of market-led interoperability	To allow customers make payment among other networks, retailers, and other institutions such as school, utilities etc.
2022	Rwanda	Integration of service providers to the national switch (ekash)	To create an organized and regulated environment for electronic communication
2022	Tanzania	Connect all operators on Instant Payment Systems (TIPS) platforms	To promote an integrated and efficient digital payment ecosystem
2022	Nigeria	National FinTech Strategy 2023	To promote the adoption and use of FinTech
2023	Algeria	National Strategy on Cybersecurity	To protect infrastructure and protect a secure digital environment

Source Authors' Computation based on Data from the Countries' Financial Websites and GSMA Reports million over five years. The program aims to strengthen the legal, regulatory and institutional framework for the telecommunications sector, deploy a resilient international network infrastructure, improve cyber resilience, and promote digital financial services, e-commerce and digital government services in the ECOWAS region. This initiative is in line with ECOWAS' vision of using ICTs to enhance economic growth and inclusion.

Source https://www.ecowas.int/ecowas-participation-in-the-digital-transformation-for-africa-western-africa-regional-digital-integration-program-declared-effective/ Accessed January, 19 2025

The Emergence of Coronavirus

COVID-19 pandemic has led to the introduction and usage of a lot FinTech application in developing economies and emerging markets, including Africa (Fu & Mishra, 2022). During that period, technology became the game changer as banks and other financial institutions integrated a number of FinTech services into their banking offerings. Today, almost every bank has a mobile app. Additionally, the use of POS has increased in Africa during the COVID-19 outbreak. In Kenya, the Central Bank took emergency measures to reduce the use of cash by allowing mobile money usage during the COVID-19 pandemic, which has fueled the growth of FinTech (Rattel, 2024).

Global Attention and Support from Development Partners

FinTech has received a global attention as it has been identified empirically that it facilitates financial inclusion (see Iddrisu et al., 2022; Salampasis & Mention, 2018). Therefore, development partners and other financiers are pumping funds into this sector especially in countries where most populations are unbanked and underserved. Africa is one of the continents that has received much funding into their FinTech Sectors. For example, the African Development Bank (AfDB) is working with Africa FinTech Network (AFN) to establish an African FinTech Hub to cater to all FinTech activities in Africa (see Box 2.5).

Box 2.5: Some Development Partners with Some African Countries to Promote FinTech

African Development Bank (AfDB) has created a funding facility such as the African Digital Finance Inclusion (ADFI) which aim to promote digital financial solutions in Africa. In August 2023, the Government of India promised to contribute US$2 million to support the facility.

AfBD has also partnered with Africa FinTech Network (AFN) to set up an institution called the Africa FinTech Hub (AFH) with a grant of US$525,000 grant. The ADFI will also provide funding and technical assistance to the AFH. AFH is a digital platform which aim to enhance partnership among FinTech associations across Africa and among others showcase the work of FinTech in the continent,

In Chad, the AfDB, through ADFI, has signed a US$650 million grant agreement with the Government of Chad to support the Microfinance Development for Women and Youth Entrepreneurship Project. The project aims to provide innovative digital financial and non-financial services to women and youth. The project has three components: (i) improving microfinance provision and developing digital finance, (ii) increasing demand for financial services, and (iii) supporting the entrepreneurial ecosystem in remote areas of Chad.

The Export–Import Bank of China has provided 155 million euros to support Ghana's rural telephony program. Launched in November 2020 by Huawei and the Ghanaian Ministry of Communications and Digitalization, the programme aims to provide voice and data services to more than 3.4 million people in these regions. In partnership with China National Technology Corporation, the project has reduced the government's cost of traditional cell sites by 70% and increased mobile phone coverage from 83 to 95%. The Ghanaian government is committed to providing affordable and reliable connectivity to all citizens.

Source AfDB, (2023a, 2023b, 2023c) and Anane-Amponsah (2024)

Emerging Market for FinTech Sector

Africa has been an emerging market for FinTech firms due as the continent's favorable demographics coupled with increasing digital adoption. This has attracted a lot of FinTech firms into Africa's FinTech Sector. This has caused some global FinTech institutions to partner with some African countries to provide FinTech services. For instance, to enhance FinTech services in Morocco, Mastercard join force with Morocco's NAPS (see Box 2.6).

Box 2.6: Mastercard Partners with NAPS of Morocco to Revolutionise Digital Platform

Mastercard and Moroccan FinTech company NAPS have formed a strategic partnership to develop innovative digital payment solutions for individuals and businesses. This collaboration builds on their long-standing relationship, aiming to revolutionize Morocco's digital payments landscape. Backed by over 30 years of experience in e-payments and biometric identification through M2M Group, NAPS will leverage Mastercard's extensive network, products, and cutting-edge technologies. The partnership seeks to strengthen NAPS' position as a leading FinTech firm and promote innovation within the company. Together, they aim to accelerate digital payment development, enhancing Morocco's role as a key FinTech hub in the Arab world and driving financial inclusion through advanced digital services.

Source FinTech Global (2023)

Start-Ups and Entrepreneurship

In Africa, there are emerging start-ups and entrepreneurs in the FinTech sector. Hence this section discusses the role these start-ups and entrepreneurs play in driving innovations in the FinTech sector. Some of the role include but not limited to niche market focus, collaboration with existing institutions, disruptive solutions, agility and experiments, and focus on SMEs.

Niche Market Focus

Start-ups and entrepreneurs often recognize opportunities as potential business ventures or identify problems and develop solutions to turn them into profitable businesses. For instance, an entrepreneur in a rural community might observe that many women struggle to read or remember mobile money passwords. In response, the entrepreneur could develop a mobile application that enables these women to use fingerprint authentication and features text-to-audio functions in their native languages. A practical example of such a start-up is MNT-Halan who provides some FinTech services for micro-lending and other financial products tailored in Egypt as shown in Box 2.7.

Box 2.7: MNT-Halan Promote FinTech Innovations in Egypt
MNT-Halan, an Egyptian FinTech start-up founded in 2018, provides financial services to the unbanked population, focusing on micro-lending and tailored financial products. Through technology, it has reached millions without access to traditional banking. The company recently raised over US$200 million from Chimera Abu Dhabi, acquiring more than 20% equity, with additional plans to secure US$60 million in primary capital. Once these investments are finalized, MNT-Halan's valuation will surpass US$1 billion, reflecting strong confidence in its value, management, and technology. This follows a US$120 million investment in 2021 by global and regional investors, including Development Partners International, Apis Growth Fund II, and Lorax Capital Partners, positioning the company for international expansion.

Source https://startuplist.africa/industry/fintech?form=MG0AV3 Accessed January 17, 2024

https://www.businesswire.com/news/home/20230131005989/en/MNT-Halan-Attracts-24400-Million-in-Largest-Funding-in-Egypt-and-the-Middle-East-in-the-Past-12-Months Accessed January 17, 2024

Collaboration with Existing Institution

Some start-ups join force with an already established financial institutions, providing them with the technology or expertise to innovative while benefiting from the institutions' regulatory frameworks and customer base. Others also partner with an existing FinTech firms or any firm who uses FinTech services to gain customers trust on their innovative products. For example, in Nigeria, Flutterwave partnered with existing firms such as Uber, MTN, Chipper, Piggyvest, 7Wise, Microsoft, Airpeace, etc. by providing services such as online remittance, shopping, and delivery, among others (see Box 2.8).

Box 2.8: Flutterwave Partners Various Established Institutions
Flutterwave, a Nigerian FinTech company, offers payment solutions that facilitate smooth transactions across Africa and globally. By partnering with

established banks, Flutterwave enhances its services through technology integration that supports online payments, mobile money, and card transactions via APIs. These collaborations also help the company navigate regulatory requirements by utilizing the banks' established frameworks. The partnerships expand Flutterwave's reach to a wider customer base, while enabling banks to leverage advanced technology to deliver modern and efficient financial services. This collaboration accelerates the adoption of FinTech solutions and strengthens the financial ecosystem. Beyond banking partnerships, Flutterwave has also teamed up with companies like Uber, MTN, Chipper, PiggyVest, 7Wise, Microsoft, and AirPeace.

Source https://flutterwave.com/gh/ Accessed January 17, 2024

Disruptive Solutions

Entrepreneurs prefer to generate a disruptive technology that challenge traditional financial institutions. These firms focus on innovative technologies which ensure efficient, accessible, and cost-alternatives. In Africa, few financial institutions engage in crypto currency investment. However, there are a lot of start-ups that ventured into such an area. For example, Moniepoint offers a comprehensive financial ecosystem that helps businesses and individuals have seamless access to payments, banking, lending, and business management tools (see Box 2.9).

Box 2.9: Moniepoint Provide Comprehensive Financial Ecosystem
In October, Nigerian FinTech start-up Moniepoint raised US$110 million in Series C equity funding to accelerate its expansion across Africa, marking its emergence as the continent's latest unicorn. Founded in 2015 by Tosin Eniolorunda and Felix Ike under the name TeamApt, Moniepoint offers a comprehensive financial ecosystem that supports seamless payments, banking, credit, and business management for 10 million businesses and individuals. As Nigeria's largest merchant acquirer, the company processes most of the country's point-of-sale (POS) transactions and handles US$17 billion in monthly transactions through its subsidiaries, operating profitably. The Series C funding round was led by Development Partners International's ADP III fund, with participation from Google's Africa Investment Fund, Verod Capital, and existing investor Lightrock.

Source https://disruptafrica.com/2024/12/23/the-top-10-african-tech-startup-funding-rounds-of-2024/?form=MG0AV3 Accessed January 17, 2024

Agility and Experiments

Start-ups thrive on agility, innovation, and risk-taking to stay ahead of the competition. They are more open to exploring new ideas and quickly iterate on changes based on customer feedback and technological advances. This agility allows them to develop business models or product offerings faster than larger, established companies with more rigid structures and slower decision-making processes. As a result, start-ups are increasingly able to capitalize on emerging trends, adapt to market changes and create effective solutions that allow them to succeed in growth and dynamic industries. For example, in Ghana, a FinTech firm called expressPay demonstrated agility and experiments that enabled a smart POS during the COVID-19 pandemic (see Box 2.10).

Box 2.10: The Journey of expressPay Depict Agility and Experiment
expressPay was established in 2012 which operates as an e-commerce marketplace and payment gateway provider. It facilitates payments for services such as school fees, hotel reservations, airtime, internet, and TV subscriptions. As an official Visa Payment Technology Provider (PTP) and a leading Visa eCommerce processor in Ghana, expressPay supports mobile money and major international card networks like Visa, MasterCard, American Express, and Discover. Serving as a comprehensive solution for e-commerce merchants' payment needs, ExpressPay meets international security standards as a PCI DSS-certified company.

expressPay initially launched as a platform to streamline online payments, enabling users to securely pay for services like utility bills, airtime, and school fees. By actively engaging with customers and business partners, expressPay gathered valuable feedback to expand its offerings. This led to the inclusion of mobile money transfers, bank transfers, and integration with international payment systems such as Visa and MasterCard. The company continuously improved its platform by adopting new technologies, optimizing security, and enhancing the user experience.

expressPay also adapted quickly to market changes, introducing online payments for government services and promoting contactless payments during the COVID-19 pandemic and meeting the rising demand for digital transactions. For example, the company introduced smart POS device in 2020.

Source https://expresspaygh.com/company Accessed January 19, 2025
https://www.modernghana.com/news/1042055/expresspay-introduces-smart-pos-devices.html Accessed January 19, 2025

Focused on SMEs

Most start-ups focus their efforts on small businesses, recognizing their unique needs and challenges. By designing tailored FinTech solutions for these businesses, start-ups provide specific services such as payment processing, financial management, and access to credit. These customized solutions not only enhance efficiency and growth for small enterprises but also drive the development of new financial technologies. As start-ups experiment with innovative tools and platforms to meet the needs of small businesses, they introduce fresh ideas and technologies into the financial ecosystem. This, in turn, promotes the continuous evolution and expansion of FinTech innovations, benefiting the broader economy.

Government and Policy Responses

This section examines the existing government and policy initiatives that have contributed to the FinTech boom in Africa.

The government and policy responses include but not limited to the interoperability, investment in digital infrastructure, provision of FinTech education and awareness, collaboration between government and development partners, implementation of FinTech based policies.

Implementation of Mobile Money Interoperability

Interoperability is the integration of different systems or product to create value for users (Rattel, 2024). Interoperability in FinTech allows different innovations to work together, creating value for users. For example, mobile money interoperability enables seamless transactions across mobile networks, bank accounts, and remittance services, while also supporting bill payments. This innovation has elevated the FinTech sector, particularly in Africa. In Ghana, mobile money interoperability led to significant growth, with transactions reaching GH¢308 million by 2019 and mobile money accounts increasing from 32.7 million in 2019 to 40.9 million by 2021. This surge highlights the pivotal role of interoperability in driving Africa's mobile money and FinTech development (Kulu & Bondzie, 2024). In first quarter of 2024, registered mobile money account increased by 3.1%[27] The GSMA study also identified that Ghana, Kenya Malawi, Rwanda, and Tanzania experienced high mobile money adoption due to mobile money interoperability especially during COVID-19 era (Rattel, 2024). Since interoperability a wide range of services, it was able to attract more FinTech firms and innovations. In Kenya for instance, apart from mobile money operators, there are lot of FinTech firms and applications which facilitate financial transactions.[28]

Increasing Investment in Digital Infrastructure

The investment and development of digital infrastructure have been crucial drivers of the FinTech boom in Africa. Enhanced connectivity through improved internet and mobile networks has expanded access to financial services, even in remote areas. For example, Ghana extended internet access to it rural through rural telephony program which aims to provide voice and data services to more than 3.4 million people (see Box 2.5). In Cape Verde, the government is investing an approximate of €35.9 million to develop a technology park which will have a Data Centre (DC), Business Continuity Plan (BCP) site, Business Centre (BC), Incubation Centre (IC), and Training Centre (TQC) (see Box 2.10). This investment in digital infrastructure has created opportunities for financial inclusion, economic growth, and innovation, making Africa a vibrant hub for FinTech development.

[27] Read more here: https://www.bog.gov.gh/wp-content/uploads/2024/05/FinTech_Sector_Report_2024-Q1-1.pdf Accessed January 19, 2025.

[28] Read more here: https://www.f6s.com/companies/FinTech/kenya/co Accessed January 19, 2025.

Box 2.11: Cape Verde invest 35.9 million Euro to develop a Technology Park

The project aims to support Cape Verde's sustainable development by advancing the Information and Communication Technology (ICT) industry, driving innovation, and promoting inclusive, green growth. It will focus on enhancing efficiency and competitiveness across various economic sectors, fostering entrepreneurship, and creating jobs. Central to the project is the development of a Technology Park in Praia, which will include a Data Centre (DC), Business Continuity Plan (BCP) site, Business Centre (BC), Incubation Centre (IC), and Training Centre (TQC). The Park will house cutting-edge computer storage and processing facilities, transforming government processes and private businesses. Located 3 kilometers from Praia International Airport, the park will be built on 8 hectares over 48 months, starting in 2013. The estimated cost of €35.9 million is funded by an Asian Development Bank (ADB) loan to the Government of Cape Verde (GoCV), and €4.4 million from Government of Cape Verde as counterpart funding. The park's sustainability will be ensured through revenue from services like cloud hosting and business partnerships. The project will benefit multiple sectors, including education, healthcare, and services, positively impacting Cape Verde, the ECOWAS sub-region, and African Portuguese-speaking countries. Direct beneficiaries include the public sector, academic institutions, and private businesses.

Source OITC Department (2013)

Support for FinTech Start-Ups

Support for FinTech start-ups has been a key driver of the FinTech boom in Africa by providing these emerging companies with the resources, mentorship, and funding needed to scale their operations. Initiatives like accelerator programs, incubators, and government-backed funding have enabled start-ups to refine their products, develop robust business models, and connect with potential investors. For instance, initiatives such as the Timbuktoo FinTech Start-up Accelerator offer mentorship, which has significantly boosted the growth potential of start-ups (see Box 2.12).

Box 2.12: Timbuktoo FinTech Start-up Accelerator Programme Support FinTech Start-ups

The Timbuktoo FinTech Startup Accelerator Programme recently entered its Acceleration Phase, following a successful Bootcamp that brought together 45 start-ups from 34 African countries. The Bootcamp equipped these start-ups with essential tools and insights to scale their businesses, offering masterclasses and workshops on topics like product refinement, business development, investment readiness, and sustainability. Participants also gained valuable fundraising skills and networked with prominent Pan-African investors, including Norrsken22, African Finance Corporation, HealthCap, and Seed Stars. Over the next five months, the Acceleration Phase will focus on scaling start-ups by refining product development and market strategies for growth across domestic and Pan-African markets, building strategic partnerships to expand impact, and enhancing investment readiness. A key highlight of the programme is the provision of US$20,000 in equity-free seed funding for each start-up. Launched in May 2024, the Timbuktoo FinTech start-up Accelerator is dedicated to supporting start-ups that use technology in financial services to address socio-economic challenges, with a focus on growth and market traction. As the program moves forward, it aims to foster innovation and position Africa as a global leader in FinTech development.

Source UNDP Nigeria (2025)

Moreover, support from development partners and investors helps start-ups enhance their product offerings and reach wider markets, both domestically and across the continent. This nurturing environment fosters innovation, leading to the creation of new, digital financial services that meet the diverse needs of African consumers and businesses, ultimately fueling the growth of the broader FinTech ecosystem.

Provision of FinTech Education and Awareness Among Users

The provision of FinTech education and awareness has played a significant role in driving the FinTech boom in Africa by equipping individuals and businesses with the knowledge and skills needed to leverage digital financial services. As more people become aware of the benefits of FinTech, such as mobile payments, online lending, and digital savings platforms, they are more likely to adopt these technologies. For instance, initiatives like the "FinTech Africa" programme have been instrumental in educating both entrepreneurs and consumers about the potential of FinTech solutions. Furthermore, awareness campaigns have helped demystify mobile banking services, leading to the success of platforms like Flutterwave and Paystack, which facilitate seamless payments for African businesses. As a result, increased understanding of digital financial services has led to greater adoption across various sectors, from retail to agriculture, fueling the rapid growth of the FinTech ecosystem on the continent.

Government and Development Partners Collaboration

Collaboration between governments and development partners has been instrumental in driving the FinTech boom in Africa by creating a supportive environment for innovation and scaling digital financial services. Governments, in partnership with international organizations and development agencies, have worked to improve the regulatory framework, promote financial inclusion, and provide funding for FinTech start-ups. Also, some government partners with some developmental partners to embark of FinTech related projects. For example, The Government of Morocco collaborated with Mastercard and Moroccan FinTech company NAPS to establish a strategic partnership aimed at developing innovative digital payment solutions for both individuals and businesses (see Box 2.6).

Conclusion

The FinTech sector is a dynamic and profitable sector that has emerged to improve the accessibility of financial services. Despite facing global and regional challenges, FinTech has experienced remarkable growth in recent years. This chapter provides an overview of the FinTech sector and its historical development in Africa. It also examines the factors behind this growth and highlights the factors that have contributed to its success. As the sector gains global recognition, it examines the role of emerging start-ups and entrepreneurs in promoting FinTech innovation across Africa. Finally, the chapter identifies and discusses government policies and responses that have influenced the growth of FinTech in Africa. The chapter identified that FinTech is simply the industry that uses technology to delivery financial services. It also identified that the FinTech sector is characterized by technologically innovative and services, unique players, global reach and disruptive and transformative. The sector has done by providing innovative finance and financial inclusion, it also creates jobs in the continents, have attracted more FDIs, promote the performance of other sectors and global connectivity. Despite this incredible performance, the sector also faces challenges such as regulatory challenges, poor ICT infrastructure, cybersecurity and customer trust and less competition among the various markets.

Historically, FinTech in Africa started with the introduction of ATMs and the adoption of EFT. This propelled the possibility of electronic banking. Despite progress made in the banking sector that originated from South Africa, the African continent as a whole faced both the challenge and the opportunity to answer the need of an underserved and unbanked population. The solution to this problem took the shape of mobile money. In 2007, mobile money was deployed in Kenya with M-PESA who diffused incrementally in many African economies and raised the world attention for the revolutionary innovation it brought to the banking sector at the time. The introduction of mobile money and the spread of mobile phones in the African societies offered a springboard for a more and more sophisticated FinTech market in a variety of African countries that partnered with Mpesa or developed their own mobile money solutions. The key drivers of FinTech growth in Africa are (1) the vast opportunity to answer the needs of an unbanked population and small-scale businesses, (2) high mobile penetration, (3) regulations and interventions, (4) COVID-19, (5) global support from development partners, and (6) an emerging market for the FinTech sector. The vibrancy around FinTech is articulated to the development of a dynamic African start-ups and entrepreneurship ecosystems. The consolidation of this ecosystem is playing a strategic role in driving innovations in FinTech sector through niche market focus notably on SMEs, collaboration with existing institutions, the introduction of disruptive solutions, agility, and experiments. The development of a thriving environment for FinTech in Africa is backed up by a coordinated governments and policy response notably led by African central banks, the implementation of mobile money interoperability within and across countries, increasing investment in digital infrastructure, support for FinTech start-ups, and provision of FinTech education and awareness by a strong base of private and public stakeholders.

Based on the discussions, the chapter outlines several policy implications for governments, regional leaders, and other stakeholders. First, considering the challenges faced by ICT infrastructure, there is a significant opportunity for investors to contribute to its development. Investors being asset owners or asset managers operating within or outside the African continent can leverage this opportunity by proposing and participating public–private partnerships (PPPs) with African governments. A proven example is Huawei's collaboration with the Ghanaian government to implement a rural telephony policy that improved access to telecommunications in underserved areas. Similar initiatives could be instrumental in enhancing ICT infrastructure across the continent. Second, while some countries are making strides in improving regulations, further efforts are needed to ensure efficient regulation that can effectively support the FinTech sector's growth. Enhancing regulation may involve governments and other stakeholders directing investments toward the development and implementation of AI-driven fraud detection systems. Third, mobile money interoperability has proven to boost FinTech performance in various countries. Therefore, nations yet to adopt such technology should prioritize its implementation. Governments could also explore innovative ways to raise funds for investments in digital infrastructure, including utilizing resource revenues to finance ICT infrastructure development. Finally, while companies and MDBs are working on training users and start-ups in FinTech activities and innovations, it is recommended that governments and policymakers in Africa partner with financial institutions and established FinTech firms to provide comprehensive training, education, and awareness programs.

References

AfDB. (2023a, April 16). *Nigeria: African Development Bank and Africa FinTech Network sign $525,000 grant to strengthen development of FinTech in Africa*. AfDB. https://www.afdb.org/en/news-and-events/press-releases/nigeria-african-development-bank-and-africa-FinTech-network-sign-525000-grant-strengthen-development-FinTech-africa-60669

AfDB. (2023b, June 9). *African Development Bank, Government of Chad sign $650,000 grant agreement to extend digital financial and non-financial services to women and youth*. AFDB. https://www.afdb.org/en/news-and-events/press-releases/african-development-bank-government-chad-sign-650000-grant-agreement-extend-digital-financial-and-non-financial-services-women-and-youth-61952

AfDB. (2023c, August 2). *India commits $2 million as new partner in Africa Digital Financial Inclusion Facility to boost digital financial inclusion across*

Africa. AfDB. https://www.afdb.org/en/news-and-events/press-releases/india-commits-2-million-new-partner-africa-digital-financial-inclusion-facility-boost-digital-financial-inclusion-across-africa-63530

AFI. (2024). Inclusive Green Finance. In *AFI*. https://www.afi-global.org/thematic-areas/inclusive-green-finance/

Anane-Amponsah, M. (2024, February 19). *1,000 Rural Telephony Sites Completed*. Graphic Online. https://www.graphic.com.gh/news/general-news/ghana-news-1-000-rural-telephony-sites-completed.html

Awanis, A., Lowe, C., Andersson-Manjang, S. K., & Lindsey, D. (2022). *State of the Industry Report on Mobile Money 2022*.

Ayyagari, M., Demirgüç-Kunt, A., & Maksimovic, V. (2017). *SME Finance*.

Batunanggar, S. (2019). *FinTech development and regulatory frameworks in Indonesia*.

Demirgüç-Kunt, A., Klapper, L., Singer, D., & Ansar, S. (2022). *The Global Findex Database 2021: Financial inclusion, digital payments, and resilience in the age of COVID-19*. World Bank Publications.

Dorfleitner, G., Hornuf, L., Schmitt, M., & Weber, M. (2017). Definition of FinTech and Description of the FinTech Industry. In *FinTech in Germany* (pp. 5–10). Springer International Publishing. https://doi.org/10.1007/978-3-319-54666-7_2

Financial Stability Board. (2023). *FinTech*. https://www.fsb.org/work-of-the-fsb/financial-innovation-and-structural-change/FinTech/

FinTech Global. (2023, June 5). *Mastercard and Moroccan FinTech NAPS join forces to revolutionise digital payments*. FinTech Global. https://FinTech.global/2023/06/05/mastercard-and-moroccan-FinTech-naps-join-forces-to-revolutionise-digital-payments/

Fu, J., & Mishra, M. (2022). FinTech in the time of COVID−19: Technological adoption during crises. *Journal of Financial Intermediation, 50*, Article 100945. https://doi.org/10.1016/j.jfi.2021.100945

Iddrisu, K., Abor, J. Y., & Banyen, K. T. (2022). FinTech, foreign bank presence and inclusive finance in Africa: Using a quantile regression approach. *Cogent Economics & Finance, 10*(1). https://doi.org/10.1080/23322039.2022.2157120

Jack, W., & Suri, T. (2011). *Mobile money: The economics of M-PESA*. https://doi.org/10.3386/w16721

Jibril, A. B., Pobee, F., Gochhait, S., & Chugh, R. (2024). Breaking boundaries: Unveiling hurdles in embracing internet banking services in Sub-Saharan Africa. *Cogent Economics & Finance, 12*(1). https://doi.org/10.1080/23322039.2024.2330436

Khalifa, D. (2024, April 4). *How Nigeria can leverage the rise of FinTech for economic progress*. World Bank Blogs. https://blogs.worldbank.org/en/psd/how-nigeria-can-leverage-the-rise-of-FinTech-for-economic-progre

Kulu, E., & Bondzie, E. A. (2024). Mobile money, credit to deposit ratio and monetary policy: Empirics from Ghana. *Transnational Corporations Review, 16*(3), Article 200060. https://doi.org/10.1016/j.tncr.2024.200060

Laghmari, S. (2020, January 16). *Digital banking in Africa: Origins and development outlook*. Infomineo. https://infomineo.com/financial-services/digital-banking-in-africa-origins-and-development-outlook/

Léon, F., & Zins, A. (2020). Regional foreign banks and financial inclusion: Evidence from Africa. *Economic Modelling, 84*, 102–116. https://doi.org/10.1016/j.econmod.2019.03.012

Maniraj Singh, A. (2004). Trends in South African Internet banking. *ASLIB Proceedings, 56*(3), 187–196. https://doi.org/10.1108/00012530410539368

Mbiti, I., & Weil, D. N. (2011). Mobile banking: The impact of M-Pesa in Kenya. In S. Edwards, S. Johnson, & D. N. Weil (Eds.), *African successes, modernization and development* (Vol. III, pp. 247–293). University of Chicago Press.

Mckinsey & Company. (2024, January 16). *What is FinTech*. Mckinsey & Company. https://www.mckinsey.com/featured-insights/mckinsey-explainers/what-is-FinTech

Morawczynski, O., & Pickens, M. (2009). *Poor people using mobile financial services: Observations on customer usage and impact from M-PESA.*

Navaretti, G. B., Calzolari, G., Mansilla-Fernandez, J. M., & Pozzolo, A. F. (2018). FinTech and banking. Friends or foes? *Friends or Foes.*

OITC Department. (2013). *Appraisal Report of Technology Park in Cape Verde*. https://www.afdb.org/fileadmin/uploads/afdb/Documents/Boards-Documents/Cape_Verde_-_Technology_Park_Project_-_Appraisal_Report.pdf

Penteriani, G. (2023). *The E-levy in Ghana: Economic Impact Assessment*. https://www.gsma.com/solutions-and-impact/connectivity-for-good/public-policy/wp-content/uploads/2023/03/E-Levy-Ghana-Economic-Impact-Assessment.pdf

Rattel, F. (2024). *The impact of mobile money interoperability on financial inclusion Evidence from five country case studies.*

Rouse, M., & Verhoef, G. (2016). Mobile banking in Africa: The current state of play. In *The book of payments* (pp. 233–257). Palgrave Macmillan UK. https://doi.org/10.1057/978-1-137-60231-2_21

Salampasis, D., & Mention, A.-L. (2018). FinTech: Harnessing innovation for financial inclusion. In *Handbook of blockchain, digital finance, and inclusion, Volume 2* (pp. 451–461). Elsevier. https://doi.org/10.1016/B978-0-12-812282-2.00018-8

Sanga, B., & Aziakpono, M. (2022). The impact of technological innovations on financial deepening: Implications for SME financing in Africa. *African*

Development Review, 34(4), 429–442. https://doi.org/10.1111/1467-8268.12668

Soni, J. (2022). *The founders: The story of PayPal and the entrepreneurs who shaped Silicon Valley*. Simon and Schuster.

Toukabri, M. T., & Ettis, S. A. (2021). The acceptance and behavior towards E-insurance. *International Journal of E-Business Research, 17*(2), 1–16. https://doi.org/10.4018/IJEBR.2021040102

Tut, D. (2023). FinTech and the COVID-19 pandemic: Evidence from electronic payment systems. *Emerging Markets Review, 54*, Article 100999. https://doi.org/10.1016/j.ememar.2023.100999

UNDP Nigeria. (2025, January 12). *20 High impact FinTech startups selected to advance to the acceleration phase of the Timbuktoo FinTech Accelerator Programme*. UNDP Nigeria.

World Bank. (2020, November 1). *Key data from regulatory sandboxes across the globe*. World Bank Group. https://www.worldbank.org/en/topic/FinTech/brief/key-data-from-regulatory-sandboxes-across-the-globe

World Bank. (2022). *Financial consumer protection and FinTech: An overview of new manifestations of consumer risks and emerging regulatory approaches*.

World Bank. (2024, April 17). *Data from the Global Findex 2021: The Impact of Mobile Money in Sub-Saharan Africa*. World Bank Group. https://www.worldbank.org/en/publication/globalfindex/brief/data-from-the-global-findex-2021-the-impact-of-mobile-money-in-sub-saharan-africa

World Economic Forum. (2023, November 21). *Here's why Africa is the world leader in digital and mobile banking*. World Economic Forum. https://www.weforum.org/stories/2023/11/africa-digital-mobile-banking-financial-inclusion/

CHAPTER 3

The Mobile Money Revolution: Transforming Payments and Financial Access in Africa

Umar Mohammed and *Ibrahim Nandom Yakubu*

Introduction

Mobile money, which uses mobile phones to deliver financial services, has offered numerous benefits, including financial inclusion, economic growth, poverty reduction, and improved remittance flows. Awuah (2025) opines that mobile money has emerged as a game-changing financial technology, providing economic participation and improving financial security. This ground-breaking financial invention has surfaced in Africa as a remedy for the restricted availability of conventional banking services. As a concept, mobile money is a financial service provided by a mobile network operator (MNO) that enables customers to manage an account

U. Mohammed (✉)
Ankara Yildirim Beyazit University, Ankara, Turkey
e-mail: ascertainus@yahoo.com

I. N. Yakubu
School of Business, University for Development Studies, Tamale, Ghana
e-mail: ibrahim.yakubu@uds.edu.gh

I. N. Yakubu (ed.), *Banking on Inclusion*, Sustainable Development Goals Series, https://doi.org/10.1007/978-3-031-96716-0_3

using a mobile device, like a phone, to pay for products and services and to send and receive money (Ericsson, 2021). A mobile money account is usually linked to their mobile phone number, and they do not need a bank account or internet to operate it. This service differs from mobile banking, which enables consumers to manage their bank account funds through internet-enabled mobile devices.

Mobile money systems, such as M-Pesa, have become prevalent in some emerging nations, allowing for large monthly transactions. Other systems, such as MTN Mobile Money and Airtel Money, have enabled smooth payments and fostered financial inclusion, economic growth, and digital innovation. With over half of the world's population (4.3 billion) owning a mobile phone (GSMA, 2023), mobile money is transforming the economic trajectories of lower-income and emerging economies.

Mobile money has revolutionized economic activity and financial transactions across Africa, transforming how individuals, organizations, and governments manage finances. In 2023, there were 1.75 billion registered mobile money accounts worldwide, with 435 million active users, 85 billion transactions volume, and a total transaction value of $1.4 trillion (Table 3.1). Sub-Saharan Africa has the highest mobile money adoption rates globally. This is evident because the region accounted for 234 million active mobile money users—more than half (53.7%) of the global total—and 62 billion and $912 billion transactions volume and values, respectively (Table 3.1). Sub-Saharan Africa alone contributed over 65% of the global mobile money transaction value, reinforcing Africa's status as a success story. Mobile money's rapid rise and growing influence can be attributed to the intersection of innovation, necessity, and strategic technological investment.

Mobile money has emerged as a transformative force in the financial sector, providing financial services to millions previously excluded from the traditional banking system, thereby fostering economic growth. Its contribution to the GDP of Sub-Saharan Africa, which exceeded $150 billion—equivalent to 3.7% of GDP growth—by the end of 2022, underscores this impact (GSMA, 2024a). Furthermore, the expansion of mobile money has positively affected GDP per capita and the growth of the financial sector in Sub-Saharan Africa (Alhassan et al., 2021).

These characteristics highlight mobile money as a revolutionary and transformative financial platform enabling financial inclusion for millions of people in urban and rural areas while reshaping banking and financial transactions. This article examines the transformative impact of mobile

Table 3.1 Mobile Money Regional Growth in 2023

Regions	*Registered account*	*Active account*	*Transaction Volume*	*Transaction Value ($)*
Global	1.75 bn	435 m	85 bn	1.4 tn
Sub-Saharan Africa	835 m	234 m	62 bn	912bn
South Asia	401 n	89 m	12 bn	214 bn
East Asia and the Pacific	374 m	77 m	9 bn	196 bn
Latin America and Caribbean	48 m	19 m	1 bn	38 bn
Middle East and North Africa	71 m	9 m	719 m	30 bn
Europe and Central Asia	26 m	6 m	391 m	7 bn

Source Authors' computations based on GSMA report (2024a)

money, particularly its role in promoting savings, supporting SMEs, facilitating payment systems, expanding financial access, and fostering inclusive economic development. Understanding the effects, challenges, and future prospects of mobile money will provide deeper insight into how it reshapes the financial ecosystem in the digital age. The remainder of the paper is structured as follows: section "The Origins and Growth of Mobile Money in Africa" provides the origins and growth of mobile money in Africa, section "Case Study: M-Pesa's Operation and Role in Financial Inclusion" looks at the case of study of M-Pesa's role in financial inclusion, section "The Impact of Mobile Money on Personal Savings, Remittances and Small Business" details the impact of mobile money on savings, remittances and small business, section "Future Trends and Sustainability of Mobile Money" presents the opportunities and challenges, and section "Conclusion and Recommendations" concludes with future trends and sustainability of mobile money.

The Origins and Growth of Mobile Money in Africa

The Origin of Mobile Money

The inception of mobile money can be ascribed to the need for financial inclusion, particularly in emerging and low-income countries where traditional banking infrastructure was either limited or nonexistent. The first mobile money service was introduced in East Asia and the Pacific in 2001. However, a major turning point in the evolution of mobile money came in 2007 when Safaricom launched M-Pesa in Kenya (Jaensson, 2018; Mugambi et al., 2014). M-Pesa, which means "Mobile Money" in Swahili, was initially developed as a pilot project to facilitate microloan repayments. However, it soon developed into a full-featured mobile money platform that enabled consumers to use their phones to pay for goods and services, make deposits, withdraw funds, and transfer funds with the Internet (Hughes & Lonie, 2007).

The shortcomings of traditional banking in Africa—such as poor infrastructure, low financial literacy, and high transaction fees—left a significant portion of the rural population without access to banking services. In effect, many people in low-income countries relied on informal financial systems, such as cash transactions, unregulated savings groups, and money couriers, which were often inefficient and insecure.

Mobile money, therefore, emerged as a more accessible, affordable, and widely adopted alternative. Suri et al. (2023) contend that the adoption of mobile money in Kenya was remarkably rapid, surpassing the adoption rates of many modern technologies in the United States. The combination of limited financial access, expanding mobile infrastructure, and corporate responsiveness to local needs contributed to the rapid spread of Safaricom's innovation, particularly in East Africa (Jang & Park, 2016). Since M-Pesa's launch in Kenya, successful mobile money businesses have widely replicated its model. MTN began operations in Rwanda in February 2010, Vodacom introduced M-Pesa in Tanzania in April 2008, and MTN launched its mobile money service in Uganda in March 2009 (McCaffrey, 2022).

Mobile money has addressed many challenges in the financial ecosystem and has become a vital part of Africa's financial system, promoting financial inclusion and expanding access to various financial services. Jaensson (2018) argues that the success of M-Pesa and its expansion into multiple countries highlighted the global potential of mobile money services.

The Growth of Mobile Money in Africa

The expansion of mobile money across Africa has followed a remarkable upward trajectory. Its growth has been particularly significant in Sub-Saharan Africa (SSA), where, by 2015, 13 countries had mobile money account penetration rates exceeding 10% (Jang & Park, 2016). The number of registered mobile money accounts has continued to rise, increasing from 469 million in 2019 to 855 million in 2023—a 45.1% growth. However, the number of active users remains lower than registered accounts. Active mobile money users grew from 181 million in 2019 to 237 million in 2023, reflecting a 23.6% increase (Fig. 3.1).

Over time, the total transaction value—the amount transferred via mobile money—has steadily increased. Between 2019 and 2023, transaction value grew to $920 billion, depicting over 50% increment. Similarly, transaction volume—the frequency of mobile money transfers—has also risen. Over the five years, transaction volume grew by 61.8%, outpacing the growth in transaction value in percentage terms (Fig. 3.2). The sharp rise in transaction volume is primarily due to the increased use of mobile money, particularly for smaller transactions. This growth was

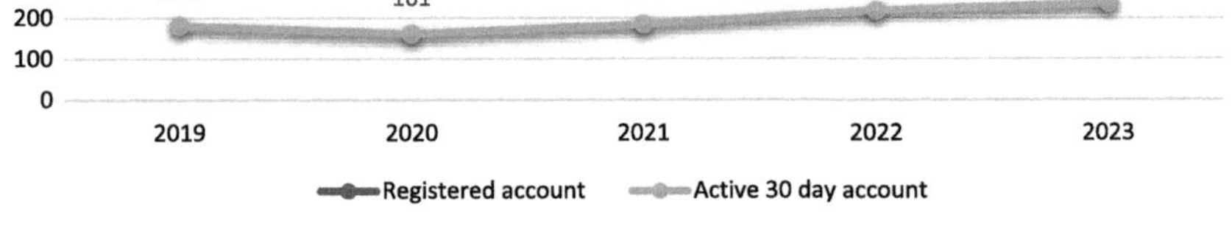

Fig. 3.1 Growth of registered and active 30-day accounts in Africa, 2019–2023 (Million) (*Source* Authors' computations based GSMA report [2024a])

most pronounced during the COVID-19 pandemic when the demand for digital transactions surged (GSMA, 2024a).

The volume and value of mobile money transactions have increased dramatically across all regions of Africa. This growth is driven by limited financial access, a rapidly expanding mobile communications infrastructure, and corporate responsiveness to local demand. Regionally, East Africa remains the epicenter of mobile money innovation, with Kenya's M-Pesa setting the benchmark in transaction volume and value of 38 billion and $488 billion, respectively. West Africa follows closely, recording a transaction value of $347 billion (Table 3.2). According to the 2024 GSMA report, West Africa had the highest percentage of newly registered and active 30-day accounts globally in 2023, with Senegal, Ghana, and Nigeria driving this growth. This trend suggests a rising number of mobile money users and a higher proportion actively using their accounts for everyday transactions (GSMA, 2024a). Similarly, transaction values in West Africa grew by 48% from 2020 to 2023, exceeding the 44% increase recorded in East Africa over the same period (Table 3.2).

Through both direct and indirect channels, mobile money plays a crucial role in supporting economic growth, particularly in countries with dispersed populations and high mobile phone penetration (Ahmad et al., 2023). Research indicates a strong positive correlation between GDP growth in Sub-Saharan Africa (SSA) and financial expansion, including mobile money activities (Alhassan et al., 2021). Additionally, the rise of

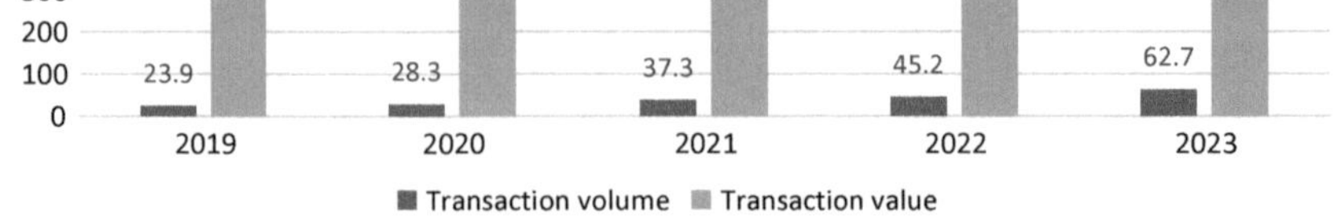

Fig. 3.2 Mobile money transaction volume and value in Africa (value in Billion $) (*Source* Authors' computations based on GSMA report [2024a])

Table 3.2 Regional transaction volume and value in Africa

Regions	*Year*	*Transaction volume*	*Transaction values ($)*
Eastern Africa	2023	38 bn	488 bn
	2020	18.6 bn	273 bn
Central Africa	2023	5 bn	72 bn
	2020	2.2 bn	35.7 bn
Southern Africa	2023	592 bn	6 bn
	2020	284 m	3 bn
Western Africa	2023	19 bn	347 bn
	2020	6.4 bn	178 bn
Northern Africa	2023	150 m	7 bn
	2020	77 m	5.4 bn

Source Authors' computations based on GSMA report (2024a)

mobile money fosters innovation by facilitating capital pooling and its allocation to productive sectors.

Case Study: M-Pesa's Operation and Role in Financial Inclusion

How M-Pesa Operates

In 2007, Safaricom, a Kenyan telecom provider, launched M-Pesa, a mobile money transfer service. Before the introduction of M-Pesa, traditional banking services were mainly inaccessible to many Kenyans due to high costs, strict regulations, and limited infrastructure. This restriction significantly constrained economic opportunities for millions, particularly low-income individuals and small business owners. M-Pesa addressed these challenges by leveraging the widespread use of mobile phones for financial transactions.

Del Torso (2019) opines that M-Pesa operates using the "mobile remote payment" method, which relies on SMS technology rather than an internet connection. This approach was chosen for several reasons. First, it enhances consumer accessibility. In 2007, smartphone penetration and internet usage in Kenya were low, making SMS a more practical option. An essential mobile phone was sufficient to access the M-Pesa platform.

Additionally, the platform's low or zero transaction costs make it affordable for individuals with modest incomes. Finally, unlike "mobile proximity payment" systems, which require internet access and are unsuitable for long-distance transactions, M-Pesa effectively facilitates remittances—one of its core functions. Safaricom's M-Pesa agents—including banks, retail shops, and airtime vendors—facilitated the buying and selling of e-money. They were crucial in managing deposits, withdrawals, and customer registration. Customers could send and receive M-Pesa e-money using the SIM Toolkit and receive an SMS confirmation from Safaricom upon successful transaction completion.

Real funds back all M-Pesa e-money in a commercial bank trust account. The total in this account always matched the e-money balance. Held under a Trust Deed, it is only accessible to M-Pesa users, not Safaricom. No funds would enter or go out of the M-Pesa trust account while customers transacted. Agents would deposit money into the trust account to buy e-money. Agents manage cash and e-money flows, ensuring users can convert between the two. M-Pesa services allow users to send and receive electronic money. For deposit, the user goes to an M-Pesa agent and gives cash in exchange for e-money and vice versa for withdrawals. M-Pesa services allow users to send and receive electronic money deposits and withdraw funds to their commercial bank accounts (if they have enrolled on such service). Users can pay bills, shop, or buy services using their M-Pesa balance.

M-Pesa Role in Financial Inclusion

Financial inclusion refers to the availability and use of affordable financial products and services that meet the needs of individuals and businesses while being delivered ethically and sustainably. Financial inclusion promotes economic growth and employment, empowers women economically, and reduces poverty (World Bank, 2025). Today, m-Pesa, Kenya's leading mobile money provider, has played a crucial role in advancing financial inclusion. For many Kenyans, it offers affordable and user-friendly services, addressing concerns about accessibility and cost (Omanga & Dreyer, 2017). Its success has been attributed to disruptive innovation, which fosters wealth creation and financial inclusion.

Kenya's financial sector has undergone a major transformation since the launch of M-Pesa in 2007. Household studies indicate a significant increase in financial inclusion over time. In 2006 only 26.7% of the population had access to formal financial services (Finaccess, 2024). By 2024, Kenya had become one of the world's most financially inclusive nations, with 90% of the population accessing financial services (Fig. 3.3). Mobile money, used by 82% of the population, remains the most popular financial product. This achievement is driven by digital technology, which nearly closed the gender gap in formal access (Finaccess, 2024). Also, financial inclusion rates have significantly increased due to the M-Pesa platform's vital role in delivering financial services to the unbanked. A sizable section of Kenyans without access to traditional financial systems have been successfully reached via M-Pesa.

To meet the evolving financial needs of consumers, businesses, and the government, M-Pesa has equally transformed over the years from a simple payment and transaction platform into a comprehensive financial ecosystem. Today, it offers wealth management, insurance, credit, savings, and investment solutions, among other financial services (Safaricom, 2024). The platform plays a crucial role in Kenya's economic growth and promotes financial well-being across the continent. Its extensive network of agents ensures that even remote areas have access to essential financial services, fostering greater financial inclusion. M-Pesa has played a transformative role in enhancing financial inclusion in Africa, particularly in Kenya, by providing accessible, secure, and efficient financial services to underserved populations.

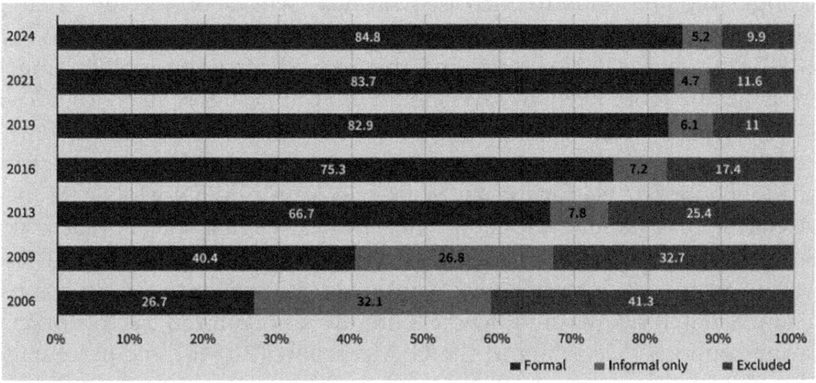

Fig. 3.3 Overall Financial Access 2006 to 2024 in Kenya (%) (*Source* Finaccess [2024])

The Impact of Mobile Money on Personal Savings, Remittances, and Small Business

The Impact of Mobile Money on Personal Savings

Savings refer to the amount of money remaining after all consumption needs have been met. People save for various reasons, including emergencies, significant future expenses, business or educational investments, and retirement. Mobile money services have significantly impacted financial inclusion in Africa, particularly in shaping savings habits among underbanked and unbanked populations. Studies indicate that mobile money increases the likelihood of saving for medical emergencies, especially among disadvantaged groups (Ky et al., 2018). Additionally, by improving access to financial services, mobile money positively influences domestic savings and fosters entrepreneurship (Okrah & Nepp, 2022).

Also, a comprehensive review of 82 studies found that mobile money provides various socioeconomic benefits, including financial development and improved household well-being (Nan et al., 2021). Research on low-income women in urban and rural areas of western Kenya revealed that access to mobile money-based savings tools can reduce their reliance on high-risk income sources, such as transactional sex (Jones & Gong, 2021). Research from Mozambique indicates that access to mobile money savings accounts leads to increased savings (Batista & Vicente, 2017). Additionally, 10.9% of mobile money users are inclined to save (MTN, 2019). Ochieng (2023) also found that individuals using mobile money are generally more likely to save and are 0.56 times more likely to have a savings product than non-users.

Millions of people now have greater access to financial services because of mobile money platforms like M-Pesa in Kenya, MTN Mobile Money in Ghana, and Orange Money in West Africa. Digital wallets that make saving easier are available through many mobile money services. These wallets frequently interface with banks and microfinance organizations, giving rural residents and workers in the unorganized sector official savings options. According to the GSMA report (2024a), the percentage of mobile money services offering savings features increased from 39% in 2022 to 44% in 2023. Additionally, in some countries, mobile money has enabled people to save. For instance, in Botswana, many users of PosoMoney mobile money accounts use them for savings, even though their balances do not earn interest. Takyi et al. (2025) also found that mobile money use generally increases savings and saving behavior among individuals in Ghana.

Sub-Saharan Africa has the highest mobile money account ownership rate, with 39% of people having saved money using their mobile money account as shown in Fig. 3.4. This rise in formal savings was primarily driven by adults who used mobile money accounts rather than traditional financial institutions. Demirgüç-Kunt et al. (2021) opine that mobile money account holders now use their accounts for various financial activities, with mobile money surpassing bank accounts as the preferred method for digitally receiving private sector salaries.

On a country basis, 37% of individuals in Ghana and Kenya and nearly 30% of adults in Senegal and Uganda reported using mobile money accounts for savings. Furthermore, the introduction of mobile money savings options almost doubled the percentage of adults who save formally in Sub-Saharan Africa (see Fig. 3.5). For example, in Kenya, over 70% of adults reported saving money in the previous year in both 2017 and 2021.

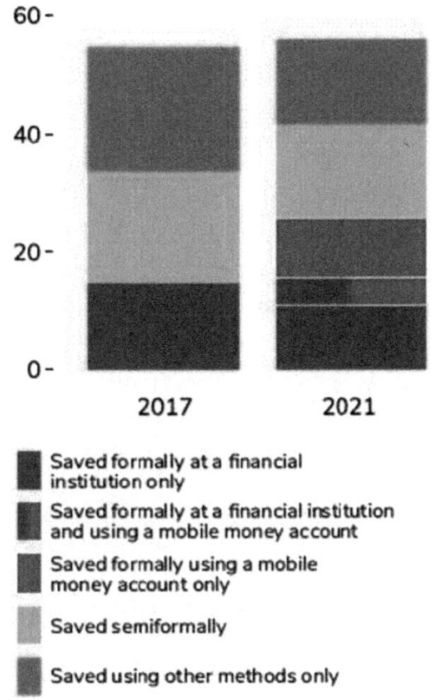

Fig. 3.4 Adults saving money in Sub-Saharan Africa (%) 2017–2021 (*Source* Global Findex Database [2021])

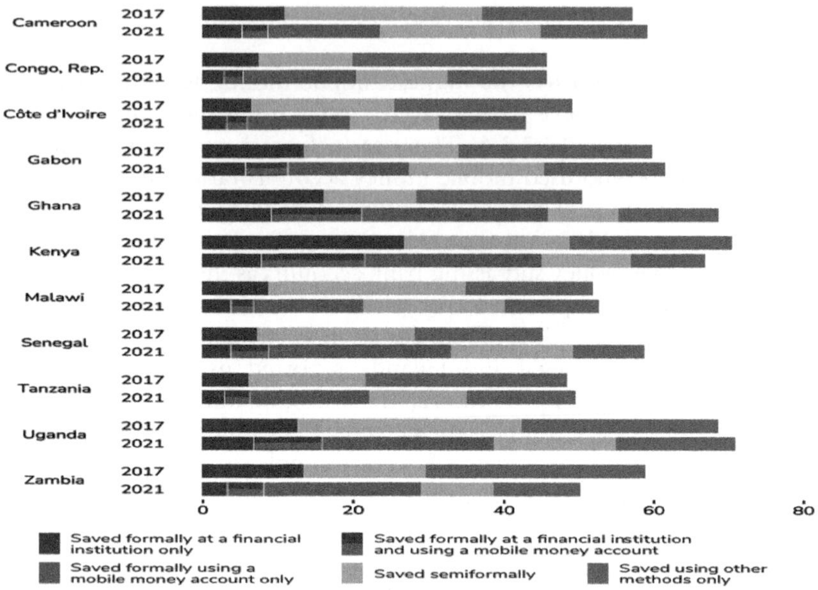

Fig. 3.5 Adults saving in selected SSA countries (%), 2017–2021 (*Source* Global Findex Database [2021])

However, the proportion of those saving formally increased from 27% in 2017 to 45% in 2021 (Demirgüç-Kunt et al., 2021).

These findings highlight the crucial role of mobile money services in enhancing financial inclusion, encouraging savings behavior, and promoting economic development in African countries by making financial services more accessible and secure for previously underserved populations. Although mobile money-based savings products have increased both the number of savers and the amount of money saved, regulations in many countries prevent mobile money providers (MMPs) from distributing interest earned on their trust accounts to individual users.

The Impact of Mobile Money on Remittances

Africa is strongly dependent on remittances from both domestic and international sources. In 2024, remittances to Sub-Saharan Africa totaled

$56 billion (World Bank, 2024a, 2024b). Mobile money has significantly transformed the remittance landscape by providing a more formal and efficient alternative to traditional informal methods. Ngaba (2021) found that individuals with mobile money accounts are less likely to use informal remittance channels. Additionally, mobile money has enhanced cross-border remittances and strengthened regional financial integration in Sub-Saharan Africa (Tembo & Okoro, 2021). While mobile remittances offer fast, convenient, and cost-effective money transfers, their potential varies across regions due to differences in banking infrastructure and regulatory frameworks among African countries (Siegel & Fransen, 2013).

Due to the high cost of sending money through official channels, many migrants rely on informal methods to remit funds at home. Sub-Saharan Africa (SSA) remains one of the most expensive remittance regions. Target 10.c of the UN Sustainable Development Goal 10 specifically intends to eliminate remittance corridors that cost more than 5% and lower remittance transaction costs to less than 3% to alleviate economic inequality across nations (United Nations, 2015). The average cost of sending $200 remittance into the Sub-Saharan Africa region increased from 7.9% in 2023 to 8.37 in the second quarter of 2024 (World Bank, 2024a, 2024b).

However, research suggests that remittance via mobile money has significantly reduced remittance transaction costs in rural Africa, leading to increased market participation and financial inclusion. For example, mobile money platforms like M-Pesa have substantially lowered remittance costs in Kenya and other African nations, potentially helping to achieve the Sustainable Development Goal (SDG) target of reducing remittance fees to 3% well before 2030 (Metzger et al., 2019). Aker et al. (2020) reveals that mobile money can reduce the cost of sending remittances as compared with traditional money transfer systems in Niger. Batista and Vicente (2023) also confirm that mobile money substantially reduces the transaction costs of remittances in rural Africa.

In the third quarter of 2024, the total charge for sending $200 via mobile money was 3.54%, reflecting a 5% decrease from the 2022 rate (see Fig. 3.6). However, the cost for smaller remittances increased, with the cost of sending $50 rising to 4.80% and $100 to 4.15% (Fig. 3.8). Despite this increasing trend for lower amounts, mobile money transfer costs remain lower than many MTO remittance services. In the second quarter of 2024, the global average charge for a $200 transfer increased to 6.65% (World Bank, 2024a, 2024b), further underscoring the cost advantages of mobile money and its role in advancing the UN Sustainable Development Goal (SDG) 10.c.

Furthermore, between 2014 and 2021, the number of financial institutions and mobile money accounts used for sending and receiving remittances grew by 50%, while reliance on cash and money transfer operators (MTOs) declined (Fig. 3.7). This trend highlights the region's increasing adoption and expansion of digital transfers and mobile money services.

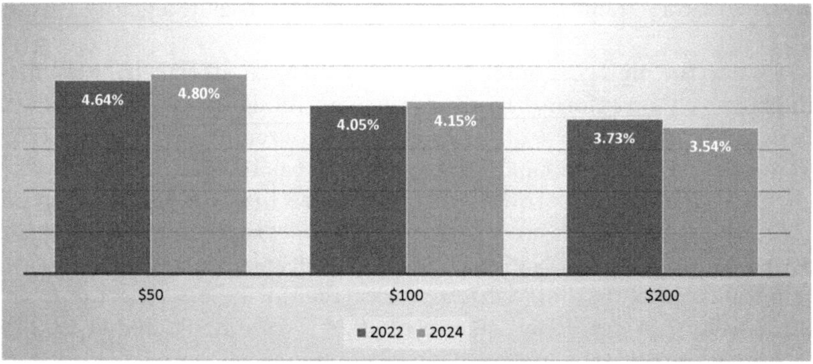

Fig. 3.6 Total fee (%) to send a cross-border mobile money remittance (*Source* Authors' Computations based on GSMA Remittances Pricing Survey [2024b])

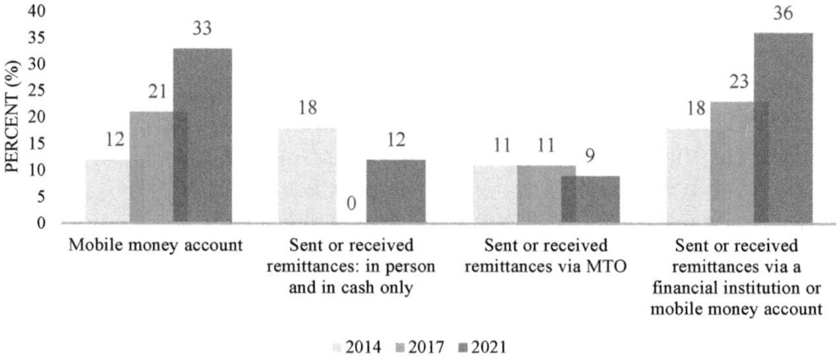

Fig. 3.7 Account ownership and digital remittances growth in Sub-Saharan Africa (*Source* Authors' computations based on Global Findex data [2022])

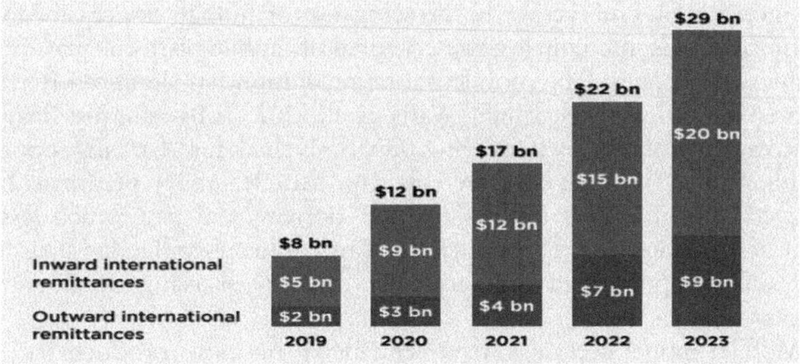

Fig. 3.8 Use of Mobile money for international remittances transaction values, 2019–2023 (*Source* GMSA state of industrial report on mobile money [2024a])

Using mobile money for international remittances has also increased the flow of remittances and impacted GDP. Research in Uganda found that using mobile money services led to a 13% increase in per capita consumption and a 36% rise in the total value of remittances received. The use of mobile money for international remittances has grown significantly over time. In 2023, the total transaction value surged by more than 70%, reaching $29 billion, up from $8 billion in 2019 (see Fig. 3.8). This rise in cross-border remittances can be attributed to the increasing adoption of mobile money for such transactions. According to GSMA (2024a), a 10-percentage-point increase in mobile money usage between 2013 and 2022 contributed to a 0.4%–1.0% rise in GDP, with mobile money and digital remittances being key drivers of this economic impact.

In summary, mobile money has revolutionized African remittances by enabling faster, more affordable, and more convenient transactions. It has also played a key role in advancing SDG 10.c, which aims to reduce remittance costs to 3%.

The Impact of Mobile Money on Small Businesses

Since millions of small businesses use mobile money for transactions, its influence on economic development and business expansion cannot be understated. Mobile money services have significantly impacted the performance of small and medium-sized businesses (SMEs) in developing nations. Micro-, small-, and medium-sized enterprises (MSMEs) are increasingly embracing the growing use of mobile devices in developing countries, recognizing the potential of mobile platforms to address business challenges. The mobile phone revolution has significantly transformed various aspects of life (Waris et al., 2024). By offering financial services to business owners who previously had few banking options, mobile money has helped close this gap. Mobile money platforms have allowed small business owners to save, borrow, and pay, which lessens their dependency on cash transactions. Entrepreneurs and individuals with few banking options can now access financial services using mobile money (Hamdan et al., 2022).

Mobile money services have enhanced business productivity and reduced transaction costs, particularly for small and medium-sized enterprises (SMEs). These services support business growth by streamlining various commercial processes, including stock purchases, payments, money transfers, and sales transactions (Chale & Mbamba, 2015). Traditional banking transactions are often associated with high costs and long processing times. However, mobile money has greatly reduced these expenses while improving efficiency. Sending and receiving money via mobile money is also more cost-effective than using cash or conventional banking methods. Instant payment processing allows businesses to operate efficiently without delays in receiving funds. Research conducted in Tanzania and Côte d'Ivoire shows that mobile money users are 37% more likely to engage in distant markets than non-users (Yao et al., 2022). This technology facilitates quick and cost-effective money transfers, helping to mitigate the risks associated with remote market participation (Yao & Shanoyan, 2018).

The convenience of mobile money payment options has enabled businesses to reach a broader audience. Accepting mobile money payments attracts more customers, including those without cash. Additionally, by extending a company's reach beyond physical locations, internet and mobile platforms have contributed to the growth of e-commerce. Islam et al. (2018) found that using mobile money positively correlates with a company's likelihood of purchasing fixed assets in Kenya, Tanzania, and Uganda. This positive impact is ascribed to reduced transaction costs, increased liquidity, and improved creditworthiness associated with mobile financial services. Equally, Studies conducted in Ghana, Somalia, Cameroon, and Tanzania indicate that mobile money enhances business growth, improves financial performance, and increases access to financial services (Chale & Mbamba, 2015; Mohamed, 2023; Talom & Tengeh, 2019; Waris et al., 2024).

Similarly, many mobile platforms now offer airtime and credit services. Businesses increasingly use digital financial records from mobile money transactions to assess creditworthiness, making it easier for small enterprises to secure loans. Access to credit enables entrepreneurs to invest in marketing, equipment, and inventory, fostering business growth. Makhandia et al. (2022) found that mobile money services also facilitate better financial management practices, such as improved savings habits and access to credit. Small businesses and entrepreneurs can expand their operations and increase profitability by investing in marketing, equipment, and inventory. Studies show that SMEs using mobile money experience improved savings practices, faster payment processing, increased sales, and more efficient stock purchases (Chale & Mbamba, 2015; Sinkala, 2023). In Somalia, a 1% increase in mobile money usage led to an 11.14% rise in business growth (Mohamed, 2023). Similarly, in Cameroon, mobile money services accounted for 73% of the variation in SME turnover (Talom & Tengeh, 2019). Also, in Kenya, mobile money services significantly positively affected SMEs' financial growth (Makhandia et al., 2022).

Mobile money has significantly impacted small businesses in Africa because it has increased financial access, decreased transaction costs, and allowed business expansion. These results demonstrate the potential of mobile money to alleviate barriers to market access and imply that measures designed to promote mobile money usage may improve smallholder farmers' market participation in developing nations.

Future Trends and Sustainability of Mobile Money

As mobile money continues to reshape the financial landscape in Africa, the focus is gradually shifting from basic transaction services to a more robust and integrated financial ecosystem. The next phase of mobile money growth will depend not only on technological advancements but also on the sector's ability to respond to emerging social, regulatory, and environmental challenges. This section explores key trends that are likely to shape the future of mobile money in Africa, as well as the factors influencing its long-term sustainability.

Expansion into Digital Financial Ecosystems

Mobile money platforms are increasingly evolving beyond peer-to-peer transfers and airtime top-ups into full-service digital financial ecosystems. Providers are integrating services such as digital credit, savings, microinsurance, investment tools, and merchant payments (Ochollah, 2025). These new offerings are particularly relevant for small businesses and informal sector actors who require flexible, low-barrier financial products. The convergence of mobile money with fintech and digital banking innovations is also enabling embedded finance models, where financial services are integrated directly into platforms used for agriculture, health, education, and e-commerce (Beck, 2024). For example, mobile money is now being linked to agricultural value chains through platforms that enable farmers to access payments, inputs, market prices, and loans via their mobile phones. In countries like Kenya and Ghana, e-wallets are transforming how farming communities manage finances and access capital.[1]

Interoperability and Platform Integration

A key future trend is the move toward greater interoperability among mobile money platforms, banks, and fintech services. As users increasingly demand seamless transactions across networks, the push for system integration is gaining momentum. Interoperability allows customers to send and receive money between different mobile operators or between mobile wallets and bank accounts, thus improving convenience, competition, and efficiency in the financial sector (Colangelo, 2024). In countries like Ghana, the Bank of Ghana has introduced regulatory frameworks encouraging cross-platform integration, and this has led to enhanced user experience and increased financial activity.[2] Regionally, cross-border mobile money initiatives are also growing, with platforms being linked

[1] https://blogs.worldbank.org/en/africacan/can-digitizing-agribusiness-payments-africa-build-ramp-financial-inclusion-farmers.

[2] Read more from here: https://thebftonline.com/2025/01/24/interoperability-digital-payment-systems-drive-financial-inclusion-to-97/.

across countries to support intra-African trade and remittances under the African Continental Free Trade Area (AfCFTA).[3]

Regulatory Evolution and Consumer Protection

As the mobile money ecosystem matures, regulatory oversight is evolving to ensure stability, security, and consumer protection. Central banks and regulatory authorities are now focusing on risk-based approaches to Know Your Customer (KYC) requirements, anti-money laundering (AML) compliance, data protection, and cybersecurity (Michael, 2025). The sustainability of mobile money hinges on maintaining user trust, particularly in the face of growing digital fraud, identity theft, and transaction disputes. Additionally, as mobile money services expand to include credit and insurance, regulators must balance innovation with safeguarding clients from predatory lending, mis-selling, or over-indebtedness. Financial consumer protection laws and effective grievance redress mechanisms will be critical in sustaining confidence in digital finance.

Green and Inclusive Mobile Finance

Sustainability also involves aligning mobile money with broader development goals, including environmental sustainability and social inclusion. There is a growing opportunity to link mobile money with green finance initiatives, such as pay-as-you-go solar systems and climate resilience insurance (GSMA, 2019). By using mobile payments to support clean energy adoption, agriculture financing, and disaster relief, mobile money can contribute to climate adaptation and the green economy transition (Foster-Collins, 2024). Moreover, future growth must address gender and geographic disparities in mobile money use. The sustainability of the sector will depend on its ability to close digital gender gaps, extend services to persons with disabilities, and ensure accessibility for remote and marginalized populations. Inclusive design, community engagement, and adaptive product development will be vital in this regard.

[3] See, for example: https://www.myjoyonline.com/ghana-and-rwanda-sign-mou-to-enhance-cross-border-fintech-agreement/.

Innovation in Infrastructure and Technology

Advances in artificial intelligence (AI), blockchain, and biometric technology are set to shape the future of mobile money. AI is already being used in credit scoring, fraud detection, and customer support through chatbots (Mundummal, 2023). Blockchain enhances transparency and security, especially in cross-border transactions and identity verification. Biometric KYC systems are emerging as secure and inclusive alternatives to traditional documentation, particularly in regions where formal ID coverage is low (Reshko, 2024). At the same time, the rollout of 5G, cloud computing, and data analytics capabilities will support more agile and efficient mobile financial services. Continued investment in digital infrastructure and internet access will be necessary to support these innovations and extend their reach to underserved communities.

Conclusion and Recommendations

The evolution of mobile money in Africa has significantly transformed the financial landscape, providing millions of previously excluded individuals with access to essential financial services. From basic peer-to-peer transfers to more complex products like microcredit and digital insurance, mobile money has emerged as a vital tool for promoting financial inclusion, especially among rural communities, informal workers, women, and youth. Its ability to overcome geographical, infrastructural, and bureaucratic barriers has enabled greater economic participation and resilience across the continent. However, as this chapter has shown, the continued growth and sustainability of mobile money services are not guaranteed and will depend on how stakeholders address critical challenges related to access, infrastructure, regulation, gender disparity, and digital literacy.

While mobile money has reached impressive levels of adoption in several African countries, extending its full benefits to the unbanked remains a pressing issue. Infrastructure gaps, especially in remote and rural areas, limited digital skills, affordability of devices, and the gender gap in access to technology are among the barriers that must be systematically addressed. Moreover, as mobile money platforms diversify into credit, savings, and insurance products, consumer protection and responsible digital finance become even more important. Without adequate safeguards, there is a risk of digital exploitation, financial exclusion, and erosion of public trust in the digital financial ecosystem.

To ensure mobile money continues to serve as a catalyst for inclusive finance, several recommendations are in order. First, governments must invest in expanding digital infrastructure, particularly in rural and underserved areas. Affordable and reliable mobile connectivity is a foundational enabler for accessing digital financial services. Second, financial and digital literacy campaigns must be scaled up and tailored to the local context. These programs should focus on vulnerable groups, including women, the elderly, and persons with disabilities, and use local languages and culturally relevant materials.

In addition, regulatory frameworks must evolve to support innovation while safeguarding users. Risk-based Know Your Customer (KYC) approaches, data privacy protections, and dispute resolution mechanisms should be embedded into the digital finance environment. Regulators should also facilitate interoperability among platforms to increase user convenience and market efficiency.

Gender-inclusive strategies are also critical. Bridging the digital gender divide requires targeted measures, such as subsidized mobile devices for women, training programs, and the design of financial products that meet women's specific needs. Partnerships between mobile network operators, fintechs, development organizations, and governments can be instrumental in achieving this.

Finally, mobile money providers should adopt user-centric approaches that prioritize affordability, transparency, and responsiveness. Product innovation should be based on a deep understanding of the daily financial realities of low-income users. Where possible, services should be bundled to offer holistic solutions, such as combining payments, savings, and microinsurance in one mobile platform.

In conclusion, mobile money remains one of Africa's most promising tools for inclusive economic transformation. Its sustainability and effectiveness will depend on the commitment of all actors (public and private) to ensure that technological advancement translates into equitable access, meaningful empowerment, and long-term development impact. Through inclusive design, enabling policy, and a focus on digital literacy and infrastructure, mobile money can continue to bridge the financial divide and support Africa's broader development aspirations.

References

Ahmad, A. H., Green, C. J., Jiang, F., & Murinde, V. (2023). Mobile money, ICT, financial inclusion and growth: How different is Africa? *Economic Modelling, 121*, Article 106220.

Aker, J. C., Prina, S., & Welch, C. J. (2020). Migration, money transfers, and mobile money: Evidence from Niger. In *AEA Papers and Proceedings* (pp. 589–593). American Economic Association.

Alhassan, T. F., Guryanov, S. A., & Kouadio, A. J. (2021). The impact of mobile money, remittances, and financial development on innovative growth in sub-Saharan Africa. Экономика региона. 2021. Том 17, выпуск 1, *17*(1), 276–287.

Awuah, E. (2025). The digital wallet revolution: Assessing mobile money's role in transforming emerging economies: A review. *Asian Journal of Economics, Business and Accounting, 25*(1), 35–43.

Batista, C., & Vicente, P. C. (2017). *Improving access to savings through mobile money: Experimental evidence from smallholder farmers in Mozambique*. Working Paper, 1705.

Batista, C., & Vicente, P. C. (2023). Is mobile money changing rural Africa? Evidence from a field experiment. *Review of Economics and Statistics*, 1–29.

Beck, S. (2024). *Understanding the role of embedded finance in the Fintech revolution*. https://www.forbes.com/councils/forbestechcouncil/2024/01/25/understanding-the-role-of-embedded-finance-in-the-fintech-revolution/

Chale, P., & Mbamba, U. O. L. (2015). The role of mobile money services on growth of small and medium enterprises in Tanzania: Evidence from Kinondoni District in Dar es Salaam Region. *Business Management Review, 17*(1), 81–96.

Colangelo, G. (2024). *Mobile wallets and interoperability: When competition meets financial inclusion*. https://ssrn.com/abstract=5039449

Del Torso, O. (2019). *Mobile payment systems and financial inclusion: The case of M-Pesa*. https://tesi.luiss.it/24994/1/212901_DEL%20TORSO_OTTAVIO.pdf

Demirgüç-Kunt, A., Klapper, L., Singer, D., & Ansar, S. (2021). *Financial inclusion, digital payments, and resilience in the age of covid-19*. World Bank Report.

Ericsson. (2021). *Mobile financial services on the rise: Exploring the consumer perspective in Sub-Saharan Africa*. https://www.ericsson.com/4ab973/assets/local/reports-papers/consumerlab/doc/11092021-mobile-money-report.pdf

Finacess. (2024). *2024 FinAccess Household Survey*. https://www.centralbank.go.ke/wp-content/uploads/2024/12/2024-FINACCESS-HOUSEHOLD-SURVEY-MAIN-REPORT.pdf

Foster-Collins, L. (2024). *How mobile money is proving to be a key technology driving development*. https://www.globalinnovation.fund/news/how-mobile-money-is-proving-to-be-a-key-technology-driving-development

Global Findex Database. (2021). *Financial inclusion, digital payments, and resilience in the age of COVID-19.*

GSMA. (2019). *Harnessing the power of mobile money to achieve the Sustainable Development Goals*. https://digitalfrontiersinstitute.org/resource/harnessing-the-power-of-mobile-money-to-achieve-the-sustainable-development-goals/

GSMA. (2023). *Smartphone owners are now the global majority, New GSMA report reveals*. https://www.gsma.com/newsroom/press-release/smartphone-owners-are-now-the-global-majority-new-gsma-report-reveals/

GSMA. (2024a). *The state of the industry report on mobile money*. https://www.gsma.com/sotir/wp-content/uploads/2024/03/GSMA-SOTIR-2024_Report.pdf

GSMA. (2024b). *Cross-border mobile money remittance cost survey: Key trends and insights*. https://www.gsma.com/solutions-and-impact/connectivity-for-good/mobile-for-development/wp-content/uploads/2024/12/Cross-border-Mobile-Money-Remittance-Cost-Survey.pdf

Hamdan, J. S., Lehmann-Uschner, K., & Menkhoff, L. (2022). Mobile money, financial inclusion, and unmet opportunities: Evidence from Uganda. *The Journal of Development Studies, 58*(4), 671–691.

Hughes, N., & Lonie, S. (2007). M-PESA: Mobile money for the "unbanked" turning cellphones into 24-hour tellers in Kenya. *Innovations: Technology, Governance, Globalization, 2*(1–2), 63–81.

Islam, A., Muzi, S., & Rodriguez Meza, J. L. (2018). Does mobile money use increase firms' investment? Evidence from Enterprise Surveys in Kenya, Uganda, and Tanzania. *Small Business Economics, 51*, 687–708.

Jaensson, J. E. (2018). The mobile money revolution. In *Marketing management in Africa* (pp. 146–158). Routledge.

Jang, J. M., & Park, H. (2016). Mobile money in Sub-Saharan Africa and its implications. KIEP Research Paper No. *World Economy Update*, 16–3.

Jones, K., & Gong, E. (2021). Precautionary savings and shock-coping behaviors: Effects of promoting mobile bank savings on transactional sex in Kenya. *Journal of Health Economics, 78*, Article 102460.

Ky, S., Rugemintwari, C., & Sauviat, A. (2018). Does mobile money affect saving behaviour? Evidence from a developing country. *Journal of African Economies, 27*(3), 285–320.

Makhandia, C. S., Miroga, J., & Otinga, H. N. (2022). Mobile money services and financial growth of small and medium enterprises in Kakamega Town, Kenya. *The Strategic Journal of Business & Change Management, 9*(2), 63–86.

Metzger, M., Riedler, T., & Pédussel Wu, J. (2019). *Migrant remittances: Alternative money transfer channels* (No. 127/2019). Working Paper.

McCaffrey, M. (2022). *Where in the world is mobile money prominent?* https://www.uncdf.org/article/7904/where-in-the-world-is-mobile-money-prominent

Michael, C. (2025). *Africa's top 10 countries in mobile money regulation*. https://businessday.ng/africa/article/africas-top-10-countries-in-mobile-money-regulation/

Mohamed, A. A. (2023). The influence of the mobile money payment on the performance of small and medium enterprises in Somalia. *Technological Forecasting and Social Change, 196*, Article 122821.

Mugambi, A., Njunge, C., & Yang, S. C. (2014). Mobile-money benefits and usage: The case of M-PESA. *IT Professional, 16*(3), 16–21.

Mundummal, S. (2023). *The future of digital payment technologies: AI, blockchain and biometrics leading the charge*. https://www.linkedin.com/pulse/future-digital-payment-technologies-ai-blockchain-charge-mundummal

MTN. (2019). *How mobile money changes the culture of saving in Africa*. https://www.mtn.com/how-mobile-money-changes-the-culture-of-saving-in-africa/

Nan, W., Zhu, X., & Lynne Markus, M. (2021). What we know and don't know about the socioeconomic impacts of mobile money in Sub-Saharan Africa: A systematic literature review. *The Electronic Journal of Information Systems in Developing Countries, 87*(2), Article e12155.

Ngaba, M. (2021). How does mobile money affect the use of informal remittance channels in Sub-Saharan Africa. *Migration et développement inclusif*, 123.

Ochieng, K. O. (2023). *The Influence of mobile money on savings behavior* (Doctoral dissertation). KDI School.

Ochollah, J. (2025). *A global perspective on mobile money in 2025*. https://www.linkedin.com/pulse/global-perspective-mobile-money-2025-judy-ochollah-ayyce

Okrah, J., & Nepp, A. N. (2022). Mobile money services: An enabler of development processes in Africa. *Journal of Applied Economic Research, 21*(4), 644–662.

Omanga, J. N., & Dreyer, J. K. (2017). Innovation and financial inclusion in Kenya innovation and financial inclusion in Kenya: A case study of M-PESA. In *Technological integration as a catalyst for industrial development and economic growth* (pp. 207–227). IGI Global.

Reshko, A. (2024). *Exploring the future: Fintech trends and innovations in digital payments*. https://fortyseven47.com/blog/future-fintech-trends-in-digital-payments/

Safaricom. (2024). *Safaricom's M-PESA Hits 34 million customers in Kenya*. https://www.safaricom.co.ke/media-center-landing/press-releases/safaricoms-m-pesa-hits-34-million-customers-in-kenya

Siegel, M., & Fransen, S. (2013). New technologies in remittance sending: Opportunities for mobile remittances in Africa. *African Journal of Science, Technology, Innovation and Development, 5*(5), 423–438.

Sinkala, N. N. (2023). Mobile money and SME growth: A Zambian perspective. *Journal of Business and Strategic Management, 8*(7), 1–18.

Suri, T., Aker, J., Batista, C., Callen, M., Ghani, T., Jack, W., Klapper, L., Riley, E., Schaner, S., & Sukhtankar, S. (2023). Mobile money. *VoxDevLit, 2*(2), 3.

Takyi, P. O., Sorkpor, C., & Asante, G. N. (2025). Mobile money for financial inclusion and saving practices: Empirical evidence from Ghana. *Journal of Economic and Administrative Sciences, 41*(1), 16–32.

Talom, F. S. G., & Tengeh, R. K. (2019). The impact of mobile money on the financial performance of the SMEs in Douala Cameroon. *Sustainability, 12*(1), 183.

Tembo, J., & Okoro, C. (2021). Mobile money and regional financial integration: Evidence from sub-Saharan Africa. *Journal of Economic and Financial Sciences, 14*(1), 13.

United Nations. (2015). *Transforming our world: the 2030 Agenda for Sustainable Development. Seventieth session, Agenda items 15 and 116*. New York

Waris, A., Nazir, S., Khan, S., Ali, M. Z., & Gorsi, M. S. R. (2024). Effects of mobile money services on the performance of small and medium size enterprises. *American Journal of Industrial and Business Management, 14*(4), 537–552.

World Bank. (2024a). *Remittance flows continue to grow in 2023 Albeit at slower pace*. https://blogs.worldbank.org/en/peoplemove/in-2024--remittance-flows-to-low--and-middle-income-countries-ar#:~:text=Growth%20in%20remittance%20flows%20in,percent%20for%20Sub%2DSaharan%20Africa.&text=Source%3A%20Authors'%20estimates.,-Note%3A%20LMICs%20%3D%20low&text=It%20is%20notable%20that%20remittances,%2D%20and%20middle%2Dincome%20countries.

World Bank. (2024b). *An analysis of trend in remittances service; Remittances Prices Worldwide Quarterly, Issue 50*. https://remittanceprices.worldbank.org/sites/default/files/rpw_main_report_and_annex_q224.pdf

World Bank. (2025). *Financial Inclusion: Financial inclusion is a key enabler to reducing poverty and boosting prosperity*. https://www.worldbank.org/en/topic/financialinclusion/overview

Yao, B. H., Shanoyan, A., Schwab, B., & Amanor-Boadu, V. (2022). Mobile money, transaction costs, and market participation: Evidence from Côte d'Ivoire and Tanzania. *Food Policy, 112*, Article 102370.

Yao, B., & Shanoyan, A. (2018). *The use of mobile money application and smallholder farmer market participation: Evidence form Cote d Ivoire and Tanzania*. https://ageconsearch.umn.edu/record/277259/?v=pdf

CHAPTER 4

Digital Banking Solutions: Enhancing Accessibility and Convenience

Yazidu Ustarz

Introduction

The banking industry globally has undergone significant transformation in the way it carries out its operations and services. Much of this transformation has been attributable to the advent of technology. Technology has made it easier for banks to carry out their mandates of financial intermediation in a more efficient manner. This chapter examines in detail the transition from traditional to digital banking in Africa, and how digital applications has helped in expanding the frontier of financial inclusion through mobile banking. The rest of the study is organised as follows: section "The Shift from Traditional to Digital-Only Banking Models" presents the shift from traditional to digital-only banking models while section "Mobile Banking Applications and Their Role in Financial Inclusion" assesses the role Mobile banking applications play in

Y. Ustarz (✉)
Department of Finance, School of Business, University for Development Studies, Tamale, Ghana
e-mail: uyazidu@uds.edu.gh

I. N. Yakubu (ed.), *Banking on Inclusion*, Sustainable Development Goals Series, https://doi.org/10.1007/978-3-031-96716-0_4

driving financial inclusion. The chapter also examined in section "Case Studies of Digital Banks Transforming Access to Services", relevant case studies on how digital banks are transforming access to services. The section "Overcoming Logistical and Infrastructural Challenges Through Digital Banking" considered how banks could overcome logistical and infrastructural challenges through digital banking with section "Regulatory Considerations for Digital Banking Expansion" looking at regulatory considerations for digital banking expansion. The chapter concludes by teasing out some implications of digital banking in a modern financial system and proffer some policy recommendations.

The Shift from Traditional to Digital-Only Banking Models

Technology has drastically transformed all aspects of human endeavour and the banking sector is not an exception (GCB, 2023; Saal et al., 2017a, 2017b). The banking industry has leveraged on advancement in technology to enhance service delivery through digital banking. Digital banking or bank has been defined as "a financial services provider with a banking license that adopts new technologies in all its operations to offer banking products and services through mainly digital channels" (Alliance for Financial Inclusion, 2021; Kerse & Staschen, 2021, 16). Unlike traditional banks that rely on their physical presence to provide financial services, digital banks could operate physically in an area or virtually depending on the regulations in a particular country (Ehrentraud et al., 2020). Traditional Banks are therefore transitioning from the traditional models of banking to integrating and adopting digital tools in order to stay competitive in the market. Five digital banks have been identified including challenger banks, digitised incumbents, non-banks, neo banks, and beta banks. The challenger banks, also known as new banks, are those who have acquired full banking licenses. These are considered as FinTechs with banking licenses who are seen as direct competitors to the traditional banks. The digitalised incumbents are existing banks that have leveraged on digital technologies to transform their operations. Their major strength is their ability to serve both traditional and digital customers through market segmentation. The non-banks are those digital banks that have no traditional banking licenses but rather rely on other means to provide financial services. The neobanks can be seen as an extension of the non-banks, who don't have a license, but rather partner a licensed banks to offer financial services. Thus, their customers are required to have accounts with a licensed existing bank. The final one is the beta banks which are either a subsidiary of an existing licensed bank or a joint venture offering financial services through a licensed parent company. They are often strategically set up to penetrate through a new market, targeting a particular consumer segment with tailored products and services (Mothibi & Rahulani, 2021).

Digital technology such as mobile and online banking help to promote efficiency in service delivery. African financial sector is largely bank driven and technology has come to assist in extending financial services to the unbanked. There is increasing demand for digital banking services due to the advent of technology. In 2023, 73% of bank's customers indicated their preference for mobile banking or app, while 13% said they preferred Internet banking (see Fig. 4.1).

There is a growing number of people moving towards digital banking. It is expected that the number will reach 3.6 billion by the end of 2024 and around 94% of this population is expected to be active users of the

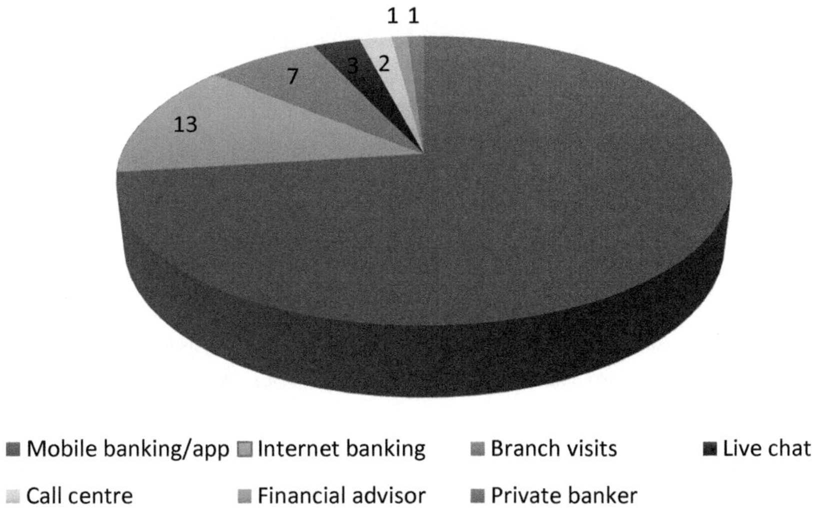

Fig. 4.1 Main modalities for accessing daily banking needs (*Source* African Banker [2023])

service.[1] By 2026, the value of digital banking platforms is also projected to reach $13.9 Billion by 2026.[2] In Africa, digital banking platforms are shaping how financial services are being delivered to meet customers' demands, stay competitive, and be able to expand market shares beyond the traditional sphere of operations. While 76% of banks in Africa recognised digitalisation as a top priority, over 60% (see Fig. 4.2) of them have digitalised most of their operations (African Banker, 2024). The adoption of digital banking is seen as a win-win for both customers and institutions.

Banks in Africa have applied different digital technologies in their operations aiming at achieving efficiency (Liang et al., 2025) and ensuring the safety of their operations (Mothibi & Rahulani, 2021), security, and maintaining and capturing market shares. Digital technologies such as Artificial Intelligence, Big data analytics, blockchain, etc. allow banks to be competitive and ensure the financial stability of their operation (Liang et al., 2025). Hence, banks have invested in one form of digital technology or the other. For instance, as indicated in Fig. 4.3, cloud computing

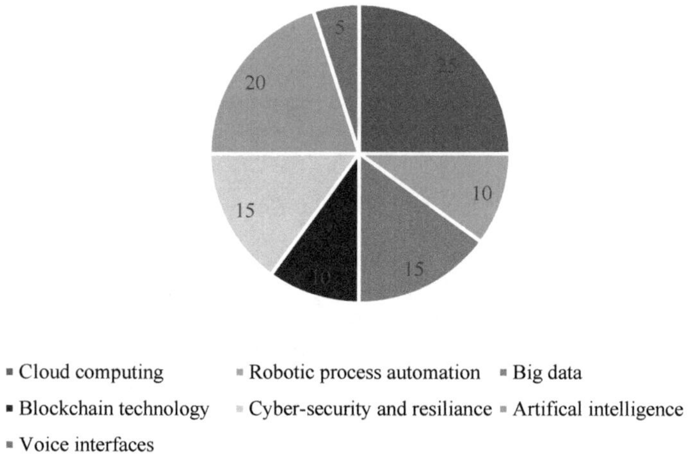

Fig. 4.2 Bank's technological priorities in Africa (percentage) (*Source* The African Digital Banking Transformation Report [2024])

[1] https://www.infopulse.com/blog/forces-shaping-banking.

[2] https://neontri.com/blog/digital-banking-transformation/.

represents the top priority technology for banks in Africa in 2024 with the highest score of 25% followed by the use of Artificial Intelligence (20%). The area of cyber-security and resilience, and Big data come as the third priority areas for banks (15% each), Robotic process automation and Blockchain technology each having a score of 10%, while Voice interfaces (5%) come as the least area of priorities for banks.

According to the African Banker Report (2024), digital banking is associated with certain benefits with customer satisfaction and loyalty having the most benefit (21.6) followed by customer engagement and personalisation (18.9) as captured in Table 4.1. Bank's ability to move faster with new products in the market and ability to impact profitability and revenue come next with 16% impact while higher customer acquisition followed with 13.5%. On the part of customers, digital banking has proven to be cost effective and convenient.

As shown in Fig. 4.3, in terms of adoption of digital banking for different areas of the bank's operations, retail banking has the highest priority of 39.5%. Banks have leveraged on internet and mobile applications to reach out to their retail customers. This is followed by the desire to target the SME sector, with a score of 26.3%. About 7.9% indicated their priority of digital banking to target Corporate and business banking, while 13.2% identified investment banking as their priority area.

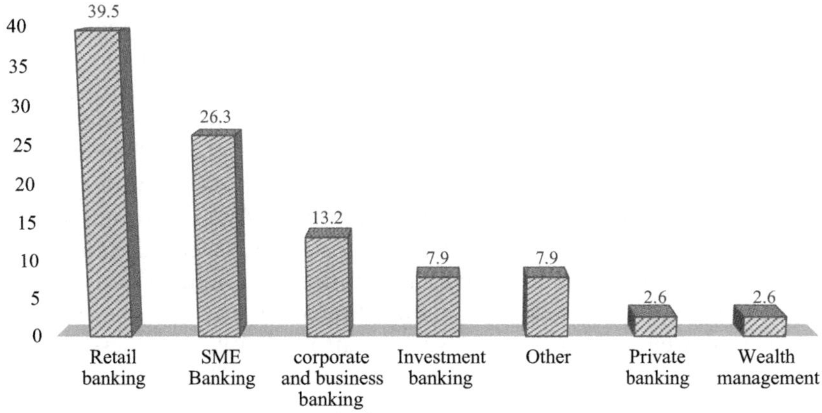

Fig. 4.3 Bank's focus on digital transformation (percentage) (*Source* The African Banker Report [2024])

Table 4.1 Benefits of adopting digital banking

Factor	*Percentage*
Better customer engagement and personalisation	18.9
Increased customer satisfaction and loyalty	21.6
Higher customer acquisition	13.5
Ability to go faster to market with new products	16.2
Lower maintenance costs	10.8
Increase in revenues and profitability	16.2
None of the above	2.7

Source The African Banker Report (2024)

Mobile Banking Applications and Their Role in Financial Inclusion

Mobile phones, though developed to serve the purpose of communication, it has become a tool that has revolutionised the provision of financial services globally and particularly in developing countries (Donovan, 2012). The number of mobile subscriptions globally in 2022 was 8.58 billion, which was higher than the world's population of 7.95 billion (World Economic Forum, 2023). Access to finance has been widely recognised as a major tool in achieving growth, reducing poverty, and inequality particularly in developing country. With access to finance being a major obstacle to achieving these objectives in Africa, policymakers have been in search of a means to deliver financial services for all in an efficient and more affordable way (Llewellyn, 2021). Mobile phone has proven to have the potential of achieving inclusivity in terms of access to varieties of financial products irrespective of one's location. Financial institutions have thus, capitalised on the widespread access to mobile phones to advance the issues of financial inclusion in Africa through mobile banking. The IMF (2020, 16) definition captures several dimensions of financial inclusion. It defines financial inclusion as 'a multifaceted concept, encompassing various dimensions, including access to and use of financial services as well as other aspects such as affordability, usefulness, quality, and awareness of financial services and products'. Thus, financial inclusion goes beyond just having access to financial services to include other dimensions such as usage, quality, and affordability, among others.

The majority of settlements in the region are rural, with greater percentage of banks concentrating in the urban areas, traditional banking services were not able to reach those residing in the area. The advent of mobile banking has breached this gap by making it possible for banks to operate virtually and be able to serve the marginalised and underserved areas of society (Kerse & Staschen, 2021). Mobile banking operates through four main channels: it can be delivered exclusively by banks, bank-led delivery in partnership with a third party such as Non-Government Organizations, it can also be delivered exclusively by Mobile Network Operators, and the last one being through a partnership between the banks and Mobile Network Operators (Singh et al., 2014).

In Africa, mobile banking has helped in deepening financial inclusion through mobile money operations. It is basically electronic fund that is stored and can be transfer by the use of a simple mobile phone. It functions in a similar fashion as a bank account which allows individuals to store, make withdrawals or even a transfer to another individual. The services are usually provided by the telecommunication companies through their agents who are physically closer to the people (Ndung'u, 2021). Mobilebanking has made it possible for the financially excluded to be reached with various financial products such as savings, insurance, credit, and remittances, among others (Donovan, 2012; Singh et al., 2014). Their services are seen to be 80% cheaper when compared with the traditional banking services, and they offer relatively higher interest on savings through their mobile money accounts (McKinsey, 2022).

The application of mobile banking particularly mobile money in Africa, has accelerated the pace of financial inclusion in Africa through the provision of digital financial services (European Investment Bank, 2024). Mobile banking apps have impacted financial inclusion in several ways: mobile apps have made it possible for people who have been financially excluded to have an account by merely possessing a mobile phone. Unlike traditional banks, the services of mobile money are delivered through their agents who are found within the communities. (Shaikh et al., 2023). The number of people globally who used mobile phones as accounts has moved to 1.75 billion in 2023 with a transaction value of 1.4 trillion annually. Of these, Africa alone accounted for over 65% (912 billion) of the value of transactions as demonstrated in Table 4.2.

These accounts allow customers to access various financial services as indicated in Table 4.3. It assists customers to mobilise funding for investment by making regular savings in their accounts. Indeed, customers earn interest by having some amount in their mobile money wallet. Customers can leverage on their accounts to borrow from the telcos which help

Table 4.2 Regional distribution of Mobile Money Services

Region	*Registered accounts (millions)*	*Active (30-day) accounts*	*Transaction volume (billion)*	*Transaction value ($ trillion)*
East Asia and Pacific	374	77	9	0.196
Europe and Central Asia	26	6	0.39	0.7
Latin America and the Caribbean	19	19	1	0.38
South Asia	401	89	12	0.214
Middle East and North Africa	401	9	0.72	0.3
World	1750	435	85	1.4
Sub-Saharan Africa	835	234	62	0..912

Source Raithatha and Storchi, 2024

customers to smoothen their consumption during adverse conditions. For instance, during COVID-19, when movements were restricted, families in financial distress were able to seek financial assistance from friends and families through mobile money (Egami et al., 2025). Services of the mobile app has gone beyond domestic transactions to include global transfer of funds such as remittances, business-to-business payments, and person-to-person. For instance, international remittance flows in Africa grew in value from about $20 billion to $29 billion between 2022 and 2023 while that of merchant payments amounted to $74 billion in 2023. With respect to remittances, the transfers is driven by remittances from West Africa and Eastern Africa which account for over 60% and 34% respectively. Another major function of the mobile money is the ease with which people and businesses are able to settle their bills without physically visiting the offices of the service provider. As indicated in Table 4.3, the West and East African countries lead when it comes to payment of bills using mobile money (Raithatha and Storchi, 2024).

The adoption of FinTech is however driven by multiple factors from both the demand and supply side. These include increasing urbanisation, a young population that is tech-savvy and the formalisation of the economy operations while the availability and affordability of smartphones, high

Table 4.3 Mobile Money services in African sub-regions

Region	*Africa*	*Northern Africa*	*Eastern Africa*	*Middle Africa*	*Northern Africa*	*Southern Africa*	*Western Africa*
Airtime top-up (millions)	1188.37	4.19	516.24	172.94	4.19	19.55	475.45
Bill payment (millions)	537.50	0.77	454.33	9.09	0.77	3.70	69.62
Bulk disbursement (millions)	216.95	0.05	93.86	4.56	0.05	2.67	115.79
Cash-in (millions)	705.64	1.63	359.82	80.26	1.63	6.62	257.31
Cash-out (millions)	591.55	0.83	269.58	67.07	0.83	5.42	248.64
International remittance (millions)	18.23	0.000594	6.12	0.96	0.000594	0.12	11.04
Merchant payment (millions)	404.41	0.21	295.29	37.74	0.21	3.75	67.41
P2P transfer (millions)	1937.09	7.05	1486.03	54.92	7.05	9.22	379.87

Source Author's compilation based on data from Raithatha and Storchi (2024).

internet connectivity constitute supply side factors (European Investment Bank, 2024). Other demands factors include high level of financial literacy, low-income earnings, and limited trust (Singh et al., 2014). These factors are the key drivers of the digital drive in ensuring financial inclusion goals are achieved. For instance, the number of smartphone subscriptions in sub-Saharan Africa rose from 33.27 million in 2012 to about 534 million in 2024, representing over a 1500 percentage growth.[3] African is said to be experiencing increasing urbanisation and is expected to reach 60% by 2050 from a figure of 47% in 2000.[4] Internet connectivity has also been a key technological innovation enabling uptake of financial inclusion products with access to broadband internet increasing

[3] https://www.statista.com/statistics/1133777/sub-saharan-africa-smartphone-subscriptions/.

[4] https://www.uneca.org/eca-events/africa-urban-forum-2024/spotlight-urbanization-africa.

to 36% in 2022. The improvement was also accompanied by a reduction in price which made it more affordable for people to access with a cost of a gigabyte of data decreasing from 10.5% of the monthly Gross National Income per capita in 2019 to about 5% in 2021 (World Bank, 2023). On the other hand, low income and financial literacy are factors also negatively affecting the potentials of FinTech to drive the financial inclusion agenda. Financial literacy in Africa is considered to be generally low with less than one-third of the population in sub-Saharan Africa being literate compared to OECD countries which have on the average, over 50% of financially literate population.[5] High financial literacy is very crucial as it influences one's ability to effectively understanding and use financial products offered through digital platforms (Yang et al., 2023).

Case Studies of Digital Banks Transforming Access to Services

Digital banking has helped in extending access to the financial services, thereby promoting financial inclusion. This section presents some evidence on the impact of digital banking, challenges, and some regulatory issues. The first case study in Box 4.1 focuses on the journey of TymeBank South Africa, a pioneer in digital banking.

Box 4.1: TymeBank-South Africa

Tyme Bank (Take Your Money Everywhere) is a pacesetter in digital Banking. Established in 2012, the bank aims to extend financial services to the underserved and financially excluded population in South Africa without having any physical branch. Operating a branchless bank, it employs the services of mobile apps and internet banking sites in collaboration with Boxer and Pick n Pay, retail outfits to provide a self-service kiosk throughout the country to facilitate the process of operating accounts and rendering of basic financial services such as savings, accounts checking

[5] https://www.cnbcafrica.com/2023/why-its-time-to-ramp-up-financial-literacy-education-across-africa/.

and debit cards.[6] This approach allows customers to transact both online and offline. The bank was fully acquired by the Commonwealth Bank of Australia in 2017, and the name was changed to TymeDigital. It was later in 2018 changed Tyme Bank Limited after it was sold to an investment firm, African Rainbow Capital (Jeník et al., 2020). It became the first digital bank in Africa to reach 10 million customers and be profitable. The bank has provided credit to the tune of $600 million to about 80,000 small businesses.[7] The success story of the banks is due to its customer and technology-cantered approach and strategic partnership. The bank strategy was to target the financially excluded with financial products and services that were secured, convenient, and user-friendly. The Bank currently has over 14 million customers.

Source Various Sources

The second case study in Box 4.2 presents the story of M-Pesa in Kenya which revolutionised mobile banking through the services of a mobile phone.

Box 4.2: The *M-Pesa*, Story

The *M-Pesa* story is one that efficiently demonstrate how financial inclusion could be achieved in developing countries setting through digitalisation. M-Pesa, which was launched in 2007 in Kenya, represents a success story of a pioneering journey of mobile money service globally. With over 34 million users and 300,000 agents across Kenya as of November 2024, M-Pesa which is owned by Safaricom commands over 93% of the market share.[8] With a successful piloting in 2006, the company engaged the key stakeholders including the Central Bank of Kenya and the Communication Commission of Kenya (CCK), with the intention of a

[6] https://en.wikipedia.org/wiki/TymeBank.

[7] https://ffnews.com/newsarticle/fintech/tymebank-reaches-10-million-customers-as-it-attracts-record-deposits-for-2024/.

[8] https://www.businessdailyafrica.com/bd/corporate/companies/safaricom-adds-500-000-M-pesa-users-in-two-months-to-34m-4847394.

nationwide rollout of the M-Pesa. Though initially faced resistance, particularly from commercial banks who viewed the move as an encroachment of their service mandate, it was eventually launched in 2007 (Ndung'u, 2021). The strength of their operation is their ability to reach the poor who have been excluded from the financial space by the formal financial institutions. Through their agents, they provided the financially excluded with an opportunity to access credit, save and transfer funds on a personal level as well as paying for services.[9] Within the first year of its operation, the number of agents moved from 307 to reach 2,329 in March 2008 while the value of transactions increased from 64 (Ksh million) to 16,756 (Ksh million) over the same period (Ndung'u, 2021). In 2014, the company launched an Android app, Safaricom M-Ledger, which allows users to check their transaction history just like a bank statement.[10]

The M-Pesa journey has been classified into five phases. The first phase had the objective of extending financial services to the poor by providing them with the means of mobilising savings and also accessing credit in times of need and consumption smoothening. Before its introduction, a large segment of the unbanked population had to rely on micro-savings whose locations were far from their communities and therefore making transactions more costly in time and cost (Ndung'u, 2021). The service contributed significantly in achieving financial inclusion goals as the adult population excluded from financial services fell from 41.3% to 11% between 2006 and 2019 (*FinAcess Survey, 2019). The second phase* witnessed the linking of customer's bank deposit and also strengthening collaboration with financial institutions. The arrangement allows the customers to make electronic retail payments for goods and services. This was followed by the third phase which saw the generation of credit scores for individuals by utilising their transactions and savings history. This was a major development aimed at addressing one major issue in accessing credit particularly by the poor; collateral (Asiamah et al., 2021). This allow

[9] https://en.wikipedia.org/wiki/M-Pesa#cite_note-2.

[10] https://en.wikipedia.org/wiki/M-Pesa#cite_note-2.

s financial institutions to evaluate the creditworthiness of borrowers. The next phase was a move to facilitate cross-border payments as well as international remittances, while the final phase was intensifying collaboration with FinTech companies to deliver financial services. (Ndung'u, 2021).

Currently, M-Pesa operates in about seven countries and contributing about 43% of Safaricom's service revenue. It continues to be a key driver of financial inclusion by extending affordable credit to the tune of $4.37 billion to over 7.5 million customers and 52,000 merchants. The company also introduced the Lipa Mdogo (a popular phone financing mechanism) which allows customers to buy smartphones on credit with a daily payment arrangement of $0.16. Further, the 'Lipa na M-PESA' allows customers to pay for goods and services electronically, thereby reducing the physical circulation of cash in the economy.[11]

The third case study shown in Box 4.3 presents the journey of mobile money (MoMo) breakthrough in Ghana pioneered by MTN.

Box 4.3: Digital Banking in Ghana

Ghana is one of the African countries that have accelerated the integration of digital banking services in its financial sector. The country has made progress on the usage of different digital banking platforms to foster financial inclusion and extend banking services to the excluded in the society. The passage of the Payment Systems Act, 2003 (Act 662), was a major turning point in laying the foundation for digital banking in the country. The Act led to the creation of the Ghana Interbank Settlement to facilitate the settlement of transactions and payments. It also transformed electronic payment systems such as the direct credit system, the electronic Cheque Truncation System and the Automated Clearing House. The pace of digital banking was accelerated with the advent of the FinTech industry, particularly mobile banking in significantly altered how financial products and services are carried out In Ghana. It allowed for receiving and sending of money just by having access to a mobile phone, thereby ensuring that the financially excluded particularly in the rural areas can participate in the financial sector.

[11] https://itweb.africa/content/raYAyqor4n2MJ38N.

The key actors in the digital banking space include banks, FinTech Companies, mobile network operators, Neo banks, G-Money, payment processors, regulatory institutions, and standards organisations.

The growth in digital banking and the acceleration of FinTech in the financial space led to a growing concern about the need for some regulations around the activities. In 2019, The Payment Systems and Services Act, 2019 (Act 987) was passed which broadened participation in the provision of financial services by different actors.[12] It also focuses on some of the enablers of the uptake of Digital banking such as financial literacy, government support, and IT infrastructure expansion, among others. The government further introduced the FinTech and Innovation Office in 2020 to drive the digitalisation agenda for the financial system. The office is responsible for issuing of licenses and regulating of activities of dedicated electronic money issuers including mobile money operators and Payment Service Providers.[13] The gains made in digital banking is being threatened by the activities of fraudsters and some unprofessional staff of these institutions. For instance, the total amount lost by electronic money issuers (EMI) due to fraudulent activities was around GHS12.8 million. The regulator has adopted a number of measures to control these fraudulent activities. These include promoting financial literacy, use of a national ID card in transactions, and the establishment of the Financial Stability Department to strengthen their oversight role (Bank of Ghana, 2021).

The efforts over the years have yielded some significant milestones, particularly with respect to financial inclusion. E-commerce activities had reached a percentage of 27.41 in 2022 and is expected to reach 37% by 2027. The number of people utilising digital payment methods had reached 8 million by 2022.

Mobile money is one area in which the country has become a giant globally. The registered number of mobile money account increased by 70.15% to reach 55.3 million between 2019 to 2022, while the active

[12] https://www.bog.gov.gh/wp-content/uploads/2019/08/Payment-Systems-and-Services-Act-2019-Act-987-.pdf.

[13] https://www.gcbbank.com.gh/research-reports/sector-industry-reports/357-digital-landscape-of-banks-2023-final-v1/file.

account stood at 20.4 million (19.3% growth). The number of active agents increased by about 123. 45% between the same period. Equally, the number of transactions increased from 200 to 488 million with a commiserating increase in the value of transactions from GHS 32.8 billion to GHS 122 billion. In 2018, Ghana elevated the digitalisation agenda by introducing the mobile money interoperability. This allows not just cross-transfer across different mobile money platforms but also linked to bank accounts. The value of transactions through interoperability rose from 1.6 million in 2019 to 2600.7 million (18.7% growth) in 2022. There are other achievements in the areas of Internet banking which also increased significantly from 2.9 in 2019 to GHS6.9 billion, representing 137.9%.[14]

Overcoming Logistical and Infrastructural Challenges Through Digital Banking

Adopting digital technology to enhance baking operations and extend financial services to the larger population comes with certain prerequisites. Key among them include the establishment of an efficient and robust infrastructure to Provide the needed foundation for reliable connectivity and security in terms of data storage (Yang and Zhang, 2025).

The development in the FinTech industry has been argued to either complement or compete with financial service delivery. FinTech as a disruptive technology has come to stay and financial banks in Africa are adopting to the technologies to enhance their operations (European Investment Bank, 2024). Some FinTech competes with banks in service delivery, particularly in the area of remittance and wealth management. However, innovations in FinTech can be of great assistance to banks in the area of risk assessment, improved efficiency by reducing transaction and investment costs, and enhanced banks' ability to capture new markets and serve their target markets better (Saal et al., 2017a, 2017b). Jeník and Zetterli (2020) have identified three different models when it comes to digital bank adaptation including, fully digital retail bank, marketplace, and the Banking as a service (BaaS). The first group of

[14] https://www.gcbbank.com.gh/research-reports/sector-industry-reports/357-digital-landscape-of-banks-2023-final-v1/file.

banks utilised digital channels to effectively reach out and service their retail customers and also their micro, small, and medium enterprises (MSMEs). Examples of Banks in this category include the TymeBank in South Africa. The Marketplace bank is where the bank leverages on a third-party platform to provide a wide range of products and services to its customers. The BaaS is rather a technology company that secures a banking license to provide some form of banking services such as payment processing, account creation and management, risk management, or providing business-to-business (B2B) services.

The impact of FinTech in the delivery of financial services affects various aspects of financial services and is not just limited to the interface of banks and customer services. It affects not just these services, but also all the different aspects of the operations of financial institutions (Saal et al., 2017a, 2017b). The FinTech landscape in Africa is evolving rapidly with a significant impact on the delivery of financial services. For instance, the percentage of people in Africa utilising digital channels for payment moved from 28% in 2014 to reach 50% in 2021 (European Investment Bank, 2024).

The spread of FinTech in the banking and other financial institutions is hampered by a number of factors ranging from weak infrastructure to financial illiteracy, low penetration of financial institutions, and an underdeveloped technological ecosystem. Infrastructure development necessary to facilitate the adoption of FinTech in the banking sector is highly limited. Infrastructure such as payment system, credit information of consumers, power and internet connectivity. The level of financial literacy, coupled with low income also affects the uptake of FinTech in the banking sector. Africa is the region with lower earnings and a higher percentage of the population not financially literate. A lot of financial transactions in Africa are dominated due to the low level of financial penetration in the region particularly in the rural areas. Lastly, FinTech drive on technology backed by funding support. The low level of technology and funding constraints hampers the expansion of financial services and FinTech development.

Regulatory Considerations for Digital Banking Expansion

The success of digital technology in driving financial inclusion depends largely on how the expansion in the sector is handled. Too strict a regulation could stifle the growth of the sector thereby limiting its impact on financial inclusion. On the other hand, a weaker regulation of the sector could erode consumer confidence due to heightened risk and possible loss of wealth. Hence, policymakers would have to strive for a balance between strengthening and relaxing regulations around FinTech operations. Two broad regulatory approaches are identified: The first is to regulate digital banking under the same regulations as Commercial banks while the second is developing a distinct rule to govern their operations taking into account risk levels and the objectives of their operations (Alliance for Financial Inclusion, 2021; Ehrentraud et al., 2020).

In employing a particular regulatory regime, policymakers should first take into account a number of factors. The first is, what the objective is for developing digital banks. Policymakers may have different objectives for promoting digital banking ranging from achieving financial inclusion, digitalisation of the financial sector of the economy to promote market competition in the delivery of financial products and services. This consideration could see the regulator relaxing some factors in terms of licencing such as minimum capital requirement, registration cost, etc. The second consideration as identified by the Alliance for Financial Inclusion (2021) is to consider the level of sophistication or maturity of the financial markets, particularly the level of digital financial literacy, the level of awareness of consumers and the target players who are likely to promote the agenda. An assessment of these factors will reveal some gaps in policy directions. The third consideration has to do with key non-financial enablers which are key drivers for the success of digital banks. For instance, the depth and the level of smartphone usage and how affordable they are will assist policymakers in determining what role digital banks can play within the economy. Also, supply-side issues such as the availability of service providers in relation to IT services as well as the number and quality of human resources to support the provision of these services are key considerations. Thus, taking into account these supply and demand factors to be considered in regulating the operations of digital banks. Finally, a good starting point in regulating the operations of digital banks is to consider an evaluation of the existing regulations to assess their adequacy so as to determine what sort of adjustment would be necessary if any to regulate the sector.

Given the crucial role digital banks play in fostering financial inclusion and inclusive and sustainable development, there is a need for specific regulation measures in order to safeguard the operations and sustainability of these banks. One such key issue has to do with risk management resulting from the activities of fraudsters. Digital banks rely on a number of key service providers which increases their exposure levels for fraudsters to gain access. In some cases, these fraudulent acts are committed with the support of the staff of companies. Many people have lost their savings and investments through these acts thereby eroding their confidence in the system. Digital banks therefore need for regulators to demand a robust system of digital banks to safeguard customers wealth. In relation to this, regulators should have specific policies when it comes to data privacy, which aspect of the data do DBs have the right to share and how that should happen. DBs can only share data that is considered private with the endorsement of the consumers in order to minimise data unbridled data sharing which increases the risk to fraudsters.

Further, due to the level of financial literacy, there is a need for regulators to demand simplifications and easy communication of the services of DB. This will ensure that there is no gap in communication and labelling of products and services. Further, there is a need to establish a clear line of communication to deal with customers' complaints and resolutions of grievances. The channel and avenue for communication should not just be limited from the customer to the bank, but also from customers to the regulator. This will enhance the regulator's understanding of the different concerns and complaints of customers and be able to be effective in regulating the activities of Development Banks. Digital banks can also rely on advancements in regtech such as Ai in monitoring their operations to enable them to detect early warning signals. This will help in minimising the operational risk of digital banks.

Conclusion

Digitalisation has transformed fundamentally the way banking and other financial services are delivered. There has therefore been a shift away from bricks and mortar structure to a virtual system where banking transactions are conducted digitally. In Africa in particular, this revolution has been led by the use of mobile technology such as mobile phone to deliver financial services particularly to the unbanked and financially excluded populations. The chapter looks at the movement from the traditional banking system to digital banking, its impact on financial inclusion, logistical constraints, and regulatory challenges. The chapter argued that digital technology such as mobile and online banking help to promote efficiency in financial service delivery. Digital technologies such as Artificial Intelligence, Big data analytics, and blockchain allow banks to be competitive and ensure the financial stability of their operation. The study further noted that mobile banking has helped shaped delivery of financial services in areas such as payment of bills, airtime purchase, cash deposit and withdrawals, and international remittances. While providing these benefits, digital banking also exposes individuals and financial institutions to considerable amount of risk. The chapter also observed that activities of fraudsters and some unprofessional staff of these institutions are threatening the gains made in digital banking. These findings have some policy implications for maximising the benefits of digital banking while ensuring the stability of the financial system in Africa. Central banks in Africa should provide the enabling environment for banks to integrate digital financial services options in their operations. To deal with cyber security concerns, policymakers should promote financial literacy to enhance financial awareness. There is also the need to ensure the use of a unified digital identity for accessing financial services across banking, non-banking, and other providers of financial services.

References

Alliance for Financial Inclusion. (2021). *Policy framework on the regulation, licensing and supervision of digital banks*. https://www.afi-global.org/publication/policy-framework-on-the-regulation-licensing-and-supervision-of-digital-banks/

Asiamah, T., Steel, W. F., & Ackah, C. (2021). Determinants of credit demand and credit constraints among households in Ghana. *Heliyon, 7*(10).

Bank of Ghana. (2021). *Banking, SDI and EMI Fraud Report: 2021 trends & statistics, financial stability, department*. Accra Ghana. https://www.bog.gov.gh/wp-content/uploads/2022/06/2021-FRAUD-REPORT-Industry-Version-For-Publication.pdf

Donovan, K. (2012). Mobile money for financial Inclusion. In T. Kelly, N. Friederici, M. Minges, & M. Yamamichi (Eds.), *Information and communications for development: Maximising Mobile, 61*(1). World Bank.

Egami, H., Mano, Y., & Matsumoto, T. (2025). Mobile money remittances to cope with aggregate shocks: Urban migrants and rural families under the COVID-19 lockdown in Bangladesh. *World Development Sustainability, 6*, Article 100197.

Ehrentraud, J., Ocampo, D. G., & Vega, C. Q. (2020, August). *Regulating Fintech financing: Digital banks and fintech platforms.*FSI Insights on Policy Implementation No. 27. https://www.bis.org/fsi/publ/insights27.pdf

European Investment Bank. (2024). *Transition finance in Africa unlocking investment in an era of digital transformation and climate transition, European Investment Bank, Luxembourg.* https://www.eib.org/attachments/lucalli/20240033_finance_in_africa_en.pdf

GCB. (2023). *Digital landscape of banks 2023, strategy and research Dept, Accra Ghana.* https://www.gcbbank.com.gh/downloads/research/sector-industry-reports/357-digital-landscape-of-banks-2023-final-v1/file

International Monetary Fund. (2020). *Measuring financial access: 10 years of the IMF financial access survey.* International Monetary Fund.

Jeník, I., Laming, M. F., & Salman, A. (2020). *Inclusive digital banking: Emerging markets case studies.* CGAP/World Bank.

Jeník, I., & Zetterli, P. (2020). *Digital banks: How can they deepen financial inclusion?* CGAP. https://www.cgap.org/research/slide-deck/digital-banks-how-can-they-deepen-financial-inclusion

Liang, Y., Wei, R., & Duan, D. (2025). Digital financial development and commercial bank stability. *International Review of Economics & Finance, 97*, Article 103749.

Llewellyn, D. T. (2021). Financial inclusion: An overview of key issues. In A. H. Ahmad, D. T. Llewellyn, & V. Murinde, (Eds.), *Inclusive financial development* (chapter 1, pp. 1–12). Edward Elgar Publishing.

McKinsey. (2022). *Fintech in Africa: The end of the beginning.* https://www.mckinsey.com/industries/financial-services/our-insights/fintech-in-africa-the-end-of-the-beginning

Mehmet Kerse, M., & Stefan Staschen, S. (2021). *Digital banks: How can they be regulated to deepen financial inclusion?* CGAP/World Bank.

Mothibi, K., & Rahulani, A. (2021). *Digital Banking Research Document, FSCA.* https://www.fsca.co.za/Regulatory%20Frameworks/FinTechDocuments/Digital%20Banking%20Research%20Document.pdf

Ndung'u, N. (2021). A digital financial services revolution in Kenya: The M-Pesa case study. *African Economic Research Consortium: Nairobi, Kenya*, 23–44.

Raithatha, R., & Storchi, G. (2024). *The State of the Industry Report on Mobile Money 2024.* FinDev Gateway.

Saal, M., Starnes, S., & Rehermann, T. (2017a). *Digital financial services: Challenges and opportunities for emerging market banks.* https://policycommons.net/artifacts/1274802/digital-financial-services/1861291/

Saal, M., Starnes, S., & Rehermann, T. (2017b). *Digital financial services: Challenges and opportunities for emerging market banks*. EMCompass| No. 42 Washington, DC, World Bank Group. http://documents.worldbank.org/curated/en/750421502949470705

Shaikh, A. A., Glavee-Geo, R., Karjaluoto, H., & Hinson, R. E. (2023). Mobile money as a driver of digital financial inclusion. *Technological Forecasting and Social Change, 186*, Article 122158.

Singh, A. S., Venkataramani, B., & Ambarkhane, D. (2014). *Role of mobile banking in financial inclusion*. Available at SSRN 2485777.

The African Banker. (2023). *The African Digital Banking Transformation Report (2024).* https://african.business/wpcontent/uploads/2023/05/Backbase_Report23_Digital.pdf

The African Banker. (2024). *The African Digital Banking Transformation Report (2024).* https://insights.african.business/ADBT_Report_2024

World Bank. (2023). *From connectivity to services: Digital transformation in Africa*.https://www.worldbank.org/en/results/2023/06/27/from-connectivity-to-services-digital-transformation-in-africa

World Bank. (2025). *Financial inclusion is a key enabler to reducing poverty and boosting prosperity*. World Bank. https://www.worldbank.org/en/topic/financialinclusion/overview

World Economic Forum. (2023). *There are more mobile phones than people in the world*. https://www.weforum.org/stories/2023/04/charted-there-are-more-phones-than-people-in-the-world/

Yang, J., Wu, Y., & Huang, B. (2023). Digital finance and financial literacy: Evidence from Chinese households. *Journal of Banking & Finance, 156*, Article 107005.

Yang, Z., & Zhang, J. (2025). Digital infrastructure construction and the development of new-quality productive forces in enterprises. *Scientific Reports, 15*(1), 24671.

CHAPTER 5

Innovative Lending Solutions for Underserved Populations in Africa

Richard Mbayo and Wynn Gemini Rajula

Introduction

Access to credit constitutes a major impediment to economic development in Africa, especially in rural areas where traditional banking infrastructure is either underdeveloped or inaccessible. Small enterprises, farmers, and low-income entrepreneurs in the countryside face significant obstacles in obtaining capital, mostly due to strict collateral requirements, absence of formal credit records, and high interest rates enforced by commercial banks (Simba et al., 2023, 285). This financial exclusion not only limits personal and business growth but also obstructs broader economic growth, trapping many communities in cycles of poverty and underdevelopment.

R. Mbayo (✉)
Department of Politics and International Affairs, Northern Arizona University, Flagstaff, AZ, USA
e-mail: rm2865@nau.edu

W. G. Rajula
School of Management, University of Electronic Science and Technology of China (UESTC), Chengdu, Sichuan, China

I. N. Yakubu (ed.), *Banking on Inclusion*, Sustainable Development Goals Series, https://doi.org/10.1007/978-3-031-96716-0_5

In Kenya, agriculture employs approximately 40% of the total population and 70% of the rural workforce. Additionally, the informal sector plays a crucial role in the country's economy, highlighting the urgent need for innovative financial solutions to empower both agricultural and informal economic activities (International Trade Administration, 2024; USAID, 2023). Traditional financing models have demonstrated insufficiency for many smallholder farmers and companies, especially due to high interest rates, inflexible collateral requirements, and rigid credit assessment methods. King and Heyer (2016) argue that rural communities in Kenya resort to informal financial sectors, such as community savings groups or predatory lenders, which operate without the protection of formal banking, and this results in unsustainable debts.

The rise of financial technology (FinTech) presents new methods for obtaining credit that are more appropriate for underserved communities such as the rural population (Tang, 2024). In Kenya, mobile technologies, alternative data sources, and decentralized lending models are used by FinTech innovators to address the funding gap among rural populations. For instance, M-Pesa mobile money services laid a foundation for this FinTech revolution to flourish. Fengler (2012) argues that Kenya is an established global leader in mobile money services, where mobile transactions constitute over 87% of the country's GDP, thereby creating a fertile environment for FinTech innovation to thrive (Fengler, 2012). These financial platforms provide numerous alternative credit scoring methods, such as mobile phone usage, transaction histories, and social network activities, to assess borrowers' creditworthiness and offer loans to individuals who have historically been marginalized from the formal financial system (*The Economist*, 2015).

Additionally, the remarkable feature of these transactions is that financial services are integrated with complementary company development tools under FinTech, as many microcredit service providers have shifted their focus from exclusively lending to incorporating business support services, market linkages, and financial literacy training as part of their products. This approach enables its clients to acquire requisite skills and resources to leverage their capital (Kodongo & Kendi, 2013). These programs encourage entrepreneurs to expand their businesses, create employment opportunities, and improve the quality of their lives. An article published by *Calibrant* shows that these innovative lending methods demonstrate effectiveness in rural regions where entrepreneurs encounter difficulties not just in securing business loans but also in establishing sustainable enterprises and markets (Calibraint, 2024).

Peer-to-peer (P2P) lending and pay-as-you-go (PAYG) models, alongside mobile money platforms, have emerged as effective ways to improve credit access for rural communities (FSD Africa, 2018). These platforms overcome the formal financial institutions' direct linkages between lenders and borrowers through mobile applications and digital platforms. As these platforms provide smaller, more accessible loans without fulfilling the collateral requirement, they hence create an opportunity for individuals who were typically excluded by the traditional banking institutions. For instance, M-Kopa, a leading pioneer in PAYG solar energy financing, demonstrates the capabilities of these models to facilitate credit access as well as promote economic activities and advance sustainable development in rural areas (Shapshak, 2016).

These FinTech innovations provide a promising future for rural populations by facilitating financial services to the underserved populations. However, digital literacy remains one of the major hurdles for many rural populations, limiting their ability to fully use these digital financial services. Moreover, regulatory frameworks lag behind the rapid development of these technologies, thereby creating uncertainties regarding data privacy, security, and consumer protection (Kodongo, 2024). Also, these FinTech innovations are at risk of creating debt traps, which are one of the key concerns among rural borrowers who have limited or no knowledge of financial literacy and therefore need to be carefully managed (Donovan & Park, 2019).

The rest of this chapter explores peer-to-peer lending, microcredits, the role of alternative credit scoring models, challenges and risks associated with these digital lending models, and policy recommendations aimed at transforming these FinTech platforms, as well as presents a conclusion on how to contribute to a more profound understanding of how FinTech is creating new opportunities for marginalized populations and what lessons can be drawn from Kenya's experience to foster inclusive financial ecosystems across the African continent.

The Rise of Peer-to-Peer (P2P) Lending and Its Impact on Small Businesses

Peer-to-peer lending is a groundbreaking FinTech evolution that involves the direct lending of funds between individuals and businesses without the involvement of financial institutions as intermediaries (Lenz, 2016). The process has disrupted the traditional banking system as it directly links borrowers and lenders through online platforms, reducing the costs, time, and complexity involved in acquiring loans (Moenninghoff & Wieandt, 2013). P2P lending has enhanced financial inclusion in emerging economies by allowing borrowers without formal credit histories and collateral to get loans. These platforms use innovative credit scoring methods that use alternative data to assess their creditworthiness, hence enabling a broader range of individuals and small businesses to access finances (Nemoto et al., 2019).

The P2P lending process involves four stages. First, registration: borrowers and lenders set up their profiles on the peer-to-peer platforms through mobile applications. In remote areas, mobile-first interfaces ensure that consumers with simple devices are able to access these services, e.g., using USSD codes. Once the user applies for a loan, the second stage takes effect. Credit assessment platforms using alternative credit rating techniques such as social media footprint, utility payment records, and smartphone usage patterns are employed for assessment to eliminate the reliance on traditional assessment criteria (Stern et al., 2017). The third stage is loan matching, in which algorithms connect borrowers with suitable lenders based on the loan specifications, interest rates, and risk assessments. Finally, the approved loan is credited to the borrower's account through the mobile network, like M-Pesa, and repayment is done using the same process to enable smooth financial transactions.

The Evolution of Peer-to-Peer (P2P) Lending in Sub-Saharan Africa

Peer-to-peer lending isn't new in sub-Saharan Africa; it dates back to the ancient colonial times and has long provided access to credit to individuals and small businesses (OECD, 2024). Self-help groups, which are frequently regarded as informal financial systems, were established on the premise of social capital, mutual support, and community support (Mashamba & Gani, 2024). Before the advent of digital peer-to-peer lending, these systems were indispensable for financial inclusion, as they established networks that enabled community members to borrow from one another. Many parts of Africa have self-help groups, like *Chamas* in Kenya, *Wazalendo* in Uganda, *Susu* from West Africa, *Stokvels* in South Africa, and *Tontines* in Francophone Africa. (Ampath Kenya, 2024; Hossein & Bonsu, 2023; Ipsos, 2024; Odhiambo, 2021; von Gaertringen, 2020; Wazalendo, 2015). These groups made it possible for people to combine their resources and lend money to one another on the basis of social connections, trust, and communal responsibility.

Marginalized socioeconomic groups, including women and youth in Kenya, have long used *Chamas* to let members save money together and get interest-free loans from the pooled resources (Odhiambo, 2021). According to recent estimates, there are over 300,000 *Chamas* in Kenya transacting over US $3 billion (Chidziwizano et al., 2020). The *Tontine* system in Francophone Africa operates as rotating savings and credit associations where members have a predetermined amount to contribute every month. Members of the *Tontine* groups are guaranteed access to a fixed amount of money based on their contribution for business growth, educational fees, and emergencies (Zambrano et al., 2023).

In West Africa, the *Susu* system employs appointed collectors to monitor payments and grant member's credit based on their savings behavior (UNCDF, 2017). In contrast, *Stokvels* in South Africa are local savings groups that collect funds for various financial purposes, such as significant purchases and investments (Ngcobo, 2021). In 2019, 45% of South Africans belonged to a *Stokvel* group, with 10 million people saving through *Stokvel* groups (Shipalana, 2019). Over the years, these 'informal' lending techniques have undergone transformations, taking into account FinTech advancements, mobile payment systems, and digital technology, and are shifting to modern P2P lending platforms that provide financial inclusion to a wider range of clientele rather than just the small communities (Hornuf et al., 2024).

Transition to Digital Peer-to-Peer Lending

Informal lending practices began to integrate with FinTech solutions as digital technologies advanced and smartphone usage increased. Mobile money services like M-Pesa (Kenya), MTN Mobile Money (West Africa), and Airtel Money (East Africa) have created a platform for digital financial transactions, hence enabling borrowers and lenders to trade money effortlessly (Piper, 2020). These mobile money services paved the way for digitizing informal lending, hence facilitating the tracking of contributions, transaction processing, and lending extension outside close-knit networks. Restrictions of traditional banks hastened the move to digital peer-to-peer lending, which excluded small businesses, informal workers, and rural communities because of high collateral criteria and rigid loan application procedures. Chitavi et al. (2021) believe that FinTech technologies have started to bridge this gap by providing alternative credit scoring models and seamless loan disbursement procedures through mobile devices.

Digital P2P lending platforms have revolutionized the lending landscape by facilitating the connection between borrowers and individual lenders through the use of big data (Philippon, 2019), artificial intelligence (AI)-driven credit assessment, and mobile payment integrations. Unlike traditional banks, which depend on collateral and formal credit records, these platforms leverage alternative data sources to gauge trustworthiness. This approach has increased financial access for the unbanked and underbanked communities by enabling them to qualify for small, short-term loans with flexible payback periods (Parlasca et al., 2022).

Moreover, financial technology has enabled real-time transactions, reduced administrative costs, and enhanced loan processing efficiency. Borrowers are able to obtain loans in hours or minutes, therefore bypassing the delays associated with traditional banking procedures. According to Finance Magnates (2023), the integration of these peer-to-peer lenders with mobile money services has enabled borrowers to accept, repay, and manage loans directly from their mobile wallets, hence simplifying the lending process. In sub-Saharan Africa, digital peer-to-peer lending services have extended financing avenues for SMEs, entrepreneurs, and underserved populations. SMEs, which constitute over 40% of GDP in several African economies, encounter a substantial financing deficit (Muriithi, 2017, 36). However, peer-to-peer lending platforms provide accessible and flexible credit alternatives that do not necessitate collateral (Sabrina & Christoph, 2020).

Such funding has allowed small firms to invest in growth, inventory, and equipment, promoting entrepreneurship and economic development, particularly among youth and women. Peer-to-peer financing has also helped to create jobs and boost local economies by allowing firms to expand and provide job opportunities (Tiony, 2024). Women, who face financial exclusion, have profited the most from these platforms, using credit to expand enterprises, pay school fees, and increase household income (World Bank, 2023).

The Future of P2P Lending in Sub-Saharan Africa

The future of peer-to-peer lending in sub-Saharan Africa seems optimistic, with various developing trends influencing its trajectory. The integration of blockchain technology with smart contracts is anticipated to improve security, transparency, and fraud prevention (OECD, 2024). AI-driven credit rating will improve loan approval and risk management, lowering default rates. Cross-border peer-to-peer lending is expected to grow, especially given that the African Continental Free Trade Agreement (AfCFTA) facilitates financial movements between countries (African Union, 2012). The next section digs deeper into microcredit platforms and their role in alleviating poverty.

Microcredit Platforms: Supporting Entrepreneurship and Poverty Alleviation

Microcredit is the provision of small, short-term loans to low-income persons, especially entrepreneurs and small business owners who do not have access to traditional banking services (Chhorn, 2020). *Muhammad Yunus*, the founder of Grameen Bank, popularized the concept of microfinance as a tool for poverty eradication (Mamun et al., 2019). Microcredit has enabled millions of individuals in developing countries to establish and maintain income-generating initiatives, thereby alleviating poverty for themselves and their communities (Makara et al., 2024). Historically, microcredit institutions were responsible for providing financial support; however, they have expanded their scope to include business advisory services, market linkages and training in vocational schools (Ijaiya, 2016). This development acknowledges that access to capital is not enough; entrepreneurs should possess the knowledge, skills, and networks necessary to manage and expand their businesses (Ofori & Kashiwagi, 2022).

Microfinance institutions (MFIs) provide advisory services to assist borrowers in optimizing their loan utilization. These services include financial literacy courses that assist business owners in the development of debt management, cash flow, and reinvestment strategies. They also provide business planning assistance, such as business plan writing, to help entrepreneurs develop viable business models (USAID, 2022). Additionally, mentorship programs provide entrepreneurs with strategic advice, ensuring they make informed decisions for sustainable business growth. Kenya Women Microfinance Bank (KWFT), for example, combines loans and business mentoring to promote women entrepreneurs and ensure long-term financial success (KWFT, 2023). Similarly, the Kenya Commercial Bank Foundation provides structured entrepreneurial training in addition to microloans and grants, fostering long-term business development (KCB, 2022).

Recognizing that many micro-entrepreneurs lack formal education, microcredit institutions are incorporating technical and business training programs to build entrepreneurial capacity (Madara, 2023). These programs focus on enhancing technical skills through vocational training, improving bookkeeping and financial management, developing marketing strategies like digital marketing, fostering customer interaction skills, and adopting technology to educate businesses on using e-commerce and mobile payments.

In addition, microcredit institutions have adopted mobile banking, artificial intelligence, and blockchain technology to enhance accessibility and efficiency (Philippon, 2019). AI-driven credit scoring employs unconventional financial data, such as mobile airtime usage and e-commerce transactions, to assess creditworthiness, hence enhancing loan evaluations (Tang, 2024). Mobile loan disbursement and repayment eliminate the necessity of in-person bank visits, thereby enhancing the convenience of financial services for borrowers. Blockchain-enabled financing enhances transparency and mitigates fraud, hence ensuring secure transactions and fostering trust in the microfinance sector (Hoque et al., 2024). Barboni (2024) shows that microcredit organizations facilitate prudent financial management and support entrepreneurs in establishing creditworthiness through structured repayment frameworks. The next section explores how M-KOPA is reshaping microcredit services in Kenya.

Case Study: M-KOPA:Transforming Microcredit with Pay-As-You-Go Financing

M-KOPA was established in 2011, with the primary objective of providing off-grid solar energy solutions to low-income households in Kenya, Uganda, and Tanzania (M-Kopa, 2024b). It is one of the leading microcredit and FinTech providers that is reshaping financial inclusion in sub-Saharan Africa by its innovative pay-as-you-go (PAYG) lending platform. Subsequently, it has expanded its product line to include smartphones, electric motorcycles, and other household necessities. According to the International Finance Corporation (2023), M-Kopa uses digital technologies and microcredit services to enable clients to purchase high-value products on credit and pay in small, manageable installments.

Unlike traditional microfinance companies that primarily provide cash loans, M-Kopa combines financing with asset ownership, allowing users to own productive assets that improve their livelihoods (Kene, 2023). The PAYG concept works through mobile money platforms, allowing customers to make daily, weekly, or monthly payments with their smartphones. This strategy eliminates the requirement for collateral, making loans more accessible to people with low or inconsistent incomes. The repayment plans' affordability ensures that debtors do not enter into unsustainable debt cycles, as payments are tailored to match their cash flow (M-Kopa, 2024a, 2024b).

M-Kopa has had a tremendous impact on entrepreneurial development and poverty eradication. Small companies in rural areas can extend their operating hours through M-Kopa's solar-powered lights, resulting in higher production and income (Rastogi, 2018, 94). In addition, M-Kopa's smartphone financing allows businesses to have access to digital markets, mobile banking, and e-commerce prospects, all of which promote business growth (Kanali, 2024). The advent of electric motorbike finance has also given thousands of riders in the *boda boda* (motorcycle) industry the ability to own their motorcycles altogether, lowering daily rental expenses and increasing long-term revenues (Mobile Money Africa, 2024).

Besides funding, M-Kopa helps its customers with business training, digital literacy initiatives, and financial management education. Such assistance guarantees that borrowers make the most of their newly acquired assets while also increasing their financial abilities (Laku, 2024). The company's unique use of AI-powered credit scoring and mobile data analytics has also increased loan availability, allowing even first-time consumers with no credit history to obtain funding.

Since its inception, M-Kopa has extended over $1.5 billion in credit to its consumers, impacting over 23 million lives (CNBCA Africa, 2024). Many consumers use M-Kopa smartphones to boost their income, with 62% reporting increased profits as a result of commercial activities facilitated by their devices. Furthermore, four out of five customers report an enhanced quality of life due to the financial inclusion provided by M-KOPA products, which helps them to meet household needs like schooling, food, and medical care. Notably, M-KOPA has introduced over 1.7 million new mobile internet users to the digital economy, thereby bridging the digital gap in sub-Saharan Africa (Laku, 2024).

M-Kopa also contributes to environmental sustainability with its clean energy products. The company has offset 2.1 million tons of CO_2 emissions by delivering solar-powered devices to houses that previously used kerosene fuel. According to a 2024 third-party carbon footprint study, M-Kopa maintains a carbon-negative status, as its operational carbon footprint is significantly outweighed by emissions that are mitigated by sustainable energy solutions (M-Kopa, 2024a, 2024b). M-KOPA is also increasing the accessibility of sustainable technology by selling more than 100,000 refurbished smartphones and second-hand devices, which are part of its circular economy solutions (M-Kopa, 2024a, 2024b).

In addition, M-KOPA is the largest financier of electric motorcycles in Kenya, having already financed approximately two-thirds of the electric bikes currently on the road. This initiative is driving Africa's transition to green mobility by reducing reliance on fuel-powered motorcycles and offering low-income earners an affordable pathway to motorcycle ownership. M-KOPA is setting new industry standards for microfinance institutions to achieve sustainability goals by integrating environmental considerations with innovative digital lending solutions.

As a result, the company has received subsequent funding linked to sustainability initiatives from organizations like the International Finance Corporation (IFC) (International Finance Corporation, 2023). The funding is intended to help M-Kopa expand its lending model and achieve environmental, social, and governance (ESG) objectives, such as the implementation of solar energy solutions to reduce greenhouse gas emissions and improve women's smartphone accessibility (M-Kopa, 2024a, 2024b).

Despite its substantial success, M-Kopa is currently facing several obstacles, such as regulatory constraints on digital lending, low smartphone penetration in rural areas, and high default rates in certain regions (International Finance Corporation, 2023). The company has successfully overcome these challenges through policy engagement, strategic partnerships with financial institutions, and continuous innovation (Kene, 2023). The potential to improve financial inclusion, empower entrepreneurs, and enrich communities is present in the combination of microcredit, technology, and business support services, as exemplified by M-Kopa. The model emphasizes the importance of integrating access to finance with productive assets and capacity-building initiatives to achieve sustainable economic development. As microcredit continues to evolve, the success of M-Kopa serves as a model for the application of FinTech to improve the economic prospects of individuals with limited resources.

The Role of Alternative Credit Scoring Models in Broadening Access to Credit

Alternative credit scoring models are techniques that assess the creditworthiness of an individual or organization by employing methods that differ from the traditional credit reports that banks and other financial institutions employ (Berg et al., 2018). These models apply an extensive range of non-financial data, sourced from digital platforms, mobile devices, and social media. The data that is employed may include:

- *Mobile Phone Data*: In Kenya, mobile money services such as M-Pesa are prevalent; creditworthiness can be assessed by analyzing data on mobile phone usage patterns, including the frequency of calls, text messages, and mobile transactions (Ngwenya, 2024). For instance, a person's history of mobile money transactions can indicate whether they consistently repay debts, which is a reliable indicator of creditworthiness (Björkegren & Grissen, 2015).
- *Utility payments*: The consistent payment of utilities, such as rent, water, and electricity, is an indicator of a borrower's ability to manage financial obligations. Since these payments are monitored by digital platforms and mobile payment systems, they are valuable data sources for alternative credit scoring models (Mallat, 2007; Naghavi, 2019).
- *Online Behavior and Social Media*: Lenders are increasingly scrutinizing individuals' online activities, such as their frequent use of online banking, online purchases, and social media usage. Berg et al. (2018) suggest that an individual's financial activity on these platforms and their reputation in online communities may provide sufficient insights into their repayment patterns and trustworthiness.

- *Purchasing Behaviors*: E-commerce and digital payment platforms maintain comprehensive records of each company's purchases, inventory, and payment history. Frost et al. (2019) argues that these records can be utilized by lenders to evaluate the financial health and loan-repayment capacity of small businesses.
- *Psychometric Scoring*: Woo and Sohn (2022) believe that lenders can utilize psychometric scoring by applying behavioral data and personality-based assessments like *Myers-Briggs* personality tests to forecast loan-repayment behaviors. An individual's character and decision-making style can offer insights into their financial reliability.

These alternative data sources enable lenders to accurately assess the creditworthiness of individuals or enterprises with minimal or zero traditional financial history, thereby overcoming the inherent constraints of traditional credit scoring techniques.

Risks and Challenges Associated with Digital Lending Platforms

Kenya's digital platform facilitates financial inclusion through rapid and expedient access to loans. However, they also present a number of risks and concerns that could potentially harm borrowers and the overall financial system. A primary challenge of digital financing in Kenya is the inflated cost of borrowing. Many digital lenders levy excessive interest rates and concealed costs, rendering loans costly (Coloma, 2021). Given that the majority of loans are unsecured and receive immediate approval, lenders rationalize these inflated expenses as remuneration for the risk of default. Nevertheless, borrowers do not understand the complete expense of the loan due to unclear terms and conditions.

The accessibility of digital loans has resulted in heightened borrowing and inadequate financial planning. Several borrowers concurrently acquire loans from different lenders, resulting in over-indebtedness (Magale, 2024). Digital lenders fail to disclose loan information to credit bureaus, enabling individuals to obtain loans from several platforms and amass debts that exceed their repayment capacity. This scenario culminates in a debt trap, as consumers acquire new loans to settle existing ones (Tetteh, 2023). Some individuals resort to informal borrowing or liquidating personal assets to settle outstanding obligations. Over-indebtedness can result in economic difficulties, mental health issues, and social problems, including familial discord, due to stress and financial instability.

Digital lending systems aggregate and retain extensive personal and financial information from users, including phone contacts, SMS records, geographical data, and expenditure patterns (Kimeu, 2022). This data aids lenders in evaluating creditworthiness, but it simultaneously subjects borrowers to considerable privacy and security vulnerabilities. Some of these digital lenders have allegedly been exploiting borrowers' data, especially during debt collection processes (Muyela, 2025). For instance, some lenders have accessed a borrower's phone contact information and sent harsh messages to their family members, colleagues, or employers, exposing them as debt defaulters, which is an unethical practice (Muyela, 2025).

The rapid growth of Kenya's digital lending platforms transcended the established regulatory mechanisms designed to protect customers. In contrast to formal banking institutions, these digital lenders operate beyond stringent regulatory supervision, enabling them to engage in exploitative lending practices (Mago & Modiba, 2024). Kenya's Central Bank implemented policies to curtail unethical behavior; however, its enforcement is not uniform, making it difficult to protect rural borrowers, as some lenders continue granting loans without evaluating risks or taking time to verify whether the borrowers understand the loan terms (Central Bank of Kenya, 2018). Therefore, the absence of a uniform dispute resolution procedure undermines borrowers' choices in case of unfair treatment.

These digital lending platforms use *AI-driven algorithms* to assess borrowers' creditworthiness through digital footprints, such as mobile money transfers, social media interactions, and online purchasing history records. According to Pazarbasioglu et al. (2020), these innovations have enabled loan access however, they have also led to discrimination of financially needy individuals, especially low-income earners, elderly rural residents and informal workers who lack adequate digital transaction histories, making it difficult for them to qualify for loans under AI-based assessment credit models.

Storchi (2025) also argues that algorithms can unjustly penalize individuals based on their historical transactions or social media behaviors, which may not accurately represent their creditworthiness and ability to repay loans. While digital lending platforms in Kenya have enabled financial inclusion, they also present significant challenges that require attention. For instance, high overnight interest rates and concealed charges burden borrowers, leading many into cycles of excessive debt (Wamalwa et al., 2019). To mitigate these challenges, we suggest a set of policy recommendations for governments, investors, digital lenders, and borrowers.

Policy Recommendations

Generally, there should be a need to reassess taxation policies on digital transactions across sub-Saharan Africa, as most of these countries' taxation policies have had unintended repercussions on the accessibility of digital financial services, which are badly needed in rural Africa. For instance, the Finance Act of 2023 in Kenya raised excise duty on mobile money transactions, increasing costs and potentially reducing FinTech adoption, particularly for low-income populations (KRA, 2023). Similar measures across the continent could disincentivize the use of FinTech solutions like mobile money and peer-to-peer (P2P) lending. Policymakers should revisit these tax policies to avoid creating barriers to financial inclusion. If such taxes are necessary for government revenue generation, countermeasures such as targeted tax relief could be considered to reduce their impact on underserved populations.

We argue that African governments need to strengthen data protection regulations for digital financial services as alternative credit scoring models become more widely used across Africa, they rely heavily on personal data, including mobile usage, social media activity, and transaction histories. To mitigate data privacy concerns, governments should develop clear, comprehensive regulations that protect consumers' sensitive data. Data protection laws should ensure that consumers have control over their information, including consent for its use in credit scoring. Ensuring that FinTech platforms adhere to strict data handling standards will build consumer trust and foster greater participation in digital financial services.

The digital divide is one of the key challenges undermining the efficiency of FinTech solutions among the rural populations in Africa. On average, mobile phone usage is increasing; however, digital literacy remains low in rural communities on the continent. Therefore, African governments and development partners should heavily invest in financial programs that will equip underserved populations with skills and knowledge to maneuver alternative credit systems effectively.

Furthermore, the government and these FinTechs should come up with an initiative to promote offline solutions such as SMS-based credit scoring or radio-based education campaigns to ensure that underserved populations without smartphones or internet access are not left out from these digital financial services aimed at strengthening economic growth.

Policymakers should come up with clearer guidelines that govern these platforms with the objective of addressing the issues of inflated interest rates and transparency, especially the lending terms and dispute resolution mechanisms in place to address these challenges. Despite the rapid expansion of P2P lending and microcredit platforms across Africa, they lack clear, comprehensive regulatory oversight, thereby exposing lenders and borrowers to risks (OECD, 2024).

African governments should foster partnerships with FinTech corporations, traditional financial institutions and development partners to accelerate financial inclusion and economic empowerment. These collaborations can aid in creating products that address the needs of underserved populations such as smallholder farmers, micro-entrepreneurs and informal sector workers. Through promoting PPP, policymakers can expand microcredit and P2P lending services in rural Africa. Collaborative efforts could also promote inclusive innovation in credit scoring and loan disbursement models, ensuring that digital finance reaches everyone.

For Lenders (e.g., MFIs, Digital Platforms)

Lenders should sign accords with mobile money platforms (like M-Pesa) and agricultural tech companies to include lending services into platforms already used daily by rural underserved populations, as this will reduce operational costs and expand reach into rural and informal sectors, as well as build trust through leveraging platforms that borrowers are already familiar with and use.

Develop a flexible, micro-tailored loan product with low-interest, short-term loans that allow flexible repayment schedules that align with seasonal or irregular income patterns (e.g., farming cycles); this reduces default risk and, at the same time, improves loyalty and financial inclusion.

For Borrowers (e.g., SMEs, Farmers, Informal Workers)

Borrowers should collaborate with NGOs to provide training on budgeting, loan management, and digital financial tools before loans are disbursed. Such activities can empower borrowers to manage credit better, reduce default rates, and facilitate sustainable borrowing, which can help avoid debt traps among rural borrowers.

Borrowers should empower themselves through community-based initiatives (e.g., SACCOs), where members pool savings and access microloans together, hence increasing their bargaining power with lenders. This approach helps to build financial resilience, improves loan negotiations, and promotes accountability and transparency among members.

Conclusion

Innovative lending solutions such as FinTech innovations in the form of P2P lending and microcredit play an important role in the rural populations, as we have seen in the Kenyan case, where over 23 million people benefit from such initiatives and these FinTechs have the capacity to comprehensively expand financial inclusion across Africa as these technologies are revolutionizing credit access by addressing the economic gap left by traditional banking institutions due to lengthy paperwork and collateral securities associated with processing a loan. Therefore, these FinTechs provide the financial resources necessary to set up small businesses, enhance livelihoods, and promote economic growth in underserved populations. Despite the tremendous benefits and roles these FinTechs play, there are concerns such as data privacy, high interest rates, unclear loan terms, limited digital literacy, and regulatory uncertainty that present dangers that can undermine their potential contributions to financial inclusion (Kimeu, 2022).

Therefore, African governments should introduce progressive policies to fix the increasing challenges of the digital financial ecosystem, ensuring that P2P lending and microcredit models can maintain their promotion of economic empowerment and financial inclusion as we seek to achieve UN SDG 1 (No Poverty) by 2030 (Mbayo & Ige, 2025, 221). This requires assessing the current taxation policies, strengthening data protection legislation, advancing financial literacy, and fostering intersectoral collaboration, as this will help bridge the digital divide between the banked and unbanked, thereby facilitating a more inclusive financial future for all Africans.

References

African Union. (2012, January). *The African Continental Free Trade Area.* African Union. Retrieved February 2, 2025, from https://au.int/en/african-continental-free-trade-area

Ampath Kenya. (2024, March 7). *Adolescent Chamas: Groups contributing to improved outcomes.* Ampath. https://www.ampathkenya.org/news-blog-feed/2024/3/7/adolescent-chamas-groups-contributing-to-improved-outcomes

Barboni, G. (2024, March 18). Innovations in the repayment structure of micro-credit contracts. *Oxford Review of Economic Policy, 40*(1, Spring), 129–138. https://doi.org/10.1093/oxrep/grae002.

Berg, T., Burg, V., Gombović, A., & Puri, M. (2018, July). On the rise of FinTechs: Credit scoring using digital footprints. *The Review of Financial Studies*, *33*(7), 2845–2897. https://doi.org/10.1093/rfs/hhz099

Björkegren, D., & Grissen, D. (2015, June). Björkegren, D., & Grissen, D. (2018). *Behavior revealed in mobile phone usage predicts loan repayment*. SSRN Electronic Journal. https://doi.org/10.2139/ssrn.2611775

Calibraint. (2024, October 10). *How to revolutionize finance in rural areas with P2P lending Software.* Calibraint. https://www.calibraint.com/blog/p2p-lending-software-rural-financial-inclusion

Central Bank of Kenya. (2018, March). *Impact of interest rate capping on the Kenyan economy.* Central Bank of Kenya. https://www.centralbank.go.ke/wp-content/uploads/2018/03/Interest-Rate-Caps_March-2018final.pdf

Chhorn, D. (2020, September 29). Microfinance illusion, poverty and welfare in Cambodia. *Journal of the Asia Pacific Economy, 26*(4), 694–719. https://doi.org/10.1080/13547860.2020.1826074

Chidziwizano, G., Wyche, S., & Kisyula, R. (2020). SmartChama: Designing collaborative digital financial systems for Chama Groups in Kenya. In *Proceedings of the 2020 International Conference on Information and Communication Technologies and Development (ICTD2020).*Association for Computing Machinery, New York.

Chitavi, M., Cohen, L., & Hagist, S. C. N. (2021, February 18). *Kenya is becoming a global hub of FinTech innovation.* Havard Business Review. https://hbr.org/2021/02/kenya-is-becoming-a-global-hub-of-fintech-innovation

CNBCA Africa. (2024, October 17). *Fintech platform M-KOPA hits 5mn customers, $1.5bn in credit distributed.* CNBCA Africa. https://www.cnbcafrica.com/media/6363370606112/fintech-platform-m-kopa-hits-5mn-customers-15bn-in-credit-distributed/

Coloma, M. G. (2021, June 9). *Digital lending in Kenya: Willingness vs. capacity to repay.* Center for Financial Inclusion. Retrieved February 2,

2025, from https://www.centerforfinancialinclusion.org/digital-lending-in-kenya-willingness-vs-capacity-to-repay/

Corporate Finance Institute. (2024, October 15). *Peer-to-Peer Lending—Overview, how it works, Pros & Cons*. Corporate Finance Institute. Retrieved February 2, 2025, from https://corporatefinanceinstitute.com/resources/wealth-management/peer-to-peer-lending/

Donovan, K. P., & Park, E. (2019, September 20). Perpetual Debt in the Silicon Savannah. *Boston Review*. Retrieved February 2, 2025, from https://www.bostonreview.net/articles/perpetual-debt-silicon-savannah/

Fengler, W. (2012, July 16). *How Kenya became a world leader for mobile money*. World Bank Blogs. Retrieved February 2, 2025, from https://blogs.worldbank.org/en/africacan/how-kenya-became-a-world-leader-for-mobile-money

Finance Magnates. (2023, April 20). *The rise of alternative lending and crowdfunding platforms in Africa*. Finance Magnates. https://www.financemagnates.com/fintech/crowdfunding/the-rise-of-alternative-lending-and-crowdfunding-platforms-in-africa/

Frost, J., Gambacorta, L., Huang, Y., Shin, H. S., & Zbinden, P. (2019, October). BigTech and the changing structure of financial intermediation. *Economic Policy, 34*(100), 761–799. https://doi.org/10.1093/epolic/eiaa003

FSD Africa. (2018, February 27). *Exploring new investment frontiers for Fintech in East-Africa*. FSD Africa. https://www.fsdafrica.org/wp-content/uploads/2018/02/18-02-27-Exploring-New-Investment-Frontiers-for-Fintech-in-East-Africa-FINAL-Report_compressed.pdf

Hoque, M. M., Kummer, T.-F., & Yigitbasioglu, O. (2024, June). How can blockchain-based lending platforms support microcredit activities in developing countries? An empirical validation of its opportunities and challenges. *Technological Forecasting and Social Change, 203*. https://doi.org/10.1016/j.techfore.2024.123400

Hornuf, L., Safari, K., & Voshaar, J. (2024). Mobile Fintech adoption in Sub-Saharan Africa: A systematic literature review and meta-analysis. *Research in International Business and Finance, 73*. https://doi.org/10.1016/j.ribaf.2024.102529

Hossein, C. S., & Bonsu, S. K. (2023). Situating the West African system of collectivity: A study of Susu institutions in Ghana's Urban center. *Rethinking Marxism, 35*(1), 108–134. https://doi.org/10.1080/08935696.2022.2159744

Ijaiya, M. A. (2016). icrofinance institutions' products and microfinance policy framework in Nigeria: An addendum. *Journal of Sustainable Development in Africa, 18*(4). https://www.jsd-africa.com/Jsda/Vol18No4-Fall21016/PDF/Microfinance%20Institutions%20Products.Muftau%20Ijaiya.

International Finance Corporation. (2023, May 15). *IFC sustainability-linked loan to M-KOPA to boost access to financial services in Eastern Africa*. International Finance Corporation (IFC). Retrieved February 2, 2025, from https://www.ifc.org/en/pressroom/2023/ifc-sustainability-linked-loan-to-m-kopa-to-boost-access-to-financial-services-in-eastern-africa

International Trade Administration. (2024, July 5). *Kenya: Agribusiness*. International Trade Administration. Retrieved January 25, 2025, from https://www.trade.gov/country-commercial-guides/kenya-agribusiness

Ipsos. (2024, March 13). *Stokvels remain the untapped 'human banks' of South Africa*. Ipsos. https://www.ipsos.com/en-za/stokvels-remain-untapped-human-banks-south-africa

Kanali, N. (2024, October 28). *M-KOPA assembles 1.5m phones in Kenya*. It Web Africa. https://itweb.africa/content/Olx4zMka3Wmv56km

KCB. (2022, October 28). *KCB commits KShs.250 billion for women entrepreneurs—KCB Kenya Website*. KCB Bank. Retrieved February 2, 2025, from https://ke.kcbgroup.com/about-us/news-room/business/kcb-commits-kshs-250-billion-for-women-entrepreneurs

Kene, T. (2023, May 15). *M-KOPA snaps up $250M+ debt, equity for its asset financing platform*. TechCrunch. Retrieved February 2, 2025, from https://techcrunch.com/2023/05/15/m-kopa-snaps-up-250m-debt-equity-for-its-asset-financing-platform/

Kimeu, C. (2022, October 12). 'Traumatising': How rogue digital loan apps in Kenya intimidate borrowers. *The Guardian*. Retrieved April 25, 2025, from https://www.theguardian.com/global-development/2022/oct/12/traumatising-how-rogue-digital-loan-apps-in-kenya-intimidate-borrowers

King, M., & Heyer, A. (2016, June 20). *The Kenyan financial transformation (2000–2015)*. The World Bank. https://blogs.worldbank.org/en/allaboutfinance/kenyan-financial-transformation-2000-2015

Kodongo, O. (2024, October 9). Financial inclusion effects of engaging with the fintech ecosystem. *International Review of Economics & Finance, 96*(103671), 1–27. https://doi.org/10.1016/j.iref.2024.103671

Kodongo, O., & Kendi, L. G. (2013). Individual lending versus group lending: An evaluation with Kenya's microfinance data. *Review of Development Finance, 3*(2), 99–108. https://doi.org/10.1016/j.rdf.2013.05.001

KRA. (2023, June 26). *The Finance Act cover*. KRA. Retrieved February 2, 2025, from https://www.kra.go.ke/images/publications/The-Finance-Act--2023.pdf

KWFT. (2023). *Business Loans—KWFT*. KWFT. Retrieved February 2, 2025, from https://kwftbank.com/business-loans/

Laku, T. (2024, September 25). *Case study: Empowering financial inclusion through technology in Africa: M-Kopa's model*. Timothy Laku. https://www.timothylaku.com/post/case-study-empowering-financial-inclusion-through-technology-in-africa-m-kopa-s-pay-as-you-go-sol

Lenz, R. (2016). Peer-to-Peer lending: Opportunities and risks. *European Journal of Risk Regulation, 7*(4), 688–700. https://doi.org/10.1017/S1867299X00010126

Madara, M. W. O. (2023, July). Training programmes and performance of Micro and Small enterprises in Western Kenya. *International Journal of Novel Research in Marketing Management and Economics, 10*(2), 38–52. https://doi.org/10.5281/zenodo.8116376

Magale, E. (2024, November 12). Kenya's Hustler Fund is a flop. Why president Ruto's plan to loan money to entrepreneurs hasn't worked. *The Conversation*. https://theconversation.com/kenyas-hustler-fund-is-a-flop-why-president-rutos-plan-to-loan-money-to-entrepreneurs-hasnt-worked-241926

Mago, S., & Modiba, F. S. (2024). The regulation and inequality nexus in microfinance and tourism sectors. *SAGE Open, 14*(2). https://doi.org/10.1177/21582440241252269.

Makara, M., Faimau, G., & Maphosa, F. (2024, November 30). Microfinance and poverty alleviation: The socio-economic contribution of SILC, a savings-led microfinance programme in Semonkong, Lesotho. *Journal of Asian and African Studies*. https://doi.org/10.1177/00219096241300433

Mallat, N. (2007, December). Exploring consumer adoption of mobile payments—A qualitative study. *The Journal of Strategic Information Systems, 16*(4), 413–432. https://doi.org/10.1016/j.jsis.2007.08.001.

Mamun, A., Bal, H., & Kabas, T. (2019, July). Microcredit and social business movement as catalyst for poverty eradication: The Grameen experience. *International Journal of Management Science and Business Administration, 5*(5), 32–42. https://doi.org/10.18775/ijmsba.1849-5664-5419.2014.55.1004

Mashamba, T., & Gani, S. (2024). Upstarts vs incumbents: The interaction between fintech credit and bank lending in Sub-Saharan Africa. *Cogent Economics & Finance, 12*(1), 1–19. https://doi.org/10.1080/23322039.2024.2375643

Mbayo, R., & Ige, K. M. (2025). *The politics of CSR in the banking sector: How does it align with the SDGs of no poverty and quality education?* In I. N. Yakubu (Eds.), *Strategic approaches to banking business and sustainable development goals*. Sustainable Development Goals Series. Spring. Springer Nature Switzerland.

M-Kopa. (2024a). *Building pathways to progress for millions of people*. M-Kopa. https://www.m-kopa.com/impact

M-Kopa. (2024b, October 24). *M-KOPA injects over KES 17bn into the local economy*. M-Kopa. https://www.m-kopa.com/newsroom/m-kopa-injects-over-kes-17bn-into-the-local-economy

Mobile Money Africa. (2024, May 1). *M-Kopa to invest Ksh.1.3 billion in electric motorcycle deal with Bolt*. Mobile Money Africa. https://mobilemoneyafrica.com/blog/kenya-m-kopa-to-invest-ksh-1-3-billion-in-electric-motorcycle-deal-with-bolt-1

Moenninghoff, S. C., & Wieandt, A. (2013). The future of Peer-to-Peer finance. *Schmalenbach Journal of Business Research, 65*(5), 466–487. https://doi.org/10.1007/bf03372882

Muriithi, S. M. (2017). African Small And Medium Enterprises (SMEs) contributions, challenges and solutions. *European Journal of Research and Reflection in Management Sciences, 5*(1), 36–48. ISSN 2056-5992.

Muyela, R. (2025, March 27). *It's illegal for banks, other lenders to call or send SMSs to your contacts after you default*. Bizna Kenya. Retrieved April 25, 2025, from https://biznakenya.com/digital-lenders-kenya-debt-collection-warning/

Naghavi, N. (2019). *State of the industry report on Mobile Money*. GSM Association.

Nemoto, N. N., Storey, D. J., & Huang, B. (2019, January 11). *Optimal regulation of P2P lending for Small and Medium-Sized Enterprises*. SSRN Electronic Journal. https://doi.org/10.2139/ssrn.3313999.

Ngcobo, L. (2021). Financial literacy and Stokvels savings of low-income households in South Africa. *International Journal of Economics and Business Administration, IX*(4), 131–139. https://ijeba.com/journal/738/download/Financial+Literacy+and+Stokvels+Savings+of+Low-Income+Households+in+South+Africa.pdf

Ngwenya, M. (2024, November). *Credit Scoring in Africa: Employing Logistic Regression on Alternative Data*. https://doi.org/10.1109/ICECCME62383.2024.10796011

Odhiambo, F. (2021, July 15). *How Chamas in Kenya Fight Poverty*. Borgen Project. https://borgenproject.org/how-chamas-in-kenya-fight-poverty/

OECD. (2024). *FinTech lending in Sub-Saharan Africa Lessons from African economies*. OECD. https://www.oecd.org/content/dam/oecd/en/topics/policy-sub-issues/digital-finance/FinTech-lending-in-Sub-Saharan-Africa

Ofori, E., & Kashiwagi, K. (2022, May 15). Impact of microfinance on the social performance of local households: Evidence from the Kassena Nankana East District of Ghana. *Sustainability, 14*(10). https://doi.org/10.3390/su14106002

Parlasca, M. C., Johnen, C., & Qaim, M. (2022, March). Use of mobile financial services among farmers in Africa: Insights from Kenya. *Global Food Security, 32*(100590), 1–10. https://doi.org/10.1016/j.gfs.2021.100590

Pazarbasioglu, C., Mora, A. G., Uttamchandani, M., Natarajan, H., Feyen, E., & Saal, M. (2020, April). *Digital financial services*. World Bank. Retrieved April 23, 2025, from https://pubdocs.worldbank.org/en/230281588169110691/digital-financial-services.pdf

Philippon, T. (2019, September). *On fintech and financial inclusion*. NBER Working Paper No. w26330. http://www.nber.org/papers/w26330

Piper, K. (2020, September 11). *How M-Pesa, Kenya's mobile money banking, transformed the lives of the poor*. Vox. Retrieved February 2, 2025, from https://www.vox.com/future-perfect/21420357/kenya-mobile-banking-unbanked-cellphone-money

Rastogi, C. (2018, June). M-Kopa Solar: Lighting up the Dark Continent. *South Asian Journal of Business and Management Cases, 7*(2), 93–103. https://doi.org/10.1177/2277977918774648

Sabrina, D., & Christoph, S. (2020). *Digitalisation and its impact on SME finance in Sub-Saharan Africa: Reviewing the hype and actual developments*. Discussion Paper, No. 4/2020. ISBN 978-3-96021-115-0. Deutsches Institut für Entwicklungspolitik (DIE), Bonn. https://doi.org/10.23661/dp4.2020

Shapshak, T. (2016, January 18). *How Kenya's M-Kopa brings prepaid solar power to rural Africa*. Forbes. https://www.forbes.com/sites/tobyshapshak/2016/01/28/how-kenyas-m-kopa-brings-prepaid-solar-power-to-rural-africa/

Shipalana, P. (2019). Digitising financial services: A tool for financial inclusion in South Africa. *South African Institute of International Affairs*, 1–38.

Simba, A., Tajeddin, M., Dana, L., & Ribeiro Soriano, D. E. E. (2023, April 21). Deconstructing involuntary fnancial exclusion: A focus on African SMEs. *Small Business Economics, 62*, 285–305. https://doi.org/10.1007/s11187-023-00767-1

Stern, C., Makinen, M., & Qian, Z. (2017, October 2). FinTechs in China—With a special focus on peer-to-peer lending. *Journal of Chinese Economic and Foreign Trade Studies, 10*(3), 215–228. https://doi.org/10.1108/JCEFTS-06-2017-0015

Storchi, G. (2025, February 24). *Does digital credit lead to over-indebtedness? Evidence from a study*. GSMA. Retrieved April 25, 2025, from https://www.gsma.com/solutions-and-impact/connectivity-for-good/mobile-for-development/uncategorized/does-digital-credit-lead-to-over-indebtedness-evidence-from-a-study/

Tang, N. (2024, October 22). P2P lending and mobile payments: Disrupting traditional banking systems and expanding financial inclusion. *Journal of Applied Economics and Policy Studies, 11*(1), 81–85. https://doi.org/10.54254/2977-5701/11/2024106

Tetteh, G. K. (2023). Local digital lending development and the incidence of deprivation in Kenya. *Financial Innovation (2023), 9*(102), 1–26. https://doi.org/10.1186/s40854-023-00507-0

The Economist. (2015, March 2). Why does Kenya lead the world in mobile money? *The Economist*. Retrieved February 2, 2025, from https://www.economist.com/the-economist-explains/2015/03/02/why-does-kenya-lead-the-world-in-mobile-money

Tiony, O. K. (2024, July). Financial technology and its role in promoting financial inclusion and economic growth in Kenya. *American Journal of Industrial and Business Management, 14*(7). https://doi.org/10.4236/ajibm.2024.147049

UNCDF. (2017, May 30). *Susu savings collectors—Competition or cooperation in Benin?* UNCDF. https://www.uncdf.org/article/2078/susu-savings-collectors

UN Global Impact. (2023, September 17). *UN Global Impact*. Small loans amount to big business for KWFT and life-enhancing outcomes for women in rural Kenya. https://unglobalcompact.org/take-action/impact/small-loans-amount-to-big-business-for-kwft

USAID. (2022, April). *Case study: Feed the future Kenya access to finance in Northern Kenya*. ACDI/VOCA. Retrieved April 27, 2025, from https://www.acdivoca.org/wp-content/uploads/2023/05/Case-Study_Access-to-Finance-in-Northern-Kenya_USAID-Feed-the-Future.pdf

USAID. (2023, May 26). *Agriculture, Food and Water Security | Kenya*. U.S. Agency for International Development. Retrieved January 25, 2025, from https://www.usaid.gov/kenya/agriculture-food-and-water-security

von Gaertringen, C. H. (2020, January 9). *La tontine—A model for the financial development in Africa*. Africa Partners. https://www.africapartners.eu/la-tontine-a-model-for-the-financial-development-in-africa/

Wamalwa, P., Rugiri, I., & Lauler, J. (2019, August). *Digital credit, financial literacy and household indebtedness*. Kenya Bankers Association. Retrieved April 25, 2025, from https://www.kba.co.ke/wp-content/uploads/2022/05/WPS-08-2019.pdf

Wazalendo. (2015, December 9). *Wazalendo savings and credit cooperative society*. Wsacco—Wazalendo savings and credit cooperative society limited. Retrieved February 2, 2025, from https://www.wazalendo.co.ug/

Woo, H., & Sohn, S. Y. (2022, May). A credit scoring model based on the Myers–Briggs type indicator in online peer-to-peer lending. *Financial Innovation, 8*(1), 42. https://doi.org/10.1186/s40854-022-00347-4

World Bank. (2023). *Using Digital Solutions to Address Barriers to Female Entrepreneurship*. Access to Finance | Gender Toolkit. Retrieved February 2, 2025, from https://digitalforwomen.worldbank.org/access-finance

Zambrano, A. F., Giraldo, L. F., Perdomo, M. T., Hernandez, I. D., & Godoy, J. M. (2023, December). Rotating savings and credit associations: A scoping review. *World Development Sustainability, 3*, 100081. https://doi.org/10.1016/j.wds.2023.100081

CHAPTER 6

Blockchain and Cryptocurrencies: Decentralized Finance for Inclusion

Ibrahim Nandom Yakubu, Mubarik Abdul Mumin, Ibrahim Osman Adam, and Rashad Saani

Introduction

Financial exclusion remains one of the most significant development challenges facing Africa in the twenty-first century. Despite notable progress in expanding access to formal financial services through mobile money and digital banking platforms, a large proportion of Africa's population remains unbanked or underbanked (Osabutey & Jackson, 2024; World Bank, 2023). According to the World Bank's Global Findex Database (2021), approximately 45% of adults in Sub-Saharan Africa do not have access to a bank account, and this figure is significantly

I. N. Yakubu (✉) · M. Abdul Mumin · I. O. Adam · R. Saani
School of Business, University for Development Studies, Tamale, Ghana
e-mail: ibrahim.yakubu@uds.edu.gh

M. Abdul Mumin
e-mail: mamubarik@uds.edu.gh

I. O. Adam
e-mail: ioadam@uds.edu.gh

I. N. Yakubu (ed.), *Banking on Inclusion*, Sustainable Development Goals Series, https://doi.org/10.1007/978-3-031-96716-0_6

higher in rural areas and among women (Iskenderian, 2025; World Bank, 2023). The lack of access to affordable, convenient, and secure financial services continues to hinder socioeconomic advancement, entrepreneurship, and resilience among vulnerable populations (Digital Frontiers Institute, 2024; Osabutey & Jackson, 2024). In this context, the emergence of blockchain technology and decentralized finance (DeFi) offers a transformative opportunity to reimagine Africa's financial landscape. Blockchain, an immutable, transparent, and decentralized digital ledger, underpins a wide range of innovations, including cryptocurrencies, smart contracts, and tokenized assets. These innovations form the foundation of DeFi, which refers to financial services built on blockchain networks that operate without traditional intermediaries like banks or credit institutions (Chainalysis, 2023a, 2023b; Odimarha, 2024). DeFi protocols enable peer-to-peer lending, borrowing, insurance, and savings schemes through programmable smart contracts, with the potential to reduce transaction costs, increase transparency, and expand financial autonomy (Avalanche, 2024; Chainalysis, 2023a, 2023b). The relevance of DeFi in the African context lies in its capacity to bypass institutional bottlenecks and extend financial services to previously excluded groups. With rising smartphone penetration, expanding internet access, and the popularity of mobile money services, Africa is well positioned to leapfrog traditional banking infrastructures and adopt decentralized financial models (GSMA, 2024; World Bank, 2023). For instance, in countries like Nigeria, Kenya, and Ghana, the adoption of cryptocurrencies for remittances, savings, and microtransactions is already growing rapidly, often driven by young, tech-savvy populations who lack trust in conventional financial systems (Chainalysis, 2023a, 2023b; Triple-A, 2023). However, the application of blockchain and cryptocurrencies for inclusive finance is not without challenges. Issues such as regulatory uncertainty, price volatility, cybersecurity risks, and digital literacy gaps must be carefully managed to avoid exacerbating existing inequalities (GSMA, 2024; Odimarha, 2024). Moreover, the decentralized nature of DeFi raises fundamental questions about consumer protection, accountability, and financial stability, especially in economies with weak institutional oversight (FSCA, 2024; Odimarha, 2024).

This chapter explores the relationship between blockchain-based financial innovations and inclusive finance in Africa. It begins by providing a conceptual overview of blockchain, cryptocurrencies, and decentralized finance. It then examines real-world applications of DeFi for promoting financial inclusion across various sectors, including remittances, lending, and digital identity. The chapter further analyzes the opportunities and risks associated with these innovations and evaluates the evolving regulatory landscape in African countries. Finally, it outlines strategic policy pathways and institutional mechanisms to harness DeFi for inclusive and equitable development.

Understanding Blockchain, Cryptocurrencies, and DeFi

Decentralized finance (DeFi) is transforming global financial systems by introducing an open, programmable, and trustless architecture built on blockchain technology (Makarov & Schoar, 2022). In Africa, where large swathes of the population remain financially excluded due to institutional, geographical, and economic barriers, DeFi offers an opportunity to leapfrog legacy banking systems (FurtherAfrica, 2022). However, to appreciate its potential and limitations, a thorough understanding of its key components, including blockchain, cryptocurrencies, and decentralized applications, is essential.

Blockchain: The Infrastructure Layer

Blockchain technology underpins decentralized finance (DeFi) by serving as a distributed ledger that securely records and verifies transactions across a peer-to-peer network (Thai et al., 2022). Unlike traditional systems managed by central authorities, blockchain is decentralized, transparent, and immutable. Transactions are validated through consensus, enhancing security and public trust (Bestas, 2023). In Africa, where weak institutions and poor recordkeeping often hinder governance, blockchain offers a credible alternative. Its transparent architecture can address systemic issues such as corruption and data inaccessibility. Projects like Bitland in Ghana use blockchain for land registration and digital identity management to enhance data integrity and empower underserved populations (see **Box 6.1**). These same attributes, including transparency, traceability, and decentralization, make blockchain well suited for enabling secure financial transactions through DeFi without relying on traditional intermediaries.

Box 6.1: Blockchain-Enabled Land Governance in Ghana
In Ghana, the Bitland Project introduced a blockchain-based land registry to tackle persistent challenges related to unclear land ownership, corruption, and poor recordkeeping. The system creates a transparent and tamper-proof ledger for documenting property transactions. Community members can voluntarily register their land claims, which are time-stamped and validated with government approval. This reduces the risk of fraud and helps individuals, particularly those from marginalized areas, gain legal recognition of their property, allowing them to use it as an economic asset. The initiative has enhanced public trust, simplified property transfers, and improved access to land records for individuals, legal practitioners, and the judiciary. As a result, legal processes have become more efficient, and land disputes have been reduced.

Source: Khwinana (2023)

Cryptocurrencies: The Exchange Layer

Cryptocurrencies are digital tokens that operate on blockchain networks, functioning as mediums of exchange, stores of value, and units of account. Bitcoin, launched in 2009, was the first cryptocurrency, followed by more advanced platforms like Ethereum that enable smart contracts and decentralized applications. In Africa, cryptocurrencies are increasingly used beyond speculation for remittances, cross-border trade, and protection against inflation. Countries such as Nigeria and Zimbabwe have seen widespread adoption, driven by currency instability, foreign exchange restrictions, and limited access to traditional banking services (Chainalysis, 2024). Despite these practical uses, central banks in several African countries remain cautious, issuing warnings about volatility, fraud, and lack of consumer protection. Nonetheless, grassroots adoption continues to rise, highlighting the growing relevance of decentralized finance in addressing systemic financial gaps.

Decentralized Finance (DeFi): The Application Layer

Decentralized finance (DeFi) refers to a suite of blockchain-based financial services such as lending, borrowing, trading, insurance, and savings that operate without traditional intermediaries like banks. Built primarily on platforms like Ethereum, these services use decentralized applications (DApps) and self-executing smart contracts. Key features include open access, user-controlled assets, and full transparency (Ozili, 2022).

DeFi offers unique potential for Africa, where many people lack formal financial access. With only an internet connection and a digital wallet, users can participate in decentralized exchanges, yield farming, and microloans. Platforms like Aave and Compound enable borrowing against digital assets without credit checks, while tools like Nexus Mutual could provide affordable insurance to smallholder farmers (Rahulani & Hlophe, 2023).

Figure 6.1 illustrates the core components of the DeFi ecosystem and how they interact to deliver decentralized financial services. Users access services through non-custodial digital wallets, interacting with smart contracts that automate lending, borrowing, trading, and insurance via decentralized applications (DApps). Liquidity pools provide the funds for transactions, while oracles supply off-chain data (e.g., prices or identity verification) to smart contracts. Governance of these protocols is often conducted by decentralized autonomous organizations (DAOs), where token holders vote on system upgrades and rules. Together, these elements form a permissionless, transparent, and programmable financial system capable of expanding access and reducing costs, especially in regions with limited traditional banking infrastructure.

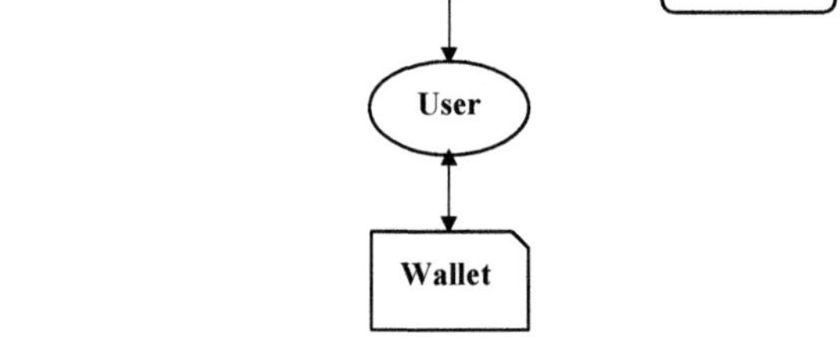

Fig. 6.1 The decentralized Finance (DeFi) ecosystem (*Source* Authors' Construct)

Summary of Key Terminologies in Blockchain and Decentralized Finance (DeFi)

As blockchain and decentralized finance (DeFi) technologies continue to evolve and gain traction within global financial systems, a growing body of specialized terminology has emerged to describe their architecture, components, and functions. **Table 6.1** provides a summary of these key terms.

Comparing Centralized and Decentralized Finance

Centralized and decentralized finance differ significantly in how financial services are delivered and controlled. While centralized finance relies on traditional intermediaries like banks, DeFi uses blockchain and smart contracts to offer user-driven, transparent services. Table 6.2 outlines the main differences between the two models, helping to assess DeFi's potential for improving financial inclusion.

Use Cases of Blockchain and Crypto for Financial Inclusion

Blockchain and cryptocurrency technologies are being increasingly deployed across Africa to tackle some of the most persistent barriers to financial inclusion, particularly high transaction costs, lack of formal identification, limited credit access, and underdeveloped financial infrastructure. This section highlights how decentralized finance (DeFi) solutions are already being applied to remittances, savings, lending, digital identity, and small business financing, offering practical pathways to inclusion.

Peer-to-Peer Remittances and Cross-Border Transfers

Remittances are a vital source of income for many African households, with Sub-Saharan Africa receiving approximately US$53 billion in remittance flows in 2022 (Bhoroma, 2023). Despite this, the region continues to face the highest remittance costs globally, averaging 8% of the transaction value, which is well above the Sustainable Development Goal (SDG) target of 3% (Okafor, 2025). Blockchain-powered remittance platforms such as BitPesa (now AZA Finance) and Yellow Card are addressing this

Table 6.1 Key terms in blockchain and decentralized finance (DeFi)

Term	*Summary definition*
Blockchain	A decentralized digital ledger that records secure and transparent transactions across a distributed network
Cryptocurrency	A digital currency built on blockchain, enabling peer-to-peer transactions without banks. Examples include Bitcoin and Ethereum
Smart Contract	Self-executing code on a blockchain that automatically enforces agreements when conditions are met
Decentralized Finance (DeFi)	A blockchain-based system offering financial services like lending and trading without intermediaries
Decentralized Application (DApp)	A blockchain-powered app that provides direct user access to DeFi services via smart contracts
Decentralized Autonomous Organization (DAO)	A user-governed organization operating through blockchain-based rules and collective decision-making
Stablecoin	A cryptocurrency pegged to a stable asset (e.g., US dollar) to reduce price volatility in DeFi transactions
Digital Wallet	Software or hardware for storing and managing cryptocurrencies and private keys
Blockchain Oracle	A tool that connects smart contracts with real-world data like weather, prices, or identity records
Liquidity Pool	A pool of crypto assets locked in a smart contract, used for decentralized trading and lending
Yield Farming	A strategy where users earn returns by staking or lending crypto assets on DeFi platforms
Gas Fees	Transaction costs paid to process activities on blockchain networks, varying with demand
Tokenization	Turning real-world assets (e.g., land, invoices) into digital tokens for easier transfer and investment
Non-Custodial Finance	A system where users fully control their funds without relying on banks or centralized platforms

(continued)

Table 6.1 (continued)

Term	*Summary definition*
Know Your Customer (KYC)	The process of verifying user identity to prevent fraud, with emerging decentralized solutions in DeFi
Cross-Chain Interoperability	The ability of different blockchain networks to communicate and share data, supporting regional integration

Source Author's compilation based on Makarov and Schoar (2022), Auer et al. (2024) andBakare et al. (2024)

challenge by enabling peer-to-peer crypto-based transfers.[1] These services bypass traditional correspondent banking networks, allowing users to send and receive funds more quickly and affordably using stablecoins or Bitcoin, which can then be converted into local currency. In countries like Nigeria, Zimbabwe, and Kenya, such solutions are gaining traction among migrant workers and freelancers who rely on international payments. **Box 6.2** illustrates how crypto remittance platforms are being used in Nigeria to overcome high transfer costs and expand financial access.

Box 6.2: Crypto Remittances in Nigeria: Lowering Transfer Costs for the Unbanked

Nigeria has recently positioned itself as a leading hub for cryptocurrency-based remittances, fueled by economic pressures and rapid digital innovation. Faced with high inflation, recurring currency devaluations, many Nigerians have embraced cryptocurrencies like Bitcoin and Ethereum as more affordable and efficient options for sending and receiving funds across borders. Peer-to-peer (P2P) platforms have become the preferred method, enabling fast and low-cost transfers while bypassing foreign exchange controls and the limitations of global payment systems that often exclude Nigerian users. Although the sector once faced regulatory pushback, including restrictions on crypto-related bank accounts, the

[1] Read more from here: https://kenyanwallstreet.com/yellow-cards-complementary-role-in-streamlining-african-cross-border-payments/ and https://www.linkedin.com/pulse/bitpesa-aza-finance-evolving-through-storm-adedayo-adebajo-4b3af.

Table 6.2 Comparison of centralized and decentralized finance

Dimension	*Centralized Finance (CeFi)*	*Decentralized Finance (DeFi)*
Control	Operated and overseen by centralized institutions such as commercial banks, central banks, and financial regulators. Users must rely on institutional trust	Operates on peer-to-peer blockchain networks without central oversight. Governance is often managed by smart contracts and decentralized autonomous organizations (DAOs)
Access Requirements	Access typically requires government-issued identification, proof of address, credit history, and a formal bank account	Open to anyone with an internet connection and a digital wallet. No need for traditional identification or credit history
Transparency	Limited transparency. Financial activities are only partially visible to regulators and auditors, and are not open to public verification	Transactions are recorded on public ledgers, allowing anyone to audit, verify, and trace financial activity in real time
Cost Structure	Involves layered fees such as service charges, maintenance fees, transfer fees, and third-party commissions	Lower operational costs due to automation and disintermediation. However, users may incur blockchain "gas" fees depending on network activity
Speed of Transactions	Often slower due to manual processing, interbank clearing, business hours, and settlement delays, especially for cross-border payments	Transactions are executed in real time or near-instantly, 24/7, using smart contracts and decentralized protocols
Trust Mechanism	Relies on regulated institutions, contractual agreements, and legal enforcement	Trust is embedded in code and enforced through blockchain consensus mechanisms such as Proof of Work or Proof of Stake
User Autonomy	Users have limited control; funds are managed and held by banks or custodial institutions	Users maintain full control over their funds and private keys. They interact directly with financial services via self-custody wallets
Risk and Security	Backed by regulatory protection (e.g., deposit insurance), but also vulnerable to institutional failures or policy constraints	Vulnerable to smart contract bugs, scams, and hacking. However, funds are non-custodial, and users are responsible for their own security

Source Author's compilation based on Kerner (2023) and OSL (2025)

government reversed course in late 2023 and introduced a clearer regulatory framework in 2024. This new approach, which placed digital assets under the Securities and Exchange Commission's oversight, has further legitimized the sector. Between July 2023 and June 2024, Nigeria received an estimated $59 billion in crypto transactions, with 85% consisting of transfers below $1 million, highlighting the practicality of crypto for everyday users. This growing trend has significantly enhanced financial access and economic participation, especially among young people and the unbanked.

Source: Adesina (2024), Mills (2024) and Clinton (2024)

Crypto-Based Lending and Savings Platforms

Access to credit remains a major hurdle for African entrepreneurs and farmers, particularly in informal economies where financial records are scant. DeFi lending protocols, such as Aave, Compound, and Africa-focused platforms like GoldFinch and Xend Finance, are helping to fill this gap. These platforms allow users to deposit collateral (in cryptocurrency or tokenized assets) and receive loans without the need for credit scores or bank approval. In addition to lending, decentralized savings protocols and staking models offer opportunities for users to earn interest on idle assets. For instance, Xend Finance, a Nigerian startup, enables users to pool their funds in stablecoins and earn higher yields compared to traditional banks, while insulating savings from local currency volatility. **Box 6.3** illustrates how Jia's blockchain lending model is being applied in Kenya, showcasing its impact on financial inclusion and SME financing.

Box 6.3: Jia's Blockchain Lending Model in Kenya

Jia is an innovative blockchain-based lending platform that has gained traction in Kenya and the Philippines between 2023 and 2024. It has disbursed over $2 million in microloans to more than 2,000 small businesses by partnering with local organizations such as Ilara Health in Kenya, which supports thousands of clinics. Jia leverages Huma Finance's on-chain credit assessment protocol and operates on the Celo blockchain, using smart contracts to streamline loan origination, repayment tracking, and the distribution of token-based rewards. Offering competitive annual interest rates of 10–12%, the platform enables borrowers to build transparent credit histories on-chain. Inspired by Kenya's traditional chama savings groups, Jia rewards timely repayments with tokens that grant borrowers access to improved loan terms and foster financial inclusion. With a default rate below 0.1% and plans to expand into West Africa and Latin America, Jia connects global stablecoin investors to underserved SMEs by converting crypto into local currency loans, mitigating exchange rate risk and addressing the massive $5 trillion credit gap in emerging markets through a transparent and decentralized finance model.

Source: Chainwire (2023), Ortiz-Bolivar (2024), Jia (2023), and Motte (2025)

Tokenized Assets and SME Financing

Small and medium-sized enterprises (SMEs) in Africa face an estimated US$330 billion financing gap (Abimbola, 2024; Mohamed, 2023). Tokenization, the process of converting real-world assets into blockchain-based digital tokens, presents a compelling solution. Entrepreneurs can tokenize receivables, agricultural produce, or equipment to raise funds through decentralized crowdfunding or asset-backed lending platforms. Tokenized crowdfunding initiatives such as Raise Africa are enabling SMEs to access capital from a broader investor base, often without incurring high interest or collateral demands. In the agricultural sector, tokenized warehouse receipts are being explored to facilitate loans for farmers who store produce in certified facilities.[2] These digital receipts, secured on a blockchain, serve as collateral for input finance or short-term credit.

Blockchain for Digital Identity and e-KYC

A major obstacle to financial inclusion in Sub-Saharan Africa is the absence of essential documentation needed to open a bank account, including government-issued identification, proof of address, and other Know Your Customer (KYC) requirements (World Bank, 2024).

[2] See for more information: https://cointelegraph.com/magazine/tokenization-projects-transforming-farmers-lives-africa/?utm_source=chatgpt.com.

Blockchain-based digital identity solutions offer a promising remedy by enabling secure, portable, and verifiable identity credentials. Projects like Kiva Protocol in Sierra Leone have piloted decentralized ID systems that enable users to access loans, mobile money accounts, or welfare programs without paper-based documentation (see **Box 6.4**). These solutions not only reduce the cost of Know Your Customer (KYC) compliance for service providers but also empower individuals to own and manage their identity data. In contexts where refugees, rural dwellers, or informal workers are excluded from formal finance due to lack of documentation, decentralized identity could serve as a powerful enabler of access.

Box 6.4: Kiva Protocol: Blockchain-Enabled Digital Identity for Financial Inclusion in Sierra Leone

The Kiva Protocol is an innovative blockchain-based digital identity and credit reporting system introduced in Sierra Leone through a partnership between Kiva, the Government of Sierra Leone, the United Nations Capital Development Fund (UNCDF), and the United Nations Development Programme (UNDP). Known as the National Digital Identity Platform (NDIP), it enables citizens to securely access and manage their national identity using biometric data such as fingerprints and ID numbers. This digital identity supports electronic Know Your Customer (eKYC) verification, allowing individuals to access financial services like loans and bank accounts without needing physical documents. Uniquely, the system consolidates credit information from both formal institutions and informal sources, such as local vendors, into a secure, blockchain-based ledger. This inclusive credit reporting framework helps the unbanked build reliable credit histories and access affordable financing. With support from the Bank of Sierra Leone, the initiative also aims to modernize the national Credit Reference Bureau and expand coverage across both formal and informal sectors. Since its public launch in 2019, the Kiva Protocol has demonstrated a scalable model for using decentralized technology to address identity and credit access challenges, offering a potential global blueprint for inclusive financial systems.

Source: Miller (2018), Davie (2019) and Hyperledger (2021)

Opportunities and Advantages for Inclusion

The integration of blockchain and decentralized finance (DeFi) into Africa's financial systems presents a unique set of opportunities to bridge longstanding gaps in inclusion, equity, and economic participation. Unlike traditional financial models that are often constrained by institutional bottlenecks, geography, and regulatory asymmetries, DeFi offers an infrastructure that is open, borderless, and disintermediated (Patel, 2024). This section outlines the major advantages of blockchain-based financial systems in advancing the financial inclusion agenda in Africa.

Lowering Transaction Costs and Entry Barriers

One of the most immediate advantages of decentralized finance (DeFi) is its potential to reduce the high costs associated with traditional financial services (Lee, 2025). In many African countries, fees for basic banking, remittances, and credit are prohibitively expensive, especially for low-income populations. DeFi platforms eliminate the need for intermediaries by enabling peer-to-peer transactions and automating services through smart contracts. This significantly reduces transaction fees and processing times (Durbin, 2025). For instance, blockchain-based remittances can be processed at a fraction of the 8% average fee charged by conventional operators in Sub-Saharan Africa.

Enhancing Financial Autonomy and Inclusion

DeFi platforms allow users to retain full control of their funds using non-custodial digital wallets. This is particularly empowering for women, youth, and informal workers who are often excluded from formal banking systems due to lack of identification, collateral, or credit history. DeFi services are accessible to anyone with a smartphone and internet connection, removing the traditional gatekeeping mechanisms that prevent underserved groups from participating in the formal economy. Alternative credit scoring models, based on blockchain transaction history or community reputation, further support inclusive access to finance.

Improving Transparency and Trust

Blockchain technology records every transaction in a publicly verifiable and immutable ledger. This transparency builds trust among users, reduces fraud, and ensures accountability in financial processes. In African contexts where institutional trust is low and corruption remains a concern, the visibility and traceability offered by blockchain can enhance confidence in financial service delivery (Boison, 2025). This is especially valuable in public sector applications such as aid disbursement, government payments, and subsidy distribution.

Enabling Cross-Border and Regional Integration

Africa's financial systems remain fragmented due to diverse currencies, regulations, and infrastructure gaps. DeFi enables cross-border transactions using cryptocurrencies and stablecoins that are not tied to any single national currency (Cellulant, 2024). This facilitates faster, cheaper, and borderless financial interactions, especially among traders, migrants, and diasporas. As the African Continental Free Trade Area (AfCFTA) promotes regional economic integration, DeFi has the potential to serve as the digital backbone for financial interoperability across the continent.

Promoting Community Finance Through DAOs

DeFi platforms support the creation of decentralized autonomous organizations (DAOs), which are digital cooperatives managed by their members through blockchain-based governance (Tang et al., 2025). These structures are modern equivalents of traditional savings groups and cooperatives, such as rotating savings and credit associations (ROSCAs). DAOs enable members to pool resources, vote on financial decisions, and share profits in a transparent and tamper-proof manner. This approach strengthens local ownership and community-driven financial empowerment.

Risks, Challenges, and Regulatory Considerations

While decentralized finance (DeFi) offers promising opportunities to extend financial access across Africa, it also presents significant risks that must be addressed to ensure safe, equitable, and sustainable adoption.

These risks span regulatory, technological, economic, and social domains. Without proactive governance and user protections, DeFi may reproduce or even worsen the very exclusions and vulnerabilities it aims to solve.

Regulatory Uncertainty and Policy Gaps

One of the most pressing challenges for DeFi adoption in Africa is the lack of clear and harmonized regulatory frameworks (Ozili, 2024). Many governments remain cautious or unclear about how to treat cryptocurrencies, smart contracts, and blockchain-based financial services. In countries like Nigeria and Kenya, regulatory bodies have issued warnings or partial restrictions on crypto activities, citing concerns about fraud, capital flight, and monetary sovereignty. This regulatory ambiguity discourages responsible innovation and limits institutional participation (PwC, 2025). Without a supportive policy environment, DeFi platforms may be forced to operate informally or offshore, reducing transparency and accountability. Furthermore, the absence of cross-border regulatory cooperation hinders regional financial integration and stifles the potential of DeFi to facilitate intra-African trade and payments.

Volatility and Lack of Consumer Protection

Cryptocurrency volatility remains a major obstacle to DeFi's reliability. Assets such as Bitcoin and Ethereum often experience significant price fluctuations, which can lead to substantial losses for users who lack risk awareness or the ability to hedge (Ahmed et al., 2024). Although stablecoins offer more predictable value, they are not entirely risk-free, as they depend on reserve assets and the solvency of issuing entities. Unlike traditional banking systems, most DeFi platforms do not offer consumer protections such as deposit insurance, dispute resolution, or fraud compensation. If a user loses funds due to a smart contract bug, scam, or transaction error, there is usually no recourse. This exposes users, especially first-time or low-income participants, to financial losses that can be devastating.

Digital Literacy and Infrastructure Constraints

Effective participation in DeFi requires a basic level of digital literacy and access to reliable infrastructure. Users must understand how to set up digital wallets, manage private keys, interact with decentralized applications, and evaluate risks. In many African contexts, especially rural areas, limited access to internet, smartphones, and digital education significantly restricts who can safely benefit from DeFi services (Domingo et al., 2024). Without deliberate interventions in education and infrastructure, DeFi could deepen digital inequality. The most vulnerable populations, who stand to benefit most from inclusive finance, may be left behind or become targets of misinformation and fraud.

Cybersecurity and Smart Contract Vulnerabilities

DeFi platforms are highly susceptible to cybersecurity threats. In 2022 alone, global DeFi-related hacks and exploits accounted for $3.8 billion in losses (Chainalysis, 2023a, 2023b). Vulnerabilities in smart contract code, phishing attacks, and fake platforms are common. In Africa, where cybersecurity infrastructure is often underdeveloped, the risk of large-scale theft or fraud could undermine user confidence and stall adoption (Benamara, 2024). Smart contracts, while powerful, are not foolproof. Coding errors or unanticipated user behavior can lead to unintended consequences. Without robust auditing and third-party verification, DeFi protocols remain exposed to critical failures that can compromise user funds and system stability.

Central Bank Digital Currencies (CBDCs) and Regulatory Competition

As African central banks explore Central Bank Digital Currencies (CBDCs), there is a growing question about how these state-backed digital currencies will coexist or compete with DeFi platforms (Alberola & Mattei, 2022). While CBDCs promise legitimacy and regulatory oversight, they often operate within centralized systems that may limit user autonomy and interoperability with DeFi applications (Murphy et al., 2024). If not carefully integrated, the rise of CBDCs could crowd out decentralized innovation or lead to overly restrictive regulations that stifle experimentation.

Strategic Pathways for Inclusive DeFi Development

The success of decentralized finance (DeFi) as a tool for inclusive development in Africa will depend not only on its technological capabilities but also on the strategies adopted to guide its growth. Realizing the full potential of DeFi requires coordinated efforts across regulatory reform, infrastructure investment, digital literacy, innovation support, and international cooperation. This section outlines strategic pathways to ensure that DeFi evolves in a manner that is inclusive, secure, and aligned with Africa's development priorities.

A critical starting point is the development of adaptive and inclusive regulatory frameworks. Many African countries currently lack clear policies to govern DeFi, which creates uncertainty for innovators, investors, and consumers. Rather than defaulting to restrictive or prohibitive measures, regulators should adopt flexible approaches that encourage responsible innovation. Regulatory sandboxes, which are controlled environments where blockchain projects can be tested under supervision, offer a promising model for experimentation. These can help authorities better understand emerging technologies while identifying and mitigating associated risks early. At the same time, consumer protection must be prioritized through clear standards on disclosure, smart contract security, dispute resolution, and risk communication. Harmonization of policies across regions, especially within ECOWAS, the Southern African Development Community (SADC), and the African Union, will also be vital for enabling cross-border DeFi services and ensuring regional financial interoperability.

Parallel to regulatory reform is the need for substantial investment in digital infrastructure. Without widespread internet connectivity, mobile network coverage, and access to affordable devices, the benefits of DeFi will remain out of reach for millions. Governments and development partners must prioritize infrastructure expansion in rural and underserved regions, ensuring that technological advancements do not deepen existing inequalities. Integrating DeFi platforms with national digital identification systems and mobile money networks will further support seamless onboarding, efficient Know Your Customer (KYC) compliance, and user convenience. Infrastructure development is thus foundational not only to expanding access but also to building user trust and confidence in digital financial systems.

Equally important is the promotion of financial and digital literacy. The accessibility of DeFi hinges on users' ability to understand and engage with blockchain applications safely and effectively. Many potential beneficiaries, particularly those in rural areas or the informal sector, lack the necessary knowledge to manage private keys, assess transaction risks, or identify fraudulent schemes. National literacy campaigns, supported by civil society organizations, educational institutions, and the private sector, must be rolled out to raise awareness and build competencies. These campaigns should be context-specific, delivered in local languages, and tailored to the needs of women, youth, and low-income groups. In addition, DeFi platforms themselves should invest in user-friendly design and embed educational resources directly within their applications.

Supporting local innovation is another essential component of a strategic DeFi development pathway. African entrepreneurs and developers are best positioned to design financial solutions that respond to local realities. Yet many face constraints in accessing funding, technical expertise, and regulatory guidance. Governments and donors should create incentive frameworks, such as grants, startup accelerators, and public procurement opportunities that encourage the development of locally relevant DeFi tools. These may include platforms for agricultural finance, cooperative lending, diaspora remittances, or blockchain-based land registries. Building robust local ecosystems for DeFi innovation will help ensure that the technology is not only adopted but adapted to serve Africa's diverse communities.

Development institutions also have a vital role to play in scaling inclusive DeFi. Organizations like the African Development Bank, United Nations Capital Development Fund, World Bank, and GIZ can provide technical assistance, co-financing, and policy advisory support to African governments and regulators. They can also serve as conveners of regional collaboration, knowledge sharing, and capacity building across the continent. By anchoring DeFi innovation within national development plans and aligning it with the Sustainable Development Goals, these institutions can help ensure that blockchain and DeFi contribute meaningfully to poverty reduction, economic resilience, and inclusive growth.

Conclusion

Decentralized finance (DeFi) is rapidly emerging as a transformative force in the global financial landscape. For Africa, where large segments of the population remain excluded from traditional financial systems, DeFi offers more than just innovation. It offers a fundamental rethinking of financial access, trust, and empowerment. Throughout this chapter, we have explored how blockchain-based financial technologies are being leveraged to address barriers related to cost, transparency, accessibility, and institutional inefficiency. From remittances and savings to lending and identity verification, the application of DeFi is demonstrating real potential in improving financial inclusion for underserved populations.

However, this potential is not without significant risks. Regulatory uncertainty, high asset volatility, limited consumer protection, cybersecurity threats, and digital literacy gaps continue to pose challenges that must be addressed with urgency and clarity. Without proactive measures, DeFi may mirror the same structural exclusions it seeks to resolve or even introduce new forms of inequality and financial vulnerability. This makes the role of governance, infrastructure, and education especially critical in shaping a future where DeFi works for everyone, not just for the technologically literate or economically privileged.

The success of DeFi in advancing inclusive finance in Africa depends on a well-coordinated approach. This includes developing flexible yet protective regulatory frameworks, investing in rural digital infrastructure, expanding financial and digital literacy, supporting locally led innovation, and encouraging regional policy harmonization. These efforts must be complemented by the active engagement of development institutions, the private sector, and civil society. All actors need to work together to ensure that DeFi aligns with national development goals and the broader Sustainable Development Agenda.

Importantly, Africa is not just a passive recipient of financial technologies developed elsewhere. Across the continent, young developers, startups, cooperatives, and grassroots innovators are already adapting DeFi tools to local needs. Their efforts underscore the continent's capacity to lead in shaping a more inclusive, decentralized, and democratized financial system. As the technology matures and adoption increases, the challenge will be to scale what works, regulate what carries risks, and design systems that center the needs of the underserved.

In a nutshell, DeFi represents a historic opportunity for Africa to bridge its financial inclusion gap and transition into a future where finance is accessible, transparent, and empowering. But this promise can only be fulfilled if the continent acts with intention by prioritizing equity, sound governance, and human-centered design. With the right strategies, decentralized finance can become more than a technological trend. It can become a cornerstone of Africa's inclusive and resilient financial future.

References

Abimbola, O. (2024). *AGF plans to bridge $300bn SME finance gap*. https://punchng.com/agf-plans-to-bridge-300bn-sme-finance-gap/

Adesina, O. (2024). *Nigeria's crypto dealings hit $59 Billion between July 2023 and June 2024*. https://nairametrics.com/2024/10/03/nigerias-crypto-dealings-hit-59-billion-between-july-2023-and-june-2024/

Ahmed, M. S., El-Masry, A. A., Al-Maghyereh, A. I., & Kumar, S. (2024). Cryptocurrency volatility: A review, synthesis, and research agenda. *Research in International Business and Finance*, 102472.

Akawak, E. (2025). *Cryptocurrency and Blockchain in Africa: Opportunities, challenges, and future prospects*. https://investafrica360.org/cryptocurrency-and-blockchain-in-africa-opportunities-challenges-and-future-prospects/?utm_source=chatgpt.com

Alberola, E., & Mattei, I. (2022). Central bank digitalcurrencies in Africa. *BIS Papers*. https://www.bis.org/publ/bppdf/bispap128.pdf

Auer, R., Haslhofer, B., Kitzler, S., Saggese, P., & Victor, F. (2024). The technology of decentralized finance (DeFi). *Digital Finance, 6*(1), 55–95.

Avalanche. (2024). *Sub-Saharan Africa: A land of DeFi opportunity*. https://www.avax.network/blog/sub-saharan-africa-a-land-of-defi-opportunity

Bakare, F. A., Omojola, J., & Iwuh, A. C. (2024). Blockchain and decentralized finance (DEFI): Disrupting traditional banking and financial systems. *World J. Adv. Res. Rev, 23*(3), 3075–3089.

Benamara, A. (2024). *Securing Africa's digital future —Are we cyber-ready?* https://techafricanews.com/2024/07/18/securing-africas-digital-future-are-we-cyber-ready/

Bestas, M. (2023). *Decentralized Finance (DeFi)*. arXiv. https://arxiv.org/abs/2304.01918

Bhoroma, V. (2023). *Remittances anchor economy*. https://www.newsday.co.zw/theindependent/business-digest/article/200013652/remittances-anchor-economy

Boison, D. K. (2025). *Leveraging digital assets to enhance trade and investment in Africa—A comparative analysis of global adoption trends*. https://www.myjoyonline.com/leveraging-digital-assets-to-enhance-trade-and-investment-in-africa-a-comparative-analysis-of-global-adoption-trends/

Cellulant. (2024). *Connect the dots: Fragmentation in Africa*. https://www.linkedin.com/pulse/connect-dots-fragmentation-africa-cellulant-n9t9f

Chainalysis. (2023a). *2022 biggest year ever for crypto hacking with $3.8 Billion stolen, primarily from DeFi protocols and by North Korea-linked attackers*. https://www.chainalysis.com/blog/2022-biggest-year-ever-for-crypto-hacking/

Chainalysis. (2023b). *Sub-Saharan Africa crypto adoption trends and analysis*. https://www.chainalysis.com/blog/africa-cryptocurrency-adoption/

Chainalysis. (2024). *Sub-Saharan Africa: Nigeria Takes #2, South Africa Grows Crypto-TradFi*. https://www.chainalysis.com/blog/subsaharan-africa-crypto-adoption-2024/

Chainwire. (2023). *Jia expands credit solution on huma to foster growth and opportunity in emerging markets*. https://chainwire.org/2023/08/01/jia-expands-credit-solution-on-huma-to-foster-growth-and-opportunity-in-emerging-markets/

Clinton. (2024). *How bitcoin and other cryptocurrencies are empowering Nigerians*. https://yellowcard.io/blog/how-bitcoin-cryptos-are-empowering-nigerians/

Davie, M. (2019). *Kiva's next frontier: Kiva protocol*. https://www.kiva.org/blog/kivas-next-frontier-kiva-protocol

Digital Frontiers Institute. (2024). *Revolutionising financial inclusion through digital financial services in Africa*. https://digitalfrontiersinstitute.org/revolutionising-financial-inclusion-through-digital-financial-services-in-africa/

Domingo, E., Muscat, S., Arnold, S., Salzinger, M., & Chetty, P. (2024). *The geopolitics of digital literacy and skills cooperation with Africa*. https://ecdpm.org/application/files/8717/1921/9245/The-geopolitics-digital-literacy-skills-coorperation-with-Africa-ECDPM-Discussion-Paper-369-2024.pdf

Durbin, S. (2025). *Decentralized finance: Reimagining the future of financial systems*. https://cfotech.co.uk/story/decentralized-finance-reimagining-the-future-of-financial-systems

Financial Sector Conduct Authority (FSCA). (2024). *Market study: Decentralised finance in South Africa*. https://www.fsca.co.za/Regulatory%20Frameworks/Documents/Market%20Study%20-%20Decentralised%20Finance%20in%20South%20Africa.pdf

FurtherAfrica. (2022). *Africa is redefining financial inclusion through decentralized finance*. https://furtherafrica.com/2022/06/21/africa-is-redefining-financial-inclusion-through-decentralized-finance/

GSMA. (2024). *The mobile economy Sub-Saharan Africa 2024*. https://www.gsma.com/mobileeconomy/sub-saharan-africa/

Hyperledger. (2021). *Kiva protocol, built on hyperledger Indy, Ursa and Aries, powers Africa's first decentralized national ID system*. https://www.lfdecentralizedtrust.org/blog/2021/01/20/kiva-protocol-built-on-hyperledger-indy-ursa-and-aries-powers-africas-first-decentralized-national-id-system

Iskenderian, M. E. (2025). Mary Ellen Iskenderian's mission to ensure one billion women have bank accounts. *Reuters*. https://www.reuters.com/sustainability/society-equity/mary-ellen-iskenderians-mission-ensure-one-billion-women-have-bank-accounts-2025-03-10/

Jia. (2023). *Using blockchain to transform financial access in emerging markets.* https://www.jia.xyz/post/jia-blockchain-emerging-markets-intro

Kerner, S. M. (2023). *Decentralized finance vs. centralized finance: What's the difference?* https://www.techtarget.com/whatis/feature/Decentralized-finance-vs-centralized-finance-Whats-the-difference

Khwinana, T. R. (2023). *Case study: Blockchain revolutionizes the land registry systems in Ghana.* https://thewill.substack.com/p/case-study-blockchain-revolutionizes.

Lee, S. (2025). *8 Quantified benefits of DeFi applications transforming finance.* https://www.numberanalytics.com/blog/benefits-defi-transforming-finance

Makarov, I., & Schoar, A. (2022). Cryptocurrencies and decentralized finance (DeFi). *Brookings*. https://www.brookings.edu/articles/cryptocurrencies-and-decentralized-finance-defi/

Miller, T. (2018). *Kiva, Sierra Leone and U.N. agencies partner to implement 'credit bureau of the future'.* https://www.kiva.org/blog/kiva-sierra-leone-and-un-agencies-partner-to-implement-credit-bureau-of-the-future

Mills, L. (2024). *Crypto in Nigeria—Surge in adoption and regulatory shifts.* https://cryptoforinnovation.org/crypto-in-nigeria-surge-in-adoption-and-regulatory-shifts/

Mohamed, D. B. (2023). *SME financing : between challenges and opportunities.* https://africa-news-agency.com/sme-financing-between-challenges-and-opportunities/

Motte, T. (2025). *Jia: blockchain-based lending for SMEs.* https://www.realisticoptimist.io/jia-blockchain-based-lending-for-smes/

Murphy, M. K. P., Sun, T., Zhou, Y. S., Tsuda, N., Zhang, N., Budau, V., Solomon, F., Kao, K., Vucinic, M., & Miggiani, K. (2024). *Central bank digital currency data use and privacy protection.* International Monetary Fund.

Odimarha, E. (2024). *Regulatory frameworks for Decentralized Finance (DeFi): Challenges and opportunities.* https://www.researchgate.net/publication/380542631_Regulatory_Frameworks_for_Decentralized_Finance_DeFi_Challenges_and_opportunities

Okafor, C. (2025). *Remittances to Sub-Saharan Africa remains over-priced.* https://africa.businessinsider.com/local/markets/remittances-to-sub-saharan-africa-remains-overpriced/dn0r47y

Ortiz-Bolivar, J. (2024). *Blockchain firm Jia records $2M in microfinance originations in the Philippines, Kenya.* https://coingeek.com/blockchain-firm-jia-records-2m-in-microfinance-originations-in-the-philippines-kenya/

Osabutey, E. L. C., & Jackson, T. (2024). Mobile money and financial inclusion in Africa: Emerging themes, challenges and policy implications. *Technological Forecasting and Social Change, 202*(4), Article 123339. https://doi.org/10.1016/j.techfore.2024.123339

OSL. (2025). *CeFi vs DeFi: A centralised and decentralised finance comparison*. https://osl.com/academy/article/cefi-vs-defi-a-centralised-and-decentralised-finance-comparison

Ozili, P. K. (2022). Decentralised finance and cryptocurrency activity in Africa. In *The new digital era: Digitalisation, emerging risks and opportunities* (pp. 1–17). Emerald Publishing Limited.

Ozili, P. K. (2024). Cryptocurrency regulation in Africa: advantages, motivation, regulatory models, challenges, consequences, and principles vs. rules-based regulation. *International Journal of Blockchains and Cryptocurrencies*, *5*(4), 294–313.

Patel, M. (2024). *A look at the future of fintech in Africa with the rise of Decentralized Finance (DeFi)*. https://www.linearloop.io/blog/future-of-fintech-in-africa-with-the-rise-of-defi

PwC. (2025). *PwC Global Crypto Regulation Report, 2025*. https://legal.pwc.de/content/services/global-crypto-regulation-report/pwc-global-crypto-regulation-report-2025.pdf

Rahulani, A., & Hlophe, N. (2023). *Market study: Decentralised finance in South Africa*. https://www.fsca.co.za/Regulatory%20Frameworks/Documents/Market%20Study%20-%20Decentralised%20Finance%20in%20South%20Africa.pdf

Tang, C., Cai, Q., Dong, C., Wang, Q., & Chen, S. (2025). Decentralised Autonomous Organizations (DAOs): An exploratory survey. *Distributed Ledger Technologies: Research and Practice*. https://dl.acm.org/doi/pdf/10.1145/3716321

Thai, P. D., Doan, M., Liu, W., Liu, T., Li, S., Zhou, H. S., & Dinh, T. N. (2022). Blockchain peer-to-peer network: Performance and security. *Handbook on Blockchain* (pp. 55–83). Springer International Publishing.

Triple-A. (2023). *Top cryptocurrency markets in Africa–2023 update*. https://africamoneydefisummit.com/top-cryptocurrency-markets-in-africa-2023-update/

World Bank. (2023). *Financial inclusion overview*. https://www.worldbank.org/en/topic/financialinclusion/overview

World Bank. (2024). *Financial inclusion in Sub-Saharan Africa—overview*. https://www.worldbank.org/en/publication/globalfindex/brief/financial-inclusion-in-sub-saharan-africa-overview

CHAPTER 7

InsurTech in Africa: Redefining Insurance for the Underserved

Khadijah Iddrisu, Joshua Yindenaba Abor, Eric Kofi Boadi, and Felix Owusu Gyebi

Introduction

Financial inclusion is recognized as a key driver of poverty alleviation, prompting the implementation of numerous policies and interventions to ensure broader access to financial services. While some continents have made significant strides in advancing financial inclusion, Africa continues

K. Iddrisu (✉)
Department of Banking and Finance, Islamic University College, Accra, Ghana
e-mail: khadijahiddris@iug.edu.gh

J. Y. Abor
Department of Finance, University of Ghana Business School, Accra, Ghana
e-mail: joshabor@ug.edu.gh

E. K. Boadi · F. O. Gyebi
Accountancy Department, Koforidua Technical University, Koforidua, Ghana
e-mail: boadikofieric@ktu.edu.gh

F. O. Gyebi
e-mail: felixo.gyebi@ktu.edu.gh

I. N. Yakubu (ed.), *Banking on Inclusion*, Sustainable Development Goals Series, https://doi.org/10.1007/978-3-031-96716-0_7

to face challenges, with nearly half of its population lacking access to formal financial services. This disparity is evident, as only about 50% of the population holds bank accounts, and insurance contributes just 3% to the continent's GDP, compared to the global average of 7% (Lamb et al., 2020). However, the presence of Information and Communication Technology (ICT) tends to change the narrative.

The advent of ICT has significantly improved operations across various industries (Cromwell & Peprah, 2025). Among the early adopters is the financial sector, which has incorporated ICT into its diverse subsectors industry (Iddrisu, Ofoeda, et al., 2025). Among the various subsectors of the financial industry, the insurance subsector has also adopted that. The application of ICT in the insurance industry is commonly referred to as Insurance Technology (InsurTech). In other words, InsurTech is the use of innovative technologies to enhance and streamline activties and operations in the insurance industry. It has enabled customers to conveniently access a range of insurance services from the comfort of their homes, including purchasing policies, obtaining quotes, calculating coverage options, and conducting personalized simulations (Ettis & Haddad, 2019).

InsurTech has gradually been accepted in most countries including the developing economies especially during the era of coronavirus disease-2019 (COVID-19). For example, during the COVID-19 period, InsurTech in Sub-Saharan Africa (SSA) saw a 19% growth in its customer base, a 6% rise in transactions, and 40% of firms reported the introduction of new products specifically tailored for the pandemic (World Bank & Cambridge Centre for Alternative Finance [CCAF], 2020). It has been established that InsurTech is delivering crop insurance coverage to 3.5 million farmers across Africa (Lamb et al., 2020). In contrast to the past, when insurance companies relied on traditional methods of service delivery, firms are now gradually embracing InsurTech by adopting mobile applications, websites, and other digital platforms to provide services. For instance, Prudential Africa has launched a mobile application linking customers directly to underwriters (Lamb et al., 2020).

As InsurTech continues to emerge across Africa, it is essential to explore its potential in promoting financial inclusion, particularly among underserved populations. This chapter examines the trends and evolution of InsurTech on the continent, highlighting the role of artificial intelligence (AI) and data analytics in advancing insurance services. Moreover, it delves into the topic of microinsurance and how InsurTech has contributed to its development in Africa. Recognizing the importance of regulatory frameworks in shaping industry growth, the chapter also reviews the regulatory landscape governing InsurTech in Africa. Also, literature on InsurTech focuses on other continent other than Africa (see Cosma & Rimo, 2024; Liu et al., 2023; Skryl & Hlushko, 2023; Sosa & Montes, 2022; Stoeckli et al., 2018). Though some African studies exist but they mostly focus on South Africa (see Antonio, 2022; Moodley, 2019; Nhlapo, 2024). While existing studies offer valuable insights, there are several notable limitations. First, conclusions drawn from studies that do not explicitly focus on Africa may be less applicable due to contextual differences such as limited ICT infrastructure, heightened cybersecurity risks, and other locational constraints. Therefore, there is a need for studies that explore how these unique characteristics influence InsurTech adoption across the continent. Second, using South Africa as a basis for inference may introduce bias, as it has a more advanced financial sector compared to most African countries, which generally have underdeveloped financial systems. Third, many of the existing studies focus on individual components of InsurTech and rely heavily on empirical models to predict its impact on insurance access. In contrast, this chapter, though not grounded in empirical modeling, draws on practical evidence such as the presence of InsurTech initiatives and the increasing number of Africans accessing insurance to offer meaningful insights. These examples span multiple African countries, providing a broader perspective on how InsurTech is enhancing insurance access across the continent.

The rest of the chapter is structured as follows: Sect. 7.2 provides a brief evolution and trend in InsurTech in Africa. Section 7.3 dicussess the role of artificial intelligence (AI) and data analytics in advancing insurance services. Also, a brief overview of microinsurance was discussed in addition to challenges that paved for the emerging InsurTech in Sect. 7.4. Section 7.5 presents how InsurTech promote microinsurance in Africa whereas Sect. 7.6 dealt with regulatory framework in Ghana. The last section concludes and provide practical implications for policymakers.

Trend and Evolution of InsurTech in Africa

Africa has embraced InsurTech in alignment with global technological advancements, following closely in the footsteps of the broader FinTech revolution. As with many sectors in Africa, mobile technology has been instrumental in transforming the insurance industry, with mobile money serving as a critical catalyst for the development of InsurTech solutions. InsurTech is progressively expanding across the continent, with its growth rooted in innovative digital platforms that address Africa's unique challenges and offer insurance services to previously underserved populations.

The widespread adoption of mobile money has been a key driver of InsurTech's growth in Africa. Mobile money platforms, such as M-PESA in Kenya, MTN Mobile Money in Ghana, and Airtel Money in Uganda, have revolutionized financial services across the continent, enabling millions of people to access banking services without traditional bank accounts (Cromwell & Peprah, 2025; Iddrisu, Yakubu, et al., 2025). Building on this foundation, InsurTech companies have integrated insurance solutions into mobile platforms, creating a seamless experience for users (Lamb et al., 2020). Through mobile payments, customers can purchase insurance policies, pay premiums, and even file claims, all from their mobile phones. This innovation has expanded access to insurance services, particularly for low-income and rural populations. Mobile technology's broad reach has made it possible to offer insurance products to individuals who were previously excluded from formal financial systems due to geographical or economic barriers. Furthermore, mobile platforms have reduced operational costs for insurers, allowing them to offer more affordable insurance solutions to a larger customer base.

InsurTech companies are embracing digital-first insurance solutions, providing a more streamlined and efficient way of delivering insurance products. Mobile platforms and applications have become vital tools in reaching underserved populations, especially in rural areas where traditional insurance coverage has historically been limited or non-existent. For example, in Ghana, SIC insurance integrated InsurTech into its activities.[1] These digital platforms enable insurers to offer a wide range of products, from life and health insurance to agricultural and microinsurance, all tailored to the specific needs of African consumers.

InsurTech also started providing microinsurance, which gained traction across Africa, providing affordable coverage for individuals and small businesses with limited financial resources. For instance, TIBA, a health financing platform, allows users to access healthcare services and insurance

[1] Read more here: https://www.ghanaweb.com/GhanaHomePage/business/SIC-to-start-e-insurance-operations-246546 Accessed February 20 2024.

coverage via mobile payments.[2] Microinsurance products are designed with the specific needs of low-income populations in mind. These products offer coverage for health emergencies, funerals, crop failures, and other risks that are highly relevant to underserved communities. The affordability and accessibility of microinsurance are helping to increase insurance penetration rates across Africa, making financial protection available to a broader segment of the population.

The collaboration between insurance companies and telecommunications providers has been a critical factor in the expansion of InsurTech in Africa. Telecom companies have extensive networks that reach millions of consumers, particularly in rural areas where traditional insurers often struggle to operate. Bima, for instance, partners with mobile network operators (MNOs) to distribute life, health, and accident insurance through mobile platforms. In Ghana, aYo has partnered with MTN MNOs to provide insurance services to the marginalized society(Punsu, 2023).

Partnering with telecom providers has helped the insurers to leverage mobile platforms to offer affordable premiums and innovative insurance products to a wider audience. These partnerships are not only enhancing financial inclusion but are also driving new business models that align with the needs of African consumers (Stanbic Bank, 2022). For example, some telecom providers are bundling insurance products with their mobile services, allowing customers to pay for insurance coverage through their mobile airtime balances. This model has proven effective in reaching low-income individuals who may not have access to traditional banking services but rely on mobile phones for their financial transactions. Moreover, by working together, insurers and telecom providers can improve operational efficiency, reduce costs, and enhance the overall customer experience. InsurTech startups are playing a key role in this ecosystem, offering innovative, customer-centric solutions that cater to the diverse needs of African consumers.

[2] For more information, visit here: InsurTech Advancements: How African Startups Are Shaping the F Accessed February 20 2024.

Data Analytics and AI in Streamlining Insurance Processes

Data analytics and artificial intelligence (AI) are playing a transformative role in streamlining insurance processes, making them more efficient, accurate, and customer-centric. These technologies are revolutionizing how insurers assess risk, price policies, process claims, and interact with customers. Below is an exploration of how data analytics and AI are reshaping the insurance industry:

Risk Assessment and Underwriting

Data analytics and AI allow insurers to move beyond traditional underwriting approaches that rely on limited historical data and a broad range of risk profiles. Insurers can leverage vast amounts of structured and unstructured data, such as social media activity, telematics, weather, and Internet of Things (IoT) data, to develop more accurate risk assessments. Specifically, data analytics and AI are used in the following ways:

i. Predictive analytics: AI algorithms analyze historical data to predict future risks, such as accidents, health conditions, and natural disasters. Insurance companies like Rexa use machine learning to process data from a variety of sources, offer insights into risk factors, and increase underwriting accuracy.
ii. Alternative data sources: Insurers use real-time data from mobile phones, satellite imagery, and wearable devices to assess risk. For example, health insurers are using fitness tracker data to offer premiums tailored to an individual's lifestyle, improving policy relevance and enhancing customer engagement. Firms such as Vitality Health Insurance uses this kind of technology (Box 7.1)

Box 7.1: Vitality Health Insurance Introduces InsurTech
Vitality Health Insurance, founded in 2004 as a partnership between Prudential and South African insurer Discovery, has since evolved into a comprehensive provider of health and life insurance. By 2014, Vitality had bought out Prudential and expanded its reach as a composite insurer.

Vitality emphasizes a member-centric approach to healthcare, focusing on prevention and well-being through its incentive-based Vitality Programme. This initiative encourages members to adopt healthier lifestyles through rewards and behavioural changes, with 25 years of success in promoting positive outcomes. Vitality is driven by a digital-first strategy, using customer insights and data-driven approaches to tailor healthcare solutions. Its "Next Best Action" initiative leverages data science to provide personalized health recommendations, addressing individual risks to enhance long-term health. The role of technology in driving customer experience, supporting claims management, and ensuring cyber security. This has expanded the scope of Vitality services to a wider range of customers. The company's holistic approach includes addressing primary care needs, traditionally outside the scope of private insurance. It also serves corporate clients by offering well-being programmes for entire workforces. Technology remains central to Vitality's operations, fostering service improvements, scalability, and employee empowerment. Vitality's dynamic culture and commitment to digital transformation enable it to adapt quickly to innovations, enhancing customer experiences and promoting a healthier society through shared value principles. The company's extensive use of AI and data analytics underpins its strategy, enhancing decision-making and service delivery at all levels.

Source: FinTech Futures (n.d.)

Customer Experience and Engagement

AI is transforming customer interactions in the insurance industry, creating a more seamless and personalized experience through the followings:

i. *Chatbots and virtual assistants*: AI-powered chatbots provide 24/7 customer support, helping with queries, policy purchases, and claims processing. miLife insurance has made it possible for customers to have interaction with the firm anywhere and anytime (see Box 7.2).

ii. *Tailored recommendations*: AI analyzes customer data and recommends insurance products and coverage options tailored to individual needs and preferences. For example, Vitality Health Insurance make tailored recommendation through the launch of Next Best Action (NBA) programme (Box 7.1)
iii. *Proactive risk management*: Insurers are using AI to inform consumers about potential risks, such as extreme weather events and health issues, so they can take preventative measures. Insurance companies such as Old Mutual and Sanlam are able to use AI to inform customers about some potential risk (TIM Group LLC, 2025).

Box 7.2: miLife Insurance Has Promoted Insurance Services in Ghana Through InsurTech

miLife Insurance in Ghana offers a diverse range of products aimed at providing financial protection and security. These offerings include the miWay Easy Mobile Insurance, which covers life, total permanent disability, critical illness, and hospitalization, with premiums conveniently paid through the MTN Mobile Money (MoMo) platform. The product also features automatic premium adjustments and cashback benefits. Additionally, MiGroup Funeral Insurance is designed for organizations, offering financial support for funeral expenses, with premiums paid via the MTN MoMo platform or other agreed methods. Both products are easily accessible and manageable through mobile platforms, allowing policyholders to conveniently handle premium payments, claims, and policy management. miLife Insurance's growth has been driven by partnerships with trade unions and leading telecom providers to deliver affordable, accessible, and customized life insurance solutions to meet the needs of Ghanaians across various income levels. With a network of over 500 retail agents powered by mobile technology, the company has reached more than 500,000 customers, 52% of whom are women, with 70% falling into the low-income bracket. Since 2016, miLife has achieved significant growth, surpassing GH¢200 million in premium income by 2022 and rising from the 17th position in 2005 to a notable 5th position in the life insurance industry rankings by 2024. The company's dedication to excellence has been recognized by the prestigious Ghana Club 100 Awards, where miLife was named the leader in the insurance industry for 2022, securing the highest rank among insurance companies and achieving the 37th position overall. This recognition underscores the commitment to delivering exceptional value to customers and driving continued growth. miLife utilizes AI-powered chatbots to offer 24/7 customer support, assisting with inquiries, policy purchases, and claims processing. These services are easily accessible through the company's website.

Source: miLife Insurance (2024)

Fraud Detection and Prevention

Insurance fraud costs billions of dollars each year and poses a significant challenge. AI and data analytics offer robust solutions to detect and prevent fraudulent claims in several key ways:

i. *Pattern recognition*: AI algorithms scan claim data to detect unusual patterns and anomalies that could signal fraud.
ii. *Natural language processing (NLP)*: NLP tools evaluate text in claim documents to identify inconsistencies or suspicious language that could indicate fraudulent activity.
iii. *Real-time monitoring*: AI systems continuously monitor the claims process and immediately flag suspicious activity for further investigation, reducing the likelihood of fraud going unnoticed.

Claims Processing and Automation

AI is revolutionizing claims processing by streamlining operations and reducing the time and cost associated with manual processes.

i. Automated claim processing: AI-powered systems can handle claims directly, eliminating the need for human intervention. For example, chatbots can guide customers through the claims process and quickly issue payments for minor incidents.
ii. Image and video analysis: AI tools can analyze visual evidence, such as photos and videos of car accidents, assess damage, and accurately estimate repair costs.

iii. Smart contracts: Blockchain-enabled smart contracts can automatically trigger claim payments when predefined conditions are met, such as flight delays or natural disasters, increasing efficiency and trust in the process.

Personalized Pricing and Product

AI and data analytics are enabling insurers to move beyond standardized policies and deliver insurance products tailored to individual needs. This is done by:

i. Dynamic pricing: In auto insurance, premiums are adjusted in real time using data such as driving behaviour and health metrics for life insurance, resulting in more accurate and personalized pricing.
ii. Usage-based insurance (UBI): Policies are priced based on actual usage, such as auto insurance that pays per mile or crop insurance that pays per harvest, offering flexibility and cost-effectiveness based on specific consumer behaviors.

Microinsurance in Africa

Microinsurance has been described in diverse ways. For instance, Morduch (2006) explained microinsurance as insurance for low-income populations, which is hailed as "the next revolution" in mitigating risks and vulnerabilities in developing nations. According to De Bock and Ontiveros (2013) microinsurance is a financial tool aimed at safeguarding low-income individuals from risks, utilizing community-based mechanisms commonly found in developing countries. Microinsurance serves underserved populations with limited financial access, benefiting from less stringent regulations (Stanbic Bank, 2022). This simplifies the sales process, creating new distribution channels and expanding reach to previously excluded segments.

In Africa, microinsurance is increasingly focused on sectors like agriculture and health, with health insurance becoming a priority due to the high cost of healthcare. Globally, health insurance is the fastest-growing type of microinsurance, with 7% and 6% growth in 2018 and 2019, respectively, and accounting for 25% of the total global premium in 2019

(Stanbic Bank, 2022). Many African governments and private institution have introduced health insurance schemes to improve access for their citizens. For instance, Vitality Health Insurance was established in 2004 to promote microinsurance but was just limited to few people in South Africa until the introduction of InsurTech (Box 7.1). Ghana's National Health Insurance Scheme (NHIS) covers either partial or full medical bills, depending on the nature of the illness, providing essential healthcare support (see Box 7.3).

Box 7.3: Ghana Set up National Health Insurance Scheme to Promote Access to Health

The National Health Insurance Scheme (NHIS) in Ghana is a social intervention program aimed at providing residents with financial access to quality healthcare. It is primarily funded through a 2.5% levy on goods and services under the Value Added Tax (VAT), 2.5 percentage points from Social Security and National Insurance Trust (SSNIT) contributions, returns from National Health Insurance Fund (NHIF) investments, and premiums paid by informal sector subscribers. The government also allocates funds to support the scheme. NHIS subscribers are classified into informal and exempt groups, with only the informal group paying premiums. Exempt individuals include SSNIT contributors, children, pregnant women, indigents, certain differently-abled persons, individuals with mental disorders, SSNIT pensioners, and those over 70. While most subscribers pay a premium and a processing or renewal fee for their ID cards, pregnant women and indigents are exempt from these fees. The NHIS credentialed healthcare facilities across various levels, including Community-based Health Planning and Services (CHPS), maternity homes, clinics, district hospitals, secondary and tertiary hospitals, pharmacies, licensed chemical shops, and diagnostic centres, to ensure access to a wide range of services. Through this infrastructure, the NHIS aims to provide comprehensive and accessible healthcare services to Ghanaians, with special provisions for vulnerable groups in the population.

Source: National Health Insurance Authority (2025)

Other example of health insurance includes Universal Health Coverage (UHC) (see Box 7.4).

Box 7.4: Universal Health Coverage of Kenya

The rollout of Universal Health Coverage (UHC) by the Ministry of Health and the National Hospital Insurance Fund (NHIF) offers a pathway for Kenyans to access essential healthcare services without facing financial difficulties. NHIF's primary role is to mobilize and register members, collect contributions, and provide health insurance benefits through tailored packages for Kenyans. With the Ministry of Health overseeing the UHC expansion, this initiative aims to ensure that all Kenyans, regardless of their socio-economic status, receive healthcare without financial strain. To prevent out-of-pocket payments that could lead to poverty, Kenyans are encouraged to secure health insurance.

Source: NHIF (2025)

In the case of agriculture, most African countries have diverse microinsurance products that enhances agriculture sector. For example, Rwanda introduced the National Agriculture Insurance Scheme (NAIS) on April 23, 2019 (Box 7.5).

Box 7.5: National Agriculture Insurance

Rwanda launched the National Agriculture Insurance Scheme (NAIS) on April 23, 2019, with the aim of mitigating risks and losses for farmers caused by natural disasters, pests, and diseases affecting their livestock and crops. Branded as "Tekana Urishingiwe Muhinzi Mworozi" (meaning "Smallholder farmer, feel safe, you are insured"), the scheme is subsidized by the government at 40%. It also enhance farmers' access to financial services and increase credit flow to the agricultural sector. In the initial phase, livestock insurance cover dairy cattle in eight selected districts, while crop insurance cover maize and rice farmers in ten districts. The crop insurance component was introduced in the 2020 farming season. The plan is to eventually scale up the scheme nationwide. Livestock insurance includes the use of microchips to prevent fraud. This scheme marks a shift from reactive post-disaster support to a proactive, budgeted agriculture insurance system. It aims to protect smallholder farmers, who account for a large portion of Rwanda's workforce and agricultural output. Agriculture represents one-third of the country's GDP and employs nearly 70% of the population. By ensuring smallholder farmers can manage risks and losses through reputable insurance providers, the scheme seeks to boost economic resilience and reduce poverty. NAIS is being implemented through a multi-agency framework involving selected insurance companies, with government oversight. The initial insurers include SONARWA, PRIME, and Radiant. The scheme's development has been supported by development partners, including Access to Finance Rwanda (AFR), which emphasized agriculture's crucial role in Rwanda's economic growth, food security, and job creation.

Source: Government of the Republic of Rwanda (n.d.)

The United Nations, through the World Food Programme (WFP), extended microinsurance support to Malawian farmers, delivering US$2.4 million in pay-outs during the 2020–2021 farming season. This initiative benefited nearly 65,000 farming households across Malawi (Box 7.6).

Although these schemes were introduced, there are some barriers to accessing microinsurance in Africa. For instance, social health coverage in Africa remained insufficient, reaching just 23.7% of the population in 2021 (International Labour Organisation [ILO], 2021). Health insurance covers medical care costs for individuals, traditionally through medical aid schemes. These plans, however, often make access to private healthcare unaffordable for those with lower incomes, leaving much of the population reliant on public facilities. As a result, preventable diseases like non-communicable diseases (heart attacks, strokes, respiratory diseases, diabetes) and curable illnesses such as malaria remain significant causes of death in Africa. For instance, the average cost to treat uncomplicated malaria in Nigeria is US$31.49, unaffordable for many, contributing to the high mortality and disability rates from the disease across SSA (Stanbic Bank, 2022).

Box 7.6: World Food Programme Provided Insurance to Farmers in Malawi

Following the devastating drought and pest infestation during the 2020–2021 farming season, nearly 65,000 farming households in Malawi have received cash pay-outs from the World Food Programme (WFP) agricultural insurance initiative of the United Nations, one of the largest crop index insurances pay-outs in Africa, totalling US$2.4 million. The programme aims to help farmers, who rely on rain-fed agriculture and mitigate the effects of climate change, which disrupts livelihoods and contributes to hunger. The Government of Malawi, in collaboration with partners, is working to empower farming communities by helping them manage climate risks. During the 2020–2021 season, farmers insured crops like maize, sorghum, rice, and groundnuts to protect their incomes from losses. These insurance policies were accessed either through cash payments or by contributing to community assets such as wells and vegetable gardens, which help farmers prepare for future climate shocks. The initiative, implemented since 2015, is part of a broader strategy to mitigate the impact of climate change on vulnerable communities. WFP is coordinating with Malawi's government and international partners, including the Adaptation Fund, Germany, and the UK, to support these efforts. At COP26, WFP advocates for better risk management systems and increased funding to help countries like Malawi adapt to climate change and improve food security. This initiative provides a springboard for farmers to continue adapting to weather-related shocks and combatting poverty and food insecurity.

Source: WFP (2021)

Barrier to Accessing Microinsurance in Africa

Several barriers hinder the majority of Africans from accessing insurance services, paving the way for the rise of InsurTech. These barriers include:

1. **High Level of Informal Sector in Africa**

Most African economy is largely shaped by the informal workforce, with 8 out of 10 people working informally across the continent (Iddrisu & Adu, 2020; Stanbic Bank, 2022). Data from the ILO suggest that since 2005 to 2024, informal sector employs about 80 to 90% and most of these are females (see Fig. 7.1). While this sector plays a crucial role in economic activity, traditional financial and insurance services remain inadequate. Microinsurance is designed to serve low-income populations, but traditional microinsurance products are inadequate to meet the unique needs of those working in the informal sector. Most traditional insurance products are skewed towards formal employment or a steady income stream, leaving the informal sectors unserved or underserved. In other words, informal workers, who are at high risk of irregular

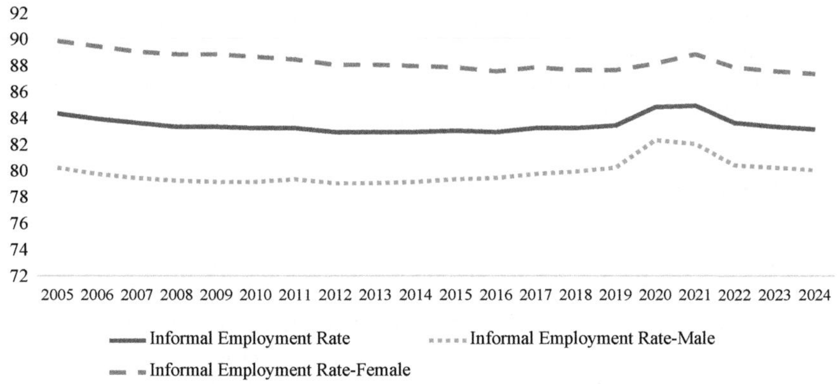

Fig. 7.1 Trend in informal employment rate by sex, 2015 to 2024 (*Source* Authors' Computation Based on Data from the ILO [2025])

income, lack social protection, and are vulnerable to unforeseen events, remain underinsured.

2. **Very Expensive**

Due to the structure of microinsurance products, which are designed for low-income populations with minimal premium values, relying on the traditional broker or agent model proves to be cost-inefficient (Stanbic Bank, 2022). The costs associated with maintaining a network of brokers and agents often outweigh the revenue generated from low premiums, making it an unsustainable model for microinsurance providers. Additionally, this conventional approach limits the scalability and accessibility of microinsurance.

3. **Lack of infrastructure**

The lack of infrastructure is a significant barrier to accessing traditional microinsurance in Africa. Many regions, especially rural and remote areas, face challenges such as limited access to financial institutions, poor road networks, and unreliable communication systems (African Monitor, 2012). These infrastructural gaps make it difficult for traditional insurance providers to reach underserved populations and effectively deliver their services. As a result, many individuals, particularly in the informal sector, are excluded from microinsurance coverage. This infrastructure deficiency not only increases operational costs for insurers but also limits the scalability and penetration of microinsurance across the continent.

4. **Complex Process**

Complex processes have long been a significant barrier to accessing microinsurance services, particularly in Africa, where many potential policyholders lack familiarity with traditional insurance systems. The intricate nature of insurance applications, underwriting, premium payments, and claims processing often deters low-income individuals and small businesses from participating in microinsurance schemes. These complexities are exacerbated by factors such as limited literacy levels, inadequate infrastructure, and a lack of trust in formal financial systems. For instance, traditional insurance processes typically require extensive paperwork, detailed documentation, and in-person interactions, which can be daunting for individuals in rural or underserved areas. Additionally, the time-consuming nature of claims processing and the lack of transparency in how claims are assessed further discourage participation. Many potential customers are also unfamiliar with insurance terminology and concepts, making it difficult for them to understand the benefits and requirements of microinsurance products.

InsurTech and Microinsurance in Africa

The emergence of InsurTech has significantly broadened the reach of microinsurance, encouraging more individuals to purchase insurance premiums for businesses, homes, vehicles, and other aspects of life. Consequently, this section explores how InsurTech has facilitated the growth of microinsurance. The integration of InsurTech into Africa's microinsurance landscape is crucial for overcoming the continent's distinct challenges and advancing financial inclusion. InsurTech harnesses digital platforms, mobile technologies, and data analytics to enhance the accessibility, affordability, and relevance of microinsurance for low-income individuals and small enterprises. InsurTech can help bridge the protection gap, providing tailored insurance products that meet the unique needs of underserved populations across the continent. This confirms to the diffusion of innovation theory by Rogers (1962) explains how new technologies or innovations spread through populations over time (Marszk & Lechman, 2021). Inspired by the diffusion of innovation theory, the growing adoption of technology, particularly InsurTech, is gradually influencing the wider population and contributing to the expansion and effectiveness of microinsurance services.

The following are practical ways through which InsurTech has facilitated the growth and accessibility of microinsurance in Africa;

1. **Data-Driven Personalization**

InsurTech uses data analytics and AI to create personalized microinsurance products that meet the unique needs of low-income individuals and small businesses. This includes UBI where premiums are adjusted based on actual usage, such as pay-per-kilometer auto insurance or pay-as-you-farm crop insurance. Also, Insurers use data from mobile phones, wearables, and satellite imagery to assess risk and tailor coverage. InsurTech enables the development of niche products, such as weather-indexed crop insurance for farmers or funeral cover for low-income families. For example, Vitality Health Insurance has bridged the gap for social care which is rare and scarce in South African's insurance sector (see Box 7.1).

2. **Simplified and Automated Processes**

InsurTech streamlines traditionally complex insurance processes, making microinsurance more user-friendly and accessible. For instance, the use of mobile platform, AI and data analytics to assess risk and approve policies in real time, reducing the need for lengthy paperwork. Customers can file claims through mobile apps or chatbots, with AI and image recognition tools used to verify and process claims quickly. Through Blockchain technology, insurers are able to ensure transparent and tamper-proof records, building trust among customers who may be skeptical of traditional insurance systems. aYo Holdings has enabled many individuals across Africa to access insurance through a mobile platform, eliminating the need for physical visits to offices or travel to insurance companies (see Box 7.7).

Box 7.7: aYo Holdings Has Streamline Insurance Process Through Technology

aYo Holdings, an InsurTech firm operating in South Africa, Uganda, Ghana, Cameroon, and Nigeria, drives financial inclusion by offering fast, convenient, and easy-to-use insurance cover directly through mobile phones. This is made possible through partnerships with MTN, MoMo, and Sanlam. The firm operates as a technology company, leveraging the rapid expansion of mobile network operators to increase accessibility, adoption, and usage of its insurance products. Insurance from aYo enables individuals to protect their families and assets affordably and conveniently against specific events. This offers many Africans their first exposure to insurance, helping them shield themselves from economic hardships that could otherwise perpetuate poverty. Since its launch in 2017, aYo Holdings has paid millions of dollars in claims across Africa. The company promotes financial inclusion by offering tailored insurance products for various market segments, from consumers to merchants, addressing specific needs. All transactions are conducted via mobile phone, eliminating the need for paperwork and providing instant, hassle-free coverage. aYo Holdings employs gamification strategies, including rewards and incentives, to engage customers and encourage consistent premium payments and policy renewals. This approach enhances customer interaction with the insurance products by making the experience more engaging and rewarding, ultimately fostering better customer retention and financial inclusion across its markets. In Ghana, aYo Holdings has paid GH¢14 million in claims to over 40,000 subscribers since its 2017 launch. With 8.2 million subscribers (25% of Ghana's population), aYo aims to reach 20 million by next year. The new 'aYo Family Cover' offers up to GH¢15,000 life cover and GH¢300 per night hospital cover for six family members, with a GH¢15 premium. Subscribers also receive 10% of the premium back if no claims are made within a year. Other products include "send with care" and "recharge with care," offering up to GH¢30,000 and GH¢6,000 life cover, respectively.

Source: aYo Holdings (2025) and Punsu (2023)

3. **Digital Distribution Channels**

InsurTech enables the distribution of microinsurance products through digital platforms, such as mobile apps, USSD codes, and web portals. This eliminates the need for physical branches and paperwork, making it easier for people in remote or underserved areas to access insurance. For example, Mobile-based platforms allow customers to purchase policies and pay premiums using their smartphones. Partnerships with MNOs and mobile money services facilitate seamless transactions, even for those without bank accounts. miLife access risks and make payment through a mobile platform especially through MTN mobile money (see Box 7.2). In the same vein, Turaco leverage on mobile platform to deliver its services (see Box 7.8).

Box 7.8: Turaco Provides Various InsurTech Products Through Partnerships

Turaco, an insurtech start-up, offers medical, life, asset, and vehicle insurance to mass-market consumers in Nigeria, Kenya, and Uganda at an average premium of around US$2 per month. Insurance is embedded into the products and services of third-party companies, including Sun King (residential solar energy systems), One Acre Fund (smallholder farmer financing), Tugende (motorcycle taxi financing), M-KOPA (pay-as-you-go access to smartphones and solar-powered appliances), and Vision-Fund (Uganda-based microfinance provider). Acting as a broker rather than an underwriter, Turaco connects insurance firms to end customers through its technology and partnerships. A recent US$10 million Series A fundraising round, led by the Cathay AfricInvest Innovation Fund and Novastar Ventures, has fueled Turaco's growth. Customers purchasing assets through partners like M-KOPA are offered insurance via call centres, and upon opting in, their coverage is activated by Turaco. Loan officers at VisionFund Uganda also notify borrowers about included insurance, with an option to upgrade to family cover. Turaco's technology platform seamlessly integrates with partners' systems through APIs, facilitating policy activation, billing, and claims administration. Offline purchases are more prevalent due to limited access to technology among the customer base. The company designs bespoke insurance bundles that cater for the underserved markets, unlocking new opportunities for insurance companies. Turaco plays a key role in the claims process, using technology such as WhatsApp integration, fraud scoring algorithms, and mobile money payment for quick turnaround. Acting as an advocate for claimants, Turaco helps expedite claims processing. With conversion rates exceeding 50%, Turaco's model proves that insurance demand in Africa is strong, particularly for base-of-the-pyramid customers who are vulnerable to financial shocks. The company's success stems from making insurance purchases frictionless, leveraging partner trust, and designing affordable, valuable

products tailored to high-risk events. Products requiring active premium payments, however, have been less successful.
Source: Maritz (2022)

4. **Affordable and Flexible Payment Options**

InsurTech introduces innovative payment models that cater to the financial realities of low-income individuals. Through some models such as Pay-As-You-Go (PAYG), customers pay small, frequent premiums linked to their usage or income cycles, making insurance more affordable. Premiums can be paid via mobile money platforms, which are widely used in Africa, even among the unbanked population. InsurTech enables insurers to offer bite-sized policies with low premiums, tailored to the specific needs and budgets of low-income customers. For example, Turaco has made it possible for citizens in Kenya, Nigeria and Uganda to get access to various PAYG such as One Acre Fund, motorcycle taxi financing and pay-as-you-go access to smartphones and solar-powered appliances (see Box 7.8).

5. **Enhanced Customer Engagement and Education**

InsurTech improves customer engagement by making insurance more interactive and understandable. AI-powered chatbots provide 24/7 support, answer customer queries, and guide users through policy purchases and claims processes. Some InsurTech platforms use gamified elements, such as rewards and incentives, to encourage regular premium payments and policy renewals. Digital platforms are used to educate potential customers about the benefits of microinsurance, addressing misconceptions and building trust in insurance products. For instance, some InsurTech firms such as Vitality Health Insurance, aYo Holdings, Turaco, and among others provides 24/7 support, guide customers and use gamified elements, such as rewards and incentives, to encourage regular premium payments and policy renewals as shown in Boxes 7.1, 7.7, and 7.8 respectively.

Challenges of InsurTech in Africa

The emergence of InsurTech in Africa has contributed to improving access to insurance and financial services more broadly. However, several challenges persist, including the following:

Low Customer Trust in InsurTech

In many African countries, the insurance sector struggles with low public trust due to historical issues such as delayed claims, lack of transparency, and limited customer engagement. This skepticism is further intensified by the introduction of digital platforms, which, while innovative, remain unfamiliar to a large portion of the population. Concerns about data security, fraud, and the impersonal nature of digital interactions contribute to user hesitation. As a result, many potential users are reluctant to adopt InsurTech solutions, preferring traditional methods or avoiding insurance altogether. Building trust through education, transparency, and user-friendly platforms is essential for greater adoption.

Low Financial and Digital Literacy

A significant portion of the population in Africa lacks both financial and digital literacy, which presents a major barrier to the effective use of InsurTech platforms. Many individuals are unfamiliar with basic financial concepts such as risk pooling, premiums, and insurance claims, making it difficult for them to understand the value and operation of digital insurance products. Additionally, limited experience with smartphones, mobile apps, and online transactions further hinders their ability to navigate digital platforms confidently. This knowledge gap not only limits adoption but also undermines trust in the system, as users may fear making mistakes or falling victim to fraud.

Limited Digital Infrastructure

Many regions across Africa continue to experience inadequate internet connectivity, frequent power outages, and limited access to affordable smartphones. These infrastructural challenges significantly hinder the scalability and accessibility of InsurTech solutions. Without reliable internet, users cannot access online platforms or receive real-time updates on policies and claims. Poor electricity supply disrupts both the operation of digital services and the ability of users to consistently engage with them. Additionally, the high cost of smartphones and data services places digital insurance solutions out of reach for many low-income individuals. As a result, InsurTech's potential to improve financial inclusion remains underutilized in these areas.

Cybersecurity and Data Privacy Concerns

As digital transactions continue to rise across the continent, InsurTech platforms are increasingly exposed to cybersecurity threats such as hacking, phishing, and data breaches. These risks pose serious challenges to the confidentiality and integrity of sensitive user information, including personal identification, medical records, and financial data. In many African countries, data protection laws are either weak, outdated, or poorly enforced, leaving users vulnerable and without clear legal guidance. This regulatory gap significantly undermines user trust and discourages broader adoption of digital insurance services. Strengthening cybersecurity measures and implementing robust data protection frameworks are essential to ensure long-term trust and growth.

Regulatory Frameworks for InsurTech in Africa

Various regulators have established regulatory frameworks to improve the efficiency of the InsurTech sector. Some of these frameworks include the following:

Regulation and Authorization

Regulators mandate that InsurTech companies secure the necessary licenses, particularly when they engage in underwriting or distributing insurance products (Chatzara, 2020). These licenses ensure that the companies comply with local regulations, maintain adequate capital reserves, and adhere to consumer protection standards. Additionally, licensing requirements help create a level playing field between traditional insurance companies and InsurTech firms, fostering trust in the market. Regulatory bodies also scrutinize the technology used by InsurTech companies to ensure it meets the required security and data protection standards, safeguarding consumers' personal and financial information.

Proper licensing is essential for promoting accountability and transparency within the InsurTech sector. In Ghana, the Insurance Act, 2021 (Act 1061), provides a structured legal framework for licensing, promoting equitable competition between conventional insurance companies and InsurTech firms. The Act outlines detailed operational guidelines for all insurance entities, including InsurTech startups, ensuring uniform regulatory adherence across the industry. The National Insurance Commission (NIC) is tasked with supervising the enforcement of these regulations and ensuring industry-wide compliance.[3]

Data Privacy and Security

As digital platforms become more prevalent, data protection regulations such as the General Data Protection Regulation (GDPR) and local data protection laws have become increasingly critical for InsurTech companies. These regulations ensure that customer data is handled securely, with privacy being a top priority. InsurTech firms must comply with these rules to protect sensitive information, prevent data breaches, and build trust with their clients. Adhering to data protection laws also promotes transparency and accountability, enabling businesses to operate more effectively while safeguarding user data and ensuring compliance with international standards in the evolving digital landscape. For instance, in Morocco, Law No. 09–08 on the Protection of Individuals Concerning the Processing of Personal Data, enacted in 2009, establishes the legal framework for data protection. The National Commission for the Control of Personal Data Protection (CNDP) is responsible for ensuring compliance and safeguarding consumer data.[4]

Investment in ICT Infrastructure

Investment in ICT infrastructure plays a pivotal role in establishing regulatory frameworks for InsurTech in Africa (Iddrisu, Yakubu et al., 2025). Enhancing digital connectivity, governments and regulatory bodies have created a solid foundation for InsurTech companies to operate efficiently.

[3] Read more here: https://nicgh.org/wp-content/uploads/2022/04/NEW-LICENCE-REQUIREMENTS.pdf?form=MG0AV3 Accessed February 25, 2025.

[4] Read more here: https://www.dgssi.gov.ma/sites/default/files/legislative/brochure/2024-07/law%2009-08%20in%20french.pdf Accessed February 20, 2025.

Robust ICT infrastructure enables better monitoring, supervision, and enforcement of regulations, ensuring that InsurTech firms comply with industry standards. Additionally, it facilitates innovation, allowing new products and services to be developed and delivered to underserved markets. As digital transformation accelerates, investment in ICT becomes essential for promoting transparency, improving customer access, and strengthening the regulatory environment for the growing InsurTech sector in Africa.

Fostering Partnership

Fostering partnership regulatory frameworks for InsurTech in Africa involves creating collaborative environments where regulators, industry players, and other stakeholders work together to promote innovation and compliance. Most regulators have encouraged insurance firms including traditional and InsurTech firms to form partnerships within or among other sectors to enhance the growth of the insurance industry (Chatzara, 2020). By encouraging partnerships between InsurTech firms, traditional insurers, technology providers, and government agencies, regulators can ensure that emerging technologies are adopted responsibly. Such frameworks facilitate knowledge-sharing, capacity-building, and the development of best practices that enhance industry standards. Collaborative efforts help align regulatory objectives with technological advancements, ensuring consumer protection, financial inclusion, and market growth. This approach strengthens the overall regulatory ecosystem, allowing InsurTech to thrive while maintaining transparency, accountability, and trust across the sector.

Conclusion

Financial inclusion remains a critical driver of poverty alleviation, yet Africa continues to lag behind other regions, with only about 50% of its population having access to formal financial services and insurance contributing just 3% to the continent's GDP. However, the advent of ICT and its integration into the financial sector, particularly through InsurTech, has begun to transform the landscape. InsurTech has enabled the delivery of innovative, affordable, and accessible insurance products to previously underserved populations, particularly in rural and low-income areas. The COVID-19 pandemic further accelerated the adoption of

InsurTech, with significant growth in customer bases, transactions, and the introduction of new products tailored to the crisis.

The integration of mobile technology, data analytics, and AI has been pivotal in this transformation. Mobile money platforms, such as M-PESA and MTN Mobile Money, have revolutionized financial services, enabling millions to access insurance products through their mobile phones. InsurTech has also facilitated the rise of microinsurance, offering affordable coverage for health, agriculture, and other critical areas, thereby addressing the unique needs of low-income populations. Furthermore, partnerships between insurers and telecommunications providers have expanded the reach of InsurTech, making insurance more accessible and affordable. Despite these advancements, significant barriers to accessing microinsurance persist, including the high level of informality in African economies, the cost of traditional insurance models, lack of infrastructure, and complex processes. InsurTech has begun to address these challenges by leveraging digital platforms, AI, and data analytics to simplify processes which is reducing costs, and enhancing customer engagement. However, the full potential of InsurTech in Africa can only be realized through supportive regulatory frameworks, investment in ICT infrastructure, and continued innovation.

Based on the review, the following policy implications were provided. First, governments and regulatory bodies should establish clear and supportive frameworks for InsurTech to ensure compliance, consumer protection, and market stability. This includes licensing requirements, data privacy regulations, and oversight mechanisms to foster trust and transparency in the sector. Also fully harnessing the potential of InsurTech, significant investment in ICT infrastructure is needed, particularly in rural and underserved areas. Improved digital connectivity will enable the expansion of InsurTech services, making insurance more accessible to a broader population.

Second, policymakers should prioritize the development of microinsurance products tailored to the needs of low-income populations, particularly in sectors like agriculture and health. This includes providing incentives for insurers to offer affordable and flexible payment options, such as PAYG models. Policymakers should work to address the structural barriers that hinder access to insurance, such as the high level of informality in African economies and the lack of infrastructure. This includes creating enabling environments for InsurTech to thrive and ensuring that regulatory frameworks are inclusive and supportive of innovation. Last, regulators should encourage the use of data analytics and AI in the insurance sector to improve risk assessment, fraud detection, and customer engagement. This will enhance the efficiency and effectiveness of insurance services, making them more relevant and accessible to consumers. Governments and industry players should invest in educational campaigns to improve financial literacy and awareness of insurance products. This will help demystify insurance concepts and encourage more people to adopt microinsurance and other financial services.

References

African Monitor. (2012). *Rural infrastructure in Africa: Unlocking the African moment* (1; Development Support Monitor—Paper Series).

Antonio, W. (2022). *The nature of project management in South African SMEs: A look at insurtech in the Western Cape Province of South Africa* [University of Cape Town]. https://open.uct.ac.za/server/api/core/bitstreams/e231f46f-d0d4-4a56-897c-8247b5cb097c/contentaYo Holdings. (2025). *What We Do.* https://ayo-holdings.com/products/

Chatzara, V. (2020). FinTech, InsurTech, and the Regulators. In P. Marano & K. Noussia (Eds.), *InsurTech: A legal and regulatory view. AIDA Europe research series on insurance law and regulation* (pp. 3–25). Springer, Cham. https://doi.org/10.1007/978-3-030-27386-6_1

Cosma, S., & Rimo, G. (2024). Redefining insurance through technology: Achievements and perspectives in Insurtech. *Research in International Business and Finance, 70*, Article 102301. https://doi.org/10.1016/j.ribaf.2024.102301

Cromwell, R. S., & Peprah, J. A. (2025). Banking business models and sustainable development: Challenges and opportunities. In I. N. Yakubu (Ed.), *Strategic approaches to banking business and sustainable development goals* (pp. 3–22). Springer. https://doi.org/10.1007/978-3-031-80744-2_1

De Bock, O., & Ontiveros, D. U. (2013). *Literature review on the impact of microinsurance* (35; Research Paper). https://www.microinsurancefacility.org/sites/default/files/repaper35.pdf

Ettis, S. A., & Haddad, M. M. (2019). Utilitarian and hedonic customer benefits of e-insurance. *International Journal of E-Business Research, 15*(1), 109–126. https://doi.org/10.4018/IJEBR.2019010107

FinTech Futures. (n.d.). *Vitality: Using technology to transform health insurance.* InsurTech Insight. Retrieved March 7, 2025, from https://www.insurtechinsights.com/vitality-using-technology-to-transform-health-insurance/?form=MG0AV3&form=MG0AV3

Government of the Republic of Rwanda. (n.d.). *Government launches a subsidized agriculture insurance scheme*. Retrieved March 6, 2025, from https://www.minagri.gov.rw/updates/news-details/government-launches-a-subsidized-agriculture-insurance-scheme?form=MG0AV3

Iddrisu, K., & Adu, K. O. (2020). *Property tax compliance in Twifo Hemang Lower Denkyira district in the Central Region of Ghana: Does distance to nearest tax office matter?*

Iddrisu, K., Ofoeda, I., Issah, O., & Iddrisu, M. (2025). Gender equality and women's empowerment in banking. In I. Yakubu (Ed.), *Strategic Approaches to banking business and sustainable development goals. Sustainable development goals series.* (pp. 179–193). Springer. https://doi.org/10.1007/978-3-031-80744-2_11

Iddrisu, K., Yakubu, I. N., & Asongu, S. A. (2025). FinTech innovations for sustainable banking. In *Strategic approaches to banking business and sustainable development goals. sustainable development goals series* (pp. 63–86). Springer. https://doi.org/10.1007/978-3-031-80744-2_4

ILO. (2021). *World social protection report 2020–22: Social protection at the crossroads—in pursuit of a better future*. https://www.ilo.org/sites/default/files/wcmsp5/groups/public/%40ed_protect/%40soc_sec/documents/publication/wcms_817572.pdf

ILO. (2025). *Informal employemnt rate by sex: ILO modelled estimates, Nov. 2023(%)-Annual*. https://rshiny.ilo.org/dataexplorer35/?region=AFRICA&lang=en&segment=indicator&id=EMP_2IFL_SEX_RT_A

Lamb, P., A2ii and Tom Herbstein, & UK's Department for International Trade. (2020). *InsurTech—shaping financial services in Sub-Saharan Africa*. Access to Insurance Initiative. https://a2ii.org/en/news/new-blog-post-insurtech-shaping-financial-services-in-subsaharan-africa

Liu, J., Ye, S., Zhang, Y., & Zhang, L. (2023). Research on InsurTech and the technology innovation level of insurance enterprises. *Sustainability, 15*(11), 8617. https://doi.org/10.3390/su15118617

Maritz, J. (2022, October 2). *Insurance for $2 a month: The business model of African start-up Turaco*. https://www.howwemadeitinafrica.com/insurance-for-2-a-month-the-business-model-african-start-up-turaco/147872/?form=MG0AV3

Marszk, A., & Lechman, E. (2021). Technological forecasting & social change reshaping financial systems: The role of ICT in the diffusion of financial innovations—Recent evidence from European countries. *Technological Forecasting & Social Change, 167*(May 2020), 120683. https://doi.org/10.1016/j.techfore.2021.120683

miLife Insurance. (2024). *About us*. https://milifeghana.com/our-story/

Moodley, A. J. (2019). Digital transformation in South Africa's short-term insurance sector: Traditional insurers' responses to the Internet of Things (IoT) and Insurtech. *The African Journal of Information and Communication, 24*, 1–16.

Morduch, J. (2006). Microinsurance: the next revolution? In A. Banerjee, R. Benabou, & D. Mookherjee (Eds.), *Understanding poverty*. Oxford University Press.

National Health Insurance Authority. (2025). *Brief introduction to the NHIS*. https://www.nhis.gov.gh/about

NHIF. (2025). *Universal health coverage*. https://www.nhif.or.ke/uhc-supa-cover/

Nhlapo, Z. (2024). *Promotion of inclusive insurance by a South African InsurTech company* [University of the Witwatersrand]. https://www.google.com/search?q=where+is+witwatersrand+university+located&oq=where+is+Witwatersrand&gs_lcrp=EgZjaHJvbWUqBwgBEAAYgAQyBwgAEAAYgAQyBwgBEAAYgAQyBwgCEAAYgAQyBwgDEAAYgAQyBwgEEAAYgAQyBwgFEAAYgAQyCAgGEAAYFhgeMggIBxAAGBYYHjIICAgQABgWGB4yCAgJEAAYFhge0gEINzk5NGowajeoAgCwAgA&sourceid=chrome&ie=UTF-8

Punsu, E. (2023, July 14). *aYo pays GH¢14m in claims*. Thebftonline.Com.

Rogers, E. M. (1962). *Diffusion of innovation* (3rd ed.). The Free Press, A Division of Macmillan Publishing Co., Inc.

Skryl, V., & Hlushko, A. (2023). Insurtech: new opportunities for the development of the insurance market. *Економіка і Регіон/ Economics and Region, 1(88)*, 144–151. https://doi.org/10.26906/EiR.2023.1(88).2877

Sosa, I., & Montes, Ó. (2022). Understanding the InsurTech dynamics in the transformation of the insurance sector. *Risk Management and Insurance Review, 25*(1), 35–68. https://doi.org/10.1111/rmir.12203

Stanbic Bank. (2022). *The Rapid Evolution of Insurance in Africa: Why it's needed and how innovation is championing new horizons for growth* . https://www.standardbank.com/static_file/StandardBankGroup/filedownloads/RapidEvolutionofInsuranceAfricaReport.pdf

Stoeckli, E., Dremel, C., & Uebernickel, F. (2018). Exploring characteristics and transformational capabilities of InsurTech innovations to understand insurance value creation in a digital world. *Electronic Markets, 28*(3), 287–305. https://doi.org/10.1007/s12525-018-0304-7

TIM Group LLC. (2025). *AI and risk assessment: How Africa is adopting new technologies for insurance*. https://tech-ceos.com/ai-and-risk-assessment-how-africa-is-adopting-new-technologies-for-insurance/?form=MG0AV3

WFP. (2021, November 3). *Farmers in Malawi receive cash in one of the largest insurance payouts in Africa*. https://www.wfp.org/news/farmers-malawi-receive-cash-one-largest-insurance-payouts-africa?form=MG0AV3&form=MG0AV3

World Bank, & CCAF. (2020). *The global covid-19 FinTech regulatory rapid assessment report*. https://www.jbs.cam.ac.uk/wp-content/uploads/2020/10/2020-ccaf-report-fintech-regulatory-rapid-assessment.pdf

CHAPTER 8

Emerging FinTech Savings and Investment Platforms in the African Financial Landscape

Khadijah Iddrisu, Farihan Alhassan, Ibrahim Nandom Yakubu, and Randolph Nsor-Ambala

Introduction

Financial Technology (FinTech) has introduced a variety of platforms and products specifically designed to cater for underserved communities (Cromwell & Peprah, 2025; Iddrisu, Yakubu et al., 2025). Some of

K. Iddrisu (✉)
Department of Banking and Finance, Islamic University College, Accra, Ghana
e-mail: khadijahiddris@iug.edu.gh

F. Alhassan
GCB Bank PLC, Accra, Ghana
e-mail: farihan@gcb.com.gh

I. N. Yakubu
School of Business, University for Development Studies, Tamale, Ghana
e-mail: ibrahim.yakubu@uds.edu.gh

R. Nsor-Ambala
Development Bank of Ghana, Accra, Ghana
e-mail: rnsor-ambala@gimpa.edu.gh

I. N. Yakubu (ed.), *Banking on Inclusion*, Sustainable Development Goals Series, https://doi.org/10.1007/978-3-031-96716-0_8

these platforms including insurance, savings and investment, regulations platforms, and among others. Currently, a range of FinTech start-ups, banks, and non-bank financial institutions are developing diverse FinTech platforms to address the needs of users, particularly those in underserved communities. Among these platforms, savings and investments platforms have been increasing. For example, in Kenya, M-Pesa's mobile money platform enables users, particularly in rural and underserved areas, to save and invest through its M-Shwari product (Safaricom, 2025). M-Shwari allows people without traditional bank accounts to save small amounts and access micro-loans, improving financial inclusion and helping individuals build financial resilience.

The onset of recent global crises, particularly the COVID-19 pandemic, has heightened people's appreciation for the convenience and services offered by FinTech savings and investment platforms. For example, during and after COVID-19, platforms like Trove, Chaka, and Bamboo have gained significant traction in Nigeria (Business World Africa, 2024). FinTech savings and investment platforms are digital services that leverage technology to offer financial solutions for saving money and investing in various assets (Iddrisu, Yakubu et al., 2025). These user-friendly platforms enable savings and investing with small amounts, often offering automated options and educational content to help users make informed financial decisions seamlessly and consistently (Iddrisu, Yakubu et al., 2025; Sanga & Aziakpono, 2022). Hence, the need to discuss how the rise of digital savings and investments promote savings and wealth creation of the underserved population in Africa.

The rest of the chapter is structured as follows: growth of digital savings and investment platforms, highlighting the key factors contributing to their increasing popularity. Section 8.3 and 8.4 discusses the impact of the rise of growth of digital savings and investment platforms on savings and wealth creation respectively. Section 8.5 discusses the challenges and way forward of rise of digital savings and investment platforms in Africa. Section 8.6 concludes and provide some practical implications for policymakers.

The Rise of Digital Savings and Investment Platforms in Africa

The introduction of M-PESA (mobile money) by Safaricom marked a pivotal moment in the rise of digital savings and investment platforms in Africa (Iddrisu, Yakubu et al., 2025; Sanga & Aziakpono, 2022). While e-banking existed prior to M-PESA, it was primarily utilized by the elite and concentrated in urban areas (see Box 8.1). However, M-PESA's adoption across various African countries revolutionized access to digital financial services, offering a platform for savings and investments that catered for both the elite and the broader population, reaching individuals in both urban and rural communities. At the time, e-banking services were limited to basic functions like checking balances and transferring funds, and were accessible only to customers with accounts at formal financial institutions, such as banks (Jibril et al., 2024).

Box 8.1: Mobile Money: The Population Savings and Investment Platform

In 2007, Safaricom, a Vodafone subsidiary in Kenya, introduced M-PESA, marking the beginning of mobile money services in Africa. Unlike most FinTech products, which were initiated by banks, M-PESA was developed by mobile operators, allowing users to transfer money and conduct financial transactions via mobile phones. The platform uses a network of agents for cash deposits, withdrawals, and transfers through SMS. Following its success, countries like Tanzania, Ghana, Uganda, and Rwanda adopted similar models. Over time, mobile money services expanded to include savings, investments, and insurance, facilitated through partnerships with financial institutions. In 2022, Sub-Saharan Africa accounted for 53% of the world's mobile money accounts, leading global growth in this sector. In 2023, out of Africa's population of about 1.18 billion, 43 percent had access to mobile phones, representing 489 million unique subscribers, while mobile internet usage reached 25 percent, with 287 million users. In Ghana alone, mobile money provided financial services to 18.4 million people by October 2021, with average monthly transactions valued at GH¢18,979.35 million.

Source: Awanis et al. (2022), Kulu and Bondzie (2024), and Laghmari (2020)

However, the introduction of M-PESA expanded the scope of digital financial services, providing more comprehensive offerings beyond traditional banking (Jibril et al., 2024). The rising demand for FinTech and others has led to the creation of diverse digital savings and investment platforms. For instance, Dalex Finance in Ghana has launched a significant product such as Dalex SWIFT, which promotes consistent and gradual contributions, helping individuals build their savings over time (see Box 8.2).

Box 8.2: Dalex SWIFT
Dalex SWIFT is a savings and investment platform offered by Dalex Finance, a prominent financial institution in Ghana. Renowned for its innovative financial solutions, Dalex Finance specializes in providing a wide range of services, particularly savings and investment products, to both individuals and businesses. Dalex SWIFT is a smart investment account designed for effortless money growth. From registration to withdrawals, customers can manage their accounts entirely through their mobile phones. With a minimum contribution of just GH ¢10, customers can make regular deposits anytime and from anywhere. The account offers compound interest rates that shield customers from market volatility, while their phone numbers serve as unique identifiers for added convenience. Best of all, there are no transaction fees. Customers can access and manage their investments directly from their mobile devices, offering maximum flexibility. In addition to the ease of managing savings, Dalex SWIFT provides the most affordable and quickest loan options. Customers can confidently rely on Dalex Finance's proven track record of reliability and safety to secure their funds. Unlike traditional banking products that impose fees for early withdrawals, Dalex SWIFT allows customers to access their funds whenever needed, without any penalties.

Source: Dalex Finance (2025)

In South Africa alone there are more than 20 savings and investment platforms including key ones such as EasyEquities, SatrixNow. Franc App, Stash by liberty, Capitec Bank App, TymeBnak Goalsave, and Old Mutual Money Account. This chapter offers insights into EasyEquities, highlighting its unique features, including the ability for users to invest in local and international stocks, ETFs, and cryptocurrencies at low fees. It caters to both novice and seasoned investors, making it an ideal platform for a wide range of users (see Box 8.3).

Box 8.3: World Trader (Pty) Ltd launched EasyEquities
EasyEquities, launched in 2014, is a financial product of the First World Trader (Pty) Ltd, a subsidiary of Purple Group. It is an authorized financial service provider and registered credit provider. It enables users to invest in a variety of securities, including whole shares and fractional security rights (FSRs). EasyEquities acts as an agent for whole shares, where the investor becomes the registered owner, gaining the right to dividends, corporate actions, and other economic benefits of share ownership. In contrast, FSRs, issued through a contract for difference (CFD), allow investors to benefit from price movements and dividends without owning the underlying share. FSRs do not come with voting rights, and as the investor accumulates enough FSRs to match a whole share, the CFD is closed, and the investor gains full ownership of the share. While EasyEquities offers a wide range of shares on its platform, the availability of shares is influenced by various factors and is not a reflection of their investment value. Prices of shares are subject to exchange delays, with South African and North American prices delayed by 15 minutes, and Australian prices by 20 minutes. The Tax-Free Savings Account (TFSA) on EasyEquities allows users to grow wealth tax-free with no monthly fees, paying only small transaction fees. It features a user-friendly interface andeducational resources. EasyEquities operates under the regulation of the Financial Sector Conduct Authority (FSCA) and ensures security by utilizing bank-grade encryption. In 2017, Sanlam Investment Holdings (SIH) purchased 30% shares of EasyEquities.

Source: EasyEquities (2025); Konnect (2025) and Tendai (2017)

Other African countries have seen also adopted diverse form of savings and investment platform. For instance, Kenya also has some platforms that seeks to serve the underserved and promote financial inclusion (see Box 8.4). This evolution is catalyzed by the convergence of several key factors, including rapid mobile phone adoption, expanding internet penetration, the rise of FinTech, and an increasing desire for financial inclusion. Digital platforms are empowering millions of previously unbanked and underbanked Africans, offering them new opportunities to save, invest, and access financial products that were once out of reach.

Therefore, this chapter discusses the factors that promote the rising savings and investments in Africa in the following sub-section.

Box 8.4: Some Savings and Investment Platforms in Kenya

There are a number of savings and investment platforms in Kenya which include the following: (i) Abacus is a Kenyan investment platform that provides access to stocks, bonds, and unit trusts. Designed for both novice and experienced investors, it offers tools and local market insights to help users make informed decisions. Abacus is integrated with the Nairobi Securities Exchange (NSE), allowing users to buy and sell stocks directly, making it a comprehensive and user-friendly platform for Kenyan investors. (ii) Bamboo enables Kenyans to invest in over 3,000 U.S. stocks and ETFs from the New York Stock Exchange and NASDAQ via mobile devices. Bamboo offers an excellent opportunity for diversification beyond the local market. Its low fees and user-friendly interface make it accessible to a wide audience, providing detailed stock information to help users make informed investment decisions. (iii) Hisa is another investment app tailored for the Kenyan market, allowing users to invest in stocks and other financial instruments listed on the NSE. It offers real-time data and analysis to keep users updated on market trends and provides educational resources for both beginners and experienced investors. With seamless integration into local payment systems, Hisa simplifies depositing and withdrawing funds, making it accessible for a broad audience. (iv) Mula is a versatile financial app offering a range of services, including bill payments, savings, and low-risk investment options like money market funds and fixed deposits. Mula's integration with mobile money platforms makes it convenient for users to manage their finances, ensuring easy transfers between accounts and providing an efficient way to invest while maintaining capital preservation. (v) Chumz focuses on promoting disciplined savings through its automated feature, encouraging users to save small amounts regularly. These savings are invested in low-risk financial instruments like money market funds, making it a practical tool for conservative investors and beginners looking to steadily grow their savings.

Source: Waceke (2024)

Catalysts for the Growth of Digital Savings and Investments Platform in Africa

The rising digital savings and investment platform in Africa is influenced by the following factors;

1. **Mobile Phone Penetration**

The widespread adoption of mobile phones in the African country has significantly increased, with a survey by the International Telecommunication Union (ITU) indicating a rise in mobile phone ownership from 53.9% in 2019 to 66.2% by 2024 (see Fig. 8.1). This surge in mobile phone penetration has created opportunities for various institutions, including banks, non-banks, FinTech start-ups, and ICT firms. These entities have leveraged the growing mobile usage to develop platforms accessible via mobile phones, enabling users to perform savings and investment activities with ease.

2. **The Presence of COVID-19**

COVID-19 prompted widespread appreciation for FinTech and its various platforms, especially among underserved populations. As activities rapidly shifted online during the pandemic, both established and new financial institutions responded by developing digital savings and investment platforms. For example, in Ghana, the country's first commercial bank, GCB, launched the G-Money app to improve financial access and

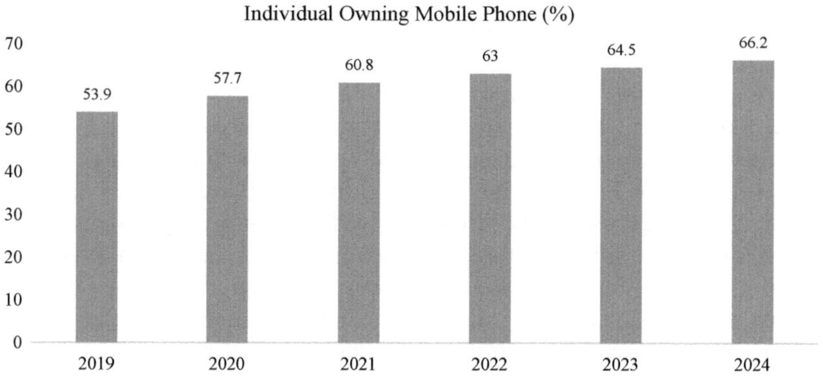

Fig. 8.1 Trend in mobile phone penetration in Africa, 2019–2024 (*Source* Authors' Computation based on Data from the International Telecommunication Union)

service delivery during this period (see Box 8.5). This digital solution enhanced the ability of individuals to save, invest, and conduct financial transactions seamlessly, reflecting how FinTech innovations supported financial inclusion and adaptation in challenging times.

Box 8.5: GCB Launched the G-Money Application
G-Money is a mobile application launched by GCB in 2020 to enhance service access and delivery during COVID-19. The app facilitates connections with third-party FinTech and technology companies, offering an open platform for broader financial integration. Unlike traditional banking apps, G-Money supports agent banking similar to mobile money, enabling customers to deposit or withdraw cash at any G-Money agent nationwide. It also allows users to link and unlink their personal bank accounts to the G-Money wallet, making seamless Bank-to-Wallet and Wallet-to-Bank transactions possible. The app supports payments for utilities, fees, and other online services, with 24/7 money transfer functionality.

Source: G-Money (2020)

3. **Investment in Information Technology**

In most African countries, governments, along with their development partners, have allocated substantial funds to enhance ICT infrastructure, fostering the growth of digital savings and investment platforms. These investments aim to strengthen broadband connectivity, mobile networks, and digital payment systems, which are crucial for supporting FinTech innovations. Governments and agencies help create an enabling environment for FinTech start-ups to thrive, enabling broader access to financial services, especially in underserved communities through investment in digital infrastructure. This commitment has been pivotal in driving financial inclusion and the adoption of digital financial solutions across the continent. For instance, the implementation of the Mobile Money Interoperability System facilitates seamless cross-network fund transfers, establishing a solid foundation for digital savings and investment platforms by improving accessibility and convenience in Ghana (see Box 8.6).

Box 8.6: Ghana Launched Mobile Money Interoperability System
The Bank of Ghana (BoG), a member of the Alliance for Financial Inclusion (AFI), launched the country's first Mobile Money Interoperability System (MMI) on May 10, 2018, through the Ghana Interbank Payment and Settlement Systems Limited (GhIPSS). The MMI system simplifies mobile money transfers across different networks and enables wallet-to-wallet, wallet-to-bank account, and wallet-to-e-zwich card transactions. It addresses challenges like opening bank accounts, high maintenance costs, and financial literacy barriers. Mobile money has grown significantly in Ghana, with active accounts increasing from 8.3 million in 2016 to 11.11 million in 2017, positioning Ghana as a leader in mobile money adoption. MMI allows customers to transfer funds directly across networks without the need for third-party payment providers, reducing costs and enhancing convenience. This system supports financial inclusion by integrating mobile money users into the financial ecosystem and promoting cashless transactions. MMI also facilitate seamless financial intermediation, allowing businesses and individuals to accept mobile money from various network users effortlessly, further boosting financial inclusion and supporting cashless transactions in the country. This pave way for FinTech firms to create platforms where payment can be made via mobile money.
Source: AFI (2018)

Similarly, multilateral organizations including Google, Convergence Partners, the International Finance Corporation (IFC), and Mitsui & Co., Ltd. entered into an agreement, committing US$100 million to invest in CSquared, a broadband infrastructure firm dedicated to developing wholesale metro fiber optic networks aimed at enhancing internet access across Africa as shown in Box 8.7. Africa has also been making significant investments in modern ICT infrastructure, including 4th Generation (4G) and 5th Generation (5G) network services (Iddrisu, Yakubu et al., 2025).

Box 8.7: Multilateral Companies Invested in CSquared to Boost ICT Infrastructure in Africa
On May 16, 2017, Google, Convergence Partners, the International Finance Corporation (IFC), and Mitsui & Co., Ltd. signed an agreement to invest in CSquared, a broadband infrastructure company focused on building wholesale metro fibre optic networks to improve internet access

in Africa. The partnership includes a capital commitment of up to US$100 million, with CSquared operating as an independent company headquartered in Nairobi, Kenya. The company already has networks in Uganda and Ghana and aims to expand further across the continent. This collaboration brings together Google's technical expertise from Project Link, which deployed fibre networks in Uganda and Ghana, with the additional capital, industry experience, and global reach of Convergence Partners, IFC, and Mitsui. Convergence Partners brings deep ICT investment experience in sub-Saharan Africa, IFC has over 40 years of telecommunications support in Africa, and Mitsui offers cross-industry capabilities and strategic investments in the ICT sector.

Africa faces significant challenges in broadband internet access, with only six percent of the population having access, hindering the region's human and economic development. Fibre optic infrastructure is essential to improve mobile networks' speed and reliability and provide direct internet access to businesses, SMEs, educational institutions, and residential estates. However, the high cost of deploying fibre infrastructure remains a barrier. By operating on a shared infrastructure model, CSquared aims to reduce costs and provide affordable wholesale services to licensed operators. CSquared's open access model allows for high-quality, cost-effective services to promote a thriving digital ecosystem. By 2017, the company had built over 800 km of fibre in Uganda and over 840 km in Ghana, connecting over 1,200 tower and commercial building sites. CSquared's efforts have enabled over 25 ISPs and mobile network operators to offer broadband and 4G services, improving internet reliability and access across the region. The partners believe this shared infrastructure model will help expand CSquared's reach and meet Africa's growing demand for quality internet networks.

Source: Convergence Partners (n.d.)

4. **Support for Fintech Startups**

FinTech start-ups have been receiving substantial support from governments, bilateral, and multilateral agencies, which has contributed to the rise of digital savings and investment platforms. Governments have introduced regulations, such as sandboxes and flexible policies, to foster FinTech growth, allowing start-ups to innovate and test digital savings platforms without strict regulations. Bilateral and multilateral agencies provide funding and grants to promote digital financial ecosystems, including savings, investment, and payment platforms. For example, Orange Ventures partner with Digital Africa to support FinTech start-ups in Africa (see Box 8.8). Through its collaboration with NVIDIA, Microsoft offers a range of support to start-ups, including funding and customized software solutions (see Box 8.9).

Box 8.8: Orange Ventures and Digital Africa Partnership to Support FinTech Start-ups

In June 2023, Orange Ventures and Digital Africa formalized a partnership at Vivatech to enhance their support for African start-ups via the Orange Digital Centers (ODC). Both organizations pledged to increase investments in start-ups accelerated by the ODC network, with the Fuzé scheme allowing for co-financing and doubling of funds from either party through joint evaluation of applications. The ODC ecosystem spans 17 countries across Africa and the Middle East, and 8 in Europe, offering free programs that include digital training, start-up incubation, and acceleration, all aimed at promoting entrepreneurship. In the first year, five start-ups such as Clinihome (Healthtech), Koree (FinTech), and Colorfol (Cultural and Creative Industries) from Cameroon, and Tolbi (Agritech) and Proboutik (FinTech) from Senegal, each received up to €50,000 in funding from Digital Africa's Fuzé program, enabling them to significantly expand their operations.

Source: À propos d'Orange (2024)

Agencies also offer technical assistance, mentorship, and capacity-building programs to support start-ups. For instance, the partnership between Microsoft and NVIDIA offers AI training for start-ups and aims to provide mentorship specifically to FinTech start-ups (see Box 8.9).

Box 8.9: Microsoft Partner with NVIDIA to Empower Start-ups in Africa

Microsoft seeks to boost the growth of African start-ups through collaboration with NVIDIA Inception, a global programme offering start-ups access to technological resources, experts, and connections with venture capitalists. It highlights local success stories like Taimba, an agritech start-up revolutionizing agricultural supply chains by linking rural farmers to urban retailers, and Zendawa, a telehealth provider offering online access to medicines and financial solutions for pharmacies. FinTech innovator Pesawise showcase how it is improving secure payment services using tools like Azure and GitHub. The Microsoft for Start-ups Founders Hub has already supported over 14,000 African start-ups, helping companies like Snark Health, Aibanc, and PCS Agri to scale their operations. Entrepreneurs benefit from mentorship, access to Microsoft Azure, GitHub, go-to-market support, technical resources, and opportunities to network and expand their solutions globally. They may also gain insights into AI technologies and collaborate with other innovators. The Microsoft Africa Development Center in Nairobi will further assist these collaborations by offering AI training for developers through virtual sessions. NVIDIA also host a workshop to guide start-ups in using generative AI tools and scaling through AI and computing resources. This initiative is designed to empower African start-ups with the support they need to thrive in the global tech landscape.

Source: Nkosi (2024)

5. **Urbanization**

Africa is experiencing significant urbanization, with many individuals from rural areas migrating to urban centers in search of better opportunities. According to World Bank data, urbanization in Africa has been steadily rising from 1999 to 2023 (see Fig. 8.2). This trend is particularly more pronounced in Western and Central Africa compared to Eastern and Southern Africa as shown in Fig. 8.2. Urbanization promotes the growth of savings and investment platforms by increasing the concentration of people in cities, where access to digital infrastructure and financial services is more readily available. As people migrate to urban areas, there is a higher demand for efficient, accessible financial tools to manage income, save, and invest. The availability of internet connectivity, smartphones, and tech-savvy populations in urban centers makes it easier for FinTech companies to reach and serve a broader audience (Mckinsey & Company, 2024). Moreover, the economic opportunities in urban areas often lead to increased disposable income, creating a need for savings and investment solutions.

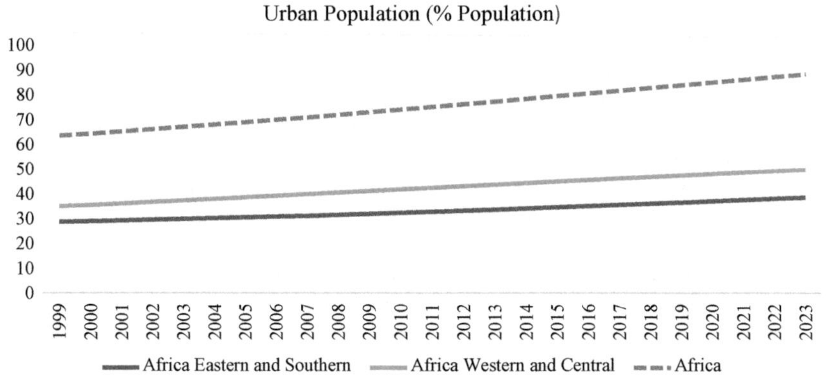

Fig. 8.2 Trend in Urbanization in Africa (1999 to 2023), by sub-region (*Source* Authors' Computation based on Data from the World Bank's WDI)

The Role of Digital Savings and Investments Platforms on the Savings of the Underserve

The rise of digital savings and investments platforms have enhanced savings in Africa. For example, in Ghana, Petra Securities Limited's digital savings and investment platform, the Achieve Mobile Platform, enabled over 30,000 Ghanaians to collectively save more than GHC12 million in 2021 alone (see Box 8.10). This confirms to some theoretical underpinnings such as the technology acceptance model (TAM), diffusion of innovation and financial inclusion theory. TAM posits that perceived ease of use and perceived usefulness drive individuals' acceptance and use of new technologies (Venkatesh & Bala, 2008). Digital savings and investment platforms enhance accessibility and convenience, encouraging adoption and increased savings behavior in Africa. Diffusion of innovation explains how new technologies and innovations spread through populations (Hussain et al., 2023; Rogers, 1962). The adoption of digital savings tools can be seen as a technological innovation that is progressively being accepted across African societies. The financial inclusion theory focuses on the mechanisms that allow underserved populations to gain access to affordable financial services. Digital platforms reduce barriers to entry, reaching unbanked populations, especially in remote and rural areas, thereby deepening financial inclusion and promoting savings.

Box 8.10: Petra Securities Limited Unveils Achieve: A Digital Platform Revolutionizing Savings in Ghana

Petra Securities Limited, a Ghanaian-owned company licensed by the Securities and Exchange Commission (SEC), launched Achieve, a mobile app making significant strides in Ghana's retail investment sector. Since its debut in August 2020, the app has enabled over 30,000 Ghanaians to save more than GHC12 million in 2021 alone. Achieve offers a convenient platform for users to save and invest towards their goals, providing access to SEC-licensed investment managers and financial experts. Users can seamlessly make deposits and withdrawals from their investment accounts via mobile money or bank accounts, while also monitoring transactions and performance in real-time.

The app's standout feature is *DigiSave*, a mutual fund-based product managed by Black Star Advisors, offering customers flexibility in saving and investing. Deposits are automatically invested in the Plus Income Fund, a licensed mutual fund, ensuring users benefit from compound interest. Mutual funds allow investors to maximize returns over time through compounding. The app's ease of use, requiring only 5 minutes to sign up without complicated paperwork or the need for large initial deposits. With as little as GHC 5, users can start saving and investing. The app also features an automated top-up option, addressing common challenges like forgetfulness and inconsistency. Available for free on both Google Play and the Apple App Store, achieve has garnered a strong user base of over 40,000 subscribers, with plans to reach one million by the end of 2022. The app's user-friendly approach and tailored goal-setting features have drawn widespread praise, with users applauding its convenience and effectiveness. Future plans for Achieve include forming partnerships to offer affordable short-term loans and expanding its investment offerings through collaborations with additional SEC-licensed entities, further contributing to the financial empowerment of Ghanaians.

Source: Adoli (2023), Business and Financial Times (B&FT, 2022) and Joyonline (2022)

While existing theories have demonstrated how emerging savings and investment platforms can enhance savings, it is equally important to highlight the practical factors that drive this impact. Below are key ways in which digital savings and investment platforms are promoting savings within these communities:

1. **Lower and No Cost, and Minimum Investment Requirement**

Conventional financial institutions typically require substantial minimum balances and impose transaction fees, rendering their services out of reach for low-income individuals. In contrast, digital platforms present cost-effective solutions with minimal entry barriers, enabling users to begin saving or investing with small amounts, often as little as a few local currencies equivalent. For example, Dalex Swift in Ghana offers fee-free savings, making it an attractive option for underserved communities (see Box 8.2). Mckinsey & Company (2024) revealed that financial services provided by FinTech companies in Africa are estimated to be up to 80% more cost-effective compared to traditional banks, while also offering interest rates on savings that are up to three times higher. This accessibility fosters regular, incremental savings habits among underserved populations.

2. **Easy to Access Financial Services**

Digital platforms enable individuals without access to traditional banking systems to save and invest conveniently using their mobile phones or the internet (Iddrisu, Yakubu et al., 2025). Unlike traditional banking, which require clients to visit physical branches and stand in queues to make deposits, digital solutions allow underserved populations to bypass these barriers (Cromwell & Peprah, 2025; Iddrisu, Ofoeda et al., 2025). This eliminates the need for physical branches and empowers them to engage in the formal financial system. Mobile money services like M-PESA and digital investment platforms like EasyEquities have proven highly successful, providing millions with access to savings and investment opportunities as shown in Boxes 8.1 and 8.2 respectively.

3. **Financial Literacy and Inclusion**

Many digital savings and investment platforms offer educational resources that enhance financial literacy, empowering users to understand savings and investments, and long-term wealth-building strategies (Iddrisu, Yakubu et al., 2025; Khalifa, 2024). When underserved populations receive this financial literacy, they gain the knowledge to appreciate the importance of savings and how different financial products operate (Iddrisu, Ofoeda et al., 2025). This understanding enables them to make informed choices, recognizing the value of setting aside even small amounts consistently. Financial education equips these individuals to manage their finances more effectively by teaching them to budget, monitor expenses, and set realistic savings goals. As a result, this knowledge promotes consistent saving habits, even among those with limited income.

4. **Flexibility**

Many underserved individuals lack trust in banks and certain financial institutions due to the challenges they face when attempting to withdraw their funds, especially during times of need, which discourages them from saving (World Bank, 2024). However, digital platforms offer 24/7 access via mobile phones, giving users the flexibility to deposit, withdraw, and manage their investments anytime, from any location. This is especially beneficial for those in remote or rural areas, as it eliminates the need for long-distance travel to access banking services, enhancing convenience and financial inclusion (Awanis et al., 2022; Iddrisu, Yakubu et al., 2025).

Impact on Financial Security and Wealth Generation

Just like savings, these digital platforms have encouraged wealth creation. This is underpinned with some theories such as the agency theory and behavioral economics theory. Behavioral economics theory explores how psychological, cognitive, and emotional factors influence economic decision-making (Kahneman & Tversky, 1979). This perspective suggests that emerging digital savings and investment platforms shape users' financial choices, encouraging them to build wealth and improve their financial security. Agency theory examines the relationship between a principal (e.g., an investor) and an agent (e.g., financial manager), where the agent is expected to act in the principal's best interest (Ozili, 2024; Shapiro, 2005). Digital savings and investment platforms reduce agency problems by providing real-time data, transparent investment options, and automated tools that empower users to make informed decisions independently (Ozili, 2024). Unlike traditional financial advisors who often involve high costs and potential conflicts of interest, digital platforms offer low-cost, automated services such as robo-advisors. These platforms also align incentives through algorithm-driven strategies tailored to users' preferences, enhancing efficiency, reducing agency costs, and supporting financial decision-making.

In practical terms, these are some of the ways in which digital savings and investment promote wealth generation in Africa.

1. **Partners with Large Finance Houses**

These platforms collaborate with both local and international finance house. Large finance houses offer a diverse array of investment opportunities, including stocks, bonds, mutual funds, and other financial instruments that may not be readily accessible to individuals on their own. By partnering with these institutions, platforms can offer users the ability to invest in a broader range of financial products, leading to higher potential returns and wealth creation. For example, PiggyVest partners with large finance houses to provide wide of investment opportunities to client (see Box 8.11).

Box 8.11: PiggyVest promote Wealth Creation in Nigeria

PiggyVest, formerly known as PiggyBank.ng, has revolutionized personal finance in Nigeria by helping over 4 million users save and invest since its inception in 2016. The platform was designed to address the financial struggles of many Nigerians who find it difficult to develop disciplined savings habits. With PiggyVest, users can automate their savings, making it easier to put money aside on a regular basis without the temptation to withdraw or spend it impulsively. The platform's automation feature ensures that users can set saving goals, whether daily, weekly, or monthly, thus building a more structured approach to their personal finance management. PiggyVest offers users opportunities to invest in low-risk, high-yield opportunities through its Investify product. Investify allows users to invest in diverse sectors like agriculture, real estate, and transportation, giving them a chance to grow their wealth over time with minimal risk. These investments are thoroughly vetted to ensure they meet safety standards, thus giving users confidence in their financial growth. In a country where financial exclusion has been a persistent issue, PiggyVest has made a significant impact by providing a secure, user-friendly platform that encourages better financial habits. Its success lies in simplifying savings and investments, empowering millions of Nigerians to take control of their financial future while promoting financial inclusion.

Source: PiggyVest (2025)

2. **Diversification**

Online platforms offer users access to a broad spectrum of investment options such as stocks, bonds, mutual funds, and exchange-traded funds (ETFs). This variety enables investors to diversify their portfolios, which is a key strategy in managing risk. By spreading investments across different asset classes, sectors, and markets, individuals can reduce the impact of poor performance in any single area. This diversification not only helps protect against losses but also provides opportunities for more stable and consistent wealth generation over time, ultimately enhancing the likelihood of long-term financial growth and security. For example, EasyEquities offers a diverse selection of both local and international organizations, encouraging members to diversify their portfolios by holding multiple investments (see Box 8.3).

3. **Lower Cost**

Digital investment platforms typically have lower fees than traditional financial advisors, allowing users to invest more of their money. For example, Robo-advisors typically offer more affordable fee structures, usually charging between 0.25% and 0.50% of assets under management. In contrast, financial advisors tend to have higher fees, often ranging from 1 to 2% or more, based on the scope and depth of services provided (IIFL Capital, 2024). This cost efficiency enhances the potential for higher returns over time, as a larger portion of funds remains invested and benefits from compounding growth. By reducing expenses, these platforms make investing more accessible and profitable for individuals, contributing to long-term wealth creation.

4. **Real-time Monitoring**

Investors can now monitor their portfolios in real-time through digital platforms, providing them with the flexibility to make informed, timely decisions based on current market conditions (World Economic Forum, 2024). This real-time visibility allows investors to react quickly to market fluctuations, capitalizing on opportunities as they arise, such as buying undervalued assets or selling before prices drop further. By staying updated with market trends and price changes, investors can adjust their strategies and portfolios as needed, optimizing their investments for greater returns. This agility is a key advantage in wealth generation, as it enables investors to be more proactive rather than passive. In fast-moving markets, where prices and opportunities can change rapidly, the ability to make swift, data-driven decisions can significantly enhance the potential for financial growth. Moreover, real-time monitoring empowers investors to better manage risks, protect their investments, and maximize their wealth creation potential in both volatile and stable market environments.

5. **Education and Awareness**

Digital platforms frequently offer a wealth of educational resources and tools, such as tutorials, articles, webinars, and financial calculators, designed to help users improve their financial literacy. These resources empower investors to understand different asset classes, market dynamics, and investment strategies, enabling them to make more informed and confident decisions. With increased knowledge, users are better equipped to assess risks, identify profitable opportunities, and tailor their portfolios to meet their financial goals. As a result, improved financial literacy through these platforms often leads to smarter investment choices and the potential for higher, more sustainable returns over time. For instance, on the website of Bamboo, there is educational resources such as calculator, financial planning tools and some economic indicators such as share prices, inflation rate and among others.

Challenges and the Way Forward for the Digital Savings and Investments Platform in Africa

Whereas these platforms are rising, there are some expected challenges and way forward.

Challenges

1. **Low Technological Literacy**

Low technological literacy poses a significant barrier to the adoption of digital savings and investment platforms in Africa, particularly in rural areas (Adel, 2024; Cromwell & Peprah, 2025; Sanga & Aziakpono, 2022). Many people lack the skills to navigate these platforms, preventing them from accessing the financial services needed to grow their wealth. Unfamiliarity with smartphones, mobile banking apps, and online transactions often leads to confusion, mistrust, and errors. This reliance on traditional financial practices makes the transition to digital systems challenging. Additionally, limited understanding of digital security increases vulnerability to fraud and cyber threats, further discouraging the use of digital platforms. Empirical study such as Hasan et al. (2023) revealed that digital literacy has impact on adoption of digital savings and investment platforms.

2. **Low ICT Infrastructure**

Despite ongoing efforts to improve ICT infrastructure in Africa, the current level of development remains insufficient to meet the demands of the continent's growing population. The limited infrastructure often results in delays and inefficiencies, particularly in digital financial transactions (Adel, 2024). For instance, users frequently experience challenges when attempting to deposit or withdraw funds, as systems may become overloaded or unreliable due to insufficient capacity. This issue highlights the gap between the high demand for ICT services and the infrastructure available to support seamless financial operations, emphasizing the need for continued investment and development in this critical area (Jayalath & Premaratne, 2021).

3. **Security Concerns**

The growth of digital platforms has raised significant concerns regarding cybersecurity and fraud. According to World Economic Forum (2025) the emergence of generative AI has dramatically expanded the scope and complexity of cybercrime, with a notable impact on identity theft and fraud. Many users are wary of the risks associated with sharing personal and financial information online, particularly in regions where digital security infrastructure is underdeveloped. Cyberattacks, data breaches, and online fraud have become increasingly prevalent, eroding trust in digital systems. Without robust security measures in place, users may fear financial losses, identity theft, or unauthorized access to their accounts. This lack of confidence can deter individuals from adopting digital investment platforms, limiting the potential for financial inclusion and broader engagement with digital financial services. For instance, FinTech Global (2025) revealed that the transition to digital banking and mobile applications has exposed South Africans to heightened risks, resulting in US$3 billion in losses due to digital crime in 2024.

4. **Economic and Political Instability**

Unstable political environments and economic volatility in some African nations can significantly deter both domestic and foreign investments. In regions marked by political instability, policy uncertainty, or civil unrest, investors often perceive higher risks of financial losses, disrupted markets, or sudden changes in regulatory frameworks. Economic volatility, including fluctuating exchange rates and inflation, further complicates investment decisions. These high-risk factors create an atmosphere of uncertainty, leading investors to adopt a cautious approach when engaging with digital platforms. As a result, many are hesitant to invest in such environments, limiting the growth and potential of digital investment platforms in these regions.

The Way Forward

The study outlines several strategies to address the challenges faced by digital savings and investment platforms in Africa, aimed at improving their efficiency. These include:

1. **Education and Awareness**

Digital literacy programs, offered through collaborations between governments, financial institutions, and NGOs, can teach basic skills like smartphone usage and online transactions, especially in rural areas. Platforms should be designed with user-friendly interfaces, incorporating local languages and visual aids to enhance accessibility. Partnering with local agents can bridge the gap for underserved populations, providing guidance and fostering trust. Public awareness campaigns about the benefits and security of digital financial services can further encourage adoption. Additionally, government support, through policies promoting digital inclusion and affordable access to technology, is essential for expanding financial literacy and inclusion across the continent.

2. **Improving ICT infrastructure**

Governments and policymakers consistently prioritize mobilizing financial resources to support infrastructure development, recognizing its critical role in driving economic growth and improving public services. By securing funding from various sources, including taxes, public–private partnerships, international loans, and grants, they aim to enhance essential infrastructure such as transportation, energy, healthcare, and communication systems. These efforts are designed to address the growing needs of urbanization, population growth, and technological advancement. Additionally, policymakers focus on creating favorable regulatory environments to attract private investment in infrastructure projects, ensuring long-term sustainability and fostering inclusive development that benefits all sectors of the economy.

3. **Promoting Cybersecurity**

Strengthening cybersecurity measures and fostering trust through transparent operations are critical to the success of digital platforms, especially in financial services. These platforms must implement robust data protection protocols, such as encryption and multi-factor authentication, to safeguard user information and prevent unauthorized access. Anti-fraud measures, including monitoring for suspicious activities and offering secure transaction processes, are also vital to maintaining the integrity of the platform. By being transparent about their security policies and demonstrating a commitment to protecting user assets, digital platforms can build trust and confidence among users, encouraging broader adoption and fostering long-term customer loyalty.

4. **Encourage Innovation**

Encouraging innovation through public–private partnerships, FinTech incubators, and targeted government support can significantly boost the development of new digital solutions that expand financial access. Public–private partnerships enable the pooling of resources and expertise to drive technological advancements, while FinTech incubators nurture start-ups focused on developing innovative financial services. Targeted government support, such as grants, tax incentives, and favorable regulations, creates an enabling environment for innovation to thrive. These innovations can provide underserved populations with greater access to investment opportunities, savings tools, and financial services, empowering them to participate more fully in the economy and promote financial inclusion on a broader scale.

5. **Enhance Regulation**

Enhanced regulation provides a strategic approach to addressing key challenges facing digital savings and investment platforms in Africa, such as consumer protection, cybersecurity, data privacy, and financial fraud. By adopting flexible and innovation-friendly frameworks, regulators can ensure the safety and trustworthiness of digital financial services while promoting responsible sector growth. This approach fosters greater accountability, builds user confidence, and supports the development of resilient and inclusive financial ecosystems across the continent.

Box 8.12: Regulatory Sandbox

A regulatory sandbox is a controlled testing environment set up by financial regulators that allows FinTech companies and other innovators to test new products, services, or business models with real customers, but under a regulator's supervision and with certain safeguards in place. It helps promote innovation in financial services; allow regulators to understand emerging technologies; ensure consumer protection and risk management and support the development of responsive and updated regulations. This innovation has been embraced by several financial regulators globally, including in African countries such as Kenya, Nigeria, South Africa, and Ghana. While challenges like fraud still persist in these countries, the adoption of regulatory sandboxes have helped reduce such risks. Moreover, it has enabled FinTech firms to better trace and identify the sources of fraudulent activities, thereby enhancing transparency and security within the digital financial ecosystem.

Source: World Bank (2020)

As such regulators should adopt innovative regulatory tools such as regulatory sandbox (see Box 8.12) and other supervision technology (SupTech) and regulation technology (RegTech) tools such as using AI and biometric authenticators to minimize fraud and other illegal activities. Countries such as Kenya, Nigeria, South Africa, and Ghana have adopted regulatory sandboxes (see Box 8.12). Other African countries may consider emulating this model and incorporating it into their regulatory frameworks to support safe and inclusive financial innovation.

Conclusion

The advent of mobile money platforms, beginning with M-PESA, has significantly transformed the financial landscape across Africa, democratizing access to savings and investment opportunities for both urban and rural populations. The integration of FinTech solutions, coupled with increasing mobile phone penetration, investments in ICT infrastructure, and government support, has catalyzed the development of digital savings and investment platforms. These platforms have not only expanded financial inclusion but also created pathways for wealth generation and financial security, particularly for underserved populations. The confluence of mobile technology, supportive government policies, and growing urbanization trends has further accelerated the expansion of these services, making financial inclusion more achievable than ever.

Based on these reviews, this chapter provides some policy implications. First, to sustain and broaden the impact of digital savings and investment platforms, governments and development partners should continue investing in ICT infrastructure, particularly in rural areas. Ensuring reliable internet access and mobile connectivity is critical for expanding the reach of these platforms to remote and underserved populations. Second, Governments and financial institutions should prioritize financial education initiatives, particularly targeting low-income individuals and rural communities. By equipping the underserved with the knowledge to understand savings, investments, and the importance of long-term financial planning, they can be empowered to make informed financial decisions. Third, Governments should maintain a flexible regulatory environment that fosters innovation while ensuring consumer protection. Regulatory sandboxes and supportive policies will enable FinTech start-ups to test and scale digital savings and investment platforms without being hampered by overly restrictive regulations. This can be in form of encouraging partnerships between FinTech start-ups and established financial institutions to provide a broader range of savings and investment products. This collaboration can help FinTech firms tap into traditional banking expertise while extending their reach to underserved markets. Governments can also provide incentives for the private sector and development partners to invest in digital financial solutions. Tax breaks, grants, or public–private partnerships can encourage further investment in FinTech, enabling more comprehensive and inclusive financial products to be developed. Last, building trust in digital platforms is essential for broader adoption. Governments and financial institutions should enhance the security of digital savings and investment platforms to mitigate concerns about fraud or data breaches. Public campaigns to highlight the safety and reliability of these platforms can also boost user confidence.

References

À propos d'Orange. (2024, May 23). *Orange Ventures and Digital Africa commit to jointly invest in startups from the "Orange Digital Centers" network in Africa and the Middle East*. https://newsroom.orange.com/orange-ventures-and-digital-africa-commit-to-jointly-invest-in-startups-from-the-orange-digital-centers-network-in-africa-and-the-middle-east/

Adel, N. (2024). The impact of digital literacy and technology adoption on financial inclusion in Africa, Asia, and Latin America. *Heliyon, 10*(24), Article e40951. https://doi.org/10.1016/j.heliyon.2024.e40951

Adoli, H. (2023, May 8). *Announcing the achieve app 2.0*. https://theachieveapp.com/announcing-the-achieve-app-2-0/

AFI. (2018, May 16). *Ghana's first mobile money interoperability system deepens financial inclusion and promotes cashless agenda*. https://www.afi-global.org/news/ghanas-first-mobile-money-interoperability-system-deepens-financial-inclusion-and-promotes-cashless-agenda/

Awanis, A., Lowe, C., Andersson-Manjang, S. K., & Lindsey, D. (2022). *State of the industry report on mobile money 2022.*

B&FT. (2022, March 2). *Meet Achieve, the digital platform making saving and investing easy*. https://thebftonline.com/2022/03/02/meet-achieve-the-digital-platform-making-saving-and-investing-easy/

Business World Africa. (2024, October 22). *Top 10 Investment Platforms in Africa for 2024*. https://businessworld.africa/top-10-investment-platforms-in-africa-for-2024/?form=MG0AV3&form=MG0AV3

Convergence Partners. (n.d.). *Google, convergence partners, international finance corporation, and mitsui co-invest in Csquared*. Retrieved February 27, 2025, from https://www.convergencepartners.com/google-convergence-partners-international-finance-corporation-and-mitsui-co-invest-in-csquared?category=

Cromwell, R. S., & Peprah, J. A. (2025). Banking business models and sustainable development: Challenges and opportunities. In I. N. Yakubu (Ed.), *Strategic approaches to banking business and sustainable development goals* (pp. 3–22). Springer. https://doi.org/10.1007/978-3-031-80744-2_1

Dalex Finance. (2025). *Dalex swift: The SMART money move*. https://dalexfinance.com/dalex-swift/

EasyEquities. (2025). *Everything you need to know about EasyEquities*. https://www.easyequities.co.za/about-us-1

FinTech Global. (2025, February 17). *How Africa's digital shift is influencing cyber threats and security measures*. https://fintech.global/2025/02/17/how-africas-digital-shift-is-influencing-cyber-threats-and-security-measures/

G-Money. (2020). *Our features*. https://www.g-money.com.gh/#home

Hasan, M., Noor, T., Gao, J., Usman, M., & Abedin, M. Z. (2023). Rural consumers' financial literacy and access to FinTech services. *Journal of the Knowledge Economy, 14*(2), 780–804. https://doi.org/10.1007/s13132-022-00936-9

Hussain, S., Gul, R., & Ullah, S. (2023). Role of financial inclusion and ICT for sustainable economic development in developing countries. *Technological Forecasting and Social Change*, *194*(September 2022), 122725. https://doi.org/10.1016/j.techfore.2023.122725

Iddrisu, K., Ofoeda, I., Issah, O., & Iddrisu, M. (2025). Gender equality and women's empowerment in banking. In I.. Yakubu (Ed.), *Strategic approaches to banking business and sustainable development goals. Sustainable development goals series.* (pp. 179–193). Springer. https://doi.org/10.1007/978-3-031-80744-2_11

Iddrisu, K., Yakubu, I. N., & Asongu, S. A. (2025). FinTech innovations for sustainable banking. In *Strategic approaches to banking business and sustainable development goals. sustainable development goals series* (pp. 63–86). Springer. https://doi.org/10.1007/978-3-031-80744-2_4

IIFL Capital. (2024, September 25). *Robo-banking versus personal advisors*. https://www.iiflcapital.com/blog/personal-finance/robobanking-vs-personal-advisors

Jayalath, J. A. R. C., & Premaratne, S. C. (2021). Analysis of key digital technology infrastructure and cyber security consideration factors for Fintech companies. *International Journal of Research Publications, 84*(1), 128–135.

Jibril, A. B., Pobee, F., Gochhait, S., & Chugh, R. (2024). Breaking boundaries: Unveiling hurdles in embracing internet banking services in Sub-Saharan Africa. *Cogent Economics & Finance, 12*(1). https://doi.org/10.1080/23322039.2024.2330436

Joyonline. (2022, March 1). *Achieve, the digital platform making saving and investing easy for Ghanaians*. https://www.myjoyonline.com/achieve-the-digital-platform-making-saving-and-investing-easy-for-ghanaians/?form=MG0AV3&form=MG0AV3

Kahneman, D., & Tversky, A. (1979). Prospect theory: An analysis of decision under risk. *Econometrica, 47*(2), 263. https://doi.org/10.2307/1914185

Khalifa, D. (2024, April 4). *How Nigeria can leverage the rise of FinTech for economic progress*. World Bank Blogs. https://blogs.worldbank.org/en/psd/how-nigeria-can-leverage-the-rise-of-fintech-for-economic-progre

Konnect. (2025). *Top 7 investment and savings apps in South Africa for 2025*. https://kashgain.net/blog/top-7-investment-and-savings-apps-in-south-africa/?form=MG0AV3&form=MG0AV3

Kulu, E., & Bondzie, E. A. (2024). Mobile money, credit to deposit ratio and monetary policy: Empirics from Ghana. *Transnational Corporations Review, 16*(3), Article 200060. https://doi.org/10.1016/j.tncr.2024.200060

Laghmari, S. (2020, January 16). *Digital banking in Africa: Origins and development outlook*. Infomineo. https://infomineo.com/financial-services/digital-banking-in-africa-origins-and-development-outlook/

Mckinsey & Company. (2024, January 16). *What is Fintech*. Mckinsey & Company. https://www.mckinsey.com/featured-insights/mckinsey-explainers/what-is-fintech

Nkosi, M. (2024, December 9). *Microsoft launches AI initiative to empower African startups*. https://www.itnewsafrica.com/2024/12/microsoft-launches-ai-initiative-to-empower-african-startups/#:~:text=TheMicrosoftforStartupsFounders,abletoscaletheiroperations

Ozili, P. K. K. (2024). Digital agency theory of financial inclusion. In E. M. Ahmed (Ed.), *Developing digital inclusion through globalisation and digitalisation* (pp. 55–72). IGI Global. https://doi.org/10.4018/979-8-3693-4111-7.ch004

piggyvest. (2025). *Invest on the go.* https://www.piggyvest.com/invest

Rogers, E. M. (1962). *Diffusion of innovations (First edition).* Free Press.

Safaricom. (2025). *M-Shwari.* https://www.safaricom.co.ke/main-m-pesa/m-pesa-services/credit-and-savings/m-shwari-mobile

Sanga, B., & Aziakpono, M. (2022). The impact of technological innovations on financial deepening: Implications for SME financing in Africa. *African Development Review, 34*(4), 429–442. https://doi.org/10.1111/1467-8268.12668

Shapiro, S. P. (2005). Agency theory. *Annual Review of Sociology, 31*(1), 263–284. https://doi.org/10.1146/annurev.soc.31.041304.122159

Tendai. (2017, August 17). *Sanlam to acquire 30% of EasyEquities.* https://www.liquidafrica.com/sanlam-to-acquire-30-of-easyequities/?form=MG0AV3&form=MG0AV3

Venkatesh, V., & Bala, H. (2008). Technology acceptance model 3 and a research agenda on interventions. *Decision Sciences, 39*(2), 273–315. https://doi.org/10.1111/j.1540-5915.2008.00192.x

Waceke. (2024, September 4). *Best investment apps for Kenyans to grow their money.* https://www.businessradar.co.ke/blog/2024/09/04/best-investment-apps-for-kenyans-to-grow-their-money/?form=MG0AV3

World Bank. (2020, November 1). *Key data from regulatory sandboxes across the globe.* World Bank Group. https://www.worldbank.org/en/topic/fintech/brief/key-data-from-regulatory-sandboxes-across-the-globe

World Bank. (2024). Financial inclusion in Sub-Saharan Africa—overview. In *The global findex database 2021.* https://www.worldbank.org/en/publication/globalfindex/brief/financial-inclusion-in-sub-saharan-africa-overview

World Economic Forum. (2024, December 20). *How digital platforms and AI are empowering individual investors.* https://www.weforum.org/stories/2024/12/digital-platforms-ai-empowering-individual-investors/

World Economic Forum. (2025, January 16). *How AI-driven fraud challenges the global economy—and ways to combat it.* https://www.weforum.org/stories/2025/01/how-ai-driven-fraud-challenges-the-global-economy-and-ways-to-combat-it/

CHAPTER 9

Leveraging Technology for Financial Education and Empowerment in Africa

Fuseini Inusah, Issah Iddrisu, and Mubarik Salifu

Introduction

Digital Financial Literacy (DFL) is a multidimensional concept that involves elements of financial and digital literacy, as well as additional elements related to access and use of digital financial services (Lyons & Kass-Hanna, 2021). The abundance of digital devices makes it relatively easier to educate the individual. According to Koskelainen et al. (2023), personal monetary management, consumer behaviour, and

F. Inusah (✉)
Department of Mathematics and ICT Education, University for Development Studies, Tamale, Ghana
e-mail: finusah@uds.edu.gh

I. Iddrisu
School of Business, University for Development Studies, Tamale, Ghana
e-mail: iiddrisu@uds.edu.gh

M. Salifu
School of Economics, University for Development Studies, Tamale, Ghana
e-mail: smubarik@uds.edu.gh

I. N. Yakubu (ed.), *Banking on Inclusion*, Sustainable Development Goals Series, https://doi.org/10.1007/978-3-031-96716-0_9

general financial services are innovative and transformative aspects of DFL. In Indonesia, a survey conducted by (Rahayu et al., 2022) relates financial behaviour to the DFL of the millennial generation. An analysis of DFL by (Yadav & Banerji, 2023) positions it as an interdisciplinary area that is very diverse and embodies areas such as demographic, behavioural, and technological factors. The behavioural factors include savings and spending, which affect the future of individuals and the economy (Setiawan et al., 2022). Adults in India are challenged with the inability to complete digital transactions and experience financial loss, as well as privacy breaches, without DFL (Ravikumar et al., 2022). In Ghana, the inadequate financial literacy and digital citizenship make people vulnerable in the digital cyber space, which affects economic growth. This affects sub-Saharan Africa in general (Osabutey & Jackson, 2024). This illustrates an interplay of knowledge in DFL, demonstrating capability and autonomy in financial decision-making and well-being.

According to (Choi, 2016) digital citizenship is the responsible and respectful use of technology to engage in the use of digital devices and online transactions. It is a necessity for effective DFL implementation and benefits. The responsible use of technology in online transactions by respecting the privacy of other Internet users enables in inclusion (Fernández-Prados et al., 2021). The abundance of digital tools enhances easy access to content, which enriches the digital citizenship of the individual. According to (Jones & Mitchell, 2016) the youth need respectful online behaviour and civic engagement to enhance their digital citizenship. In using the internet and demonstrating global citizenship, there is a need for ethical and critical use of electronic media (Choi, 2016). The impact of DFL and digital citizenship on inclusion and empowerment is necessary for growth and development. Despite the relevance of DFL and digital citizenship, digital platforms do not integrate these two components but rather focus on DFL more. The main goal of this work is to ascertain the impact of DFL platforms as a technology on users' digital citizenship which empowers them in Africa. The following are the specific research questions to achieve the goal:

1. What are the main features of digital financial literacy platforms as a technology to improve digital citizenship?
2. How do the components of digital financial literacy platforms impact digital citizenship?

The remaining part of this work is organised in related works, which constitute literature available on research works, the methodology, which specifies the scientific procedures employed in this research to accrue the findings, presentations of the results obtained, the findings, and the conclusions drawn from the work.

Related Works

Several research works on the DFL platforms as a technology on user's digital citizenship focus on financial inclusion and other economic factors. Behaviour influences economic management, and general financial discipline as a basic requirement for a nation's economic growth are the major factors given attention.

Relevance of Digital Financial Literacy in Financial Inclusion

The ability to handle finances by demonstrating knowledge of financial technology is necessary in the digital age (Respati et al., 2023). As technology improves and is massively adopted to handle real-life problems, knowledge of DFL is needed to make an individual productive in society irrespective of gender (Hasan et al., 2023). This is evidence for enhancing DFL to improve productivity in society (Koomson et al., 2020). DFL helps in easily achieving financial inclusion (Khan et al., 2022). It also influences decision-making (Mishra et al., 2024). Countries including China adopts DFL as a booster for economic growth by leveraging mobile technology. In brief, it is a technology that spices digital payments making it easier for individuals and businesses to transact business (Seldal & Nyhus, 2022). This knowledge can easily be acquired through social media (Al-shami et al., 2024) making it the easy approach to improving financial technology which is a necessary factor for improving DFL (Ferilli et al., 2024). Developing countries benefit more from DFL in making business transactions (Uthaileang & Kiattisin, 2023).

Relevance of Digital citizenship in Financial Inclusion

Educating individuals to be useful in the digital age is vital to achieving digital inclusivity (Emejulu & McGregor, 2019). Nations owe citizens the responsibility to educate with sustainable learning practices for effective digital citizenship (Ghosn-Chelala, 2019). Responsible use of technology is vital in achieving digital citizenship (Hollandsworth et al., 2017). Society needs adequate citizenship education to bring the required change (Ribble, 2012). The youth need this knowledge as they dominate social media and DFL (Fernández-Prados et al., 2020). This knowledge should go beyond the online presence (Monteiro et al., 2022). Early education of the younger generation at the childhood stage can maximise competencies in digital citizenship (Lauricella et al., 2020). The perception of educators on the practices of digital citizenship should also be a factor in achieving the goals of digital citizenship to address the challenges of DFL (Martin et al., 2019). Different disciplines can therefore contribute to achieving digital citizenship as a learner progresses(Chen et al., 2021). In all these, there will be civility and morality in the online behaviour of the users of digital platforms regarding decision-making and their choices (Harrison & Polizzi, 2022).

Relationship Between DFL and Digital Citizenship

There exists a strong positive relationship between DFL and digital citizenship through digital rights, citizenship, and literacy as the core elements bonding them (Pangrazio & Sefton-Green, 2021). Globalisation necessitates financial citizenship, which broadens FL through democratic procedures (Khalil, 2020). The digital skills influence the DFL of an individual, which strongly influences his digital citizenship (Gutiérrez-Aguilar et al., 2024). Digital skills and digital citizenship have an intricate interrelationship (Gutiérrez-Aguilar et al., 2024). The effect is a positive application in managing the economy both at the individual and institutional levels (Görög & Udvari, 2023). Digital citizenship skills enhance sustainable development through DFL skills (Sayed Abdellatif et al., 2024). With strong digital citizenship skills and good moral values, cybercrime will be minimised (Althibyani & Al-Zahrani, 2023). Good digital citizenship development.

Digital Platforms and Mobile Apps for Financial Education

Integrating systems for effective management is important for enhancing efficiency(Inusah et al., 2023a, 2023b). Individuals and Businesses need systems for financial decision-making(Inusah & Amponsah, 2018). It is applicable in general resource management, where predictive tools can be used for forecasting and identifying future needs (Inusah et al., 2021).

The impact of digital technologies on individual decision-making and general public service is impressive (Iddrisu & Fuseini, 2025). Several DFL platforms promote responsible individual and cooperative financial management (Panos & Wilson, 2020). Some of the platforms are targeting early childhood to enhance comparative studies (Fitriah et al., 2023). These platforms have become a means for financial inclusion by delivering financial literacy (Boldar et al., 2022). Digital platforms are crucial factors for economic development in Africa (Vovchenko et al., 2018). Social media platforms play a major role in this task (Kaur Chhabra & Shilpi Gupta, 2023). Accurate data and proper imaging of the financial well-being of an individual or corporate institution can easily be ascertained through digital platforms (Ekpo et al., 2022). Artificial intelligence makes it easier (Murugesan & Manohar, 2019). Enough evidence points to the relevance of financial digital platforms in educating the individual (Lusardi, 2019).

Relevant Case Studies for Financial Literacy Campaigns Using Digital Tools

According to Uthaileang and Kiattisin (2023), developing countries need to increase their capabilities in financial literacy to enable financial inclusion. This was for the case of an online loan for small entrepreneurs. Researchers such as Mancone et al., (2024) sees financial literacy programs impacting the lives of the youth by changing their behaviours on how they use money. Cases on women empowerment in DFL and the possibility of leveraging knowledge in financial literacy for financial inclusion are dominant (Mishra et al., 2024). According to Chidiogo et al. (2024), it is more applicable to small and medium enterprises (SMEs). Knowing the literacy level of financial education programs also helps in identifying the strength of the program (Méndez-Prado et al., 2023). Digital payment technologies influence financial vulnerability and financial literacy (Seldal & Nyhus, 2022). Evidence from Chinese households reveals a strong relationship between digital finance and financial literacy through the use of digital tools (Yang et al., 2023).

The Importance of Financial Literacy in Fostering Sustainable Financial Inclusion

Sustainable financial inclusion is a term that describes individuals and businesses having access to and using affordable financial products and services that meet their needs, which are delivered responsibly and sustainably (Ozili, 2022). The relevance of financial literacy in fostering sustainable financial inclusion can be seen in (Pandey et al., 2022), where North India is used as a case study. In Asia, it assists in improving inclusivity to alleviate poverty despite the digital divide(Tay et al., 2022). This calls for an intensive financial inclusion through digital training (Koomson et al., 2020). For the effective achievement of financial inclusion, households need digital financial literacy (Dash & Mohanta, 2024). This can be integrated into education for poverty alleviation. In Kenya, it serves as a financial literacy delivery channel (Boldar et al., 2022). The availability of social media makes it easily achievable (Al-Shami et al., 2024). Digital financial literacy influences Small and Medium Enterprises (Kulathunga et al., 2020). Financial inclusion cannot be achieved without financial education and DFL (Das, 2024). Using DFL training programs is the best approach to financial inclusion (Choudhary & Jain, 2023).

Methodology

This is case study research for the top five (5) DFL platforms in Africa. It explores the DFL Platforms to identify the key elements of DFL that promote digital citizenship. A critical examination of the components as well as the design of the online platform is used to determine the key components. Contextually, platforms for African users have been selected for exploration.

Research Design

This work is an exploratory sequential design which makes use of both qualitative and quantitative data. An initial exploration of the DFL platforms to collect qualitative data was done, which builds on quantitative data collection and analysis before the discussion. Figure 9.1 is a diagram illustrating the design.

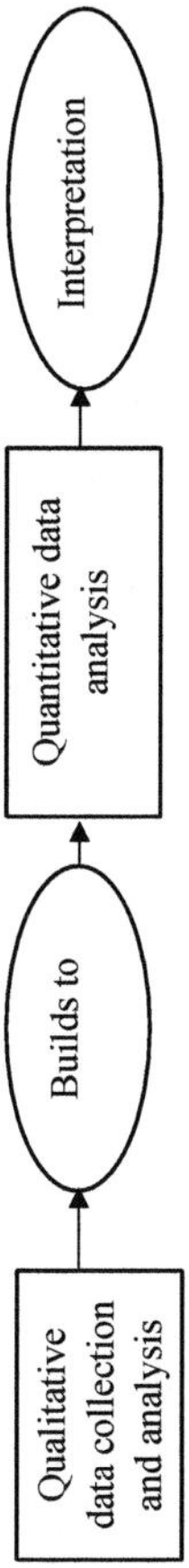

Fig. 9.1 Exploratory sequential design framework (*Source* Adapted from Creswell and Clark [2011])

Data Collection

Mixed data (qualitative and quantitative) is used in this research. The qualitative data is the evidence collected from observing the DFL platforms and the features that constitute those platforms. Some qualities of the features and how they can impact digital inclusion. The quantitative data emerges from the analysis of the qualitative data. The numeric values of the features identified and the impacts of the features on digital inclusion are presented.

Population and Sample

In Sensor Tower's space, the target DFL applications are those widely used by Africans through the Android operating system. Selected among these are the top five downloaded within the third quarter of 2024. The applications identified in this category are: Ocean Plus- Save Money, Money Tracker Expense Tracker, Cash Book -Daily Expenses, Hustler Pesa, and MKOPO CHAPCHAP.

Results and Findings

The work's results are divided into two categories: the results of the qualitative data collected and the results from the quantitative data obtained from the qualitative data analysed. The presentation is based on the research questions guiding the work.

What are the main features of digital financial literacy platforms as a technology to improve digital citizenship?

This research question was answered by the qualitative data from exploring the five (5) platforms. A checklist was designed to identify the relevant features of the platforms based on the DFL needs.

In the third quarter of 2024, the top personal finance budgeting and planning applications on the Android platform in Africa demonstrated varied performance metrics, as reported by Sensor Tower.

"Ocean Plus—Save Money saw consistent weekly downloads, hovering around 9000 to 11,000 throughout the quarter, peaking at 11,300 in the week of September 9. The application maintained a strong user base with weekly active users growing from approximately 88,000 at the start of July

to over 102,000 by the end of September. Money Tracker Expense Tracker experienced a noticeable increase in downloads and active users. Downloads rose from 4300 in early July to over 13,300 by September. The application's weekly revenue also climbed steadily, reaching $92 by the end of the quarter, while active users increased from about 12,800 to over 25,000. Cash Book-daily expenses maintained modest download numbers, fluctuating between 2700 and 6800. The application's active user count saw an upward trend, starting from 39,000 and reaching over 46,000 by the end of September, with steady revenue of around $1 weekly.

Hustler Pesa exhibited a mixed download performance, starting with 4000 in early July, dipping mid-quarter, and then rising to nearly 6000 by the end of September. Unfortunately, this application had no revenue or active user data. Lastly, MKOPO CHAPCHAP recorded a volatile download trend, with numbers ranging from as low as 15 to peaking at 7900 in early September. Like Hustler Pesa, no revenue or active user data was available." (Top 5 Personal Finance Apps on Android in Africa, Q3 2024).

In Table 9.1, six (6) aspects were considered when identifying the platform features. The aspects are Access, which is about the availability and the amount of memory space needed in a device to run the application, the design of the interface of the application, the descriptive analytics tools, the level of literacy required, the ethical and security issues and the offline capabilities of the platform. Ocean-plus is a free-to-download application that requires about 12 MB. It has a straightforward interface with income and expenditure targets as the main components. Reports are presented in simple graphs that an average user can understand. Its multi-user offline functionality makes it the most preferred platform, giving it the highest downloads. Money tracker is the second with about 100 thousand downloads within the period, and is also free to download, with about 15 Mb in size. It has a more detailed calendar feature for income, expenses and balance with reports presented in the form of charts. An average user needs financial accounting and bookkeeping knowledge, and there is higher privacy as no data is shared with a third party. The application can still function without internet connectivity. Cash Bank Daily Expenses is another application with a file size of 14 Mb and is free to download with cash-in and cash-out features for weekly, monthly, and yearly and has very detailed account reporting for all account transfers and summaries. Users of this application require detailed accounting and bookkeeping knowledge as well as digital banking skills. It has strict security measures in place to prevent hackers. Effectively, the application requires internet connectivity for synchronisation. Hustler Pesa is another free-to-download application with a 14 Mb file size, a user-friendly interface and core features such as income and expenditure accounts, custom budget, and business calculator. Reports are generated using graphs and percentages, and average knowledge in creating accounts and using digital devices is needed, with third-party data encryption to prevent data loss. The app can run offline, but internet connectivity is needed for synchronisation. The MKOPO CHAPCHAP application is also free to download with user-friendly features such as income, expenditure, and custom budget categories, with a business calendar having graphical reports with charts and percentages. Knowledge of ledger management and digital computing is a requirement. Consent of the user is sought in data collection and deletion, with good encryption to prevent attacks. Figure 9.2 is the graphical representation of the downloads.

How Do the Components of Digital Financial Literacy Impact Digital Citizenship?

The interrelationship of the components of the digital platforms and how they enhance digital citizenship is presented in this research question. Three (3) major digital citizenship components are identified in this work. They are digital security, integrity, and responsibility. These components demonstrate the core digital citizenship as it spells out the protection of the digital landscape and the practice of digital hygiene in the digital civic space of Africa. Figure 9.3 is a diagram of the DFL and Digital citizenship.

A DFL platform requires these three tiers as a test for propagating digital citizenship: looking at the authenticity and credibility of the sources of information, taking appropriate measures to protect the information, and reporting inappropriate content and abusive behaviours online.

Digital Integrity

Protecting users' rights in the digital realm is necessary for effective digitalization. The physical and moral rights of the individual should not be compromised during online presence. Users must act freely without any fear or favour. This will enable easy trust of DFL platforms and enhance accessibility without limitations. The integrity of the individual should

Table 9.1 Checklist results for the features of the top five DFL platforms from sensor tower

Name of platform	*Access*	*Design of the interface*	*Descriptive analytical tools*	*Level of literacy required*	*Ethical and security issues*	*Offline capability*
Ocean Plus save money	Free to download Takes about 12 MB of memory space. The language is in English	Very simple with income target and spending target as the main components	Simple graphs and percentages	Average user	It can be multi-user with privacy and privileges settings No data shared with third-party Data is encrypted in transit	It can be used without internet connectivity
Money Tracker Expense Tracker	Free to download and instal with about 15 MB	More detailed with calendar features for income expenses and balance	Records, charts, and reports based on the schedule	Requires basic business accounting and book-keeping knowledge	No data shared with third-party Data is encrypted in transit	Data can be entered offline but needs internet connectivity to synchronise
Cash Book -Daily Expenses	Free to download and instal with about 14 MB	Cash in and cash out are the main components with daily, weekly, monthly, and yearly details availability	The very detailed reporting system for all accounts, transfers, and summaries	Requires more accounting and book-keeping knowledge as well as digital banking	Strict security measures to prevent attacks from hackers	It is highly recommended to have the app running online for easy synchronisation

(continued)

Table 9.1 (continued)

Name of platform	*Access*	*Design of the interface*	*Descriptive analytical tools*	*Level of literacy required*	*Ethical and security issues*	*Offline capability*
Hustler Pesa	Free to download and instal with about 4 MB	It has a user-friendly interface. It has core functionalities such as adding income and expense accounts, creating custom budget categories, and even using a business calculator	Reports are generated using graphs and percentage	Average knowledge in creating accounts and use of digital devices	There is third-party data encryption to prevent data loss	The app can run offline but internet connectivity is needed for synchronisation
MKOPO CHAPCHAP	Free to download with about 7 MB	It has user-friendliness with features such as income, expenditure and custom budget categories with a business calendar	Graphical reports with charts and percentages	Knowledge in ledger management and digital computing	No third-party data collection No data is collected without the consent of the user. Data is encrypted in transit and data cannot be deleted without the user's knowledge	App requires internet connectivity for effective functionality of the components

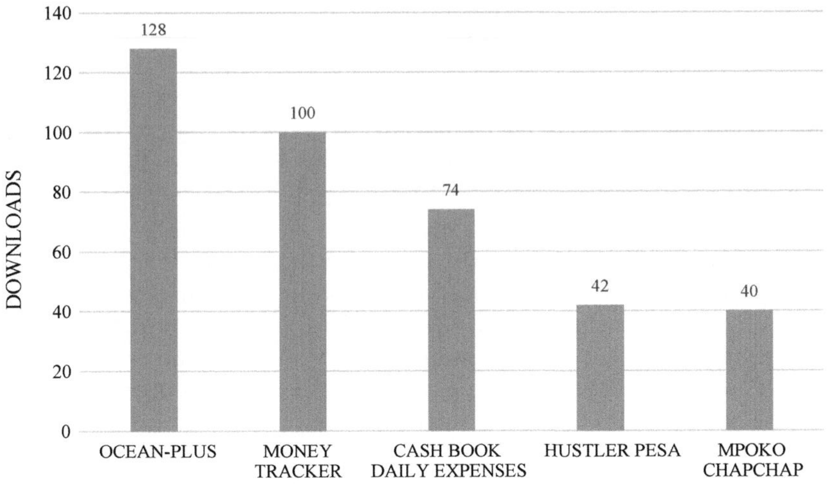

Fig. 9.2 Bar graph of the applications and downloads for the period (*Source* Authors' Compilation)

Fig. 9.3 The DFL and digital citizenship (*Source* Authors' Construct)

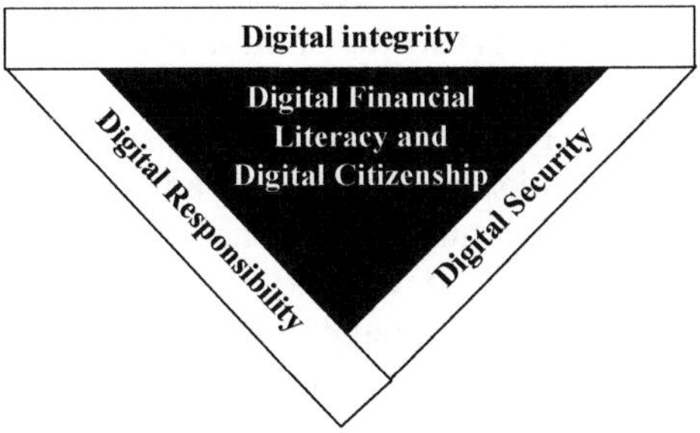

not be compromised when using a DFL platform. Both the user and the platform must demonstrate true integrity by enhancing good data management. The five (5) platforms explored in this work all demonstrate utmost good faith in protecting the integrity of the user through the privacy and security measures to protect user data. Honesty and sincerity in providing input from the user perspective and the production of outputs in the form of reports by the platforms are key in this scenario.

Digital Security

The protection of individual user accounts after signing up for the platform is crucial to providing security. Security rules on passwords as well as the authentication mode for verification of accounts, are very important. Online Security measures to safeguard digital assets from both the user and platform perspectives should be put in place. The confidentiality of the users and the platforms strongly depends on the security measures. As indicated in Fig. 2, digital security goes with the responsibility of usage to enhance the integrity of the data. Security of the platforms includes access control for the management of the views of the system, and the application security, which dwells much on the prevention of vulnerabilities, the services and protocols for hosting the platform, and the endpoint security for the devices that connect to the platforms.

Digital Responsibility

The responsible use of technology protects resources and helps in understanding the sustainability of technological solutions. These solutions should be ethical and moral enough to enhance peaceful co-existence. The DFL platforms should be free from harm. Both the user and the service providers should ensure responsible usage to protect the rights of others. The service providers have the responsibility of ensuring the platform works to serve the needs of the users. This can be done through proper optimisation to enable different users at different locations and with different devices to enjoy the services. The responsible use of digital platforms can enhance the confidentiality and integrity of both the users and the service providers of the platforms.

Discussion of Results

The importance of DFL in the digital landscape of Africa is noticeable in the digital civic space. Effective use of technological devices to enjoy the services of DFL platforms has helped improve the lives of individuals and helped them gain financial inclusion and independence. As indicated in (Mancone et al., 2024). Careful spending by the younger generations will assist in easy financial management through the DFL platforms. For responsible individual and corporate financial management, knowledge of DFL is very crucial. This can only be achieved through DFL platforms (Panos & Wilson, 2020). The free accessibility of DFL platforms as well as the user-friendly interface for effective utilisation, makes it easy for a novice to use the DFL platform. This informs the choice of DFL platforms by many users. Careful design is therefore a factor to consider in DFL platform development. This should go with the management of space or file size of the application.

The level of skill needed in using the DFL platform is very important in the inputs to generate the desired output. The descriptive analytic tools that summarise the output for the user are essential in determining the type of DFL platform users choose. A clear understanding of the information is very crucial in enhancing DFL. This goes with the level of literacy of the user of the platform. A good DFL platform should be designed for the use of an average literate. Technical language for experts should be carefully explained to the ordinary user.

Financial issues are often embedded with fraudulent activities as a result of fraudsters' activities. Ethical and legal issues are considerations for the choice of DFL platforms. This constitutes a chunk of the security needed to build trust. A secure DFL platform should respect the ethics of the domain in which it is developed. Data privacy should be a priority to ensure the platform does not allow third-party access to information. Appropriate data encryption should be used for data in transit and at rest.

As indicated in (Ghosn-Chelala, 2019), it is the responsibility of nations to educate citizens to be good users of DFL platforms. This education should span across all domains of DFL to ensure safe practices of the people to protect the rights and interests of users. The youth should be the main targets for this (Fernández-Prados et al., 2020). Responsible use of technology to address the challenges of society is a catalyst for growth and development. As the youth's quest for financial stability increases, DFL platforms should embed digital citizenship to help educate users on the need to adhere to ethics. Nations can integrate digital citizenship at the early grade level (Lauricella et al., 2020). There is a strong relationship between digital citizenship and DFL(Lauricella et al., 2020). This strong positive relationship drives how individuals and institutions respect the rights of others in digital cyberspace. Knowledge of digital devices and content management should go with ethics to ensure decency in the digital landscape.

Already existing case studies indicate the relevance of DFL in assisting individuals and institutions to exhibit financial discipline (Mancone et al.,

2024). This discipline serves as a foundation for the growth of businesses and the enhancement of the financial inclusion of individuals, making it the best tool for women's empowerment. Even households need this knowledge to enhance their financial security (Dash & Mohanta, 2024). The importance of DFL is, therefore, outstanding and should be the pivot for citizenship education in a country. The surge in mobile application development and patronage is a culmination for DFL if digital citizenship can be at the forefront of application development.

The three major factors identified for proper integration of DFL with digital citizenship are digital integrity, security, and responsibility. The interrelationship between these three components produces a glowing digital citizenship that informs the growth and development of DFL. The true integrity of the DFL platform can be achieved through proper security measures embedded in the application. This will monitor the responsible use of the platform to strengthen the trust users have for DFL platforms. As females are the most vulnerable in the digital civic space, boasting digital security, integrity, and responsibility will help in active female participation in the DFL platforms. This will enhance financial inclusion to bring more sustainability in finance.

Practical Implication

The direction in the design and implementation of DFL platforms is needed to enhance the digital well-being of users. As investment and decision-making are crucial, institutions and individuals must look for features that will improve their digital citizenship before choosing a DFL platform. As security is a major responsibility that impacts integrity, stakeholders must adopt DFL platforms based on security standards. Service providers should use this as a criterion for standardisation, and individual users should also consider these features for their safety in the digital landscape. This will manifest in a positive impact. As part of digital policies for nations, digital citizenship should be prioritised to enable the achievement of DFL goals. Accountability and integrity of the financial sector will easily be achieved through this. Financial inclusion and empowerment will therefore be easily attainable. Individuals and institutions will be motivated to invest as decision-making will improve for financial stability.

Conclusion

Technology is a tool for the efficient utilisation of the DFL. Enhancing digital citizenship through the DFL platforms is the best approach since all manner of people can access and utilise DFL platforms through their mobile devices. Key features for the identification of good DFL platforms include the digital integrity of the platform, which dwells much on the protection of the information and its reliability. Another factor is digital security, which dwells much on the protection of information from third-party access through encryption. The responsible use of the DFL platforms is also a key factor as it helps in protecting the rights of other users of the platform. A user has a responsibility to protect other users' privacy. This will enhance proper dependency on DFL platforms to strengthen the bonds and empower all manner of people in DFL to improve the financial security of society.

References

Akpuokwe, C. U., Chikwe, C. F., & Eneh, N. E. (2024). Leveraging technology and financial literacy for women's empowerment in SMEs: A conceptual framework for sustainable development. *Global Journal of Engineering and Technology Advances*, *18*(3), 020–032. https://doi.org/10.30574/gjeta.2024.18.3.0041

Al-shami, S. A., Damayanti, R., Adil, H., Farhi, F., & Al mamun, A. (2024). Financial and digital financial literacy through social media use towards financial inclusion among batik small enterprises in Indonesia. *Heliyon*, *10*(15). https://doi.org/10.1016/j.heliyon.2024.e34902

Althibyani, H. A., & Al-Zahrani, A. M. (2023). Investigating the effect of students' knowledge, beliefs, and digital citizenship skills on the prevention of cybercrime. *Sustainability (Switzerland)*, *15*(15). https://doi.org/10.3390/su151511512

Boldar, J. D. S., Omanwa, C., & Baimwera, B. (2022). Role of digital platforms as financial literacy delivery channels for promotion of financial inclusion in commercial banks in Kenya. *International Journal of Professional Practice (IJPP)*, *10*(1).

Chen, L. L., Mirpuri, S., Rao, N., & Law, N. (2021). Conceptualization and measurement of digital citizenship across disciplines. In *Educational Research Review* (Vol. 33). Elsevier Ltd. https://doi.org/10.1016/j.edurev.2021.100379

Choi, M. (2016). A concept analysis of digital citizenship for democratic citizenship education in the internet age. *Theory and Research in Social Education, 44*(4), 565–607. https://doi.org/10.1080/00933104.2016.1210549

Choudhary, H., & Jain, H. (2023). Addressing financial exclusion through financial literacy training programs: A systematic literature review. *Empirical Research in Vocational Education and Training, 15*(1). https://doi.org/10.1186/s40461-023-00147-9

Creswell, J. W., & Clark, V. L. (2011). *Designing and conducting mixed methods research* (2nd ed.). Sage Publications.

Das, S. (2024). *Financial literacy and education in enhancing financial inclusion and poverty alleviation* (pp. 127–144). https://doi.org/10.1007/978-3-031-67523-2_8

Dash, A., & Mohanta, G. (2024). Fostering financial inclusion for attaining sustainable goals: What contributes more to the inclusive financial behaviour of rural households in India? *Journal of Cleaner Production, 449*. https://doi.org/10.1016/j.jclepro.2024.141731

Ekpo, A. E., Drenten, J., Albinsson, P. A., Anong, S., Appau, S., Chatterjee, L., Dadzie, C. A., Echelbarger, M., Muldrow, A., Ross, S. M., Santana, S., & Weinberger, M. F. (2022). The platformed money ecosystem: Digital financial platforms, datafication, and reimagining financial well-being. *Journal of Consumer Affairs, 56*(3), 1062–1078. https://doi.org/10.1111/joca.12458

Emejulu, A., & McGregor, C. (2019). Towards a radical digital citizenship in digital education. *Critical Studies in Education, 60*(1), 131–147. https://doi.org/10.1080/17508487.2016.1234494

Ferilli, G. B., Palmieri, E., Miani, S., & Stefanelli, V. (2024). The impact of FinTech innovation on digital financial literacy in Europe: Insights from the banking industry. *Research in International Business and Finance, 69*. https://doi.org/10.1016/j.ribaf.2024.102218

Fernández-Prados, J. S., Lozano-Díaz, A., & Ainz-Galende, A. (2021). Measuring digital citizenship: A comparative analysis. *Informatics, 8*(1). MDPI AG. https://doi.org/10.3390/informatics8010018

Fernández-Prados, J. S., Lozano-Díaz, A., & Cuenca-Piqueras, C. (2020). Digital citizenship and education: State of the art and bibliometric analysis. *ACM International Conference Proceeding Series*, 174–178. https://doi.org/10.1145/3395245.3396430

Fitriah, N., Degeng, M. D. K., Degeng, I. N. S., & Praherdhiono, H. (2023). Enhancing early childhood financial literacy through FinSOLEkid Indonesia: A comparative study of digital platforms. *Golden Age: Jurnal Ilmiah Tumbuh Kembang Anak Usia Dini, 8*(3), 171–181. https://doi.org/10.14421/jga.2023.83-06

Ghosn-Chelala, M. (2019). Exploring sustainable learning and practice of digital citizenship: Education and place-based challenges. *Education, Citizenship and Social Justice, 14*(1), 40–56. https://doi.org/10.1177/1746197918759155

Görög, V., & Udvari, B. (2023). How to assess responsible digital citizenship? Economics students in the digital world. *Society and Economy, 45*(2), 112–135. https://doi.org/10.1556/204.2022.00028

Gutiérrez-Aguilar, O., Turpo-Gebera, O., Chicaña-Huanca, S., Laura-de-la-Cruz, K. M., Pérez-Postigo, G., Diaz-Zavala, R., & Ccoya, I. O. (2024). Digital skills and digital citizenship education: An analysis based on structural equation modeling. *Journal of Technology and Science Education, 14*(3), 738–755. https://doi.org/10.3926/jotse.2436

Harrison, T., & Polizzi, G. (2022). (In)civility and adolescents' moral decision making online: Drawing on moral theory to advance digital citizenship education. *Education and Information Technologies, 27*(3), 3277–3297. https://doi.org/10.1007/s10639-021-10710-0

Hasan, R., Ashfaq, M., Parveen, T., & Gunardi, A. (2023). Financial inclusion—does digital financial literacy matter for women entrepreneurs? *International Journal of Social Economics, 50*(8), 1085–1104. https://doi.org/10.1108/IJSE-04-2022-0277

Hollandsworth, R., Donovan, J., & Welch, M. (2017). Digital citizenship: You can't go home again. *TechTrends, 61*(6), 524–530. https://doi.org/10.1007/s11528-017-0190-4

Iddrisu, I., & Fuseini, I. (2025). The impact of digital technologies on public service delivery: The role of organizational structures and decision-making. *International Journal of Organizational Analysis*. https://doi.org/10.1108/IJOA-10-2024-4918

Inusah, F., & Amponsah, A. A. (2018). An expert system to assist businesses in financial decision making to enhance efficiency. *International Journal of Computer Applications, 181*(7).

Inusah, F., Missah, Y. M., Najim, U., & Twum, F. (2023a). Agile neural expert system for managing basic education. *Intelligent Systems with Applications, 17*, Article 200178. https://doi.org/10.1016/j.iswa.2023.200178

Inusah, F., Missah, Y. M., Najim, U., & Twum, F. (2023b). Integrating expert system in managing basic education: A survey in Ghana. *International Journal of Information Management Data Insights, 3*(1), Article 100166. https://doi.org/10.1016/j.jjimei.2023.100166

Inusah, F., Missah, Y. M., Ussiph, N., & Twum, F. (2021). Expert system in enhancing efficiency in basic educational management using data mining techniques. In *IJACSA) International Journal of Advanced Computer Science and Applications* (Vol. 12, Issue 11). www.ijacsa.thesai.org

Jones, L. M., & Mitchell, K. J. (2016). Defining and measuring youth digital citizenship. *New Media and Society, 18*(9), 2063–2079. https://doi.org/10.1177/1461444815577797

Kaur Chhabra, K., & Shilpi Gupta, P. (2023). *Impact of digital media platforms on personal financial literacy.*

Khalil, M. (2020). Financial citizenship as a broader democratic context of financial literacy. *Citizenship, Social and Economics Education, 20*(1), 3–16. https://doi.org/10.1177/2047173420948411

Khan, F., Siddiqui, M. A., & Imtiaz, S. (2022). Role of financial literacy in achieving financial inclusion: A review, synthesis and research agenda. *Cogent Business and Management, 9*(1). Cogent OA. https://doi.org/10.1080/23311975.2022.2034236

Koomson, I., Villano, R. A., & Hadley, D. (2020). Intensifying financial inclusion through the provision of financial literacy training: A gendered perspective. *Applied Economics, 52*(4), 375–387. https://doi.org/10.1080/00036846.2019.1645943

Koskelainen, T., Kalmi, P., Scornavacca, E., & Vartiainen, T. (2023). Financial literacy in the digital age—A research agenda. *Journal of Consumer Affairs, 57*(1), 507–528. https://doi.org/10.1111/joca.12510

Kulathunga, K. M. M. C. B., Ye, J., Sharma, S., & Weerathunga, P. R. (2020). How does technological and financial literacy influence SME performance: Mediating role of ERM practices. *Information (Switzerland), 11*(6). https://doi.org/10.3390/INFO11060297

Lauricella, A. R., Herdzina, J., & Robb, M. (2020). Early childhood educators' teaching of digital citizenship competencies. *Computers and Education, 158*,. https://doi.org/10.1016/j.compedu.2020.103989

Lusardi, A. (2019). Financial literacy and the need for financial education: Evidence and implications. *Swiss Journal of Economics and Statistics, 155*(1). https://doi.org/10.1186/s41937-019-0027-5

Lyons, A. C., & Kass-Hanna, J. (2021). A methodological overview to defining and measuring "digital" financial literacy. *Financial Planning Review, 4*(2). https://doi.org/10.1002/cfp2.1113

Mancone, S., Tosti, B., Corrado, S., Spica, G., Zanon, A., & Diotaiuti, P. (2024). Youth, money, and behavior: the impact of financial literacy programs. In *Frontiers in Education* (Vol. 9). Frontiers Media SA. https://doi.org/10.3389/feduc.2024.1397060

Martin, F., Gezer, T., & Wang, C. (2019). Educators' perceptions of student digital citizenship practices. *Computers in the Schools, 36*(4), 238–254. https://doi.org/10.1080/07380569.2019.1674621

Méndez-Prado, S. M., Rodriguez, V., Peralta-Rizzo, K., Everaert, P., & Valcke, M. (2023). An assessment tool to identify the financial literacy level of financial education programs participants' executed by Ecuadorian financial institutions. *Sustainability (Switzerland)*, *15*(2). https://doi.org/10.3390/su15020996

Mishra, D., Agarwal, N., Sharahiley, S., & Kandpal, V. (2024). Digital financial literacy and its impact on financial decision-making of women: Evidence from India. *Journal of Risk and Financial Management*, *17*(10). https://doi.org/10.3390/jrfm17100468

Monteiro, A., Teixeira, E. G., Leite, C., Barros, R., Fernandes, P., & Soares, F. (2022). Education towards literacy and digital citizenship of young people: Beyond "being online." *Revista Conhecimento Online*, *2*, 89–107. https://doi.org/10.25112/RCO.V2.2991

Murugesan, R., & Manohar, V. (2019). AI in financial sector—A driver to financial literacy. *Shanlax International Journal of Commerce*, *7*(3), 66–70. https://doi.org/10.34293/commerce.v7i3.477

Osabutey, E. L. C., & Jackson, T. (2024). Mobile money and financial inclusion in Africa: Emerging themes, challenges and policy implications. *Technological Forecasting and Social Change, 202*. https://doi.org/10.1016/j.techfore.2024.123339

Ozili, P. K. (2022). Financial inclusion and sustainable development: An empirical association. *Journal of Money and Business, 2*(2), 186–198. https://doi.org/10.1108/jmb-03-2022-0019

Pandey, A., Kiran, R., & Sharma, R. K. (2022). Investigating the impact of financial inclusion drivers, financial literacy and financial initiatives in fostering sustainable growth in North India. *Sustainability (Switzerland)*, *14*(17). https://doi.org/10.3390/su141711061

Pangrazio, L., & Sefton-Green, J. (2021). Digital rights, digital citizenship and digital literacy: What's the difference? *Journal of New Approaches in Educational Research, 10*(1), 15–27. https://doi.org/10.7821/NAER.2021.1.616

Panos, G. A., & Wilson, J. O. S. (2020). Financial literacy and responsible finance in the FinTech era: capabilities and challenges. *European Journal of Finance, 26*(4–5), 297–301. Routledge. https://doi.org/10.1080/1351847X.2020.1717569

Rahayu, R., Ali, S., Aulia, A., & Hidayah, R. (2022). The current digital financial literacy and financial behavior in Indonesian millennial generation. *Journal of Accounting and Investment*, *23*(1), 78–94. https://doi.org/10.18196/jai.v23i1.13205

Ravikumar, T., Suresha, B., Prakash, N., Vazirani, K., & Krishna, T. A. (2022). Digital financial literacy among adults in India: Measurement and validation. *Cogent Economics and Finance*, *10*(1). https://doi.org/10.1080/23322039.2022.2132631

Respati, D. K., Widyastuti, U., Nuryati, T., Musyaffi, A. M., Handayani, B. D., & Ali, N. R. (2023). How do students' digital financial literacy and financial confidence influence their financial behavior and financial well-being? *Nurture, 17*(2), 40–50. https://doi.org/10.55951/nurture.v17i2.154

Ribble, M. (2012). Digital citizenship for educational change. *Kappa Delta Pi Record, 48*(4), 148–151. https://doi.org/10.1080/00228958.2012.734015

Sayed Abdellatif, M., Issa Idris, A., Hasan, M., Al-Abyadh, A., Saeed, A., & Al-Budaiwi, F. (2024). *Digital Citizenship Skills and the Attitudes Towards Sustainable Development among University Students. 12*(1), 2051–4883. https://doi.org/10.58262/ks.v12i1.192

Seldal, M. M. N., & Nyhus, E. K. (2022). Financial vulnerability, financial literacy, and the use of digital payment technologies. *Journal of Consumer Policy, 45*(2), 281–306. https://doi.org/10.1007/s10603-022-09512-9

Setiawan, M., Effendi, N., Santoso, T., Dewi, V. I., & Sapulette, M. S. (2022). Digital financial literacy, current behavior of saving and spending and its future foresight. *Economics of Innovation and New Technology, 31*(4), 320–338. https://doi.org/10.1080/10438599.2020.1799142

Tay, L. Y., Tai, H. T., & Tan, G. S. (2022). Digital financial inclusion: A gateway to sustainable development. *Heliyon, 8*(6). Elsevier Ltd. https://doi.org/10.1016/j.heliyon.2022.e09766

Top 5 Personal Finance Apps on Android in Africa, Q3 2024. (n.d.). Retrieved April 19, 2025, from https://sensortower.com/blog/2024-q3-android-top-5-personal%20finance%20budgeting%20and%20planning-units-africa-63e363f0e1714cfff1979caa

Uthaileang, W., & Kiattisin, S. (2023). Developing the capability of digital financial literacy in developing countries: A Case of online loan for small entrepreneurs. *Heliyon, 9*(12). https://doi.org/10.1016/j.heliyon.2023.e21961

Vovchenko, N. G., Galazova, S. S., Danchenko, E. A., Ivanova, O. B., & Kostoglodova, E. D. (2018). Improvement of financial literacy as a crucial factor of economic development. In *European Research Studies Journal: Vol. XXI* (Issue 1).

Yadav, M., & Banerji, P. (2023). A bibliometric analysis of digital financial literacy. *American Journal of Business, 38*(3), 91–111. https://doi.org/10.1108/ajb-11-2022-0186

Yang, J., Wu, Y., & Huang, B. (2023). Digital finance and financial literacy: Evidence from Chinese households. *Journal of Banking and Finance, 156*. https://doi.org/10.1016/j.jbankfin.2023.107005

CHAPTER 10

Cybersecurity and Data Protection in FinTech: Ensuring Safe and Inclusive Financial Services

Ibrahim Nandom Yakubu, Ibrahim Osman Adam, and Mubarik Abdul Mumin

Introduction

The ongoing digital revolution is reshaping global financial systems, and nowhere is its transformative potential more evident than in the rapidly expanding FinTech sector (Rivera, 2025). From mobile money and digital banking to blockchain applications and peer-to-peer lending, financial technology has opened new frontiers for delivering financial services in innovative, efficient, and inclusive ways. In Africa and

I. N. Yakubu (✉) · I. O. Adam · M. Abdul Mumin
School of Business, University for Development Studies, Tamale, Ghana
e-mail: ibrahim.yakubu@uds.edu.gh

I. O. Adam
e-mail: ioadam@uds.edu.gh

M. Abdul Mumin
e-mail: mamubarik@uds.edu.gh

I. N. Yakubu (ed.), *Banking on Inclusion*, Sustainable Development Goals Series, https://doi.org/10.1007/978-3-031-96716-0_10

other emerging markets, where traditional banking infrastructure remains limited, FinTech is proving particularly powerful, offering low-cost, accessible financial solutions to the previously unbanked and underbanked (Skamser, 2025). In Ghana, Kenya, Nigeria, and South Africa, for instance, millions of individuals now access savings, credit, insurance, and payment platforms using nothing more than a mobile phone (GSMA, 2025). This digital leapfrogging is revolutionizing how people transact, save, invest, and participate in the economy, especially in underserved rural and informal economies.

However, the same digital systems that are promoting financial inclusion also create new risks and vulnerabilities (Umoga et al., 2024). As financial services migrate online and digital platforms handle ever-growing volumes of sensitive user data and transactions, the FinTech ecosystem becomes increasingly susceptible to cyber threats. The nature of these threats is complex and evolving, ranging from malware and phishing attacks to large-scale data breaches, ransomware incidents, and sophisticated digital fraud schemes (Dieu, 2024). Unlike traditional banks that have legacy systems and extensive internal controls, many FinTech startups are small, under-resourced, and technologically exposed. These firms often lack robust cybersecurity protocols, making them attractive targets for cybercriminals. Furthermore, their reliance on third-party cloud services, open APIs, and mobile platforms adds additional layers of cyber risk (Goater, 2025).

More troubling is the impact of these risks on financial inclusion and user trust. For low-income users who are new to digital finance, a single cyber incident such as a hacked account or an unauthorized withdrawal can result in catastrophic financial losses (Anthony et al., 2024; Bosco & Totolo, 2024). In many cases, these users have little legal recourse or awareness of how to protect themselves online. Digital illiteracy, language barriers, and weak consumer protection frameworks further exacerbate the situation. As such, cyber threats do not affect all users equally; they disproportionately harm those the FinTech revolution aims to uplift (Thimot, 2022). Without deliberate efforts to embed cybersecurity and data protection into the architecture of digital finance, there is a risk that technological innovation will reproduce or even deepen existing inequalities.

Closely intertwined with cybersecurity is the issue of data protection. FinTech platforms rely extensively on user data for decision-making, product design, and credit scoring. While data-driven finance enables personalized services and alternative credit models, it also introduces serious concerns around privacy, surveillance, and informed consent (Hariharan, 2024). In many African countries, legal frameworks for data protection are either nascent or poorly enforced, allowing for unchecked data harvesting, algorithmic bias, and data exploitation (Mhlanga, 2024). This raises critical ethical questions: Who owns the data? How is it used? Are users aware of the implications of their digital footprints? And importantly, how do we ensure that data-driven innovation does not come at the cost of user autonomy and dignity?

Cybersecurity and data protection, therefore, are not merely operational or compliance matters. They are fundamental pillars of digital trust and financial inclusion. They determine whether FinTech will serve as a bridge to broader economic participation or as a barrier that excludes the most vulnerable (Khullar, 2025). For governments, regulators, developers, and civil society, the challenge is to strike a balance: fostering innovation while safeguarding users; encouraging data use while enforcing privacy rights; scaling digital services while managing systemic risk.

This chapter examines these critical dynamics in detail. It begins with a review of the cybersecurity threat landscape in FinTech, highlighting the nature and scope of digital risks. It then analyzes the legal and regulatory frameworks shaping cybersecurity and data protection globally and in selected African countries. The discussion progresses to strategies for building cyber-resilient FinTech ecosystems and the ethical dimensions of digital data governance. Finally, the chapter provides strategic policy and institutional recommendations aimed at creating a safer, more inclusive, and trust-based digital financial future.

The Cyber Threat Landscape in FinTech

As FinTech platforms increasingly handle sensitive financial data and real-time transactions across digital networks, they are becoming prime targets for cybercriminals. The rise of mobile money, digital wallets, lending apps, and neobanking services has opened new channels for access but also created vulnerabilities that malicious actors can exploit (Dieu, 2024; Katariya, 2025). Unlike traditional banks, many FinTech firms operate in regulatory gray zones or lack the financial and human capital to invest in robust cybersecurity infrastructure. The combination of innovation and fragility makes this sector particularly exposed to digital threats, with far-reaching implications for consumer trust, financial stability, and national security (Bonini, 2025).

Common Cyber Threats Targeting FinTech Services

FinTech platforms are exposed to a wide spectrum of cyber risks, some inherited from broader digital systems and others specific to financial technologies. Among the most common and damaging threats are phishing, ransomware, denial-of-service (DoS) attacks, identity theft, data breaches, SIM swap fraud, and insider attacks. These threats can compromise customer funds, leak personal data, disrupt platform services, and severely damage a company's reputation. **Table 10.1** summarizes some of the major cyber threats facing FinTech platforms, their mechanisms, and potential impacts.

These cyber threats often interact with one another. For instance, a successful phishing attempt may lead to unauthorized fund transfers, which can then expose broader data vulnerabilities. In mobile-first environments, where most transactions rely on phones and USSD codes, attackers have increasingly targeted telecom networks and mobile interfaces, highlighting the importance of a holistic cybersecurity framework that spans across sectors (Sen, 2024).

Unique Vulnerabilities in Mobile and App-Based FinTech Models

In many African and Asian countries, FinTech innovation is closely tied to mobile technology. Users primarily interact with digital financial services via mobile applications, mobile money platforms, and USSD codes (Mngoma, 2024). While this model enhances accessibility, it also introduces specific cyber risks. These include poor app permissions, outdated operating systems, unsecured Wi-Fi usage, and limited encryption on low-end devices. Many users, particularly those in low-income or rural settings, may lack basic cybersecurity awareness, increasing the likelihood of falling victim to social engineering attacks (BDO, 2024; Shebalkov, 2024). Additionally, many mobile apps do not follow secure development practices. In some cases, developers fail to encrypt data at rest or during transmission. Others integrate with third-party ad libraries or analytics tools that harvest user data without adequate consent. This creates a situation where platforms designed to promote inclusion may inadvertently

Table 10.1 Common cyber threats in FinTech ecosystems

Threat type	*Description*	*Impact on FinTech*
Phishing	Fraudulent emails or SMS messages tricking users into disclosing credentials	Unauthorized access to user accounts, identity theft
Ransomware	Malware that encrypts system files until a ransom is paid	Business interruption, data loss, financial extortion
Data Breaches	Unauthorized access to user databases and transaction records	Leakage of sensitive information; regulatory penalties
SIM Swap Fraud	Fraudsters duplicate a victim's SIM card to access mobile money or SMS codes	Account takeovers, mobile wallet theft
Denial-of-Service	Overwhelming servers with traffic to disable services	Downtime for apps and platforms, customer dissatisfaction
Insider Threats	Malicious activities by employees or contractors with system access	Manipulation of systems, leaking sensitive company or user data
Bot Attacks	Automated scripts targeting APIs or login portals for exploitation	Disruption of services, data scraping, credential stuffing
Third-party Risks	Vulnerabilities introduced through vendors, APIs, or cloud providers	Breaches through integrations; regulatory compliance failure

Source Authors' compilation based on Dixon (2024), Katariya (2025), and Alexander (2025)

facilitate exploitation. **Box 10.1** highlights a 2017 incident in Kenya, where Safaricom's M-Pesa platform was targeted through a SIM swap attack that briefly compromised customer funds before being contained.

Box 10.1: Cybersecurity Breach Attempt on M-Pesa in Kenya
In April 2017, Safaricom, Kenya's largest telecommunications provider, successfully thwarted a sophisticated cyberattack targeting its M-Pesa mobile money platform. The attackers attempted to exploit a SIM swap method to gain control of a user's mobile account, managing to access KES 266,000 before Safaricom's risk management team detected the breach. The company quickly refunded the stolen amount and reassured customers that no funds were ultimately lost. Safaricom referred the case to law enforcement, leading to legal action against the suspects, demonstrating its firm stance on cybersecurity. The incident revealed critical

vulnerabilities in mobile money systems and emphasized that, despite M-Pesa's essential role in Kenya's economy, digital fraud remains a persistent challenge.

Source: Proshare (2017)

The Human Factor and Behavioral Vulnerabilities

While technical systems can be fortified with firewalls, encryption, and multifactor authentication, human behavior remains a major source of risk (Kost, 2025). Users often reuse weak passwords, click suspicious links, and share PINs or authentication codes unknowingly. In underserved populations, digital financial literacy is often low, and users may not fully understand cybersecurity risks. Moreover, the informal nature of transactions (e.g., sending money via mobile to unregistered vendors) can create gray areas in responsibility when things go wrong. FinTech companies themselves may also contribute to behavioral vulnerabilities, as some platforms prioritize rapid user acquisition and interface simplicity over security features (Gallagher, 2025). For example, they may delay implementing two-factor authentication to avoid friction in the onboarding process, thereby exposing users to account takeover risks. Similarly, vague or complex privacy policies discourage users from understanding how their data is collected and processed.

Regulatory and Legal Frameworks for Cybersecurity and Data Protection

As FinTech reshapes the financial landscape, regulators are racing to catch up with the speed and complexity of its evolution. Effective regulation is critical to ensuring that digital financial services are not only innovative and inclusive, but also secure and rights-based (Rimon & Shabana, 2024). Without clear legal frameworks governing cybersecurity and data protection, FinTech users, especially those from low-income and marginalized groups, remain vulnerable to exploitation, fraud, and data misuse. This section explores the global, regional, and national regulatory efforts aimed at strengthening cybersecurity and safeguarding user data within the FinTech ecosystem.

Global Frameworks: Guiding Principles for Digital Security and Data Governance

At the international level, several frameworks have emerged to guide countries in developing their cybersecurity and data protection strategies. The *General Data Protection Regulation (GDPR)*, implemented by the European Union in 2018, has become the gold standard for data privacy legislation globally. It emphasizes principles such as informed consent, data minimization, user access rights, and accountability (Matinou, 2024). While not legally binding outside the EU, the GDPR has influenced many African data protection laws, including those in Nigeria, Kenya, and South Africa.[1]

In the area of cybersecurity, global standards such as the *ISO/IEC 27,001* provide a systematic approach to managing sensitive company and customer data. These standards help organizations establish, implement, maintain, and continually improve information security management systems (ISMS). International organizations such as the World Bank, International Telecommunication Union (ITU), and the Organisation for Economic Co-operation and Development (OECD) have also developed cybersecurity toolkits and guidance to support national-level digital resilience.[2]

However, global frameworks often require significant institutional capacity and resources to implement, which many FinTech startups and regulators in low- and middle-income countries lack (Joshi, 2025). Therefore, a localized and context-sensitive approach to regulation is essential.

African Context: National Laws and Regulatory Diversity

Across Africa, the legal landscape for cybersecurity and data protection is highly varied. Some countries have enacted comprehensive legislation, while others are still in the process of drafting bills or have no legal framework at all. **Table 10.2** outlines the status of selected African countries in relation to data protection and cybersecurity laws.

[1] Read more from here: https://gdprlocal.com/gdpr-and-data-protection-laws-in-africa-a-comparison/#:~:text=Scope:,GDPR%20or%20another%20African%20standard).

[2] https://www.worldbank.org/en/results/2025/01/29/-enhancing-cyber-resilience-in-developing-countries.

Table 10.2 Cybersecurity and data protection landscape in selected African countries

Country	*Cybersecurity law*	*Data protection law*	*Regulatory body*
Ghana	Cybersecurity Act (2020, Act 1038)	Data Protection Act (2012, Act 843)	Data Protection Commission and Cyber Security Authority (CSA)
Nigeria	Nigeria Cybercrime Act (2015)	Nigeria Data Protection Regulation (NDPR, 2019)	NITDA (pending Data Protection Commission)
Kenya	Computer Misuse and Cybercrimes Act (2018)	Data Protection Act (2019)	Office of the Data Protection Commissioner
South Africa	Cybercrimes Act (2021)	Protection of Personal Information Act (POPIA)	Information Regulator
Uganda	Computer Misuse Act (2011)	Data Protection and Privacy Act (2019)	National Information Technology Authority
Senegal	Law on Cybercrime (2008)	Data Protection Act (2008, amended 2016)	Commission de Protection des Données

Source Authors' compilation

As **Table 10.2** shows, many African countries now have baseline legal instruments in place, although enforcement remains inconsistent. Ghana's Cybersecurity Act (2020, Act 1038), for instance, establishes the Cyber Security Authority (CSA) to regulate cybersecurity activities and protect critical information infrastructure. The act mandates FinTech companies and digital platforms to report cyber incidents and comply with national cybersecurity standards. Additionally, the country's Data Protection Act (2012, Act 843) requires all data controllers, including FinTech platforms, to register with the Data Protection Commission and adhere to principles of lawful processing.

Kenya's Data Protection Act (2019) and South Africa's POPIA are also considered progressive, aligning with GDPR-style provisions. They provide for data subject rights, lawful data processing, restrictions on cross-border data transfers, and enforcement mechanisms. However, regulatory capacity and technical know-how to oversee compliance in FinTech remain limited, particularly outside major urban centers.

Regulatory Sandboxes and Innovation Hubs

Recognizing the need to support innovation while safeguarding users, several African countries have introduced regulatory sandboxes, which are controlled environments where FinTech firms can test products under the supervision of regulators (Gilbert, 2025). These sandboxes offer a middle ground, allowing authorities to observe risks in real time while providing innovators with space to refine security and data protection protocols before scaling. These regulatory innovations promote "learning by doing," enabling agile responses to new threats while shaping policy through evidence. However, for sandboxes to be effective, there must be post-testing regulatory clarity and continued oversight to ensure that pilot-stage protections are maintained once solutions enter the broader market (Kálmán, 2025). **Figure 10.1** presents a four-phase operational model of a regulatory sandbox, outlining the key steps from initial application to post-testing scale-up and regulatory alignment.

As adoption grows, sandbox models are enabling regulators to develop evidence-based policy responses, adapt to fast-changing innovations, and enhance financial inclusion. **Boxes** 10.2, 10.3 and 10.4 present selected country experiences that highlight different approaches to sandbox design and implementation across the continent.

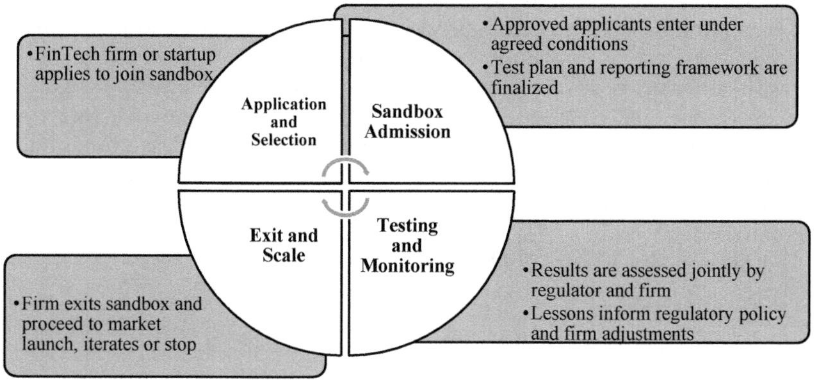

Fig. 10.1 Operational phases of a regulatory sandbox (*Source* Authors' Construct)

Box 10.2: Sierra Leone's FinTech Sandbox for Inclusive Innovation
Launched in 2018 by the Bank of Sierra Leone (BSL), the regulatory sandbox is one of Africa's first in a fragile state setting, aimed at expanding financial inclusion through FinTech innovation. The program allows selected firms to test their solutions over a 12-month period under close regulatory oversight. It is aligned with the country's National Financial Inclusion Strategy and prioritizes products that serve underserved populations. Participating companies must be locally registered with at least 10% Sierra Leonean ownership. Managed by a dedicated team within BSL and supported by UNCDF and FSD Africa, the sandbox helps regulators adapt policies through real-world learning. Strong institutional commitment underscores its value as a model for inclusive digital finance regulation.

Source: Massally and Duff (2018)

Box 10.3: Nigeria's Regulatory Sandbox for Payments Innovation
The Central Bank of Nigeria (CBN) launched its regulatory sandbox in January 2021 to support innovation in the payments sector while protecting consumers and maintaining financial stability. The sandbox allows FinTechs, licensed institutions, and telecom firms to test new products in a controlled environment for up to 12 months. Its goals include promoting financial inclusion, accelerating time-to-market, and improving regulatory clarity. Applicants must identify risks and propose safeguards, with assessments covering areas such as monetary stability, AML/CFT compliance, and data privacy. The sandbox uses digital infrastructure by Emtech for real-time supervision. Although the framework is promising, limited public disclosure about participants and outcomes remains a challenge, raising concerns about transparency and the broader impact of the initiative.

Source: Bisi-Afolabi (2022)

Box 10.4: Ghana's Regulatory Sandbox for Digital Financial Innovation
The Bank of Ghana (BoG), in partnership with EMTECH Service LLC, launched a regulatory and innovation sandbox pilot on February

25, 2021, to foster a supportive environment for FinTech growth and financial inclusion. The sandbox focuses on emerging digital financial services and business models not yet covered by existing regulation. It prioritizes innovations in blockchain, remittances, crowdfunding, e-KYC, regtech, suptech, digital banking, and solutions aimed at MSMEs and women's financial inclusion. Eligible participants, including startups and licensed institutions, are granted a six-month testing window, extendable upon review. The pilot transitioned into a full launch in August 2022, reinforcing BoG's long-term commitment to innovation and regulatory oversight. Foreign applicants must register locally with at least 30% Ghanaian ownership to participate.

Source: Moody's (2023) and Mate-Kole and Bentsi-Enchill (2023)

Gaps and Challenges in the Current Legal Environment

Despite progress in strengthening regulatory frameworks for digital financial services, major challenges persist. First, many FinTech firms operate across borders, creating jurisdictional complexities when it comes to enforcement. A mobile lending app developed in Nigeria but used in Ghana may not be subject to the same data protection laws, raising questions about whose rules apply and how violations are redressed. Second, many laws do not adequately address emerging risks such as algorithmic bias, AI-based profiling, or the use of biometric data. Third, enforcement remains a major bottleneck. Regulatory agencies are often under-resourced, lack technical expertise, and face political interference. Additionally, informal FinTech services, such as unlicensed mobile lenders or digital investment schemes, often operate outside the regulatory radar, exposing users to significant cyber and data risks. These gaps highlight the need for regional cooperation and capacity building.

Integrated Cyber Resilience Strategies for FinTech Ecosystems

The security and sustainability of FinTech platforms depend not only on technological innovation but also on how well they anticipate, prevent, and respond to cyber threats (Techcabal, 2024). As digital financial services become more embedded in the daily lives of users, especially in low-income and underserved regions, the need for an integrated and inclusive cyber resilience strategy becomes urgent. Resilience in this context refers to the ability of FinTech systems to withstand cyberattacks, recover from incidents, and adapt to evolving threats without compromising user trust, operational continuity, or regulatory compliance (Montini, 2025).

Cyber resilience must be built across three interrelated levels: the platform level, where technical systems and products interface with users; the institutional level, where organizational policies, governance, and human capital shape internal risk management; and the ecosystem level, where laws, partnerships, infrastructure, and multi-stakeholder coordination determine the broader security landscape. Each of these levels involves unique actors, tools, and objectives, yet they are mutually reinforcing. A vulnerability at any one level can compromise the entire ecosystem. For this reason, FinTech stakeholders must adopt a multi-layered strategy that aligns platform design, institutional governance, and ecosystem collaboration.

Table 10.3 presents a structured framework mapping out specific focus areas, recommended strategies, responsible actors, and the anticipated impact for each layer of resilience. It is designed to guide FinTech companies, regulators, development partners, and telecom operators in formulating robust security approaches tailored to emerging market realities.

Data Protection and Digital Trust in Inclusive Finance

As FinTech platforms collect, process, and store increasingly large volumes of personal data, concerns around data protection and digital trust have moved to the forefront of the financial inclusion debate (Odeyemi, 2025). While data is the lifeblood of digital finance, enabling risk assessments, tailored product offerings, and faster service delivery, it can also become a tool of exploitation and exclusion when not governed responsibly. In inclusive finance, where users are often low-income, low-literacy, and digitally inexperienced, the stakes of poor data practices are even higher. This section explores key dimensions of data protection and digital trust in the inclusive finance landscape.

Table 10.3 Integrated cyber resilience strategies for FinTech ecosystems

Resilience level	*Focus area*	*Key strategies and tools*	*Actors involved*	*Expected impact*
Platform Level	Secure Development Practices	Implement secure coding standards, use end-to-end encryption for data storage and transmission, and conduct regular vulnerability assessments	Financial technology developers, independent cybersecurity experts	Reduces technical vulnerabilities and enhances platform security
	Fraud Detection	Deploy artificial intelligence-driven transaction monitoring, behavioral user verification, and fraud analytics systems	Financial technology companies, data science service providers	Prevents financial fraud, enhances transaction integrity
	Data Privacy and Consent	Integrate privacy-focused design, use clear and localized consent forms, and ensure compliance with national data protection laws	Application developers, legal compliance teams, data privacy officers	Promotes user trust and ensures lawful data usage
Institutional Level	Governance and Compliance	Appoint a cybersecurity lead at executive level, perform regular risk audits, and establish compliance with national and international standards	Senior executives, internal compliance teams	Strengthens internal control and regulatory accountability
	Human Capital	Deliver staff training on phishing awareness, cyber hygiene, and role-specific access control	Human resource departments, information technology trainers	Minimizes insider risk and human error

(continued)

Table 10.3 (continued)

Resilience level	*Focus area*	*Key strategies and tools*	*Actors involved*	*Expected impact*
	Incident Management	Maintain an incident response plan, ensure daily system backups, and test recovery capabilities through simulations	Risk management officers, operations departments	Enhances operational resilience and ensures business continuity
Ecosystem Level	Regulation and Oversight	Set cybersecurity minimum standards for financial technology companies, require reporting of cyber incidents, and adopt regulatory technology for monitoring	Central banks, national cybersecurity authorities	Improves ecosystem-wide security and fosters regulatory compliance
	Collaborative Infrastructure	Establish industry-wide partnerships for information sharing, develop national computer emergency response teams, and foster collaboration with telecommunications providers	Telecommunications operators, financial regulatory agencies, national alliances	Supports rapid response to emerging threats and enhances sector readiness
	Innovation and Research	Promote secure innovation through regulatory testing environments, invest in privacy-enhancing technologies, and support academic research on local cybersecurity needs	Technology innovation hubs, academic institutions, international development organizations	Enables responsible innovation and builds context-specific resilience

Source Authors' Compilation based on insights from World Economic Forum (2020), Oluokun et al. (2024) and Nelson (2024)

The Centrality of Data in FinTech Innovation

Data lies at the heart of modern FinTech innovation. It enables platforms to deliver financial services to individuals previously excluded from traditional banking systems by generating insights from non-traditional data sources such as mobile usage patterns, social media activity, geolocation, and digital transaction histories (Thompsett, 2025). These innovations have made it possible to assess credit risk, verify identities, and tailor financial products with remarkable efficiency. However, this data-centric approach also introduces significant vulnerabilities. When personal data is collected without transparency or stored without adequate protection, users are exposed to financial fraud, identity theft, and discriminatory practices. Moreover, the monetization of user data by some platforms, often without clear consent, turns personal information into a commodity, creating a power imbalance that favors institutions over individuals (Dixon, 2024).

User Consent and Informed Participation

A cornerstone of ethical data governance is the principle of informed consent. Users should not only be aware of what data is being collected, but also understand how it will be used, stored, and potentially shared. Unfortunately, many FinTech platforms fail to meet this standard (Surya, 2024). Consent forms are often written in complex legal language, presented in dominant languages that many users may not understand, or designed in ways that pressure users into compliance. These problems are particularly visible in mobile-based digital lending (Aldboush & Ferdous, 2023). Several platforms require access to users' contact lists, call records, and device metadata as a condition for offering loans. In some instances, this data has been misused to harass borrowers or shame them publicly when they default. Such practices are not only unethical, they also erode user trust and deter participation in digital financial systems (Hariharan, 2024).

Algorithmic Bias and Data-Driven Exclusion

The automation of financial decision-making through machine learning and artificial intelligence offers great promise but also significant risk (Vohra, 2025). Algorithms trained on biased or incomplete datasets can reinforce patterns of social exclusion (Satoh, 2024). For instance, if a credit scoring model relies heavily on formal employment data, rural dwellers, informal workers, or women, who are less likely to be formally employed, may receive low credit scores or be denied access altogether. Because many FinTech firms treat their algorithms as proprietary, there is often little transparency or accountability in how decisions are made. This lack of visibility, often referred to as the "black box" problem, makes it difficult for users to challenge unfair outcomes or understand why they were denied a loan or charged a higher fee (Nallakaruppan et al., 2024). Inclusive finance must therefore ensure that algorithmic systems are transparent, regularly audited, and equipped with accessible grievance mechanisms for affected users.

The Risk of Surveillance and Overreach

Beyond consent and bias, another major challenge is the creeping normalization of surveillance in digital financial ecosystems. In some markets, FinTech platforms and their corporate partners track user behavior across apps and websites, collect location data, and analyze personal interactions for commercial purposes (Cazarin, 2025). While marketed as personalization, such practices often amount to unregulated surveillance and data commodification. This is particularly dangerous in regions with limited regulatory oversight or weak democratic safeguards (Anthony et al., 2024). For instance, biometric data like fingerprints and facial scans are increasingly used for digital onboarding and Know Your Customer (KYC) compliance. However, these data types, once compromised, cannot be changed or revoked. Without clear rules governing storage, sharing, and protection, the use of biometric data poses profound risks to privacy and security. As highlighted in **Box 10.5**, the cases of Nigeria and India show how unregulated lending apps have exploited personal data and prompted regulatory reforms aimed at safeguarding user rights and restoring digital trust.

Box 10.5: Data Privacy and Consumer Protection Challenges in Digital Lending: Lessons from Nigeria and India

In both Nigeria and India, the rapid growth of digital lending applications has led to a significant erosion of public trust, largely due to unethical handling of user data. Investigations uncovered that certain platforms accessed users' contact lists without permission and used the information to intimidate borrowers by sending harassing messages to their acquaintances. In response, Nigeria's Federal Competition and Consumer Protection Commission (FCCPC), alongside the Nigeria Data Protection Commission (NDPC), implemented stricter enforcement measures under the Nigeria Data Protection Regulation (NDPR), including mandatory registration of digital lenders and comprehensive rules on data use and consent. Likewise, the Reserve Bank of India introduced robust digital lending regulations in 2022 to govern data practices, promote transparency, and shield consumers from exploitative behaviors. These regulatory actions underscore the urgent need for enhanced data protection frameworks, greater accountability, and stronger user rights in the fast-evolving fintech lending landscape.

Source: Etiebet and Matthew (2022), Crystalite Solicitors (2024) and Digital Policy Alert (2022)

Conclusion

The digital transformation of financial services has opened a new frontier for inclusive finance, with FinTech innovations playing a pivotal role in expanding access to credit, savings, insurance, and payment services across underserved populations. However, alongside these benefits lie serious risks that, if not managed effectively, threaten to undermine the very progress digital finance aims to achieve. This chapter has examined how cybersecurity and data protection constitute the backbone of safe and inclusive FinTech ecosystems, especially in emerging markets where regulatory maturity, user awareness, and institutional capacities are often limited.

The analysis has highlighted the multiplicity of cyber threats facing FinTech platforms including phishing attacks, SIM swap fraud, ransomware, and insider risks all of which compromise user safety, disrupt platform operations, and erode digital trust. Vulnerabilities are particularly pronounced in mobile-first environments, where applications may lack robust security features and users often have limited digital literacy. Moreover, the growing reliance on personal data and algorithmic systems introduces complex ethical challenges related to privacy, informed consent, and exclusionary practices. In the absence of comprehensive data governance frameworks and strong enforcement mechanisms, users, particularly those in low-income or marginalized communities, are exposed to risks of exploitation, surveillance, and harm.

Despite the adoption of national data protection laws and cybersecurity strategies in countries like Ghana, Nigeria, Kenya, and South Africa, enforcement gaps persist, and many FinTech firms continue to operate without adequate oversight. Regulatory sandboxes, while useful for experimentation, must be supported by clear compliance pathways, sector-wide accountability, and cross-border collaboration. Furthermore, cyber resilience must be institutionalized not just at the technical level, but also within governance structures, human capital systems, and ecosystem partnerships.

Strategic Recommendations

To safeguard the future of inclusive digital finance and to ensure that FinTech evolves as a trustworthy and equitable solution for underserved populations, a set of coordinated and multi-level strategic actions is required. These recommendations are directed toward regulators, policymakers, FinTech companies, civil society, and international development partners.

First, there is an urgent need to strengthen regulatory frameworks for cybersecurity and data protection across African and other emerging markets. National governments should ensure that comprehensive legislation aligned with international best practices such as the GDPR is not only enacted but rigorously enforced. Regulatory bodies must be adequately funded and staffed with technical experts capable of conducting audits, investigating breaches, and imposing penalties for non-compliance. Where possible, harmonization of data protection standards across regions through Economic Community of West African States (ECOWAS) or the African Union (AU) frameworks will help reduce jurisdictional inconsistencies in a digital ecosystem that is inherently cross-border.

Second, capacity building within regulatory institutions must be prioritized. Many data protection commissions and cybersecurity agencies in Africa lack the technical tools, forensic capacity, and legal infrastructure needed to oversee fast-evolving FinTech markets. Development partners can play a catalytic role by investing in regulator training programs, establishing knowledge exchange networks, and supporting the creation of compliance toolkits tailored to small and medium-sized digital finance providers.

Also, FinTech companies themselves must adopt a security-by-design and privacy-by-design approach to innovation. This means integrating cybersecurity features such as two-factor authentication, encryption, and regular patch updates into the core of digital services, not as afterthoughts. At the same time, companies must embed ethical data governance practices, ensuring that users are provided with clear, accessible, and multilingual information about how their data is collected, stored, and used. Consent processes must be simplified and meaningful rather than tokenistic.

Moreover, to build resilience beyond individual firms, collaborative cyber ecosystems must be developed. Public–private partnerships involving telecom companies, financial regulators, CERTs (Computer Emergency Response Teams), and cybersecurity service providers can facilitate the sharing of threat intelligence, coordinate responses to breaches, and set common industry standards. Platforms such as the Smart Africa Alliance and Africa Cybersecurity Alliance offer models for how regional cooperation can scale cybersecurity readiness.

Furthermore, user awareness and digital literacy programs are essential. Many data breaches and fraud cases are enabled by user behavior such as weak passwords, unsecured devices, or falling for phishing scams. Targeted awareness campaigns, delivered through radio, SMS, social media, or in-person training, can empower users with the knowledge to protect themselves and make informed choices about their digital financial participation.

Finally, regulators and industry actors must ensure algorithmic accountability and fairness in automated decision-making systems. With the increasing use of AI and machine learning in credit scoring, fraud detection, and customer segmentation, there is a risk that opaque algorithms may reproduce historical biases or exclude certain groups. Mandating algorithm audits, transparency reporting, and user appeal mechanisms will help make FinTech systems more inclusive and just.

References

Aldboush, H. H., & Ferdous, M. (2023). Building trust in fintech: An analysis of ethical and privacy considerations in the intersection of big data, AI, and customer trust. *International Journal of Financial Studies, 11*(3), 90.

Alexander, N. (2025). *Lessons on fintech breaches from the frontlines*. https://www.bobsguide.com/lessons-on-fintech-breaches-from-the-frontlines/

Anthony, A., Sambuli, N., & Sharma, L. (2024). *Security and trust in Africa's digital financial inclusion landscape*. Carnegie Endowment for International Peace. https://carnegieendowment.org/research/2024/03/security-and-trust-in-africas-digital-financial-inclusion-landscape

BDO. (2024). *Unlocked potential Fintech in Africa*. https://www.bdo.co.za/getmedia/0a92fd54-18e6-4a18-8f21-c22b0ae82775/Fintech-in-Africa-Report-2024_June.pdf

Bisi-Afolabi, M. (2022). *The Central Bank of Nigeria is launching a Regulatory Sandbox. Here's what to know!* https://paystack.com/blog/operations/cbn-regulatory-sandbox

Bonini, S. (2025). *Top cybersecurity threats for Fintech in 2025*. https://blog.clovrlabs.com/en/top-cybersecurity-threats-for-fintech-in-2025/

Bosco, F., & Totolo, E. (2024). *Cybersecurity: A crucial ingredient for responsible finance and consumer protection*. https://www.centerforfinancialinclusion.org/cybersecurity-a-crucial-ingredient-for-responsible-finance-and-consumer-protection/

Cazarin, I. (2025). *Big banks, big tech, big data: People left vulnerable to the relentless commodification of their sensitive data*. https://ourfinancialsecurity.org/2025/01/blog-big-banks-big-tech-big-data-people-left-vulnerable-to-the-relentless-commodification-of-their-sensitive-data/

Crystalite Solicitors. (2024). *Data protection: Legal remedy to loan apps menace*. https://crystalitesolicitors.com/data-protection-legal-remedy-to-loan-apps-menace/

Dieu, L. C. (2024). *The Fintech cyber seas: Challenges and solutions for secure navigation*. https://smartdev.com/the-fintech-cyber-seas-challenges-and-solutions-for-secure-navigation/

Digital Policy Alert. (2022). *India: RBI released regulatory framework for digital lending including provisions on data protection*. https://digitalpolicyalert.org/event/6423-rbi-released-regulatory-framework-for-digital-lending-including-provisions-on-data-protection

Dixon, D. (2024). *Top cyber threats in Fintech and how to reduce cyber risk*. https://cyberlab.co.uk/2024/09/11/top-cyber-threats-in-fintech/

Etiebet, I., & Matthew, U. (2022). *The online lending boom and data privacy concerns in Nigeria*. https://vlex.com/vid/the-online-lending-boom-901058141

Gallagher, C. (2025). *The cybersecurity landscape of 2025: Human behavior as the first line of defense*. https://www.linkedin.com/pulse/cybersecurity-landscape-2025-human-behavior-first-line-gallagher-eabqe

Gilbert, P. (2025). *The role of African regulatory sandboxes in the age of AI*. https://www.connectingafrica.com/ai/the-role-of-african-regulatory-sandboxes-in-the-age-of-ai

Goater, D. (2025). *Cyber threats in finance: Your strategic guide for 2025*. https://www.lepide.com/blog/cyber-threats-in-finance-your-strategic-guide/

GSMA. (2025). *The state of the industry report on mobile money 2025*. https://www.gsma.com/sotir/wp-content/uploads/2025/04/The-State-of-the-Industry-Report-2025_English.pdf

Hariharan, A. (2024). *Data privacy & compliance in financial services: The role of consent governance*. https://ibsintelligence.com/blogs/data-privacy-compliance-in-financial-services-the-role-of-consent-governance/

Joshi, A. (2025). *The growing complexity of global cybersecurity: Moving from challenges to action*. https://www.weforum.org/stories/2025/01/growing-complexity-global-cybersecurity-from-challenges-action/

Kálmán, J. (2025). *The role of regulatory sandboxes in FinTech innovation: A comparative case*.

Katariya, J. (2025). *Fintech cybersecurity: Protecting financial data in the digital age*. https://www.moontechnolabs.com/blog/fintech-cybersecurity/

Khullar, A. (2025). Data breaches and cybersecurity in Fintech—A comprehensive analysis. *International Journal of Innovative Science and Research Technology, 10*(4), 1116–1127. https://ijisrt.com/assets/upload/files/IJISRT25APR1107.pdf

Kost, E. (2025). *Human factors in cybersecurity in 2025*. https://www.upguard.com/blog/human-factors-in-cybersecurity

Massally, T. K., & Duff, S. (2018). *What can we learn from Sierra Leone's new regulatory sandbox?* https://www.cgap.org/blog/what-can-we-learn-sierra-leones-new-regulatory-sandbox

Mate-Kole, E. S., & Bentsi-Enchill, J. (2023). *The bank of Ghana regulatory sandbox*. https://thebftonline.com/2022/09/13/the-bank-of-ghana-regulatory-sandbox/

Matinou, S. K. (2024). *The influence of the GDPR on African data protection standards: A path toward digital sovereignty or a new form of regulatory dominance?* https://www.linkedin.com/pulse/influence-gdpr-african-data-protection-standards-path-samuel-frank-exewf

Mhlanga, D. (2024). The role of big data in financial technology toward financial inclusion. *Frontiers in Big Data, 7*, 1184444.

Mngoma, F. (2024). *The rise of Fintech in Africa: Bridging the gap to financial inclusion and economic growth*. https://www.mandg.co.za/insights/articlesreleases/the-rise-of-fintech-in-africa-bridging-the-gap-to-financial-inclusion-and-economic-growth/

Montini, H. (2025). *Cybersecurity trends: How to be cyber resilient in 2025*. https://www.provendata.com/blog/cyber-security-trends/

Moody's. (2023). *BOG launches regulatory sandbox in Ghana*. https://www.moodys.com/web/en/us/insights/regulatory-news/bog-launches-regulatory-sandbox-in-ghana.html

Nallakaruppan, M. K., Chaturvedi, H., Grover, V., Balusamy, B., Jaraut, P., Bahadur, J., Meena, V. P., & Hameed, I. A. (2024). Credit risk assessment and financial decision support using explainable artificial intelligence. *Risks*, *12*(10), 164.

Nelson, E. (2024). *Fintech compliance and how to maintain it*. https://hyperproof.io/resource/fintech-compliance-and-how-to-maintain-it/

Odeyemi, A. A. (2025). *Digital trust in finance: Why data security is your competitive advantage in 2025*. https://www.linkedin.com/pulse/digital-trust-finance-why-data-security-your-2025-odeyemi-fca-acti-wl89f

Oluokun, A., Ige, A. B., & Ameyaw, M. N. (2024). Building cyber resilience in fintech through AI and GRC integration: An exploratory Study. *GSC Advanced Research and Reviews*, *20*(1), 228–237.

Proshare. (2017). *Safaricom foils attempted cyber attack on M-Pesa platform*. https://proshare.co/articles/safaricom-foils-attempted-cyber-attack-on-m-pesa-platform?menu=Technology&classification=Read&category=Fintech

Rimon, L. L., & Shabana, G. (2024). *Fintech focus: How regulatory events of 2023 should guide financial institutions' New year's resolutions for 2024*. https://www.jenner.com/en/news-insights/publications/fintech-focus-how-regulatory-events-of-2023-should-guide-financial-institutions-new-years-resolutions-for-2024

Rivera, C. (2025). Digital transformation in global finance: How technology is shaping the financial landscape. *Academy of Accounting and Financial Studies Journal*, *29*(S1), 1–3.

Satoh, Y. (2024). *Navigating the risks of AI in finance: Data governance and management are critical*. https://blogs.cfainstitute.org/investor/2024/09/03/navigating-the-risks-of-ai-in-finance-data-governance-and-management-are-critical/

Sen, S. (2024). *Mobile security threats in 2025: How to protect your devices*. https://www.analyticsinsight.net/security/mobile-security-threats-in-2025-how-to-protect-your-devices

Shebalkov, M. (2024). *'Mobile money and huge growth potential'—Mikhail Shebalkov on Fintech in Africa*. https://www.vanguardngr.com/2024/08/mobile-money-and-huge-growth-potential-mikhail-shebalkov-on-fintech-in-africa/

Skamser, C. (2025). *The current state of the FinTech industry: Insights, trends, and expectations for 2025*. https://www.linkedin.com/pulse/current-state-fintech-industry-insights-trends-2025-charles-skamser-1jv6c

Study of the UK, Singapore, and Hungary. https://www.preprints.org/frontend/manuscript/574aeff623b6c648e30cc24fefb99a49/download_pub

Surya, N. (2024). *The ultimate guide to data quality governance in the financial services industry*. https://www.acceldata.io/blog/the-ultimate-guide-to-data-quality-governance-in-the-fintech-industry

Techcabal. (2024). *Building cyber resilience: Navigating the future of cybersecurity in Nigeria's banking and Fintech sectors*. https://techcabal.com/2024/12/24/building-cyber-resilience-navigating-the-future-of-cybersecurity-in-nigerias-banking-and-fintech-sectors/

Thimot, T. (2020). *Cyber threats to the fintech industry a growing concern*. https://fintechmagazine.com/financial-services-finserv/cyber-threats-fintech-industry-growing-concern

Thompsett, L. (2025). *Data analytics: Empowering Fintech and Regtech capabilities*. https://fintechmagazine.com/articles/data-analytics-empowering-fintech-and-regtech-capabilities

Umoga, U. J., Sodiya, E. O., Amoo, O. O., & Atadoga, A. (2024). A critical review of emerging cybersecurity threats in financial technologies. *International Journal of Science and Research Archive, 11*(1), 1810–1817.

Vohra, D. K. (2025). *Exploring risk assessment with machine learning in finance*. https://www.hyperstack.cloud/blog/case-study/exploring-risk-assessment-with-machine-learning-in-finance

World Economic Forum. (2020). *Systems of cyber resilience: secure and trusted FinTech*. https://www3.weforum.org/docs/WEF_Systems_Cyber_Resilience_2020.pdf

CHAPTER 11

Islamic FinTech and Ethical Finance: Opportunities for Inclusive Finance in Africa

Ibrahim Nandom Yakubu, Abdallah Abdul-Salam, Abdul-Hamid Abdul-Wahab, and Alhassan Bunyaminu

Introduction

Financial inclusion remains a formidable development challenge across the African continent, where large segments of the population continue to be excluded from formal financial systems. According to the World Bank Global Findex Database (2021), about 45% of adults in Sub-Saharan Africa do not have access to a formal bank account, with exclusion rates

I. N. Yakubu · A. Abdul-Salam · A.-H. Abdul-Wahab
School of Business, University for Development Studies, Tamale, Ghana
e-mail: ibrahim.yakubu@uds.edu.gh

A. Abdul-Salam
e-mail: abdallah.abdulsalam@uds.edu.gh

A.-H. Abdul-Wahab
e-mail: abdulhamid@uds.edu.gh

A. Bunyaminu (✉)
University of Professional Studies, Accra, Ghana
e-mail: alhassan.bunyaminu@upsamail.edu.gh

I. N. Yakubu (ed.), *Banking on Inclusion*, Sustainable Development Goals Series, https://doi.org/10.1007/978-3-031-96716-0_11

significantly higher in rural areas and among women. The reasons for this include lack of trust in conventional banks, absence of physical infrastructure in remote areas, high transaction costs, and religious or cultural reservations, particularly among Muslim communities. In this context, the emergence of Islamic finance as an ethical, interest-free alternative presents a unique opportunity to extend financial services to underserved populations (Soage, 2020).

Islamic finance is based on principles of equity, justice, and risk-sharing as prescribed by Shariah law. It prohibits interest (*riba*), gambling (*maysir*) excessive uncertainty (*gharar*), and unethical investments, while promoting socially responsible financial transactions (Sarwar, 2024; Shahariman et al., 2024). These principles align closely with the values of many African communities, especially in regions with significant Muslim populations such as Northern Nigeria, Sudan, Somalia, and parts of East and West Africa (Abib, 2020). However, the traditional model of Islamic banking has not been fully effective in overcoming infrastructural, regulatory, and accessibility constraints that hinder outreach to low-income populations (Hamzat & Nwankwo, 2023; Salaudeen & Zakariyah, 2022). This is where financial technology, or FinTech, becomes a game-changer.

FinTech, through mobile banking, digital payments, peer-to-peer lending, and blockchain-based services, offers new tools to address long-standing barriers to finance (Dangkeng, 2025). When applied within the framework of Islamic finance, FinTech solutions can create products that are both Shariah-compliant and accessible to underserved groups. For example, mobile-based Islamic microfinance platforms can provide small-scale, interest-free loans to informal entrepreneurs in rural Ghana or Kenya, while digital zakat (charity) platforms can efficiently distribute funds to the needy during times of crisis (Wahyudi et al., 2024). Such innovations demonstrate how the convergence of technology and Islamic ethics can unlock inclusive financial ecosystems tailored to African realities.

Moreover, the ethical dimension of Islamic finance is not only relevant to Muslims. Its emphasis on social justice, transparency, and avoiding exploitation makes it a valuable model for developing inclusive and responsible financial systems more broadly (Lesmana et al., 2024). In recent years, there has been a growing global interest in ethical finance, driven by concerns over inequality, financial misconduct, and climate risks (Brogi & Lagasio, 2024). In this broader movement, Islamic FinTech represents a distinctive value proposition, particularly in Africa where the informal sector dominates and trust in conventional finance is often limited (Alam, Gupta, & Zameni, 2019).

This chapter aims to explore the role of Islamic FinTech in advancing inclusive finance in Africa. It begins by providing foundational insights into the principles of Islamic finance and their intersection with modern FinTech innovations. The chapter then examines various Islamic FinTech models and their applications in African contexts, highlighting case studies and emerging trends. It also maps the existing market potential and identifies institutional opportunities and regulatory gaps. Finally, the chapter discusses the challenges facing Islamic FinTech in Africa and proposes strategic pathways to scale its impact.

Foundations of Islamic Finance and FinTech

Core Principles of Islamic Finance

Islamic finance is built upon a framework of ethical and religious guidelines that prioritize justice, fairness, and social responsibility in economic transactions (Hassan & Kayed, 2009; Shahariman et al., 2024). Unlike conventional finance, which allows for the charging of interest (*riba*) and speculative investments, Islamic finance prohibits such practices in favor of asset-backed, risk-sharing arrangements that reflect real economic activity (Abiola-Adams et al., 2025). It also mandates that all financial dealings be transparent and free of ambiguity (*gharar*) to prevent unjust enrichment and exploitation (Sarwar, 2024). These principles are outlined in Table 11.1, which summarizes the key components of Islamic finance and their implications in practice.

These principles make Islamic finance not only a religiously guided system but also an ethical and inclusive financial model. In many African countries, where financial trust is low and religious observance is high, this ethical alignment can play a pivotal role in extending financial services to marginalized groups.

FinTech: Transforming Financial Services

FinTech, or financial technology, refers to the digital transformation of financial services through tools such as mobile banking, digital payments, blockchain, and artificial intelligence (Kumari & Devi, 2022). It is

Table 11.1 Key principles of Islamic finance and their practical implications

Principle	*Definition*	*Practical implication in finance*
Riba (Interest)	Prohibition of predetermined or guaranteed returns on loans	Interest-based loans are not allowed; institutions use profit-sharing contracts like ***mudarabah*** and ***musharakah***
Gharar (Uncertainty)	Avoidance of excessive ambiguity in contracts	Contracts must specify clear terms and eliminate speculative conditions
Haram activities	Prohibition of activities harmful to individuals or society	No investment in gambling, alcohol, pornography, or arms
Risk sharing	Parties in a contract must share risks and rewards Fairly	Use of partnership-based finance (e.g., joint ventures)
Asset-backing	Transactions must be linked to tangible assets	Prohibits synthetic or speculative products; encourages real-sector activity

Source Authors' compilation based on Ismayil (2012) and Bertillo and Salando (2013)

rapidly reshaping the global financial landscape by reducing transaction costs, eliminating geographical barriers, and expanding access to unbanked populations (Ediagbonya & Tioluwani, 2023; JIE, 2024). In Africa, where mobile phone penetration is high and traditional banking infrastructure is limited, FinTech has emerged as a powerful tool for democratizing finance (Dahi & Enweruzo, 2024).

FinTech applications have significantly advanced financial inclusion in countries like Kenya and Ghana, where mobile money systems such as M-Pesa and MTN Mobile Money have become mainstream (Abbey, 2024). These platforms have brought millions of individuals into the formal financial system, enabling them to send and receive money, pay bills, and access microcredit from basic mobile devices (Agarwal & Assenova, 2024). The benefits of FinTech also apply to Islamic finance institutions, which can adopt similar models to reach Muslim populations with faith-compliant products. As FinTech enables more customized financial products, the integration of Islamic principles into digital tools provides an opportunity to develop inclusive services that are both ethical and technologically advanced (Risza, 2024). The distinctions between conventional and Islamic FinTech approaches are shown in Table 11.2, illustrating the operational and ethical differences.

The Emergence of Islamic FinTech

Islamic FinTech represents a convergence of two powerful trends: the digital revolution in finance and the resurgence of interest in Shariah-compliant financial products (Alshater et al., 2022). It refers to technology-driven financial innovations that adhere to Islamic legal and ethical standards (Alshater et al., 2022). This emerging sector has given rise to platforms for Shariah-compliant crowdfunding, interest-free lending, digital zakat distribution, Islamic investment screening, and blockchain-based sukuk issuance (Dawood et al., 2022; Hassan et al., 2022). These innovations are not only theoretically interesting but also practically operational in several African and global contexts. Table 11.3 highlights notable Islamic FinTech platforms and their use cases, many of which could be replicated or scaled in Africa, where demand for ethical and inclusive finance is growing.

Blockchain and Smart Contracts in Islamic Finance

Blockchain technology, with its attributes of decentralization, immutability, and transparency, is well suited to support Islamic finance principles (Dahdal et al., 2022). The technology can facilitate real-time auditing, prevent fraud, and enhance trust, which are key concerns for financial institutions in low-trust environments (Gandhi Maniam et al., 2024). Smart contracts, which are self-executing digital agreements, can enforce compliance with Shariah rules automatically. For example, a smart contract could disburse a microloan only if the investment purpose is verified as halal, or calculate and deduct zakat contributions based on income thresholds and rules set by a Shariah board (Rabbani et al., 2025; Rahim et al., 2019). Furthermore, blockchain technology supports the tokenization of assets and sukuk issuance, which can be particularly relevant for African governments or corporations seeking to raise funds in a Shariah-compliant manner (Kharitonova, 2021; Mousavi et al., 2025). By reducing issuance costs and democratizing participation, blockchain-based sukuk platforms can attract diaspora investors and small-scale savers.

Table 11.2 Comparison between conventional FinTech and Islamic FinTech

Dimension	*Conventional FinTech*	*Islamic FinTech*
Underlying Principles	Based on conventional finance principles, including interest-based transactions	Based on Shariah principles prohibiting interest (*riba*), speculation (*gharar*), and unethical investments
Financial Instruments	Utilizes debt-based tools such as loans, credit cards, and derivatives	Utilizes Shariah-compliant contracts such as *Murabaha*, *Mudarabah*, *Musharakah*, *Ijara*, and *Sukuk*
Revenue Model	Primarily earns through interest, fees, commissions, and capital gains	Earns profit through cost-plus sale, fee-based services profit-sharing arrangements and lease-based financing, while avoiding interest income
Risk Sharing	Risk is typically transferred to the borrower or third parties	Emphasizes risk-sharing between parties (e.g., profit-and-loss sharing models)
Regulatory Oversight	Governed by secular financial authorities and global financial standards	Subject to both secular financial regulators and Islamic finance regulators such as IFSB and AAOIFI
Ethical Screening	No mandatory exclusion of unethical industries	Mandatory exclusion of activities involving alcohol, gambling, pork, arms, and non-halal activities
Target Market	Broad market focus regardlessof religious or ethical preferences	Focused on Muslim consumers and ethical investors seeking Shariah-compliant financial solutions
Technology Usage	Employs digital platforms, blockchain, AI, and data analytics	Also employs modern technologies, but integrated with Shariah-compliant logic and contracts
Examples of Services	Robo-advisory, peer-to-peer lending, digital wallets, neobanks	*Zakat* calculation apps, halal investment platforms, Islamic crowdfunding and digital *sukuk* issuance
Governance and Assurance	Corporate governance with focus on legal compliance	Dual governance: corporate + Shariah governance to ensure religious compliance

Source Authors' compilation based on Kılıç and Türkan (2023), Sedania (2021), Suciati et al. (2024)

Table 11.3 Selected Islamic FinTech use cases and platforms

Service type	*Platform*	*Country/Region*	*Description*
Crowdfunding	EthisX, Beehive, ITHBAR, Rawafid, Tameed, DubaiNext, Bambucorn	MENA region (KSA, UAE, Oman, Bahrain, Malaysia, Singapore, Indonesia, Saudi Arabia, others)	Islamic crowdfunding platforms offering Shariah-compliant investment opportunities avoiding prohibited sectors and high-risk speculative investments
Digital Zakat	Al-Arafah Bank digital platforms, Baznas digital zakat platforms	Bangladesh, Malaysia, Indonesia	A digital platform that enables users to make Zakat, Sadaqah, and Waqf contributions online, ensuring Shariah compliance and transparency
Sukuk on Blockchain	Blossom SmartSukuk™	Global (Ethereum blockchain)	A platform for issuing blockchain-based Sukuk, enhancing transparency and efficiency in Islamic capital markets
Islamic Microfinance	Niyah (United Kingdom), Islamic equity crowdfunding and peer-to-peer financing platforms	United Kingdom, Malaysia, Southeast Asia	Digital platforms providing Shariah-compliant microfinance and SME funding, offering interest-free banking products and alternative financing for MSMEs
Takaful (InsurTech)	Ouch!	Malaysia	First digital takaful operator offering simple, cost-effective, and fully digital Shariah-compliant life insurance products with fast claims processing via mobile app

Source Authors' compilation based on Finance (2020), Perzhanovskiy (2023), Abdeldayem and Aldulaimi (2022), Rahman (2025) and TechNodeGlobal (2023)

As illustrated in Box 11.1, platforms like HAQQ Network are pioneering the use of blockchain and smart contracts to revolutionize Islamic capital markets, particularly in the area of sukuk issuance and management.

Box 11.1 HAQQ Network and Tokenized Sukuk
HAQQ Network represents a Shariah-compliant, community-governed blockchain platform aimed at transforming Islamic capital markets through the use of decentralized finance (DeFi). It facilitates the issuance, trading, and management of tokenized sukuk by employing smart contracts and Shariah Oracles, which ensure compliance with Islamic finance principles such as profit-sharing and asset-backing. Through its user-friendly HAQQ Wallet, the platform enables fractional ownership and global investor participation, particularly among retail investors and diaspora communities. By lowering issuance costs and eliminating geographic barriers, HAQQ makes sukuk more accessible. Moreover, its plans to introduce gold-backed stablecoins and tokenized securities integrate tangible assets with blockchain, offering ethical and efficient alternatives to traditional Islamic financial products. This innovation not only advances financial inclusion but also enhances the transparency and liquidity of Islamic financial instruments.

Source HAQQ Insights (2024) and Mathew (2024)

Ethical and Inclusive Potential of Islamic FinTech

Islamic finance, although rooted in religious doctrine, is increasingly recognized for its universal ethical appeal. Its emphasis on social justice, transparency, and community-oriented finance aligns with broader global movements toward sustainable and responsible finance (Mousavi et al., 2025). In Africa, where poverty, inequality, and informality limit financial access, Islamic FinTech offers tools to design affordable and socially grounded financial solutions (World Bank, 2020). For instance, a mobile-based platform offering *qard hasan* (benevolent loans) can support women in rural areas to start small businesses without the burden of interest (Ok, 2025). Similarly, blockchain-enabled zakat distribution platforms can ensure that charitable resources reach the most vulnerable in a timely and accountable manner (Ibrahim & Zakaria, 2021). To better understand the scope for Islamic FinTech, Table 11.4 presents data on Muslim populations and financial inclusion levels in selected African countries.

Table 11.4 highlights key opportunities and challenges for Islamic FinTech across diverse African markets. Countries with high Muslim populations like Sudan, Senegal, and Nigeria show strong or growing

Table 11.4 Muslim population and financial inclusion in selected African countries

Country	*% Muslim population*	*Banked Adults*[1] *(%)*	*Islamic finance presence*
Nigeria	*Over 50%*	*45%*	*Presence of Islamic banks and growing fintech platforms*
Senegal	Over 90%	56%	Strong Islamic finance presence with Islamic banks and microfinance institutions active
Kenya	About 11%	79%	Emerging Islamic finance sector including Islamic banking windows and fintech platforms
South Africa	About 1.5%	85%	Limited Islamic finance presence, some Islamic banking and takaful offerings
Sudan	Over 90%	32%	Well-established Islamic banking sector; Islamic finance is dominant

Source Authors' compilation based on World Bank Global Findex Database (2021) and Galal (2024)

Islamic finance ecosystems; however, financial inclusion remains uneven, especially in Sudan and Nigeria, where less than half of adults are banked (Acheampong & Disman, 2024; Omer, 2023). This creates significant space for Shariah-compliant digital financial services to bridge inclusion gaps. In contrast, Kenya and South Africa, with smaller Muslim populations but higher banked rates, indicate potential for niche Islamic FinTech solutions tailored to minority Muslim communities within broader digital finance landscapes (Salim, 2017). Overall, the table suggests that Islamic FinTech can play a critical role in expanding access to ethical finance, particularly in underbanked yet religiously aligned regions, by leveraging mobile platforms and inclusive technologies.

Islamic FinTech Innovations for Inclusion

The emergence of Islamic FinTech is reshaping the contours of financial inclusion across Africa and other developing regions (Arcot et al., 2024). By merging Shariah-compliant finance with digital technologies, Islamic FinTech is enabling access to ethical and culturally aligned

[1] Based on the World Bank Global Findex Database 2021 (bank account ownership among adults).

financial services for individuals and communities historically excluded from the formal financial system (Rabbani et al., 2025; Rahim et al., 2019). These innovations address three critical dimensions of inclusion: everyday financial access, social redistribution, and long-term investment. This section discusses Islamic FinTech innovations grouped under three thematic umbrellas: digital financial services, platforms for social finance, and investment infrastructure.

Shariah-Compliant Digital Financial Services

Islamic FinTech is reshaping financial access by delivering Shariah-compliant services through digital platforms. It avoids interest-based transactions and promotes ethical finance through models like *mudarabah* (profit-sharing) and non-interest digital wallets (Kasujja, 2018). Peer-to-peer lending and crowdfunding platforms, using structures such as *musharakah* and *qard hasan*, enable small businesses and entrepreneurs to access capital without collateral (BEKHTI, 2025). These community-driven platforms support halal enterprises and real estate projects, particularly for underserved African MSMEs. Additionally, *takaful* (Islamic cooperative insurance) is now offered via mobile apps, providing affordable coverage for health, agriculture, and businesses (Nazarov & Dhiraj, 2019). Rooted in mutual assistance, these innovations make Islamic financial services more accessible to low-income and underbanked populations. As illustrated in Box 11.2, the use of *muzara'ah*-based Islamic crowdfunding in Mali demonstrates how faith-driven financial innovation can address agricultural financing gaps, promote inclusive rural development, and align with both Shariah principles and broader sustainability goals (Sylla, 2023).

Box 11.2 Muzara'ah-Based Islamic Crowdfunding in Mali
In Mali, Islamic crowdfunding platforms are leveraging the *muzara'ah* profit-sharing model to deliver Shariah-compliant financing to smallholder farmers. Rather than earning interest, investors participate in peer-to-peer digital crowdfunding by funding agricultural ventures and receiving a share of the harvest profits. These platforms integrate blockchain technology to enhance transparency and are guided by Shariah advisory boards to ensure adherence to ethical and Islamic principles. This financing model offers rural farmers affordable, interest-free capital, fostering sustainable

agriculture, employment opportunities, and poverty alleviation. While infrastructural and regulatory challenges remain, the initiative reflects the core Islamic values of risk-sharing and social equity, highlighting the capacity of Islamic FinTech to support marginalized communities in Africa's farming sector.

Source Sylla (2023)

Platforms for Islamic Social Finance and Philanthropy

Islamic social finance, particularly through *zakat* and *waqf*, is being transformed by digital technology to enhance poverty reduction and social equity (Atah et al., 2018). Digital zakat platforms automate calculations and disbursements, using tools like blockchain to ensure transparency, accountability, and real-time donation tracking (Khairi et al., 2024). Platforms such as Global Sadaqah increase donor trust and improve the impact of charitable giving. Similarly, modern waqf platforms are introducing asset tokenization and smart contracts, enabling communities to co-invest in development initiatives while preserving the integrity of endowments (Aini et al., 2024). This innovation is especially valuable in Africa, where many dormant waqf assets could be reactivated to support sectors like education, healthcare, and rural development.

As shown in Box 11.3, Nigeria's adoption of the Qitmeer blockchain demonstrates the potential of digital infrastructure to transform Islamic philanthropic systems by improving governance, accountability, and the social impact of zakat distribution.

Box 11.3 Nigeria's Qitmeer Blockchain for Transparent Zakat Management

In Nigeria, the Qitmeer blockchain network is being used to improve zakat distribution by promoting transparency, traceability, and accountability in the management of zakat funds. The platform records every transaction on an immutable public ledger and automates zakat calculations in line with Shariah guidelines, thereby enhancing trust and reducing the risk of fraud. Each zakat contributor is assigned a unique identification number, and the system integrates with government databases to verify recipient eligibility, ensuring more accurate and efficient fund allocation. This technology-driven model has boosted donor confidence, curbed corruption, and enhanced the impact of poverty reduction initiatives, serving as a strong example of how blockchain can modernize and strengthen zakat administration across Africa.

Source Al-Taani et al. (2024)

Investment and Infrastructure Innovations

Islamic FinTech is increasingly channeling ethical investment into infrastructure and development projects through Shariah-compliant tools like sukuk and halal investment apps (Cherqaoui, 2022). Digital sukuk platforms use blockchain to issue asset-backed Islamic bonds that fund projects such as roads, hospitals, and schools, offering returns through profit-sharing instead of interest (Shahariman et al., 2024). Countries like Senegal and Nigeria are adopting sukuk to finance public infrastructure and attract diaspora investment (Mousavi et al., 2025). Meanwhile, Shariah-compliant robo-advisors and investment apps are making ethical investing more accessible by screening out non-halal sectors and customizing portfolios based on users' risk preferences (BEKHTI, 2025). These innovations are expanding financial inclusion, especially among young, urban Africans seeking secure and faith-aligned investment options via mobile technology.

Market Landscape and Potential in Africa

The African continent offers fertile ground for the expansion of Islamic FinTech. With a growing Muslim population, widespread mobile technology adoption, and persistent financial exclusion, the region presents both a moral imperative and a market opportunity for inclusive, Shariah-compliant financial solutions (Naima, 2024). However, realizing this potential requires a holistic understanding of the demographic, institutional, and infrastructural landscape across different countries and regions. This section explores the evolving market dynamics that shape the potential of Islamic FinTech in Africa, focusing on population trends, financial access indicators, mobile infrastructure, and the current state of Islamic financial institutions. It also highlights key countries leading the Islamic FinTech charge and identifies emerging opportunities for growth.

Demographic and Financial Inclusion Trends

Africa is home to a significant and growing Muslim population, with an estimated 50% of the continent's people identifying as Muslim (Galal, 2024). Countries like Nigeria, Egypt, Sudan, Senegal, Mali, and Somalia have Muslim populations ranging from 50 to over 90 percent. These demographics create a strong demand base for financial services that align with Islamic values. Despite this potential, financial inclusion remains low across many African countries as reported by the World Bank Global Findex Database (2021). Among Muslim communities, barriers to inclusion are not only economic and infrastructural but also cultural and religious. Many Muslims avoid conventional banks due to the prohibition of *riba* (interest) and the lack of halal financial options (Andani, 2021). This gap presents an opportunity for Islamic FinTech to address both faith-based and structural barriers to inclusion by offering digital, Shariah-compliant financial products tailored to local needs.

Mobile and Digital Readiness

One of Africa's greatest assets in driving financial innovation is its mobile-first ecosystem. According to GSMA (2023), Sub-Saharan Africa is home to 527 million unique mobile subscribers which is expected to rise to 751 million by 2030, and mobile internet penetration is growing rapidly, particularly among young people (Gurara, 2024). Mobile money platforms such as M-Pesa in Kenya, MTN Mobile Money in Ghana, and Orange Money in West Africa have already demonstrated the transformative potential of mobile technology in financial inclusion (Kitimbo, 2021).

Islamic FinTech platforms can leverage this infrastructure to deliver services such as Islamic digital banking, mobile takaful, crowdfunding, and zakat distribution without the need for costly physical branches (Wahyudi et al., 2024). The ubiquity of mobile phones allows even rural and nomadic populations to engage with financial services via USSD codes, SMS, and lightweight apps, making FinTech a powerful enabler of inclusive Islamic finance (Muneeza & Mustapha, 2021). Countries like Kenya, Nigeria, Egypt, and South Africa already have robust mobile ecosystems and high FinTech activity, providing a foundation for expanding Shariah-compliant digital products.

Islamic Financial Institutions in Africa

While Islamic finance remains underdeveloped in many African countries compared to regions like the Middle East and Southeast Asia, the last two decades have seen steady growth in institutions offering Shariah-compliant services. As at year 2020, there were more than 80 Islamic financial institutions operating across Africa, including full-fledged Islamic banks, Islamic windows within conventional banks, takaful operators, and microfinance institutions (Moody's Investors Service, 2020). Nigeria, for instance, is home to Jaiz Bank, the country's first Islamic bank, which has grown its customer base to over 500,000 clients. Sudan operates a fully Islamized financial system, while Senegal and Morocco have established regulatory frameworks to support Islamic banking (Soetan & Mogaji, 2024). In Kenya, Islamic windows within banks such as Gulf African Bank and First Community Bank provide Shariah-compliant services alongside takaful products (Kiyalu, 2022). However, these institutions are often limited in reach and constrained by regulatory fragmentation, low public awareness, and a shortage of Shariah-compliant product offerings. Islamic FinTech has the potential to fill this gap by expanding outreach, automating compliance, and introducing innovative products at lower costs.

Key Market Drivers and Enablers

Remittances and regulatory reforms are key enablers of Islamic FinTech growth in Africa. Many African countries receive substantial remittance inflows from Muslim-majority nations, particularly in the Gulf region (Bakar & Ahmad). This creates a strong market for Shariah-compliant remittance services and diaspora investment platforms that align with Islamic principles. By offering halal financial channels, Islamic FinTech firms can enhance financial inclusion while tapping into this cross-border economic link (Muneeza & Mustapha, 2021). On the regulatory front, several African countries are taking steps to create enabling environments for Islamic finance. Nigeria, Senegal, Morocco, and Tunisia have initiated reforms to support Shariah-compliant financial services, while Ghana is also considering the introduction of Islamic banking (Conteh et al., 2022). These efforts signal growing institutional support for Islamic FinTech, paving the way for more inclusive and diversified financial systems across the continent. Additionally, growing awareness of Islamic social finance tools such as zakat and waqf offers further opportunities for digital innovation that aligns with faith and social justice (Zahari et al., 2024).

Challenges and Regulatory Considerations

While Islamic FinTech holds significant promise for addressing financial exclusion and promoting ethical finance across Africa, its growth is impeded by a complex array of structural, institutional, and regulatory challenges (Koanda, 2025). These constraints not only limit the reach and scalability of innovative solutions but also expose gaps in policy, compliance, infrastructure, and capacity. Understanding these challenges is essential to designing interventions that can support the safe and sustainable development of Islamic FinTech across diverse African contexts. This section outlines some key challenges to the adoption of Islamic FinTech.

Limited Regulatory Frameworks

Across Africa, most countries lack integrated frameworks that address both Islamic finance and digital financial services (Abubakar & Aysan, 2023). While some nations have Islamic banking laws or FinTech regulations, very few combine them to guide Islamic FinTech operations. This absence of clarity forces startups into regulatory grey zones, making licensing, product approval, and compliance uncertain. Regulatory sandboxes often exclude Shariah-compliant models, limiting experimentation (Kismawadi, 2024). Inconsistent or outdated legal provisions discourage innovation and external investment. Additionally, the divergence in legal interpretations across jurisdictions complicates cross-border operations. This fragmented and underdeveloped policy environment remains a major obstacle to formalizing and scaling Islamic FinTech initiatives.

Shariah Compliance and Governance

Shariah compliance is central to Islamic FinTech credibility, yet most countries lack structured mechanisms to oversee and enforce it (Muhamad Sori & Perwiragama, 2025). There is a shortage of Shariah scholars who understand both Islamic law and emerging technologies, which weakens product validation. Many startups operate without Shariah boards or rely on ad hoc advisory services, resulting in inconsistent interpretations and practices (Salam et al., 2023). National financial regulators often have limited capacity to assess or verify Shariah compliance in digital contexts. The absence of standardized guidelines and audit tools undermines consumer trust and market coherence. These governance gaps make it difficult to ensure authenticity, transparency, and accountability.

Cybersecurity and Consumer Protection

Islamic FinTech platforms are increasingly exposed to digital threats, but cybersecurity and consumer protection frameworks remain underdeveloped (Rabbani et al., 2025). Many startups lack robust encryption systems, secure data storage, or user authentication protocols. In environments with low digital literacy, users are vulnerable to fraud, phishing scams, and identity theft. Trust in financial systems, especially in religious contexts, is fragile, and breaches can have reputational or even spiritual consequences (Kulshrestha et al., 2022). Platforms handling sensitive funds such as zakat or waqf are particularly at risk if systems are compromised. Furthermore, most jurisdictions lack comprehensive consumer protection laws tailored to the specific risks posed by Islamic digital finance.

Low Public Awareness and Digital Literacy

A significant barrier to Islamic FinTech adoption is the limited public awareness of both Islamic finance principles and digital financial tools (Alshater et al., 2022). Many potential users, particularly in rural or underserved communities, remain unfamiliar with halal finance concepts such as mudarabah, qard hasan, or takaful (Shahariman et al., 2024). Simultaneously, low levels of digital literacy prevent users from confidently navigating mobile platforms, interpreting contracts, or managing financial risks (Ogunola et al., 2024). This dual knowledge gap disproportionately affects women, older adults, and informal sector workers. Mistrust of financial institutions, past experiences with fraud, and misinformation about digital Islamic finance further hinder uptake across various demographic and cultural groups.

Infrastructure and Connectivity Constraints

Basic infrastructure deficits in many African countries hinder the effective delivery of Islamic FinTech services. In rural and peri-urban areas, mobile network coverage is limited, electricity supply is unreliable, and internet access is often expensive or unavailable (Kainja, 2023). These limitations disrupt real-time financial transactions, digital onboarding, and mobile-based takaful or zakat platforms. The absence of foundational digital infrastructure such as biometric ID systems or interoperable payment gateways also constrains integration with national financial ecosystems (Smith, 2025). Poor infrastructure particularly affects the populations Islamic FinTech aims to serve: low-income, remote, and informally employed individuals. Without dependable digital access, financial inclusion remains largely aspirational.

Jurisdictional Fragmentation

Regulatory fragmentation across African jurisdictions limits the cross-border expansion and interoperability of Islamic FinTech platforms (Salami, 2024). Each country applies different interpretations of Shariah law and maintains distinct rules regarding financial licensing, taxation, consumer data protection, and electronic transactions. These variations increase legal uncertainty and raise the cost of compliance for startups seeking regional reach. A crowdfunding platform or Islamic investment app certified in one country may face disqualification in another due to conflicting legal or religious standards (Sudarwanto et al., 2023). The lack of shared frameworks or mutual recognition between regulators undermines market integration. As a result, Islamic FinTech remains siloed within national boundaries.

Strategic Pathways and Policy Recommendations

As Islamic FinTech continues to gain traction across Africa, the realization of its full potential depends not only on technological innovation but also on strategic policy actions, regulatory reform, and cross-sector collaboration (Alshater et al., 2022). The challenges outlined in the previous section highlight the urgent need for coordinated and forward-looking interventions. This section proposes strategic pathways and policy recommendations to create a robust, inclusive, and Shariah-compliant digital finance ecosystem in Africa.

A foundational step is the development of integrated regulatory frameworks that accommodate both Islamic finance principles and digital financial innovations. National financial regulators, including central banks and securities commissions, must work closely with Shariah advisory councils, Islamic finance practitioners, and FinTech associations to establish clear, coherent, and innovation-friendly policies. These frameworks should define licensing procedures for Islamic digital platforms, establish guidelines for Shariah-compliant digital products, and include Islamic FinTech in regulatory sandboxes. By codifying rules around smart contracts, profit-sharing structures, and permissible financial assets, regulators can reduce legal ambiguity and encourage investor participation.

Equally important is the standardization of Shariah compliance practices. Countries should establish or strengthen centralized Shariah supervisory boards that provide oversight and accreditation for Islamic FinTech products. These boards must be equipped with digital tools to conduct real-time audits and provide guidance on emerging technologies such as blockchain, artificial intelligence, and smart contracts. Regional collaboration through institutions like the African Union can also help harmonize Shariah interpretations and reduce inconsistencies that currently fragment the market. Standardization will build public trust and facilitate cross-border interoperability among Islamic FinTech platforms.

To strengthen user confidence and ensure ethical integrity, cybersecurity and consumer protection policies must be prioritized. Governments should mandate minimum digital security standards for all FinTech providers, including two-factor authentication, data encryption, and anti-fraud systems. Consumer protection regulations should be adapted to Islamic contexts, especially for services that involve charitable funds like zakat or waqf. These regulations must include disclosure rules, grievance mechanisms, and Shariah-consistent dispute resolution channels. Educational campaigns to raise user awareness of digital risks and ethical safeguards will further strengthen the ecosystem.

Addressing the issue of low public awareness and digital literacy is critical to mainstreaming Islamic FinTech. Policymakers, financial institutions, and religious leaders should collaborate to design targeted financial education programs. These initiatives should explain the principles of Islamic finance, the functionalities of digital platforms, and the responsibilities of users. Mass media, mosques, and community-based organizations can serve as effective channels for delivering localized and culturally relevant messages. Additionally, FinTech providers should adopt user-centered design approaches to create interfaces that are intuitive, multilingual, and accessible to individuals with low literacy or digital experience.

Investing in digital infrastructure and identity systems is essential for scaling Islamic FinTech to underserved regions. Governments must prioritize expanding mobile broadband access, improving electricity supply, and reducing data costs in rural areas. At the same time, robust national digital identity systems integrated with financial platforms will facilitate secure onboarding, targeted zakat distribution, and efficient claims management for takaful. Interoperability between identity, payment, and regulatory systems will also reduce compliance burdens and transaction costs for providers, enabling innovation to thrive even in low-resource settings.

Finally, there is an urgent need for regional regulatory harmonization to support the growth of Islamic FinTech across borders. As part of the African Continental Free Trade Area's broader agenda of financial integration, member states should work toward mutual recognition of Islamic FinTech licenses, joint Shariah compliance standards, and cross-border dispute resolution mechanisms. Regional innovation hubs, knowledge-sharing platforms, and public–private partnerships can further accelerate the development of inclusive Islamic FinTech models tailored to Africa's diverse economic, legal, and cultural landscapes.

Conclusion

The rise of Islamic FinTech marks a transformative moment for inclusive finance in Africa. By combining the ethical foundations of Islamic finance with the reach and efficiency of digital technologies, Islamic FinTech has the potential to reshape how financial services are designed, delivered, and experienced, particularly for populations that have long remained excluded from the formal financial system. As this chapter has demonstrated, Islamic FinTech goes beyond providing financial access; it offers culturally grounded, socially responsible, and economically empowering alternatives that resonate with millions of people across the continent.

Africa's rapidly growing Muslim population, widespread mobile penetration, and vibrant entrepreneurial ecosystem present fertile ground for

Islamic digital finance. Innovations such as Shariah-compliant mobile banking, crowdfunding platforms, blockchain-based zakat distribution, and digital takaful are already gaining traction in countries like Nigeria, Senegal, Kenya, and Sudan. These tools address not only structural barriers to finance but also religious and cultural sensitivities that have historically deterred many from using conventional banking products. As such, Islamic FinTech is emerging as a vital instrument in advancing financial justice and resilience in both Muslim-majority and mixed-faith societies.

However, unlocking the full promise of Islamic FinTech requires more than technological adaptation. Persistent challenges, such as fragmented regulations, inconsistent Shariah oversight, low financial literacy, and inadequate infrastructure, must be systematically addressed. Without robust legal frameworks, harmonized standards, and strong consumer protection mechanisms, Islamic FinTech risks remaining fragmented, underutilized, or misaligned with its core ethical principles. The integrity and sustainability of this emerging sector depend on proactive governance and inclusive policy design that reflects Africa's unique demographic, cultural, and economic realities.

Looking ahead, Islamic FinTech holds immense potential to contribute to broader development goals, including poverty reduction, gender equity, and the deepening of financial markets. Its emphasis on fairness, transparency, and shared prosperity aligns with Africa's aspirations for inclusive growth and ethical transformation. As African countries continue to explore innovative financial models to serve their people, Islamic FinTech offers a compelling blueprint, one rooted in values, enabled by technology, and oriented toward collective well-being.

References

Abbey, S. N. A. (2024). *The Role of technology in financial inclusion—A case study mobile money penetration in Ghana.*

Abdeldayem, M. M., & Aldulaimi, S. H. (2022). *Financial technology application and Islamic crowdfunding.* Paper presented at the 2022 ASU International Conference in Emerging Technologies for Sustainability and Intelligent Systems (ICETSIS).

Abib, A. (2020). *Sources of development funds for Somalia with reference to blended finance.* Hamad Bin Khalifa University (Qatar).

Abiola-Adams, O., Azubuike, C., Sule, A. K., & Okon, R. (2025). The impact of Islamic finance on global asset and liability management practices. *Gulf Journal of Advance Business Research, 3*(1), 186–200.

Abubakar, J., & Aysan, A. F. (2023). Islamic specialized FinTech for inclusive and sustainable growth in Sub-Saharan Africa. In *Islamic Finance, FinTech, and the road to sustainability: Reframing the approach in the post-pandemic era* (pp. 283–307): Springer.

Acheampong, K., & Disman, D. (2024). Empowering the poor through financial and social inclusion in Africa an Islamic perspective. By Abdelrahman Elzahi Saaid Ali (Ed.), Switzerland: Springer Nature. 2022.£ 130.00 (pbk). ISBN: 9783031009259. In: Wiley Online Library.

Agarwal, A., & Assenova, V. A. (2024). Mobile money as a stepping stone to financial inclusion: How digital multisided platforms fill institutional voids. *Organization Science, 35*(3), 769–787.

Aini, S. N. M., Roslan, S. N. I. B., Nazuki, N. N., Helmi, F. I. M., & Dahlan, A. R. A. (2024). 'Sadaqahnow' project business model: Trusted fundraising mobile application for enhancing the well-being of local & global communities. *Journal of Information Systems and Digital Technologies, 6*(1), 54–73.

Al-Taani, A. H. M., Al-Zaqeba, M. A. A., Maabreh, H. M. A., & Jarah, B. A. F. (2024). Exploring the impact of digital accounting and digital zakat on improving business sustainability in the Middle East and Malaysia. *International Journal of Advanced and Applied Sciences, 11*(1), 56–67.

Alam, N., Gupta, L., & Zameni, A. (2019). *Fintech and Islamic finance*. Springer.

Alshater, M. M., Saba, I., Supriani, I., & Rabbani, M. R. (2022). Fintech in Islamic finance literature: A review. *Heliyon, 8*(9).

Andani, H. M. (2021). *Financial exclusion due to religious reasons: Examining sociodemographic factors*. Hamad Bin Khalifa University (Qatar),

Arcot, P. P., Sayed, G., Parekh, B., Balasubramanian, J., & Sudheer, V. (2024). The interplay of ethics, culture, and society in the age of finance digital transformation. *Journal of Southwest Jiaotong University, 59*(2), 139–163.

Atah, U. I., Nasr, W. M. A., & Mohammed, M. O. (2018). *The role of zakat as an Islamic social finance towards achieving sustainable development goals: A case study of Northern Nigeria*. Paper presented at the E-Proceedings of the Global Conference on Islamic Economics and Finance.

Bakar, M. D., & Ahmad, A. U. F. Professor Dr Mohammad Hashim Kamali, Founding CEO.

BEKHTI, D. (2025). *In module Financial Technology: Handout directed to second-year master's students in business economics*.

Bertillo, J. B., & Salando, D. J. (2013). Principles and practice of Islamic finance systems. *Available at SSRN 1880028*.

Brogi, M., & Lagasio, V. (2024). New but naughty. The evolution of misconduct in FinTech. *International Review of Financial Analysis, 95*, 103489.

Cherqaoui, S. (2022). *islamic finance growth a catalyst for financial development.* Hamad Bin Khalifa University (Qatar).

Conteh, S., Sano, M. A. A., Sawaneh, K., Shuaib, B. L., & Hassan, R. (2022). Regulatory framework of Islamic finance in selected West African countries. In *Islamic Finance in Africa* (pp. 44–67). Edward Elgar Publishing.

Dahdal, A., Truby, J., & Ismailov, O. (2022). The role and potential of blockchain technology in Islamic finance. *European Business Law Review, 33*(2).

Dahi, M. B., & Enweruzo, C. O. (2024). Fintech's role in empowering SMEs financing with a focus on Mauritania. *Open Journal of Business and Management, 12*(03), 1477–1487.

Dangkeng, A. (2025). Fintech and financial inclusion: How digital payment systems empower small entrepreneurs. *Journal of Indonesian Scholars for Social Research, 5*(1), 46–55.

Dawood, H., Al Zadjali, F., Al Rawahi, M., Karim, S., & Hazik, M. (2022). Business trends & challenges in Islamic FinTech: A systematic literature review. *F1000Research, 11*, 329.

Ediagbonya, V., & Tioluwani, C. (2023). The role of fintech in driving financial inclusion in developing and emerging markets: Issues, challenges and prospects. *Technological Sustainability, 2*(1), 100–119.

Finance, B. (2020). Blockchain microfinance sukuk wins 2 awards, yields 15.5% despite covid-19 stress. *Blockchain microfinance Sukuk wins 2 awards, yields 15.5% despite covid-19 stress.*

Galal, S. (2024). *Muslim population in Africa 2024, by country*. Retrieved from https://www.statista.com/statistics/1368589/muslim-population-in-africa-by-country/

Gandhi Maniam, P. S., Acharya, N., Sassenberg, A.-M., & Soar, J. (2024). Determinants of blockchain technology adoption in the Australian agricultural supply chain: A systematic literature review. *Sustainability, 16*(13), 5806.

GSMA. (2023). *The mobile economy Sub-Saharan Africa 2023.* Retrieved from https://www.gsma.com/solutions-and-impact/connectivity-for-good/mobile-economy/sub-saharan-africa/

Gurara, M. (2024). *Why women choose homebirth with traditional birth attendants and the effectiveness of interventions to promote institutional childbirth in rural Gamo zone, Southern Ethiopia, 2017–2022.* University of Antwerp,

Hamzat, M. A., & Nwankwo, T. (2023). Islamic banking and financial inclusion of women in Lagos. *FinTech and AI in Finance (FinTAF), 1*(1).

HAQQ Insights. (2024). Retrieved from https://www.haqq.network/blog/haqq-insights-understanding-defi-sukuk

Hassan, M. K., & Kayed, R. N. (2009). The global financial crisis, risk management and social justice in Islamic finance. *Risk Management and Social Justice in Islamic Finance*.

Hassan, M. K., Rabbani, M. R., Rashid, M., & Trinugroho, I. (2022). Islamic fintech, blockchain and crowdfunding: current landscape and path forward. In *FinTech in Islamic financial institutions: Scope, challenges, and implications in Islamic Finance* (pp. 307–340). Springer.

Ibrahim, A., & Zakaria, M. (2021). Using blockchain for managing zakat distribution: A juristic analytical study. *Al-Hikmah International Journal of Islamic Studies and Human Sciences, 4*(2), 1–25.

Ismayil, S. I. (2012). *The principles of Islamic finance*. Eastern Mediterranean University (EMU).

JIE, T. (2024). *Unlocking potential: The impact of financial technology (FinTech) on financial inclusion*.

Kainja, J. (2023). Legal and policy gaps affecting digital rights in Malawi. *Journal of Humanities, 31*(1), 1–19.

Kasujja, K. M. (2018). *Technology and financial disintermediation with a special reference to blockchain and Islamic Finance*. Hamad Bin Khalifa University (Qatar).

Khairi, K. F., Laili, N. H., & Ahmad, A. (2024). The newly developed of blockchain architecture on Zakat collection in Malaysia: A case in MAIW-PPPZ, Malaysia. *Global Business & Management Research, 16*(2).

Kharitonova, A. (2021). *Capabilities of blockchain technology in tokenization of economy*. Paper presented at the 1st International Scientific Conference" Legal Regulation of the Digital Economy and Digital Relations: Problems and Prospects of Development" (LARDER 2020).

Kılıç, G., & Türkan, Y. (2023). The emergence of Islamic fintech and its applications. *International Journal of Islamic Economics and Finance Studies, 9*(2), 212–236.

Kismawadi, E. R. (2024). Islamic fintech: Navigating the regulatory framework and promoting financial inclusion in Gulf Cooperation Council (GCC) countries. *Journal of Islamic Marketing, 16*(6), 1742–1769.

Kitimbo, A. (2021). Mobile money and financial inclusion of migrants in sub-Saharan Africa. In *Research handbook on international migration and digital technology* (pp. 251–266). Edward Elgar Publishing.

Kiyalu, H. (2022). *Strategies adopted by Islamic banks to increase their profits in Kenya*. University of Nairobi.

Koanda, Y. (2025). Financial technologies in fragile environments: Triumphs and trials in Africa and the Middle East. In *The Palgrave handbook of FinTech in Africa and Middle East: Connecting the dots of a rapidly emerging ecosystem* (pp. 1–34). Springer.

Kulshrestha, P., Gautam, R., & Singh, A. (2022). *Cyber crime, regulation and security: Contemporary issues and challenges*. Libertatem Media Private Limited.

Kumari, A., & Devi, N. C. (2022). The impact of fintech and blockchain technologies on banking and financial services. *Technology Innovation Management Review, 12*(1/2).

Lesmana, M., Afif, M., Husni, N. I., Raihan, F., & Maulana, I. (2024). Integrating Islamic finance principles and the digital disruptive age to support global sustainability. *International Journal of Advanced Research in Economics and Finance, 6*(2), 204–216.

Mathew, J. (2024). *Blockchain network HAQQ reveals plans for gold-backed stablecoin, tokenised sukuk to boost Islamic interbank market*. Retrieved from https://www.arabianbusiness.com/industries/banking-finance/blockchain-network-haqq-reveals-plans-for-gold-backed-stablecoin-tokenised-sukuk-to-boost-islamic-interbank-market

Moody's Investors Service. (2020). *Cross-sector—Islamic Finance: GCC and Malaysia will drive growth across Sharīʿah-Compliant Products in 2020*. March, pp. 1–19.

Mousavi, S. H., Tohidinia, A., & Mousavi, S. M. (2025). Transforming Islamic finance: The impact of blockchain and Smart Sukuk. *Access Journal, 6*(1), 184–201.

Muhamad Sori, Z. B., & Perwiragama, S. A. (2025). *Enhancing transparency and governance: Implementing Sharia compliance framework in Indonesia's IPF sector*.

Muneeza, A., & Mustapha, Z. (2021). Islamic fintech and financial inclusion. *Islamic FinTech: insights and solutions*, 173–190.

Naima, U. (2024). *Bridging the digital gender divide through digital financial inclusion: A case of low-income Bangladeshi Muslim women in South East Queensland*. Queensland University of Technology.

Nazarov, I. I., & Dhiraj, N. S. (2019). A conceptual understanding and significance of takaful (Islamic insurance): History, concept, models and products. *International Journal for Innovation Education and Research, 7*(4), 280–298.

Ogunola, A. A., Sonubi, T., Toromade, R. O., Ajayi, O. O., & Maduakor, A. H. (2024). *The intersection of digital safety and financial literacy: Mitigating financial risks in the digital economy*.

Ok, E. (2025). *Comparative analysis of Islamic and conventional microfinance approaches*.

Omer, A. M. (2023). *The impact of financial inclusion on poverty alleviation through Islamic banks= İslami bankalar aracılığıyla Finansal Kapsayıcılığın yoksulluğun azaltılmasına etkisi*. Sakarya Üniversitesi.

Perzhanovskiy, N. (2023). Retrieved from https://lenderkit.com/blog/top-10-islamic-crowdfunding-platforms-and-how-to-build-one/

Rabbani, M. R., Bawazir, H., Khan, S., Karim, S., & Chebab, D. (2025). Smart contract-based Islamic Fintech model for Mudaraba financing. *International Journal of Business Innovation and Research, 36*(2), 248–262.

Rahim, N. F., Bakri, M. H., & Yahaya, S. N. (2019). Fintech and Shariah principles in smart contracts. In *FinTech as a disruptive technology for financial institutions* (pp. 207–220). IGI Global.

Rahman, M. (2025). Retrieved from https://www.thedailystar.net/supplements/swipe-celebrate/news/digital-zakat-faith-meets-fintech-3852991

Risza, H. (2024). *The intention of young muslim generation using the Islamic E-Wallet services in Indonesia.*

Salam, S. A., Salleh, H. M., Muflih, B. K., & Jaiyeoba, H. B. (2023). Roles of Islamic Shariah scholars in The Halal Assurance system. *Journal of Halal Science and Technology, 2*(1), 40–47.

Salami, I. (2024). *Financial technology law and regulation in Africa.* Taylor & Francis.

Salaudeen, A. O., & Zakariyah, H. (2022). Challenges hindering Islamic microfinance banks' sustainable financial inclusion: A case of al-hayat microfinance bank in Ogun State, Nigeria. *El Barka: Journal of Islamic Economics and Business, 5*(1), 24–50.

Salim, I. M. (2017). Expanding the Islamic financial services frontier: Lessons from Islamic finance sector in Kenya. *Journal of Islamic Banking and Finance, 5*(1), 1–6.

Sarwar, M. (2024). Financial risk management: It's implications and compliance with Shari'ah standards. *Al-Marjān, 2*(3), 1–17.

Sedania. (2021). How Fintech is different from Islamic Fintech? *sed.* Retrieved from https://www.sedaniainnovator.com/post/how-fintech-is-different-from-islamic-fintech

Shahariman, A. A. B., Asari, N., Sulaiman, N., & Marzuki, N. (2024). *Islamic principles and their application in personal financial decision making. Accessed* December 15.

Smith, B. (2025). *A novel digital payment architecture: A unified payment interface and its systematic transformation of financial infrastructure.*

Soage, A. B. (2020). An overview of Islamic finance: History, instruments, prospects. *Journal of the Sociology and Theory of Religion, 9*, 60–81.

Soetan, T. O., & Mogaji, E. (2024). Financial services providers in Nigeria. In *Financial services in Nigeria: The path towards financial inclusion, economic development and sustainable growth* (pp. 49–103). Springer.

Suciati, R., Setiawan, D., & Misdawita, M. (2024). Comparison analysis of Sharia financial technology with conventional financial technology in Indonesia. *Jurnal Ilmiah Ekonomi Islam, 10*(1), 313–317.

Sudarwanto, A. S., Kharisma, D. B., & Cahyaningsih, D. T. (2023). Islamic crowdfunding and Shariah compliance regulation: Problems and oversight. *Journal of Financial Crime, 31*(4), 1022–1036.

Sylla, M. (2023). Muzara'ah-based crowdfunding for financing small farmers in Mali. *Journal of Islamic Economics, 3*(1), 31–45.

TechNode Global. (2023). *Insurtech Ouch! enters market as the first digital Takaful operator in Malaysia*. Retrieved from https://technode.global/2023/08/17/insurtech-ouch-enters-market-as-the-first-digital-takaful-operator-in-malaysia/

Wahyudi, I., Amalia, E., & Rini, R. (2024). Revamping tradition with Tech: Guiding innovation in Zakat for social good. *Al-Risalah: Jurnal Studi Agama dan Pemikiran Islam, 15*(1), 18–40.

World Bank. (2020). Leveraging Islamic fintech to improve financial inclusion. *Leveraging Islamic Fintech to Improve Financial Inclusion.*

World Bank Global Findex Database. (2021). Financial inclusion, digital payments, and resilience in the Age of COVID-19. *The Global Findex Database*. https://doi.org/10.1596/978-1-4648-1897-4

Zahari, S. A., Shahimi, S., Alma'amun, S., & Ismail, A. G. (2024). Ethics in focus: A bibliometric and content analysis of Islamic banking and finance research. *Journal of Islamic Monetary Economics and Finance, 10*(2), 249–276.

CHAPTER 12

Regulatory Framework and Policy Challenges in FinTech-Driven Financial Inclusion

Richard Stephens Cromwell, James Atta Peprah, Khadijah Iddrisu, and Osman Issah

Introduction

One of the global agendas development partners and policymakers are fighting towards achieving is financial inclusion. Financial inclusion can be seen as equal access to all financial services and product by businesses and individuals in an efficient way. Some development partners such as African Development Bank (AfDB) has some financial products such as Affirmative Finance Action for Women in Africa (AFAWA) to promote financial inclusion for women in Africa (Iddrisu et al., 2025b). Also, World Bank

R. S. Cromwell (✉)
Institute of Oil and Gas, University of Cape Coast, Cape Coast, Ghana
e-mail: richard.cromwell@stu.ucc.edu.gh

J. A. Peprah
School of Economics, University of Cape Coast, Cape Coast, Ghana
e-mail: jpeprah@ucc.edu.gh

I. N. Yakubu (ed.), *Banking on Inclusion*, Sustainable Development Goals Series, https://doi.org/10.1007/978-3-031-96716-0_12

has a programme such as Financial Inclusion Support Framework (FISF) that seek to enhance financial inclusion (World Bank, 2022b). Some of these deliberate efforts have been initiated, recognising financial inclusion as a key driver of shared prosperity and sustainable growth. One of the robust ways to promote financial inclusion is the emergence of financial technology (FinTech) (Cromwell & Peprah, 2025; Iddrisu et al., 2022; Iddrisu et al., 2025c; World Bank, 2020). Global FinTech investment increased by 8% in the first half of 2022 compared to the same period in 2021, with venture capital funding totalling US$63.8 billion.[1]

FinTech plays a crucial role in promoting financial inclusion, particularly by enabling individuals and small businesses to access financial resources in a more efficient, convenient, and affordable manner. Through innovations such as mobile money (MoMo), digital banking platforms, and mobile apps, FinTech has significantly reduced the barriers to accessing financial services, especially in underserved and remote areas. By leveraging technology, these platforms offer savings, credit, insurance, and investment services to those previously excluded from the formal financial system. However, despite these advancements, regulatory challenges continue to persist. Issues such as data privacy, cybersecurity, consumer protection, and compliance with anti-money laundering (AML) and know-your-customer (KYC) requirements remain critical concerns. The rapid pace of technological development often outpaces the ability of regulatory frameworks to adapt, creating gaps that could undermine trust and stability in the sector. Therefore, this chapter discusses the regulatory challenges and provide best practices to minimize these challenges.

The rest of the chapter is structured as follows: Sect. 12.2 discusses FinTech-driven financial inclusion; Sect. 12.3 also captures regulatory

K. Iddrisu
Department of Banking and Finance, Islamic University College, Madina, Ghana
e-mail: khadijahiddris@iug.edu.gh

O. Issah
Department of Accounting, School of Business, University for Development Studies, Tamale, Ghana
e-mail: oissah@uds.edu.gh

[1] Read more here: https://chatgpt.com/c/67f48254-c62c-8010-a6dd-fdec7a5ed34e, Accessed April 3, 2025.

framework of FinTech. Policy Challenges in FinTech Regulation is also discussed in Sect. 12.4. This chapter discussed some policy recommendation and best practices in Sect. 12.5. The chapter also provided a concluding remark which is presented in Sect. 12.6.

FinTech-Driven Financial Inclusion

Scope of Financial Inclusion

Financial inclusion is mainly concerned with efficient and effective access of formal financial services and products by individuals and business. Some scholars and institutions also provide different dimensions of financial inclusion. For example, Sarma and Pais (2011) describe financial inclusion as the process that ensures the ease of access, availability and usage of formal financial system for all members of an economy. Khan (2011) revealed that financial inclusion is the process of ensuring that vulnerable populations such as low-income groups and marginalized communities, have access to essential financial services and timely, adequate credit at an affordable cost. Some other scholars such as Allen et al. (2016) and Ozili (2018) also explain financial inclusion as the process of ensuring individuals, especially poor people have access to basic financial services in the formal sector. According to World Bank (2025), financial inclusion entails ensuring that individuals and businesses can access and effectively utilize affordable financial products and services tailored to their needs, delivered in a responsible and sustainable manner.

Financial inclusion acts as a catalyst for sustainable development by fostering inclusive economic growth and reducing vulnerabilities. Below are some key ways it contributes to advancing sustainable development.

1. **Financial inclusion empowers women**

Access to financial services empowers women by providing them with the tools and resources needed to achieve economic independence (Iddrisu et al., 2025b). With the ability to start and grow businesses, women can contribute more significantly to their families' financial stability and well-being. Furthermore, financial inclusion allows women to manage household finances effectively, make informed investment decisions, and plan for the future. This empowerment not only enhances their personal economic capacity but also strengthens their ability to contribute to broader community development, fostering long-term positive impacts on society (World Bank, 2022b, 2024a, 2025).

2. **Support entrepreneurship and business growth**

Financial inclusion promotes entrepreneurship and business growth by providing individuals and small enterprises with access to essential financial services such as credit, savings, insurance, among others (Demirgüç-Kunt & Singer, 2017). This access enables entrepreneurs to secure the capital needed to start or expand their businesses, manage financial risks more effectively, and improve operational efficiency. Formal financial services also facilitate better financial planning and record-keeping, which are crucial for business sustainability and attracting investment. Moreover, digital financial tools open up new market opportunities and reduce transaction costs, allowing businesses to scale more easily. Overall, financial inclusion fosters a more enabling environment for innovation, productivity, and economic empowerment.

3. **Enhance energy consumption**

Financial inclusion promotes energy consumption by enabling households and businesses, particularly in underserved areas, to access financial resources needed to invest in modern energy solutions. Through access to credit, savings, and microfinance, individuals can afford clean energy technologies such as solar panels, energy-efficient appliances, and clean cooking solutions. Financial services also support small-scale energy providers in expanding infrastructure to remote communities. Additionally, digital payment platforms facilitate pay-as-you-go models for electricity, making energy more accessible and affordable. By removing financial barriers, financial inclusion drives greater adoption and consumption of reliable, sustainable energy, contributing to improved livelihoods and economic development. An empirical study by Koomson and Danquah (2021) in Ghana revealed that high level of financial inclusion reduces energy poverty. In Kenya, Mbate and Fall (2025) showed that financial inclusion promote energy access.

4. **Financial inclusion strengthens resilience to climate-related shocks**

Financial inclusion plays a vital role in building resilience by enabling individuals and businesses to invest in climate-smart infrastructure, adopt sustainable agricultural techniques, and implement energy-efficient technologies (Cromwell & Peprah, 2025; Iddrisu et al., 2025c; World Bank, 2025). These actions not only support adaptation but also contribute to climate mitigation efforts. Additionally, access to savings and insurance products enhances households' and enterprises' ability to recover from natural disasters more swiftly, reducing long-term economic setbacks and fostering greater stability in vulnerable communities. More than 80% of the world's 1.4 billion adults without access to formal financial accounts live in regions highly vulnerable to climate change, heightening their exposure to economic and environmental shocks (World Bank, 2025). Therefore, enhancing financial inclusion can strengthen resilience to climate-related and other economic shocks.

Despite financial inclusion serving as a catalyst for sustainable development, there exist some challenges.[2] These include the following:

1. **Limited access to financial institutions**

Many individuals, especially those residing in rural or remote areas, faced significant barriers to accessing banks and formal financial services due to inadequate infrastructure and limited branch networks (Cromwell & Peprah, 2025). These regions often lacked essential infrastructure such as paved roads, reliable transportation, electricity, and internet connectivity, which made it challenging and financially unfeasible for financial institutions to establish and maintain physical branches. In the absence of these services locally, residents were forced to travel long distances to reach the nearest bank, which not only added substantial travel costs but also resulted in considerable time burdens. For many, the journey could take hours, making it impractical for frequent banking needs. The geographical and infrastructural isolation of these areas exacerbated financial exclusion, leaving millions of people without access to basic financial services such as savings accounts, loans, and insurance.

[2] Most of these challenges have been solved with FinTech.

This exclusion hindered economic opportunities, perpetuated poverty, and reinforced inequality in rural and underserved communities.

2. **Stringent documentation requirements**

Many potential customers were excluded from the formal financial system due to their inability to meet the standard requirements imposed by traditional financial institutions, such as formal identification, credit history, or proof of income (Iddrisu et al., 2025b; World Bank, 2024a). In many developing regions, a significant portion of the population works in the informal sector, where income is often irregular, unpredictable, and undocumented. This irregular income makes it difficult for individuals to provide the necessary proof of financial stability required by banks to assess creditworthiness. Additionally, many people in these regions lack government-issued IDs or verifiable residential addresses, further complicating their ability to open bank accounts or access credit and insurance services. Without a recognized financial footprint, these individuals are often classified as high-risk by financial institutions (Gormley, 2010; Iddrisu et al., 2022; Léon & Zins, 2020). This exclusion prevents them from benefiting from financial services that could support entrepreneurial ventures, facilitate savings, and enhance economic resilience, perpetuating cycles of poverty and limiting economic growth in these communities.

3. **High transactional cost**

Traditional banking services often came with high fees, such as account maintenance charges, transaction costs, and interest rates, making them unaffordable for low-income individuals and small businesses (Ayyagari & Beck, 2015; Ayyagari et al., 2017). These fees created a significant financial barrier, especially for those with limited financial resources or irregular incomes, as they found it difficult to meet the required costs of accessing basic services. Small businesses, in particular, struggled to secure loans due to prohibitive interest rates and stringent collateral requirements, further limiting their growth and potential. For low-income individuals, even basic banking services like savings or checking accounts were often beyond reach due to the associated fees, leaving them financially excluded. In the absence of affordable banking options, many people turned to informal financial systems, such as local savings groups or informal lenders. However, these alternatives lacked the security, regulation, and scalability of formal banking systems, exposing individuals and businesses to greater risks and financial instability.

4. **Gender and social barrier**

Women and marginalized groups frequently encountered substantial socio-cultural and legal barriers when trying to access financial services (Iddrisu et al., 2025b). In many societies, deeply entrenched gender norms and cultural practices severely restricted women's ability to control or manage finances, often leaving them unable to access essential financial products such as bank accounts, loans, or credit. These norms reinforced the notion that financial decision-making was a male prerogative, hindering women's economic independence. Legal barriers also played a significant role, with women in some regions required to obtain consent from male guardians or spouses before they could open accounts or apply for credit, further undermining their autonomy. Marginalized groups, including ethnic minorities and rural populations, similarly faced exclusion and discrimination. Many lacked the necessary documentation or were socially stigmatized, making it difficult for them to engage with formal financial systems. Furthermore, financial services were often not tailored to meet their unique needs, leaving them vulnerable to economic instability and further marginalization.

5. **Low financial literacy**

A widespread lack of awareness and understanding of financial products and services significantly limited their usage and undermined trust in formal financial systems (Iddrisu et al., 2025a; World Bank, 2024b). Many individuals, particularly in low-income and rural areas, lacked familiarity with basic banking concepts such as savings accounts, loans, and insurance, which are essential for financial planning and security. This financial illiteracy created a significant barrier to adopting formal financial services, as individuals were uncertain about how these products worked, their potential benefits, or even how to access them. Moreover, a deep-seated distrust in formal financial institutions further discouraged engagement with the system. This mistrust often stemmed from past negative experiences, perceived exploitation, or a lack of transparency in banking practices. Without clear and accessible information, many people remained skeptical, leading to a preference for informal financial systems or opting out of financial services altogether. As a result, cycles of financial exclusion and economic vulnerability were perpetuated, hindering broader economic growth and stability.

While these challenges persist and caused low level of financial inclusion, a break-through solution came up which is FinTech. Hence, the next sub-section discusses how FinTech drive financial inclusion.

Key FinTech Innovations Enhancing Inclusion

FinTech has enhanced the level of financial inclusion in a lot countries including the emerging economies. The ownership of accounts in formal financial institutions rose from 51% in 2011 to 76% in 2021 (Cevik, 2024). Account ownership in developing countries increased by 30 percentage points, reaching 71% (World Bank, 2023). The greatest advancements in financial inclusion due to FinTech have been recorded in **Africa and Asia–Pacific**. The level of financial inclusion increases based on the type of innovation used. Hence, this sub-section discussion the key FinTech innovations that spike the level of financial inclusion. These include the following:

1. **Mobile money**

This FinTech innovation has illuminated the financial sector in emerging economies. While various innovations have emerged, MoMo has set a remarkable pace, driving significant progress. Since the launch of the first mobile money provider in East Asia and the Pacific in 2001, the introduction of M-PESA in Kenya in March 2007 marked a transformative milestone that propelled the global adoption of the mobile money model (Iddrisu et al., 2025c). M-PESA in Kenya, combines "M" for mobile phone and "PESA," meaning money in Swahili. The core idea behind M-PESA is to leverage widespread mobile phone usage to bridge the gap between the unbanked population and formal financial services. Users can deposit funds into an account linked to their mobile device, which can then be accessed or transferred via Short Message Service (SMS). Additionally, MoMo relies on a network of agents who act as intermediaries for transferring and withdrawing funds, further enhancing accessibility and convenience. Mobile network service providers (MNOs) have indeed been key initiators and drivers of mobile money services, particularly in regions where traditional banking infrastructure is limited.

Mobile money has experienced significant global growth, reaching 1.6 billion registered accounts in 2022, a 13% increase from the previous year (Awanis et al., 2022). Africa alone accounted for 781 million of these accounts, growing at 17% annually. Transaction values climbed by 22% from 2021 to 2022, hitting US$1.26 trillion. From 2013 to 2022, mobile money contributed over US$150 billion to Africa's GDP, adding around 3.7% (Awanis et al., 2022). SSA, as of 2024, leads in mobile money adoption, with major platforms like M-PESA, Orange Money, MTN Mobile Money, and Airtel Money dominating the region. These services allow users to transfer funds, pay bills, and access digital services. With over 144 providers in SSA, mobile money now offers financial access to over 60% of previously unbanked individuals (GSM Association, 2024). By the end of 2023, there were approximately 435 million active mobile money accounts, reflecting a 9% growth rate, slower than the 13% in 2022 and 15% in 2023 (GSM Association, 2024).

2. **Bank and other financial institution applications**

The rise of bank and other financial institution applications (apps) have significantly advanced financial inclusion by making banking services more accessible, convenient, and affordable. These digital platforms allow users to open accounts, transfer funds, pay bills, access credit, and monitor their finances anytime and anywhere through smartphones or tablets. For individuals in remote or underserved areas, these apps eliminate the need to travel long distances to physical bank branches. They also reduce transaction costs and waiting times, thereby encouraging greater use of formal financial services. In many emerging economies, these apps have enabled millions of unbanked individuals especially youth, women, and informal workers, to integrate into the formal financial system. Furthermore, the ability to access microloans, insurance, and savings tools through apps empowers small businesses and entrepreneurs to grow. These apps are playing a vital role in bridging the financial divide and promoting inclusive economic development. For example, Fidelity mobile app promotes financial inclusion by empowering about 1.5 million new customers in Ghana (Box 12.1).

Box 12.1 Fidelity Mobile App Enhances Financial Inclusion in Ghana
The Fidelity Mobile App has significantly enhanced financial inclusion in Ghana by providing convenient access to banking services. Fidelity Bank has pioneered Agency Banking, allowing people in remote areas to access banking services at community locations, such as pharmacies and mobile money vendors. This initiative has brought essential financial services closer to underserved populations. Additionally, Fidelity Bank introduced Smart Accounts, which require minimal documentation and can be opened in just five minutes, further enabling financial access for previously unbanked individuals. The bank's expansive agency network, now comprising over 6,000 active agents, has empowered more than 1.5 million new customers, contributing to a deposit growth exceeding half a billion Ghana Cedis.

Source Fidelity Bank (2024)

In Nigeria, FairMoney mobile app promotes financial inclusion by allowing up to ₦3,000,000 without the need for collateral (Box 12.2).

Box 12.2 FairMoney Promotes Financial Inclusion in Nigeria
FairMoney is a prominent microfinance app that provides users with a range of financial services, including instant loans, savings, and traditional banking services. One of its key features is the provision of instant loans, allowing users to access up to ₦3,000,000 without the need for collateral. Additionally, FairMoney offers savings and investment options, with the potential to earn up to 28% interest per annum on fixed deposits, making it an attractive choice for savers. The app also enables users to make utility bill payments, purchase airtime and data, often with discounts. Banking services, such as free transfers, secure transactions, and ATM card delivery, further enhance the convenience and accessibility of financial services. Another notable microfinance app is Sparkle, which focuses on digital banking solutions that include payment services, savings tools, and business management features, offering a comprehensive platform for individuals and small businesses alike.

Source Microfinance Bank (2025)

3. FinTech Innovations by Start-Ups

FinTech start-ups have emerged as key drivers of financial inclusion by leveraging technology to deliver innovative, affordable, and user-friendly financial solutions to underserved populations. Unlike traditional financial institutions, start-ups are often more agile and responsive to market needs, developing platforms that cater specifically to the unbanked and underbanked. Innovations such as digital wallets, peer-to-peer (P2P) lending, micro-investment platforms, blockchain-based remittances, and AI-driven credit scoring have revolutionized access to financial services. These start-ups reduce entry barriers by eliminating the need for physical branches, paperwork, and credit history, making it easier for individuals in rural areas, informal workers, and marginalized groups to access savings, credit, and insurance. Some of the innovations introduced by these start-ups include MoMo, financial institution apps, and other digital solutions. These innovations have effectively brought capital markets closer to citizens. For instance, Akaboxi offers an innovative financial service that fosters financial inclusion (Box 12.3). In South Africa, Bright On Capital delivers innovative financial solutions designed to empower small businesses and accelerate their growth (Box 12.4).

Box 12.3 Akaboxi, a FinTech Start-Up Innovation

Akaboxi is a digital financial inclusion system designed to support smallholder farmers in managing and monitoring their savings collectively. The platform replaces the traditional method of storing savings in boxes or at home with a more secure, efficient, and easily monitored digital solution. It works with existing savings groups in rural areas and also helps establish new ones where they do not yet exist. These groups typically meet weekly, consisting of around 30 members, 95% of whom are women. Each member receives an Identity Card (ID) with demographic details, embedded with Near Field Communication (NFC) technology for transaction identification and processing, such as savings and borrowing.

The system offers several key features, including tracking weekly savings for both individual members and Village Savings and Loan Associations (VSLA) groups, issuing transaction receipts for transparency, and integrating with existing mobile money platforms for direct deposits into group accounts. It sends SMS alerts for transactions, generates reports on loan portfolios, arrears rates, and savings, and maintains a social networking feature to share information. The platform is simple, user-friendly, and customized for Akaboxi clients, subscribers, and partners. The vision is to become the leading provider of digital financial inclusion systems for farmers in Africa, with a mission to deliver affordable and appropriate services to financially excluded individuals, especially in rural areas, in compliance with relevant laws.

Source Akaboxi (2025)

Box 12.4 Bright on Capital Innovations Provide Loans to Small Business

Bright On Capital is a online lender that provides affordable working capital and funding solutions to small and emerging businesses with sustainable growth potential in South Africa. The institution offers four core lending products tailored to support business growth and cash flow management. These include Invoice Finance, which advances up to 80% of the value of selected invoices with the remainder paid upon customer settlement; Purchase Order Finance (Supply and Deliver), offering up to 70% of purchase order value within 24 hours; Purchase Order Finance (Manufacture and Assemble), which supports businesses executing orders requiring manufacturing or assembly; and Buy Now, Pay Later, a credit facility enabling businesses to purchase from Merchant Partners and repay after order completion and customer payment.

Bright On Capital adopts an innovative approach to small business lending by assessing each enterprise's products and services, operational capacity, and cash flow patterns. This enables the structuring of funding solutions that align with the business's financial needs and growth trajectory. Small businesses with a proven track record of supplying corporate or public-sector clients can access revolving credit facilities of up to R2.5 million to execute procurement opportunities from qualifying large organisations. This financing empowers entrepreneurs to accept larger contracts and expand operations. Bright On Capital is an Authorised Financial Services Provider and a Registered Credit Provider (NCRP7586), committed to inclusive economic participation and enterprise development

Source Bright On Capital (2025)

Regulatory Framework for FinTech

Principle of FinTech Regulation

To ensure the effectiveness of the regulation of FinTech, there are four main principles of FinTech regulation. These include the following:

1. **Legal Certainty**

Legal certainty is a fundamental principle in effective regulation, particularly for FinTech. Clear regulatory boundaries and consistent application of laws prevent regulatory arbitrage and support both financial innovation and investor confidence (Amstad, 2019). However, legal certainty in FinTech faces three major challenges. First, the rapid evolution of FinTech outpaces traditional regulatory processes, which are often slow and involve broad stakeholder consultations. Second, regulatory fragmentation across multiple institutions such as central banks, financial supervisors, tax authorities, and anti-money laundering bodies can lead to overlaps and confusion, especially around digital assets. Third, FinTech increasingly requires regulators and market participants to understand coding and technology, beyond traditional legal and financial expertise. To address these challenges, many jurisdictions have introduced regulatory sandboxes, allowing innovators to test products in a controlled environment. Others have established specific FinTech licenses or developed legislation for distributed ledger technologies (DLTs), aiming to provide flexibility while maintaining oversight and legal clarity in a fast-evolving financial landscape.

2. **Proportionality**

The principle of proportionality in FinTech regulation emphasizes that regulatory requirements should be tailored to the size, nature, complexity, and risk level of the financial activity or institution (Amstad, 2019). This approach is especially critical in fostering innovation and promoting financial inclusion by ensuring that smaller FinTech start-ups and new market entrants are not subject to the same rigorous and costly regulatory burdens as large, well-established financial institutions. Applying overly stringent rules to small players can stifle innovation, discourage entry, and limit competition, ultimately slowing down the development of inclusive financial services. Proportional regulation allows regulators to strike a balance ensuring that basic consumer protection, anti-money laundering, and data security standards are met without imposing unnecessary barriers. This approach also encourages experimentation and agility in product development, supporting dynamic growth while maintaining the overall safety, transparency, and stability of the financial system. By adjusting requirements to fit risk profiles, proportionality helps create a more inclusive and innovation-friendly regulatory landscape.

3. **Technological Neutrality**

Technology neutrality is a key principle in effective FinTech regulation. It means that regulatory frameworks should not favor or discriminate against any particular technology or method of delivery (Amstad, 2019). Whether financial services are offered through traditional brick-and-mortar institutions or via digital platforms such as mobile apps or blockchain, the same rules and standards should apply. This ensures a level playing field, where innovation can thrive based on the quality and utility of a service rather than regulatory advantage. A technology-neutral approach enables regulators to focus on the actual function and associated risks of financial activities—such as lending, payments, or asset management—rather than how they are delivered. It also helps maintain consistency in consumer protection, market conduct, and financial stability. Importantly, this approach encourages innovation while minimizing regulatory arbitrage and fragmentation. As FinTech evolves rapidly, neutrality ensures that regulations remain adaptable and future-proof, supporting sustainable development of financial ecosystems across both traditional and digital sectors.

4. **Risk-Based Approach**

A risk-based approach to FinTech regulation involves assessing and addressing the specific risks posed by FinTech activities, such as operational, cybersecurity, fraud, and financial crime risks. Instead of applying one-size-fits-all regulatory measures, this approach allows regulators to focus on areas of higher risk, ensuring that resources are allocated efficiently and regulatory actions are proportionate to the threat.[3] For example, financial services that handle sensitive data or large sums of money may be subject to stricter cybersecurity measures compared to lower-risk applications. Similarly, the likelihood of fraud or money laundering activities may dictate the level of scrutiny a service receives. By prioritizing regulatory efforts according to the severity and likelihood of harm, a risk-based approach helps prevent regulatory overload while safeguarding the financial system. It also enables regulators to stay adaptive and responsive to the fast-paced evolution of technology, ensuring that emerging risks are swiftly identified and addressed before they can cause widespread harm.

Policy Regulations for FinTech

FinTech firms must comply with various regulations to ensure they positively impact sustainable banking. These include anti-money laundering and counter-terrorism financing, customer protection, operational risk management and governance, and authorization and vetting requirements.

1. **Anti-Money Laundering and Counter-Terrorism Financing**

Policies regulating AML and Counter-Terrorism Financing (CTF) aim to prevent the misuse of FinTech services for illicit activities, such as money laundering and financing terrorism. These regulations ensure that FinTech platforms, including digital payment systems, peer-to-peer lending, and cryptocurrency exchanges, do not facilitate the transfer of illicit funds. FinTech companies are required to adopt comprehensive Know Your Customer (KYC) procedures, monitor transactions for suspicious behavior, and report any potential illegal activities. Additionally, due diligence is necessary, especially for large or cross-border transactions. Compliance with AML and CTF regulations safeguards the financial ecosystem, ensuring that FinTech services operate securely and legally. Some examples of AML and CTF is the Financial Action Task Force

[3] Read more here: https://www.neotas.com/risk-based-approach-rba/.

(FATF) which is the global watchdog against money laundering and terrorist financing (Box 12.5).

Box 12.5 Financial Action Task Force (FATF) Recommendations

The Financial Action Task Force (FATF), established in 1989 and based in Paris, serves as the global standard-setter and watchdog in the fight against money laundering, terrorist financing, and the financing of weapons of mass destruction. Its comprehensive set of Recommendations, initially adopted in 2012 and most recently updated in November 2023, forms the cornerstone of global efforts to detect and deter financial crimes. These Recommendations promote legislative, regulatory, and operational measures tailored to the legal and institutional frameworks of individual countries, encouraging reforms through international cooperation and political advocacy.

FATF comprises 40 member countries and has influence over more than 200 jurisdictions committed to upholding its standards. It addresses serious threats such as drug trafficking, illicit arms trade, corruption, and cyber-enabled financial crimes by ensuring a harmonized international response. The FATF's framework includes not only its Recommendations but also Interpretive Notes and a Glossary, providing clarity and guidance to member states. On 24 February 2023, FATF suspended Russia's membership, underscoring its commitment to ethical governance and global security. Through collaborative action, FATF enhances resilience against organized crime and fosters global financial integrity.

Source FATF (2023)

Another notable example is the Bank Secrecy Act (BSA), which requires financial institutions to maintain detailed records and submit specific reports that support investigations. This regulatory framework plays a critical role in assisting law enforcement agencies in detecting and preventing money laundering, terrorist financing, and tax evasion by ensuring transparency in financial transactions and enabling the tracking of suspicious activities (Box 12.6).

Box 12.6 Bank Secrecy Act in the USA

The Bank Secrecy Act (BSA), enacted by the U.S. Congress in 1970, was the first major legislative effort to combat money laundering in the United States. The BSA requires financial institutions and certain businesses to maintain records and file reports that are valuable for criminal, tax, and regulatory investigations. These obligations help law enforcement agencies detect, investigate, and prevent illegal financial activities, including those related to organized crime, terrorist financing, and tax evasion. A core component of the U.S. National Money Laundering Strategy, the Internal Revenue Service (IRS) plays a dual role by enforcing compliance and providing educational support to affected entities. Key BSA provisions include the requirement to file Form 8300 for cash payments exceeding US$10,000, reporting obligations for foreign financial accounts, and specific compliance measures for money services businesses (MSBs). Additionally, a dedicated helpline is available to assist institutions with compliance inquiries, ensuring continued transparency and accountability in the financial system.

Source Internal Revenue Service (2024)

At the regional level, the European Union has implemented policies like the Anti-Money Laundering Directive (AMLD) to strengthen the fight against money laundering and terrorist financing. This directive is designed to enhance global security, safeguard the integrity of the financial system, and promote financial stability. By fostering greater transparency and accountability, the AMLD also supports sustainable economic growth across EU member states. (Box 12.7).

Box 12.7 European Union Anti-Money Laundering Directive

The Anti-Money Laundering Directive (AMLD) is a comprehensive regulatory framework developed by the European Union (EU) to combat money laundering and terrorist financing across its member states. Introduced in 1990 and regularly updated, the AMLD aligns closely with the Financial Action Task Force (FATF) standards. It requires member countries to incorporate these regulations into their national legal systems, ensuring consistency and uniformity in preventing the misuse of the financial system for illicit activities. Core obligations under the AMLD include customer due diligence (CDD), monitoring of financial transactions, and the reporting of suspicious activities to relevant authorities.

The directive is continuously revised to address emerging risks such as virtual assets, cryptocurrencies, and crowdfunding platforms. It works in tandem with complementary regulations, including the Markets in Crypto-Assets Regulation (MiCA) and the Regulation on the Traceability of Transfers of Funds (TFR), which will come into force in December 2024 to strengthen the traceability and verification of crypto-asset transfers. The European Commission plays a supervisory role, coordinating with member states to ensure effective implementation and adaptation. AMLD's evolving structure seeks to create a coherent, secure, and resilient financial ecosystem across the EU, bolstering financial integrity and global security.

Source European Commission (2024a)

2. Consumer Protection

Policies have also been established to enhance consumer protection within the FinTech ecosystem. These regulations aim to shield consumers from fraud, exploitation, and unfair practices by ensuring that FinTech services operate transparently and responsibly. Essential elements include clear pricing structures and easily understood terms, enabling users to make informed financial decisions. Firms are required to implement strong protections against data breaches and identity theft, particularly in digital payment and lending platforms. Additionally, effective dispute resolution mechanisms and compensation procedures must be in place for instances of fraud or service errors. Guidelines on truthful and non-misleading advertising further support consumer confidence. Collectively, these policies foster trust, fairness, and security in digital financial services. Among these policies is the Payment Services Directive (PSD2), introduced by the European Commission, which grants the Commission the authority to adopt delegated and implementing acts. These acts are designed to provide detailed guidance and ensure effective compliance with PSD2 requirements by both regulatory authorities and market participants (see Box 12.8).

Box 12.8 Payment Services Directive Protect Consumers

The Payment Services Directive (PSD2) empowers the European Commission to adopt delegated and implementing acts that support effective compliance with PSD2 obligations by both competent authorities and market participants. These acts provide specific technical and procedural standards that ensure a harmonized and transparent regulatory environment across the European Union.

Key regulatory acts include:

1. Commission Delegated Regulation (EU) 2019/411 (Art. 15(4))—This sets the technical standards for the creation, operation, and maintenance of the electronic central register for payment services, ensuring public access to relevant data.
2. Commission Implementing Regulation (EU) 2019/410 (Art. 15(5))—It outlines the structure and content of the information that national competent authorities must submit to the European Banking Authority (EBA) concerning payment service providers.
3. Commission Delegated Regulation (EU) 2017/2055 (Art. 28(5))—This regulation defines standards for cooperation and information sharing between authorities when payment institutions operate across borders or under the freedom to provide services.
4. Commission Delegated Regulation (EU) 2021/1722 (Art. 29(6))—It specifies the supervisory cooperation framework between home and host country authorities overseeing cross-border payment and electronic money institutions.

Together, these acts strengthen regulatory clarity, enhance supervision, and promote cross-border cooperation across the EU's financial landscape.

Source European Commission (2024b)

Another example of consumer protection is the U.S. Consumer Financial Protection Bureau (CFPB), which works to safeguard consumers in financial matters by establishing and enforcing regulations that prevent deceptive, unfair, and abusive practices within the financial industry (see Box 12.9).

Box 12.9 US Consumer Financial Protection Bureau

The Consumer Financial Protection Bureau (CFPB) was created by the Dodd-Frank Wall Street Reform and Consumer Protection Act in 2010, following the 2007–08 financial crisis, to combat predatory and deceptive practices in the financial sector. Senator Elizabeth Warren played a key role in its development, and the bureau officially began operations in July 2011, with Richard Cordray serving as its first director. The CFPB's core mission is to protect consumers in financial matters by creating and enforcing rules to prevent deceptive, unfair, and abusive practices. It also handles consumer complaints, monitors financial markets for risks to consumers, and provides financial education tools and resources.

Led by a director appointed by the president and confirmed by Congress, the CFPB is currently under the leadership of Rohit Chopra as of May 2024. The agency operates with six divisions, each focusing on various aspects of consumer protection and financial regulation. Funded through quarterly transfers from the Federal Reserve, the CFPB has secured over US$20 billion in consumer relief and collected US$4 billion in penalties. However, it has faced criticism for potential overreach and a perceived lack of accountability. Critics point to the agency's director independence and the special court deference it receives, complicating oversight. Despite these challenges, the CFPB remains a critical entity for safeguarding consumers and promoting financial literacy.

Source Marquit (2024)

3. **Operational Risk Management and Governance**

Risk management and governance are critical pillars of FinTech regulation aimed at ensuring operational resilience, financial stability, and consumer protection (Iddrisu et al., 2025b). Regulatory policies require FinTech firms to establish robust internal control systems, risk assessment frameworks, and effective governance structures (Zetzsche et al., 2017). These include board oversight, compliance functions, and procedures for managing financial, operational, cybersecurity, and third-party risks. Firms must also adopt risk mitigation strategies aligned with the nature and complexity of their services. Proper governance ensures accountability, transparency, and sound decision-making, while effective risk management protects against systemic vulnerabilities. Together, these measures strengthen trust and safeguard the broader financial ecosystem from emerging threats.

4. **Licensing and Registration Requirements**

The objective of regulatory authorization for FinTech companies is to ensure they operate legally and meet minimum standards before offering services (Iddrisu et al., 2025c; Li et al., 2023; World Bank, 2022a). This involves establishing a licensing process tailored to the nature of services provided, such as payment services, lending, crowdfunding, or blockchain-based services, ensuring firms meet operational, financial, and legal requirements (Li et al., 2023). Additionally, periodic registration with regulators is necessary to confirm ongoing compliance with applicable laws, guidelines, and standards. This framework helps protect consumers, ensure financial stability, and maintain the integrity of the financial system, fostering a regulated environment that supports sustainable and secure FinTech operations.

Regulatory Approaches

Three key regulatory innovations include sandboxes and innovation hubs, regulatory technology (RegTech) and supervisory technology (SupTech), and cross-border coordination mechanisms.

1. **Sandboxes and Innovation Hubs**

Regulatory sandboxes and innovation hubs have emerged as key tools for enabling FinTech experimentation within a controlled regulatory environment (Arner et al., 2017; World Bank, 2020). A regulatory sandbox allows FinTech firms to test new technologies, products, or business models without immediately complying with the full spectrum of regulatory requirements. This flexibility enables innovation while ensuring consumer protection and financial stability. Innovation hubs, on the other hand, offer a platform for regulators and innovators to engage, share information, and collaborate on addressing regulatory challenges. These mechanisms are particularly effective in promoting financial inclusion by providing a testing ground for novel solutions to reach underserved populations. Most regulators are adopting sandboxes as shown in Fig. 12.1.

2. **RegTech and SupTech**

RegTech and SupTech are technological innovations that significantly enhance both regulatory compliance and supervision within financial

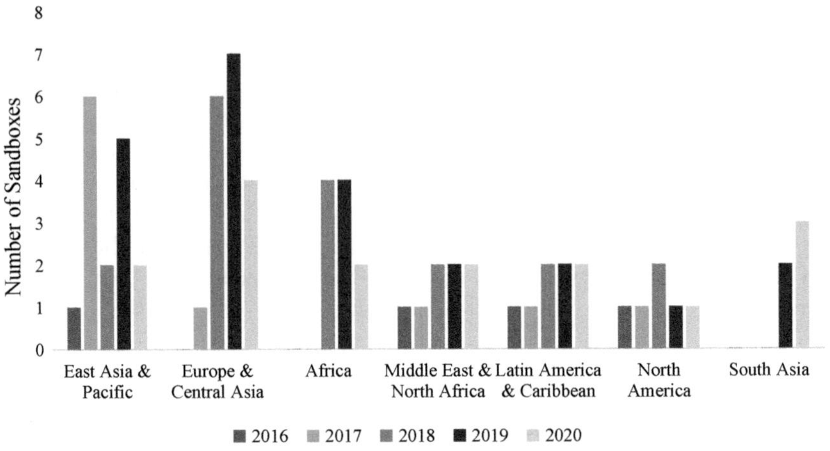

Fig. 12.1 Global Sandbox Adoption, 2016–2020, by region (*Source* Authors' Construct Based on Data from World Bank (2020))

markets. RegTech enables financial institutions to streamline their compliance processes by automating routine tasks such as compliance checks, risk assessments, transaction monitoring, and reporting (Arner et al., 2017). It also helps in adhering to AML laws and other regulatory requirements, reducing operational costs and mitigating human errors. SupTech, on the other hand, empowers regulators by providing advanced tools to gather, analyze, and interpret large volumes of data, which improves their ability to monitor market activities, detect emerging risks, and ensure effective oversight. By utilizing technologies like big data analytics, artificial intelligence, and machine learning, SupTech helps regulators stay ahead of evolving financial landscapes and emerging threats, ensuring that regulatory frameworks remain robust and adaptive. Both RegTech and SupTech play a crucial role in promoting financial stability while fostering innovation in the financial sector (Li et al., 2023).

3. **Cross-Border Coordination Mechanisms**

As FinTech activities often transcend national borders, regulatory authorities face challenges in managing cross-border risks, ensuring consistent consumer protection, and fostering international cooperation. Cross-border coordination mechanisms involve collaboration between regulators across jurisdictions to establish common standards, share information, and harmonize regulatory approaches. This is especially important for global financial systems, where inconsistent regulations can create fragmentation and regulatory arbitrage opportunities. These mechanisms help ensure a level playing field, mitigate risks like money laundering or cyber threats, and facilitate the seamless operation of cross-border FinTech services. One example of this mechanism is the Pan-African Payment and Settlement System (PAPSS), which facilitates instant or near-instant transfer of funds to beneficiaries across different African countries (Box 12.10).

Box 12.10 Pan-African Payment and Settlement System
The Pan-African Payment and Settlement System (PAPSS) serves as a pivotal mechanism in enhancing financial integration across the African continent. By enabling the instant or near-instant transfer of funds between beneficiaries in different African countries, PAPSS significantly reduces the time and cost associated with cross-border transactions. This system supports multiple currencies and is designed to streamline payments across 41 African countries, ultimately promoting trade and economic growth. According to the African Union, the system aims to facilitate intra-African trade, which accounts for less than 20% of the continent's total trade. PAPSS is expected to reduce transaction costs by up to 80%, contributing to the realization of the African Continental Free Trade Area (AfCFTA) goals and fostering greater economic cooperation across the region.
Source PAPSS (2025)

Policy Challenges in FinTech Regulation

1. **Managing Risks Related to Digital Lending, Fraud, and Identity Theft**

The growth of digital lending platforms and peer-to-peer lending has significantly transformed the way individuals and businesses access credit, providing opportunities for those who might not qualify for traditional loans due to a lack of credit history. However, this new form of lending introduces several risks (IND Momey, 2023). Without the typical credit assessment processes, there is a heightened risk of loan defaults, as borrowers may not be adequately evaluated for their ability to repay. This lack of thorough assessment increases the probability that individuals or businesses with insufficient financial stability or creditworthiness could access loans, which ultimately leads to higher default rates. In addition, the digital nature of these lending platforms, while offering convenience and accessibility, exposes them to various vulnerabilities. These platforms are particularly susceptible to fraudulent activities, including identity theft, scams, and data breaches. Cybercriminals can exploit the digital infrastructure, gaining unauthorized access to sensitive financial information or manipulating borrower data for malicious purposes (Jimmy, 2024). As a result, these risks not only jeopardize the financial stability of the platform but also threaten the security and trust of borrowers.

2. **Balancing Innovation with Financial Stability and Consumer Protection**

One of the most pressing challenges in FinTech regulation is finding the right balance between encouraging innovation and ensuring financial stability (Iddrisu et al., 2025c). FinTech innovations, including digital banking, blockchain technology, and mobile payments, offer significant benefits, such as enhancing financial inclusion and increasing efficiency in financial transactions. However, the fast pace of technological advancements can often outstrip current regulatory frameworks, creating gaps that may expose the financial system to risks. Regulators must ensure that these new innovations are embraced without compromising consumer protection, market integrity, or systemic stability. This involves crafting a regulatory environment that fosters innovation while putting in place necessary safeguards to mitigate potential risks, such as fraud or market volatility. Striking this balance ensures that FinTech growth contributes positively to the economy and society, without undermining trust in the financial system or exposing consumers to undue harm.

3. **Challenges in Anti-Money Laundering and Combating the Financing of Terrorism Compliance**

FinTech companies, especially those engaged in digital currencies and cross-border payments, are increasingly exposed to significant risks related to AML and Combating the Financing of Terrorism (CFT) (World Bank, 2022a). The anonymity that often accompanies digital transactions makes it difficult for regulators to track and identify illicit activities, such as money laundering or terrorist financing. This challenge is further intensified by the rapid pace of innovation within the FinTech sector, with new products, services, and technologies continuously emerging. As these innovations often outpace existing regulatory frameworks, it becomes increasingly difficult for authorities to implement effective oversight and ensure compliance with AML and CFT regulations (Salampasis & Samakovitis, 2024). This regulatory gap poses significant risks to both financial stability and security.

3. **Regulatory Arbitrage and Uneven Development Across Jurisdictions**

The global nature of FinTech presents a significant challenge in the form of regulatory arbitrage, where firms exploit differences in regulatory standards across jurisdictions (Nwafor & Ayodele, 2024). Inconsistent regulations create an uneven playing field, as companies may relocate to regions with more lenient regulations, bypassing essential oversight. This can lead to regulatory gaps, allowing harmful practices to flourish and increasing risks for consumers and financial markets. Moreover, such discrepancies can undermine the stability of the global financial system, creating an environment where firms are incentivized to avoid stronger regulatory regimes. To address this, international coordination and cooperation are essential to establish harmonized rules and standards that promote fairness, transparency, and stability across borders. This ensures that FinTech innovations can thrive while maintaining adequate consumer protection, market integrity, and financial stability worldwide.

The Way Forward and Best Practices

1. **Strengthening Digital Infrastructure and Legal Identity Systems**

For FinTech to truly drive financial inclusion, building robust digital infrastructure is essential. Governments need to prioritize expanding reliable internet connectivity, especially in rural and underserved regions, to bridge the digital divide (World Economic Forum (WEF), 2025; World Bank, 2022a). This ensures that everyone, regardless of location, has access to essential digital financial services. Additionally, strengthening legal identity systems is critical in enabling individuals, particularly those without traditional bank accounts, to engage with the formal financial sector. Secure, universally recognized digital identities are key in facilitating access to services such as credit, insurance, savings accounts, and digital wallets. By establishing these systems, marginalized groups often excluded from financial systems can fully participate in the digital economy, fostering greater economic inclusion and empowering individuals to better manage their financial lives. Some countries have already built digital infrastructure.

2. **Promoting Financial Consumer Protection and Grievance Redressal Mechanisms**

Consumer protection must be a fundamental aspect of any FinTech regulatory framework. As digital financial services continue to expand, it is vital that consumers have access to clear, transparent, and fair financial products (Cromwell & Peprah, 2025; Iddrisu et al., 2025a, b). Regulators should establish robust mechanisms to safeguard consumers from fraud, exploitation, and unethical practices. This includes implementing user friendly grievance redressal systems where individuals can easily report issues, seek compensation, and resolve disputes swiftly. Ensuring transparency, fairness, and accountability in financial services will foster greater trust in the FinTech sector, leading to broader adoption and enhanced financial inclusion. Furthermore, regulators must ensure that all financial service providers adhere to strict standards that prioritize the protection of consumer rights, ensuring that innovation does not come at the expense of user welfare. These measures will ultimately build a safer, more inclusive financial ecosystem.

3. **Developing Adaptive and Inclusive Regulatory Frameworks**

To effectively regulate the rapidly evolving FinTech sector, regulators must create adaptive and flexible frameworks capable of accommodating technological advancements while fostering innovation. These frameworks should be inclusive, ensuring that underserved populations, such as low-income groups and women, have equitable access to financial services. A risk-based approach is crucial, allowing regulations to be tailored to the size, scope, and risk profile of different FinTech entities, ensuring proportional oversight. Additionally, regulations must be periodically reviewed and updated to reflect emerging trends like blockchain technology and digital currencies. This ongoing revision is vital to maintaining a regulatory environment that is both relevant and supportive of sustainable innovation. By adapting to changes in technology and market dynamics, regulators can ensure that FinTech remains a powerful tool for financial inclusion while managing potential risks effectively. This balance will be key to the long-term success of the sector.

4. **Encouraging Public–Private Collaboration**

Public–private partnerships play a crucial role in developing a vibrant FinTech ecosystem. Regulators should collaborate with FinTech companies, financial institutions, and other key stakeholders to encourage innovation while ensuring adherence to regulatory standards. This cooperation helps identify emerging risks, address market gaps, and co-create solutions that drive financial inclusion. By working together, the public and private sectors can pool resources, expertise, and technology to design more effective policies and services. Governments can further support these partnerships by offering tax incentives, grants, and backing regulatory sandboxes, which allow FinTech start-ups to test new business models in a secure environment. Such collaborations foster industry growth and innovation, while maintaining a stable, secure financial system that benefits consumers and businesses alike. This synergy between regulators and the private sector will be crucial in realizing the full potential of FinTech to enhance financial inclusion globally.

5. **Enhancing Regulatory Capacity and Digital Literacy**

To effectively navigate the complexities of the FinTech sector, regulators must enhance their capacity by investing in specialized training, resources, and expertise. It is essential for regulators to understand the technologies and business models driving FinTech innovations, enabling them to craft informed and effective regulations. In addition, fostering digital literacy among both regulators and the general public is crucial. Increased awareness and understanding of FinTech services empower consumers to make informed financial decisions and safeguard themselves against fraud. Governments should collaborate with educational institutions, industry players, and technology experts to develop comprehensive programs aimed at improving digital and financial literacy across diverse demographics. This initiative ensures that both regulatory bodies and consumers are equipped to handle the evolving landscape of FinTech, promoting sustainable innovation and protecting the interests of all stakeholders involved.

Conclusions

FinTech has played a crucial role in advancing financial inclusion, offering significant opportunities for underbanked individuals and businesses. In spite these advancements, several regulatory challenges hinder the full potential of FinTech. This chapter explores these challenges and provides policy recommendations and best practices. It begins by examining the role of financial inclusion in promoting sustainable development, with findings indicating that financial inclusion empowers women, supports SMEs, fosters business growth, increases energy consumption, and strengthens resilience to climate-related shocks. Despite various policy initiatives, financial inclusion remained limited until the widespread adoption of FinTech, primarily due to factors such as limited access to financial institutions, stringent documentation requirements, high transactional costs, gender and social barriers, and low financial literacy.

While FinTech has significantly boosted financial inclusion, certain key innovations have played a pivotal role in this progress. These include mobile money platforms (e.g., MoMo), banking applications, and various innovations from FinTech start-ups. The chapter also delves into the regulatory framework for FinTech, outlining principles such as legal certainty, proportionality, technological neutrality, and a risk-based approach. It also discusses policy regulations, including AML and combating the CFT, consumer protection, operational risk management, governance, and licensing requirements. The regulatory approaches covered include sandboxes, innovation hubs, RegTech, SupTech, and cross-border coordination mechanisms.

The chapter identifies several regulatory challenges faced by authorities, such as managing risks related to digital lending, fraud, and identity theft, balancing innovation with financial stability and consumer protection, ensuring AML and CFT compliance, and addressing regulatory arbitrage and uneven development across jurisdictions. In response, the chapter offers policy recommendations and best practices to address these challenges. These include strengthening digital infrastructure and legal identity systems, promoting consumer protection and grievance redressal mechanisms, developing adaptive and inclusive regulatory frameworks, encouraging public–private collaboration, and enhancing regulatory capacity and digital literacy.

References

Akaboxi. (2025). *About Akaboxi*. http://www.akaboxii.com/about/akaboxi/

Allen, F., Demirguc-Kunt, A., Klapper, L., & Peria, M. S. M. (2016). The foundations of financial inclusion: Understanding ownership and use of formal accounts. *Journal of Financial Intermediation, 27*, 1–30. https://doi.org/10.1016/j.jfi.2015.12.003

Amstad, M. (2019). *Regulating Fintech: Objectives, principles, and practices* (1016; ADBI Working Paper Series). https://www.adb.org/sites/default/files/publication/533791/adbi-wp1016.pdf

Arner, D. W., Barberis, J., & Buckley, R. P. (2017). *FinTech and RegTech in a Nutshell, and the Future in a Sandbox*. https://rpc.cfainstitute.org/sites/default/files/-/media/documents/article/rf-brief/rfbr-v3-n4-1.pdf

Awanis, A., Lowe, C., Andersson-Manjang, S. K., & Lindsey, D. (2022). *State of the industry report on mobile money 2022.*

Ayyagari, M., & Beck, T. (2015). *Financial inclusion in Asia: An overview* (449; Economics Working Papers). https://www.adb.org/sites/default/files/publication/173377/ewp-449.pdf

Ayyagari, M., Demirgüç-Kunt, A., & Maksimovic, V. (2017). *SME Finance.*

Bright On Capital. (2025). *About us.*

Cevik, S. (2024). *Promise (Un)kept? Fintech and financial inclusion* (2024/131; IMF Working Papers).

Cromwell, R. S., & Peprah, J. A. (2025). Banking business models and sustainable development: Challenges and opportunities. In I. N. Yakubu (Ed.), *Strategic approaches to banking business and sustainable development goals* (pp. 3–22). Springer. https://doi.org/10.1007/978-3-031-80744-2_1

Demirgüç-Kunt, A., & Singer, D. (2017). *Financial inclusion and inclusive growth: A review of recent empirical evidence.*

European Commission. (2024a). *Anti-money laundering and countering the financing of terrorism at EU level.* https://finance.ec.europa.eu/financial-crime/anti-money-laundering-and-countering-financing-terrorism-eu-level_en

European Commission. (2024b). *Implementing and delegated acts - PSD 2.* https://finance.ec.europa.eu/regulation-and-supervision/financial-services-legislation/implementing-and-delegated-acts/payment-services-directive_en

FairMoney Microfinance Bank. (2025). *We are building the mobile bank for the next 2 Billion.* https://fairmoney.io/

FATF. (2023). *The FATF recommendations.* https://www.fatf-gafi.org/en/publications/Fatfrecommendations/Fatf-recommendations.html

Fidelity Bank. (2024, November 13). *A decade of breaking barriers: Fidelity bank's financial inclusion journey in Ghana.* https://www.fidelitybank.com.gh/news/752-a-decade-of-breaking-barriers-fidelity-banks-financial-inclusion-journey-in-ghana

Gormley, T. A. (2010). The impact of foreign bank entry in emerging markets: Evidence from India. *Journal of Financial Intermediation, 19*(1), 26–51. https://doi.org/10.1016/j.jfi.2009.01.003

GSM Association. (2024). *The state of the industry report on mobile money 2024.*

Iddrisu, K., Abor, J. Y., & Banyen, K. T. (2022). Fintech, foreign bank presence and inclusive finance in Africa: Using a quantile regression approach. *Cogent Economics & Finance, 10*(1). https://doi.org/10.1080/23322039.2022.2157120

Iddrisu, K., Boadi, E. K., Giamporcaro, S., & Doku, J. N. (2025a). Ethical banking and growth of small and medium enterprises in emerging economies. In I. Yakubu (Ed.), *Strategic approaches to banking business and sustainable development goals. Sustainable development goals series* (pp. 157–178). Springer. https://doi.org/10.1007/978-3-031-80744-2_10

Iddrisu, K., Ofoeda, I., Issah, O., & Iddrisu, M. (2025b). Gender equality and women's empowerment in banking. In I. Yakubu (Ed.), *Strategic approaches to banking business and sustainable development goals. Sustainable development goals series*(pp. 179–193). Springer. https://doi.org/10.1007/978-3-031-80744-2_11

Iddrisu, K., Yakubu, I. N., & Asongu, S. A. (2025c). FinTech innovations for sustainable banking. In *Strategic approaches to banking business and sustainable development goals. Sustainable development goals series* (pp. 63–86). Springer. https://doi.org/10.1007/978-3-031-80744-2_4

IND Momey. (2023, October 26). *Peer-to-peer lending: Opportunities and risks for market investors.*

Internal Revenue Service. (2024). *Bank secrecy act*. https://www.irs.gov/businesses/small-businesses-self-employed/bank-secrecy-act#:~:text=CongresspassedtheBankSecrecy,%2C%20tax%2C%20and%20regulatorymatters

Jimmy, F. (2024). Cybersecurity threats and vulnerabilities in online banking systems. *International Journal of Scientific Research and Management (IJSRM), 12*(10), 1631–1646.

Khan, R. (2011, November 4). Financial inclusion and financial stability: Are they two sides of the same coin? *BANCON 2011*. https://www.bis.org/review/r111229f.pdf

Koomson, I., & Danquah, M. (2021). Financial inclusion and energy poverty: Empirical evidence from Ghana. *Energy Economics, 94*, Article 105085. https://doi.org/10.1016/j.eneco.2020.105085

Léon, F., & Zins, A. (2020). Regional foreign banks and financial inclusion: Evidence from Africa. *Economic Modelling, 84*, 102–116. https://doi.org/10.1016/j.econmod.2019.03.012

Li, J., Maiti, A., & Fei, J. (2023). Features and scope of regulatory technologies: Challenges and opportunities with industrial Internet of Things. *Future Internet, 15*(8), 256. https://doi.org/10.3390/fi15080256

Marquit, M. (2024). *What is the Consumer Financial Protection Bureau (CFPB)?* https://www.britannica.com/money/Consumer-Financial-Protection-Bureau

Mbate, M., & Fall, E. H. (2025). Financial inclusion and energy access: Evidence from Kenya. *Innovation and Green Development, 4*(2), Article 100219. https://doi.org/10.1016/j.igd.2025.100219

Nwafor, K. C., & Ayodele, E. A. (2024). Regulatory challenges and innovations in financial technology: Safeguarding against fraud while maximizing ROI. *International Journal of Research Publication and Reviews, 5*(10), 4983–4994. https://doi.org/10.55248/gengpi.5.1024.3125

Ozili, P. K. (2018). Impact of digital finance on financial inclusion and stability. *Borsa Istanbul Review, 18*(4), 329–340. https://doi.org/10.1016/j.bir.2017.12.003

PAPSS. (2025). *About us*. https://papss.com/about-us/

Salampasis, D., & Samakovitis, G. (2024). Regtech frontiers: Innovations, trends, and insights redefining compliance. In H. Baker, G. Filbeck, & G. Filbeck (Eds.), *The emerald handbook of Fintech* (pp. 65–87). Emerald Publishing Limited. https://doi.org/10.1108/978-1-83753-608-520241008

Sarma, M., & Pais, J. (2011). Financial inclusion and development. *Journal of International Development, 23*(5), 613–628. https://doi.org/10.1002/jid.1698

WEF. (2025, April 1). *Developing countries are struggling to achieve their technology aims. Shared digital infrastructure is the answer*. https://www.weforum.org/stories/2025/04/shared-digital-infrastructure-emerging-economies/

World Bank. (2020, November 1). *Key data from regulatory sandboxes across the Globe*. World Bank Group. https://www.worldbank.org/en/topic/fintech/brief/key-data-from-regulatory-sandboxes-across-the-globe

World Bank. (2022a). *Regulation and supervision of Fintech: considerations for EMDE policymakers*. https://documents1.worldbank.org/curated/en/099735204212215248/pdf/P173006033b45702d09522066cbc8338dcb.pdf

World Bank. (2022b, July 11). *Financial Inclusion Support Framework (FISF)*. https://www.worldbank.org/en/topic/financialinclusion/brief/financial-inclusion-support-framework

World Bank. (2023, February 2). *Latest global findex data chart 10 years of progress in financial inclusion*. https://www.worldbank.org/en/news/feature/2023/02/02/latest-global-findex-data-chart-10-years-of-progress-in-financial-inclusion

World Bank. (2024a). Financial inclusion in Sub-Saharan Africa—overview. In *The Global Findex Database 2021*. https://www.worldbank.org/en/publication/globalfindex/brief/financial-inclusion-in-sub-saharan-africa-overview

World Bank. (2024b, April 17). *Data from the Global Findex 2021: The impact of mobile money in Sub-Saharan Africa*. World Bank Group. https://www.worldbank.org/en/publication/globalfindex/brief/data-from-the-global-findex-2021-the-impact-of-mobile-money-in-sub-saharan-africa

World Bank. (2025, January 27). *Financial inclusion: Financial inclusion is a key enabler to reducing poverty and boosting prosperity*. https://www.worldbank.org/en/topic/financialinclusion/overview

Zetzsche, D. A., Buckley, R. P., Barberis, J. N., & Arner, D. W. (2017). Regulating a revolution: From regulatory sandboxes to smart regulation. *Fordham Journal of Corporate and Financial Law, 23*, 31.

CHAPTER 13

Collaborative FinTech Models for Advancing Financial Inclusion: Public–Private Partnerships and Beyond

Khadijah Iddrisu, Simplice A. Asongu, Muazu Ibrahim, and Richard Stephens Cromwell

Introduction

The literature indicates that financial inclusion drives the attainment of the Sustainable Development Goals (SDGs) (Demirgüç-Kunt et al., 2022; Fouejieu et al., 2020; Hussain et al., 2023; Iddrisu et al., 2022). Financial inclusion is the process of ensuring that individuals and businesses, especially those traditionally underserved or excluded, have access to affordable, timely, and appropriate financial products and services such as savings, payments, credit, insurance, and investment options (Doku et al., 2023; Iddrisu et al., 2022, 2023; Salampasis & Mention, 2018). Governments, development partners, and policymakers have actively worked to

K. Iddrisu (✉)
Department of Banking and Finance, Islamic University College, Madina, Ghana
e-mail: khadijahiddris@iug.edu.gh

S. A. Asongu
School of Economics, University of Johannesburg, Johannesburg, South Africa

I. N. Yakubu (ed.), *Banking on Inclusion*, Sustainable Development Goals Series, https://doi.org/10.1007/978-3-031-96716-0_13

advance financial inclusion. A key initiative identified in this effort is the use of financial technology (FinTech) to accelerate financial inclusion. In Africa, a significant FinTech product, mobile money (MoMo), has been utilized to enhance financial inclusion in some unbanked regions. For instance, MoMo adoption has been significantly boosted in several countries, including Kenya (69%), Rwanda (61%), Ghana (60%), Tanzania (45%), Malawi (34%), and others in 2024 (Iddrisu et al., 2025b). This has translated into an increase of financial inclusion. For instance, financial inclusion in Ghana rose to 58% in 2017 and further increased to 68% in 2021 as a result of MoMo.[1] M-PESA facilitates over US$314 billion in transactions annually by its customers (Vodafone Group, 2025).

Several MoMo initiatives, including M-PESA and MTN MoMo, were launched in Africa through collaborative models. Several Multilateral Development Banks (MDBs) and development institutions, including the African Development Bank (AfDB), promote FinTech by launching initiatives like the Africa FinTech Hub, which aims to support and foster FinTech innovations across select African countries (AfDB, 2022a). The United Nations Development Programme (UNDP) Nigeria collaborates with investors to support the training of FinTech start-ups through initiatives like the Timbuktoo Fintech start-ups Accelerator Programme (UNDP Nigeria, 2025). Therefore, this chapter seeks to discuss the collaborative FinTech models in the quest to promote financial inclusion.

Although MoMo, a widely adopted FinTech solution in Africa, has significantly advanced financial inclusion in the areas of remittance, transfers and payments, it offers limited focus on investment opportunities compared to emerging FinTech platforms that prioritize savings and investment (Iddrisu et al., 2025b; Sanga & Aziakpono, 2022). It is essential to foster greater collaboration among firms and other stakeholders

M. Ibrahim
Economics Department, World Bank, Washington, DC, USA
e-mail: imuazu@uds.edu.gh

R. S. Cromwell
Institute of Oil and Gas, University of Cape Coast, Cape Coast, Ghana
e-mail: richard.cromwell@stu.ucc.edu.gh

[1] Read more here: https://www.bog.gov.gh/wp-content/uploads/2023/01/Governors-Remarks-Ghana-FinTech-Awards-2022-27-01-23.pdf Accessed March 1, 2025.

to drive FinTech innovations that broaden financial inclusion, extending beyond remittances, transfers, and payments to encompass a wider range of financial services. The chapter further discusses strategies for scaling more FinTech solutions through partnerships.

The rest of the chapter is structured as follows: Sect. 13.2 discusses some successful Public–Private Partnership (PPP) collaborative models. The role of development organizations and NGOs in fostering collaboration is also discussed in Sect. 13.3. The chapter also discusses the strategies for scaling FinTech solutions through partnerships in 13.4. The chapter ends with a concluding remark which include policy implications.

Successful PPP Models Accelerating Financial Inclusion

Promoting FinTech innovations to advance financial inclusion requires substantial investment, which governments alone cannot fully support. As a result, various African governments through PPP enhanced FinTech development, with the goal of expanding financial inclusion. Therefore, this section discusses some of these models and show how these promote financial inclusion in Africa. Although numerous successful PPP models have advanced FinTech and promoted financial inclusion, this chapter focuses on a few key examples. Some initiatives share similarities, such as the launch of MoMo in various countries following the M-PESA model. As a result, only M-PESA is discussed, while similar models are not covered. The selection was made to avoid redundancy, choosing one representative model from those with similar characteristics.

These models primarily focus on developing innovative financial solutions, investing in ICT infrastructure, establishing agencies and networks to support FinTech, and providing capacity building and training. For instance, M-PESA represents an example of innovative financial solutions, while the Africa Fintech Network emphasizes the creation of agencies and collaborative networks.

The Launch of M-PESA

One of the successful PPP FinTech models is the launch of M-PESA, the first MoMo initiative in Africa and even the world (see Box 13.1). This financial innovation has promoted financial inclusion in Kenya.

For instance, from 2006 to 2021, M-PESA increased financial inclusion from 26% to 84% (Mckinsey & Company, 2022a, b). Leveraging strong partnerships with major money transfer operators like MFS Africa, Western Union, World Remit, MoneyGram, Remitly and M-PESA serves as the primary platform for over US$1.5 billion in annual remittances. This includes handling 60% of formal remittances to Kenya and 20% to Tanzania (Vodafone Group, 2025).

Box 13.1 Creation of M-PESA by Public–Private Partnership

M-PESA, an innovative mobile money (MoMo) service, emerged through a strategic Public–Private Partnership (PPP) that involved collaboration between key public and private sector entities. The private sector, spearheaded by Safaricom and its parent company Vodafone, provided the technological infrastructure and innovative capabilities essential for developing the platform. Commercial Bank of Africa (CBA) managed the trust account that safeguarded customer funds, ensuring that all electronic money was fully backed by physical cash. Faulu Kenya, a microfinance institution, initially suggested utilizing airtime for loan repayments, which evolved into the M-PESA concept. Technical and financial support was provided by MicroSave and the UK Department for International Development (DfID) who contributed £1 million through the Financial Deepening Challenge Fund. From the public sector, the Central Bank of Kenya (CBK) played a crucial regulatory role, addressing settlement, liquidity, and anti-money laundering concerns. The Communications Commission of Kenya (CCK) and the Ministry of Information and Communication provided policy guidance and ensured adherence to telecommunications regulations. This partnership enabled the creation of a secure, efficient, and widely accessible mobile money platform. M-PESA's development began in 2002 with experiments in using airtime as a form of currency. By 2005, Safaricom, Vodafone, CBA, Faulu Kenya, and MicroSave collaborated to pilot the mobile payment service. The passage of the Communications Act of 2006 facilitated the conversion of money into electronic units, paving the way for M-PESA's official launch in 2007. The service allowed users to deposit, withdraw, and transfer money via mobile phones through Safaricom's agent network. Regulatory oversight by the CBK, including the trust account managed by CBA, ensured the security of customer funds. This PPP model successfully overcame initial challenges and became a transformative tool for financial inclusion, reshaping access to financial services both in Kenya and internationally. In early 2020, Safaricom and

Vodacom concluded the acquisition of the M-PESA brand from Vodafone Group through a new joint venture establishment. This partnership provides Vodacom and Safaricom with full control over the M-PESA brand, service support and product development, positioning them to drive the platform's growth across Africa and expand into new markets on the continent.

Source Ndung'u (2021) and Vodafone Group (2025)

NIBBS Instant Payment

Nigerian Inter-Bank Settlement System (NIBSS), a PPP between licensed banks and the Central Bank of Nigeria, developed the NIBSS Instant Payment (NIP) system as a FinTech innovation designed to promote financial inclusion (see Box 13.2). NIP enables instant, 24/7 interbank transfers, enhancing financial accessibility in remote areas by allowing real-time transactions through mobile and digital channels as shown in Box 13.2. For instance, transaction volumes surged to 3.4 billion by 2021 from 371 million in 2017, while transaction values grew from US$135 billion to US$655 billion during the same period. This significant increase in NIP usage was largely traceable to the coronavirus diseases 2019 (COVID-19) pandemic, which heightened the need for digital payment solutions as individuals increasingly sought contactless alternatives for conducting financial transactions (Box 13.2).

Box 13.2 Nigeria Inter-Bank Settlement System Plc (NIBSS) Launched Instant Payment

The Nigerian Inter-Bank Settlement System (NIBSS) in 2011 introduced the NIBSS Instant Payment (NIP) system to facilitate real-time interbank payments and support economic growth through faster, more efficient retail transactions. NIP reduces financial barriers, lowers transaction costs, and enhances convenience, making financial services more accessible to both urban and rural populations. It supports instant electronic funds transfers (EFTs) across various channels such as internet banking, mobile banking, Point of Sales (POS), Automated Teller Machines (ATMs),

Unstructured Supplementary Data (USSD), web platforms, and third-party agents, ensuring immediate value for person-to-business, person-to-person, and business-to-business transactions. Despite initial challenges in securing bank adoption, NIP launched with two small commercial banks. By 2012, all 22 commercial banks, 20 microfinance banks, and six mobile money operators (MMOs) in Nigeria had joined the platform. NIP, initially supporting only credit transfers, expanded to include debit EFTs, mobile wallets, card networks, and proxy identities for improved convenience. In 2014, NIBSS introduced the Bank Verification Number (BVN) to mitigate fraud risks, followed by upgrades that included card interoperability, USSD functionality, QR code integration through the New Quick Response (NQR) platform, and increased settlement cycles. NIBSS continues to upgrade NIP every two to three years, ensuring enhanced performance and monitoring transaction times. In 10 seconds or less, most transactions are processed, with a maximum processing time of 45 seconds.

Transaction volumes increased to 3.4 billion in 2021 from 371 million in 2017, while transaction values rose to US$655 billion in 2021 from US$135 billion in 2017. The rise in NIP usage was accelerated by the coronavirus disease 2019 (COVID-19) pandemic, which significantly boosted the demand for digital payment solutions as people sought contactless methods of conducting financial transactions. NIP's seamless integration into various financial institutions' channels has helped to make it Nigeria's most efficient and reliable real-time funds transfer service, driving increased financial inclusion and economic activity across the country.

Source AfricaNenda (2022) and NIBSS (2025)

Korea Telecom Rwanda Networks' 4G Service

Korea Telecom Rwanda Networks (KTRN), owned by the Government of Rwanda and Korea Telecom, expanded its 4G network in Rwanda (see Box 13.3). This expansion opened up new opportunities for FinTech companies and start-ups, enabling them to drive further innovation and scale their operations. By 2020, KTRN achieved over 96% 4th Generation (4G) coverage in Rwanda, significantly boosting financial inclusion. Formal financial services access grew from 48 to 93% between 2014 and 2020. Enhanced 4G infrastructure facilitated MoMo adoption, with 86%

of adults using services like Airtel Money and MTN MoMo by 2021 (Box 13.3).

Box 13.3 Korea Telecom Rwanda Networks (KTRN) Extended 4G in Rwanda

In 2013, the Rwandan government and Korea Telecom (KT) entered into a transformative partnership, forming Korea Telecom Rwanda Networks (KTRN) to launch 4th Generation (4G wholesale services in Rwanda. This Public–Private Partnership (PPP) aimed to accelerate the country's digital transformation and promote financial inclusion by providing widespread access to high-speed internet. The Rwandan government owns 49% of KTRN, while Korea Telecom holds the remaining 51%. Through this venture, Korea Telecom invested US$140 million and contributed its technological expertise, while the government leveraged its national fibre optic network assets, spectrum, and granted KTRN a 25-year wholesale-only operator license. KTRN partnered with Squire Technologies to enhance its 4G Long-Term Evolution (LTE) network by deploying value-added services, including an Short Message Service Center (SMSC), Unstructured Supplementary Data (USSD) Gateway, and Short Message Service (SMS) campaign portal. These services enable bulk SMS functionality, Application-to-Person (A2P) messaging, and integration with KTRN's IP Multimedia Subsystem (IMS) core, supporting various messaging protocols for seamless communication across networks. This partnership had a profound impact on Rwanda's Information and Communication Technology (ICT) infrastructure, significantly improving internet connectivity across the country. Over 700 base stations across Rwanda have been installed by KTRN, covering above 98% of the population.

By 2020, KTRN had achieved over 96% population coverage for 4G services, making Rwanda one of the best-connected countries in Africa. This widespread internet access has been fundamental in boosting financial inclusion, as more Rwandans have gained access to digital financial services, especially in underserved and rural areas. Between 2014 and 2020, Rwanda saw the proportion of adults having access to formal financial services grow from 48 to 93%. The expansion of mobile money services like MTN Mobile Money and Airtel Money, facilitated by enhanced 4G infrastructure, enabled people to use mobile phones in conducting financial transactions. By 2021, mobile money penetration in Rwanda had reached 86% of the adult population, with transactions exceeding RWF 6 trillion (approximately US$5.8 billion). KTRN's contribution to Rwanda's digital ecosystem has not only bridged the digital divide but also supported the country's financial inclusion goals by providing reliable internet connectivity that enables digital financial services, thus fostering economic growth and development. KTRN increases 4G coverage from 5% in 2014 to 98.5% by 2018. KTRN promotes healthy competition, benefits consumers and enterprises, and supports Rwanda's transformation into East Africa's ICT hub. Despite its achievements, KTRN continues to pursue even more transformative projects for society. Although KTRN initially held a monopoly on delivering 4G services, the government, in 2023, ended this exclusivity and invited other private sector players to participate in the provision of 4G services.

Source Sehloho (2023) and Burkitt-Gray (2023)

Konza Technopolis Project

Through PPP agreement, the Government of Kenya collaborated with private sector partners in the development of a technology hub, the Konza Technopolis (see Box 13.4). The Konza Technopolis Project is a visionary undertaking by the Kenyan government to establish a smart city and innovation hub approximately 64 kilometres southeast of Nairobi. Aligned with Kenya's Vision 2030, this strategic initiative aims to elevate the nation into a middle-income, knowledge-driven economy. This initiative is expected to boost the adoption of FinTech innovations, ultimately advancing financial inclusion.

Box 13.4 Kenya Embarks on Konza Technopolis Project

Konza Technopolis, known as "Africa's Silicon Savannah," is a flagship Public–Private Partnership (PPP) project in Kenya, aligned with the country's Vision 2030 economic development strategy. The Konza Technopolis Development Authority, a government entity in Kenya, is responsible for overseeing the development of the Technopolis and managing investments within the project. Situated about 60 kilometers south of Nairobi, Konza is envisioned as a world-class technology hub, designed to attract tech companies, start-ups, and research institutions. The development spans a 5,000-acre greenfield site and is planned in phases over 20 years. It includes multi-use office spaces, residential areas, and city amenities to support a thriving information, communications, and technology (ICT) sector. The partnership between the Kenyan government and private sector investors is expected to mobilize substantial private investment and creating thousands of jobs. Konza Technopolis has formed strategic alliances with key partners such as Tetra Tech, a global city development leader providing consulting services; HR&A Advisors, a real estate and economic development firm leading master planning efforts; and Gauff Consultants, a German engineering company with international project experience. Konza Technopolis contributes to financial inclusion by fostering an environment conducive to investment and innovation. The project aims to drive economic growth by attracting businesses that create job opportunities. It also supports financial inclusion by providing access to affordable financing and long-term credit to investors, helping bridge the digital divide and promoting economic participation across different sectors of society.

Source Business Today (2023) and Konza Technopolis (2024)

International Financial Inclusion Conference in Nigeria

To promote financial literacy, training and capacity building, Central Bank of Nigeria host an annual International Financial Inclusion Conference (IFIC). In 2023, the Bank partnered with Interswitch to host the 2nd IFIC in Lagos (see Box 13.5).

Box 13.5 CBN Partners with Interswitch to Host Financial Inclusion Conference

The Central Bank of Nigeria (CBN) has collaborated with Interswitch to strengthen training and capacity building through its annual conference. Interswitch, a leading provider of integrated payment and digital commerce solutions in Africa, served as the Platinum Sponsor of the second edition of the International Financial Inclusion Conference (IFIC). This high-profile event, organized by the CBN at the Landmark Event Centre in Lagos, took place on October 5th and 6th, 2023. The IFIC serves as a vital forum for thought leaders, regulators, financial service providers, development partners, and other principal stakeholders in the financial inclusion space to explore emerging trends, tackles principal issues, and develop strategies for creating a more inclusive financial ecosystem. The conference featured networking opportunities, exhibitions showcasing innovative financial inclusion solutions, the prestigious Financial Inclusion Awards, and a series of expert-led panel discussions, including one on 'Fintech-Enabled Financial Inclusion: Last Mile Solutions.' Themed 'Financial Inclusion for All: Global Insights for Local Impact,' the conference reaffirmed CBN's commitment to broadening access to financial services for underserved and excluded communities. Interswitch's sponsorship of the event reflects its commitment that is evolving in view of promoting financial inclusion as well as and supporting sustainable economic development.

Source Interswitch (2023)

The conference focused on advancing financial inclusion through various activities, entailing networking sessions, and exhibitions displaying innovative financial inclusion solutions, the esteemed Financial Inclusion Awards, and engaging panel discussions led by industry experts.

Mobile Money Interoperability in Ghana

The Bank of Ghana, in partnership with Ghana Interbank Payment and Settlement Systems (GhIPSS), MoMo operators, and FinTechs, launched the MoMo Interoperability (MMI) service to streamline fund transfers across mobile networks, bank accounts, and e-zwich cards. Rolled out in two phases in 2018, MMI enables seamless wallet-to-wallet, wallet-to-bank, and wallet-to-e-zwich transactions (Box 13.6). MMI has significantly increased transaction volumes and enhanced Ghana's digital financial ecosystem with a unified, cost-effective system for users. For instance, Ghana's MoMo transactions reached GH¢308 million, making it a leader in Africa's MoMo market in 2019.

Box 13.6 The Launch of Mobile Money Interoperability in Ghana

The Bank of Ghana, in collaboration with Ghana Interbank Payment and Settlement Systems (GhIPSS), mobile money operators, and FinTechs, launched the Mobile Money Interoperability (MMI) service to enable seamless fund transfers across different mobile networks and financial platforms. MMI facilitates direct transfers between mobile money wallets, as well as between wallets, bank accounts, and e-zwich cards, creating a unified financial ecosystem. The rollout occurred in two phases. Phase I, launched on May 10, 2018, introduced seamless transfers between mobile money wallets across different networks and allowed transfers from mobile wallets to bank accounts. Phase II, launched on November 28, 2018, expanded this functionality by enabling transfers between mobile money wallets and e-zwich cards, as well as between e-zwich cards and bank accounts. MMI supports multiple transaction types, including wallet-to-wallet transfers, which allow users to send funds between mobile money platforms. It also enables wallet-to-bank account transfers, making it easier for users to move funds directly into their bank accounts. Additionally, wallet-to-e-zwich card transfers allow direct fund movement from mobile wallets to e-zwich cards. This interoperability has significantly boosted transaction volumes, with the "receiver pays" pricing model adopted to ensure a standardized fee structure. This model recognizes that interoperable payments often flow from smaller providers to larger ones. As a result, MMI has contributed to the growth and efficiency of Ghana's digital financial ecosystem, providing users with more convenient, cost-effective options for financial transactions across networks and platforms.

By 2019, mobile money transactions in Ghana reached GH¢308 million, positioning the country as one of Africa's leading mobile money markets. In 2021, the number of mobile money accounts saw a significant rise, growing from 32.7 million to 40.9 million, reflecting the rapid expansion and adoption of mobile financial services. The launch of MMI contributed significantly to the rise in financial inclusion in Ghana, which grew from 58% in 2017 to 68% by 2021. By 2023, MTN had more than 15.2 million active subscribers to its MoMo service, reflecting a significant increase from approximately 12.7 million subscribers the previous year. Following the introduction of the levy in May 2022, mobile money usage in Ghana dropped by 25%, with smaller transactions seeing reductions of up to 48%. Transaction volumes and revenues declined by 20% to 35%, while cash-out transactions, exempt from the levy, increased by 25% in volume and 61% in value.

Source AFI (2018a, b), Cromwell and Peprah (2025), Iddrisu et al. (2025a), Kulu and Bondzie (2024) and Rattel (2024)

MoMo accounts grew from 32.7 million in 2019 to 40.9 million in 2021, driven by MMI, which boosted financial inclusion from 58 to 68%. MTN's MoMo service had 15.2 million active users in 2023. However, after the 2022 levy, mobile money usage especially transfer dropped by 25%, while cash-out transactions increased significantly (see Box 13.6).

The Creation of African FinTech Network

The Africa FinTech Network (AFN) was established on January 24, 2018, in Lagos, Nigeria, during a FinTech leaders' roundtable, and formally inaugurated on December 4, 2018, at the first Africa FinTech Festival by Nigeria's Vice President and key representatives from regional and global institutions. Officially launched on March 24, 2019, during UNECA's conference, AFN aims to foster connections between Africa and the global fintech community. AFN has 41 member countries and 25 strategic partners with the aim to promote financial inclusion and fintech innovation. Through this network, Africa Fintech Hub (AFH) is created through an agreement between AFN and AfDB who committed US$525,000 grant. The Hub aims to promote knowledge exchange and foster collaboration.

Box 13.7 Africa FinTech Network promote Financial Inclusion Through FinTech Solutions

The Africa FinTech Network (AFN) was conceived on January 24, 2018, during a roundtable of African Financial Technology (fintech) leaders and regulators from seven countries in Lagos, Nigeria, prior to the National Fintech Conference. It was formally inaugurated on December 4, 2018, as the first Africa Fintech Festival by Nigeria's Vice President, the President of the African Development Bank, and key representatives from International Monetary Fund (IMF), United Kingdom Department for International Development (UK-DFID), United Nations Economic Commission for Africa (UNECA), and others. Following strong support from regional and global institutions, the network was officially launched on March 24, 2019, during the UNECA Conference of Ministers of Finance & Economic Planning in Marrakesh, Morocco, coordinated by the Executive Secretary of UNECA. The network's goal is to foster connections between Africa and the global community, enabling open dialogue, building synergies, and creating opportunities in Fintech. It seeks to drive Africa-led Fintech solutions, catalysing the continent's digital economy. The network boasts 41 African member countries, 25 strategic partners, 4 FinTech festivals, and 21 board members. 25 strategic partners include African Union, Ecobank, BFA Global, African Development Bank, Africa Export Import Bank, Korea-Africa Foundation and among others.

AFN's flagship event, the FinTech Festival, promotes financial inclusion by bringing together industry leaders, innovators, and policymakers, fostering dialogue, collaboration, and knowledge exchange within the fintech ecosystem. The African Development Bank, through the Africa

Digital Financial Inclusion Facility (ADFI), has signed a US$525,000 grant agreement with the AFN to establish the Africa Fintech Hub in 2023. This online platform serves as a central resource for fintech activities across Africa, facilitating collaboration, knowledge sharing, and showcasing fintech innovations, including those led by women. The Hub is managed by AFN, with technical support from Cenfri, focusing on innovation, research, and knowledge creation to strengthen Fintech associations and partnerships across the continent. The initiative aims to enhance financial inclusion and support Fintech growth in Africa. AFN also partnered with Cenfri to conduct a study, as part of their African Fintech Radar initiative, assessed 100 FinTech's across 17 African countries. The findings reveal that African Fintechs face a range of challenges, including difficulties in accessing markets, securing funding, navigating regulatory landscapes, and developing products that effectively meet the needs of financially underserved market segments.

Source AFN (2024a, b)

Development Organizations and NGOs in Fostering Collaboration

Development organizations and NGOs play a pivotal role in fostering collaboration for financial inclusion through FinTech by acting as catalysts in creating inclusive ecosystems that address financial disparities, particularly in emerging economies. Their roles can be understood in several key areas such as advocacy and policy support, capacity building and technical assistance, funding and investment, the creation of collaboration platforms, research and data collection, awareness and education and innovative pilots and prototypes.

Advocacy and Policy Support

Development organizations and NGOs work to influence policies that create an enabling environment for FinTech growth, ensuring regulations support innovation while protecting vulnerable populations. They often advocate for policies that encourage the use of digital financial services, reduce barriers to entry for FinTech providers, and promote financial literacy. For instance, an institution like the Consultative Group to Assist the Poor (CGAP)[2] advocacy to support FinTechs in reaching low-income populations (Baur-Yazbeck, 2021). Other institutions such as the Alliance for Financial Inclusion (AFI)[3] also promote financial inclusion through their FinTech policies such as Inclusive Green Finance, National Financial Inclusion Strategy (NFI), Financial Inclusion Data (FID), Digital Financial Services (DFS), and Gender Inclusive Finance (GIF). AFI has introduced a policy framework on FinTech supervision in the African region to support the implementation of financial inclusion policies within its member countries across the AFI network (AFI, 2023). The United Nations Environment Programme Finance Initiative (UNEP FI)[4] promotes and supports policy development through its frameworks, including the Principles for Responsible Banking (PRB), Principles for Responsible Investment (PRI), Principles for Sustainable Insurance (PSI), and the Sustainable Blue Economy Finance Principles (SBEFP) (UNEP FI, 2024).

Capacity Building and Technical Assistance

These organizations provide training and capacity-building initiatives aimed at both FinTech start-ups and underserved communities. They help FinTech companies understand the unique challenges faced by low-income or rural populations and offer technical assistance to enhance the

[2] CGAP is a global partnership of over 30 development organizations, founded in 1995 and housed at the World Bank, dedicated to advancing financial inclusion for the poor. It promotes innovative financial services, conducts research, and fosters partnerships to improve financial access in developing countries.

[3] AFI is a global network of central banks and financial regulators from 84 countries working to advance financial inclusion. Over 15 years, AFI members have introduced 1,130 policies, benefiting 850 million people. AFI's cooperative model fosters knowledge exchange and peer engagement, promoting country-specific policies. Through working groups, events, and reports, AFI supports effective financial inclusion strategies. Its Global Policy Forum, the largest of its kind, connects 700 policymakers annually, while partnerships enhance institutional capacity.

[4] UNEP FI unites banks, insurers, and investors to drive sustainable finance and global economies. For over 30 years, it has connected financial institutions with the UN to shape the sustainability agenda, establishing key frameworks like the Principles for Responsible Banking and Sustainable Insurance. With more than 500 members managing assets over US$170 trillion, UNEP FI provides guidance to help institutions transition to sustainable practices. Founded in 1992, it fosters leadership and promotes sustainability worldwide across all regions.

scalability of FinTech solutions tailored to these groups. For example, AfDB provided technical assistance and capacity building to small financial sectors who focus on SMEs (Box 13.8).

Box 13.8 African Development Bank Support Smaller Financial Institutions

The project seeks US$3.98 million from the Fund for African Private Sector Assistance (FAPA) to provide capacity building to up to 25 smaller financial institutions (FIs) as wall as Technical Assistance (TA) focused on SMEs in Africa, especially in Fragile States and in Low Income Countries. This is part of the AfDB's Africa SME support program, which includes both a funding and TA component. The funding component extends US$125 million in medium- to long-term loans to the FIs, while the TA component strengthens operational efficiencies in areas such as credit assessment, management information systems (MIS) and risk management. The initiative is also linked to the Enhanced Private Sector Assistance (EPSA), a collaboration between the Government of Japan and the AfDB, enhancing the effect of the programme on Africa's private sector development. The TA component is essential to addressing the operational weaknesses of the FIs, enabling them to better serve SMEs. The programme aligns with the Bank's Private Sector Development Strategy, which aims to improve SME access to finance through combined financial and technical support, and supports the Bank's Long-Term Strategy (2013–2022) to deepen financial markets and promote private sector growth in Africa.

Source AfDB (2013)

Funding and Investment

Development organizations and NGOs often act as intermediaries for funding FinTech startups focused on financial inclusion. They can provide grants, seed funding, or facilitate partnerships with impact investors. By doing so, they help FinTech firms develop innovative solutions that cater for unbanked or underbanked populations.

Box 13.9 Microsoft Supporting 10,000 FinTech Start-up
Microsoft, through its Africa Transformation Office (ATO), has announced initiatives to boost investment in Africa's FinTech startup ecosystem over the next five years which will entail the acceleration of the growth of 10,000 African FinTech startups. The global Founders Hub of the company, now available to African startups via the ATO, offers resources such as mentorship, skilling content, Microsoft Azure and GitHub tools, and business support. Additionally, Microsoft is establishing new partnerships with incubators and accelerator in Africa, including Grindstone, FlapMax, Greenhouse, and Seedstars, in order to provide startups with technical skills, access to markets, and funding opportunities. These collaborations will help startups scale by co-selling with Microsoft, gaining access to technology, and co-innovating with Microsoft's engineering and product teams. To further accelerate growth, Microsoft is establishing industry partnerships and alliances with venture capital investors, facilitating access to US$500 million in potential funding for African startups. This investment will be channeled through a network of venture capital investors, including Banque Misr, Global Ventures Capital, and Get Funded Africa, who are committed to supporting start-ups within Microsoft's ecosystem. Over the next five years, Microsoft aims to expand this investor network to scale up African startups and foster economic growth across the continent.

Source Microsoft News Center (2022).

For instance, Techstars, which has invested in approximately 3,000 start-ups worldwide, resulting in a collective graduate market capitalization of US$73 billion, is now expanding its investment focus to Nigeria (Vota, 2022). As part of this shift, Techstars is funding 12 promising startups selected from a competitive pool of applicants, further strengthening the country's entrepreneurial ecosystem (Vota, 2022). Other institutions like Microsoft provided new initiatives to support 10,000 African FinTech startups over 5 years (Box 13.9).

Collaboration Platforms

By fostering collaboration between various stakeholders (including governments, financial institutions, fintech companies, and local communities), NGOs and development organizations help create synergistic relationships. These platforms encourage knowledge-sharing, partnership opportunities, and joint ventures that align FinTech innovations with financial inclusion goals. For instance, an NGO focused on financial inclusion partners with a local government, a major bank, a FinTech startup, and community leaders in a rural region where access to formal financial services is limited. AFN is an example of a collaboration of various NGOs, development organization and most African countries to promote FinTech which in effect promote financial inclusion (Box 13.7).

Research and Data Collection

Development organizations and NGOs often lead in gathering data on financial exclusion and assessing the effectiveness of FinTech solutions in different contexts. By sharing insights and research findings, they help fintech firms design products that meet the specific needs of marginalized populations and measure the impact of their services. For example, European Investment Bank (EIB) conducted research on start-ups and SMEs which helped to outline challenges start-ups and SMEs face and suggest ways to overcome it (EIB, 2024). Also, the AFN collaborated with Cenfri to conduct a study on the challenges faced by FinTech start-ups. AFN and Cenfri revealed that these startups encounter obstacles such as securing funding, navigating regulatory frameworks, and developing products that cater to the needs of financially underserved market segments (Box 13.7).

Awareness and Education

NGOs and development organizations conduct awareness campaigns and financial literacy programmes that educate underserved populations about FinTech solutions. These efforts help build trust in digital financial services and empower individuals to use technology to manage their finances. An example is Brac International, which established a regional office in Nairobi, Kenya, and has been actively conducting various awareness campaigns and financial literacy programmes aimed at educating underserved populations about fintech solutions (Brac, 2025).

Innovative Pilots and Prototypes

Development organizations often sponsor pilot projects that test new FinTech solutions for underserved markets. These pilots help assess the feasibility of new technologies, such as mobile money platforms or blockchain-based services, and provide valuable lessons that can be scaled. For instance, in Mozambique, the World Bank supported a pilot project to test the use of MoMo platforms for social cash transfers. The project aimed to provide low-income households with access to digital wallets, enabling them to receive government payments and conduct transactions more efficiently (Chimal & Machado, 2022). Also, the AfDB is assisting Liberia with a pilot study on an innovative financial inclusion framework aimed at supporting the formalization of artisanal and small-scale mining operations (AfDB, 2022b).

Strategies for Scaling Fintech Solutions Through Partnerships

Scaling fintech solutions through partnerships requires well-defined strategies to leverage synergies, expand market reach, and enhance operational efficiency. Here are key strategies:

1. **Public–Private Partnerships**

Governments and FinTech companies can work together to foster an environment conducive to FinTech innovation by developing comprehensive frameworks that include supportive regulations, infrastructure, and policies (Iddrisu et al., 2022; Iddrisu et al., 2025a). Governments can encourage the growth of FinTech startups while ensuring consumer protection and financial stability through establishing clear and flexible regulatory guidelines. Additionally, investing in digital infrastructure such as high-speed internet and secure payment systems is crucial for the success of FinTech solutions. Collaborative efforts in crafting policies that promote innovation, financial inclusion, and competition can further drive FinTech development, creating a more dynamic and accessible financial ecosystem for businesses and individuals alike. For instance, the Government of Ghana through the Ministry of Communication and digitalisation partnered with some ICT firms including Huawei to expand ICT infrastructure into the rural areas (Box 13.10).

Box 13.10 Ghana Rural Telephony and Digital Inclusion Project Extend ICT Infrastructure to Rural Areas

The Ghana Rural Telephony and Digital Inclusion Project, launched in 2020 with a €155-million facility from the China EXIM Bank, is a collaboration between the Government of Ghana, Huawei and the China National Technical Import and Export Corporation (CNTIC). Local partner Ascend Digital Solutions was also engaged. The project aims to extend mobile telephony services to underserved and unserved rural communities by constructing 2,016 rural telephony sites, ultimately benefiting around four million residents. As of February 2024, 1,010 sites had been built, with 618 operational, providing essential voice and data services to 1,620 rural communities. This initiative has significantly improved connectivity, enhancing access to information, communication, and digital services, and positively impacting the social and economic activities in rural areas.

Source Anane-Amponsah (2024) and Ministry of Information (2024)

2. **Collaboration with Banks and Microfinance Institutions**

FinTech companies can collaborate with traditional banks and microfinance institutions (MFIs) to develop hybrid solutions that blend digital innovation with well-established financial services. Traditional banks and MFIs can enhance their service offerings, making financial products more accessible, efficient, and user-friendly through leveraging the digital capabilities of FinTech, such as mobile banking apps, online lending platforms, and data analytics. This partnership enables traditional institutions to tap into new customer segments, such as underserved populations, while benefiting from the agility of FinTech innovations. In turn, FinTech firms gain from the banks' extensive customer bases, regulatory expertise, and market credibility, creating a mutually beneficial relationship. For instance, FINCA Mobile came into realization due to the partnership between MoMo operators and FINCA Tanzania, a MFI (Box 13.11).

Box 13.11 FINCA Mobile launched via partnership between FINCA Tanzania and MNOs.
In 2013, FINCA Tanzania introduced FINCA Mobile, a mobile banking platform, in collaboration with three mobile network operators (MNOs): Vodacom, Airtel, and Tigo. The goal was to leverage the extensive agent networks of these MNOs to offer FINCA's low-income clients more convenient and affordable financial services, as traveling long distances to branches posed a financial burden. Through FINCA Mobile, clients could conduct various transactions at MNO agents, including deposits, bill payments, transfers, airtime purchases, withdrawals, loan repayments, and request mini-statements. Beside mobile banking aimed to mitigate operational costs, it also grow FINCA Tanzania's customer base, and broaden its outreach. However, partnering with MNOs introduced new risks, such as liquidity management and Know Your Customer (KYC) procedures, which were handled by the MNO agents. Revenue sharing was also implemented, with 60% of commissions going to FINCA and 40% to the MNO agents. FINCA Mobile enhanced the customer experience by eliminating long queues at branches and significantly reducing wait times. Operational costs also decreased, with each transaction costing FINCA US$0.50 at an MNO agent, relative to US$0.85 at FINCA agents and US$1.21 at FINCA branches.

Source AFI (2018a)

3. **Partnerships with Educational Institutions**

FinTech companies can collaborate with universities and training institutions to foster talent development and drive innovation in the FinTech sector. FinTech firms can help design specialized courses, internships, and certification programmes that equip students with the necessary skills in areas such as blockchain, artificial intelligence, data analytics, and digital payments when partner with academic institutions. This collaboration ensures a steady pipeline of skilled professionals to meet the growing demands of the industry. Additionally, universities serve as hubs for research and development, enabling FinTech companies to explore cutting-edge solutions and innovations, advancing the sector while bridging the gap between academia and industry.

4. Engaging with Incubators and Accelerators

Partnering with accelerators and incubators offers FinTech companies some valuable mentorship, business support, and access to new markets. These programmes provide startups with expert guidance from seasoned professionals, helping them navigate the complexities of scaling a business and addressing regulatory challenges.

Box 13.12 Some Incubators and Accelerators in Africa

The Google for Start-ups Accelerator Africa is a three-month program designed for seed to Series A startups across Africa, focusing on those incorporating machine learning and AI into their solutions. Startups from countries including Algeria, Botswana, Cameroon, Côte D'Ivoire, Egypt, Ethiopia, Ghana, Kenya, Morocco, Nigeria, Rwanda, Senegal, South Africa, Tanzania, Tunisia, Uganda, and Zimbabwe are eligible to apply. The accelerator offers equity-free support, mentorship from Google experts, product credits, early access to new Google tools, and advanced technical project partnerships, along with other valuable benefits.

AB Accelerator, launched by Arab Bank, is a FinTech-focused corporate accelerator aimed at developing solutions using emerging technologies within the bank. It enables start-ups to have their solutions tested via a proof-of-concept, with a likelihood for a pilot agreement with Arab Bank. Startups can also integrate with the bank's systems via its open banking developer portal. Applications are accepted on a rolling basis, and those selected undergo validation based on the bank's investment thesis and business needs. Sponsors work closely with applicants during the proof-of-concept development, defining scoping, deliverables, success criteria, and timelines, over a period of three to six months.

Likewise, the Accelerator programme in Egypt by Flat6Labs from 1864, operated in collaboration with Barclays Bank Egypt, targets FinTech startups. The program provides mentorship, office facilities, entrepreneurship training, subject matter sessions, and various benefits from partners. In addition, the accelerator organizes ideation sessions, a FinTech hackathon, a business bootcamp, and workshops. For a duration of three months, the 1864 Accelerator focuses on creating a minimum viable product, acquiring customers, and exploring potential pivots. The programme culminates in a demo day where startups present their ideas to venture capital investors, angels, entrepreneurs, and partners.

GreenHouse Lab (GHL), a leading FinTech accelerator by GreenHouse Capital in Nigeria, targets early-stage FinTech startups offering solutions in financial services, insurance, and remittances. Participating startups can secure up to US$10,000 in funding from GreenHouse Capital. The six-week accelerator features specialised seminars led by experts on topics such as strategy, growth, data analysis, and machine learning. Additionally, startups gain access to GreenHouse Capital's investor and corporate network, alongside exclusive sessions and product credits from partners like AWS, InsiderPR, and Google for startups.

Fintech is a key focus area of the ASIP Accelerator by Startupbootcamp AfriTech (SBC AfriTech) in South Africa, supported by anchor partner Telecel Group. Targeted at startups with a mobile tech emphasis, the three-month remote program offers over EUR 500,000 in benefits, including credits from Google Cloud, AWS, and others, including EUR 15,000 in funding from SBC. The focus of the program entails areas such as alternative finance, cross-border payments, regtech and KYC, and financial inclusion. Startups also have the chance to pilot and test proof-of-concept projects with corporate partners, potentially leading to long-term commercial agreements.

MEST Africa, based in Ghana, offers three incubation and acceleration programmes for early-stage startups. Its Seed Programme provides 18 to 24 months of incubation at MEST hubs, granting access to an internal seed fund with investments ranging from US$50,000 to US$250,000. With the MEST Express programme, participants benefit from 20 weeks of practical workshops and guidance from professionals, with the experience ending in a pitch for equity-free grant funding. Lastly, the MEST Scale programme is a venture accelerator focused on supporting SMEs in Ghana by enhancing operations, addressing technology gaps, and facilitating growth.

These accelerators and incubators provide significant opportunities for fintech start-ups to develop and refine their solutions, offering guidance, resources, and access to potential investors or bank partnerships.

Source FinTech News Network (2025)

FinTechs benefit from tailored advice on product development, marketing strategies, and fundraising, significantly improving their chances of success. In addition, accelerators and incubators often have extensive networks of investors, industry leaders, and potential customers, providing FinTechs with crucial market access and opportunities for collaboration. This partnership can accelerate growth, drive innovation, and position FinTech startups for long-term sustainability and success. There are some incubators and accelerators in Africa (see Box 13.12) where FinTech firms and startups can partner with.

5. **Cross-Border Partnerships**

FinTech companies can establish cross-border partnerships to broaden their market presence and offer interoperable financial solutions across multiple countries. FinTech firms can overcome geographical barriers and tailor their services to meet diverse regulatory requirements and consumer needs in different regions when collaborate with international financial institutions, technology providers, and regulatory bodies. Cross-border partnerships enable the development of seamless digital payment systems, mobile banking platforms, and other fintech innovations that work across national boundaries. These collaborations not only expand the customer base but also enhance financial inclusion by making services more accessible to underserved populations in emerging markets, fostering economic growth and integration. For instance, dLocal partnered with AZA Finance to promote efficient cross-border payment in Africa (Box 13.13).

Box 13.13 dLocal and AZA Finance Collaborate to Enhance Cross-Border Payment in Africa

dLocal, a leading cross-border payment platform, has partnered with AZA Finance, a prominent African FinTech specialising in payments and foreign exchange. This strategic collaboration aims to enhance both companies' offerings through mutual cross-selling by combining dLocal's global payment infrastructure with AZA Finance's extensive regional licenses and foreign exchange expertise. Customers will benefit from more efficient payment processing, expanded market reach, and improved financial services. This partnership will streamline international transactions, offering seamless foreign exchange conversion and faster cross-border payments in key African markets such as Nigeria, Kenya, South Africa, Ghana, Egypt, Cameroon, and Zambia. AZA Finance is recognized for its leadership in African remittances, while dLocal's "One dLocal" platform simplifies global payments by providing a single API, contract, and settlement solution for merchants connecting with consumers in emerging markets.

Source FinTech Magazine Africa (2025)

6. **Partnerships with Local Communities**

FinTech companies can directly engage with local communities to co-create financial solutions that are tailored to their specific needs and challenges. When community members are involved in the design and development process, FinTech firms can better understand local economic conditions, cultural preferences, and barriers to financial access. This collaborative approach ensures that the resulting products and services, such as mobile banking apps, micro-lending platforms, or payment solutions, are user-friendly and responsive to real-world demands. Engaging communities foster trust and drive adoption, while also empowering local populations to participate in shaping FinTech innovations that improve financial inclusion, economic empowerment, and sustainable development. For example, Tosin Eniolorunda founded Moniepoint, formerly known as TeamApt, through a collaborative partnership with the local community (Tech Culture Africa, 2025).

7. **Partnerships with International Organizations**

FinTech companies can partner with international organizations such as the World Bank, AfDB, and UNDP to gain access to critical funding, technical assistance, and expert knowledge. These organizations offer financial support through grants, loans, and investment programmes that can help FinTech firms scale their operations and develop innovative financial solutions. Additionally, they provide technical assistance in areas like regulatory compliance, market entry strategies, and capacity building. Partnering with these global institutions also opens opportunities for knowledge exchange and collaboration on projects that aim to advance financial inclusion, digital transformation, and economic development in emerging markets, fostering long-term growth and impact. For example, the partnership between IFC and C2FO aim to boost financing for local enterprise (Box 13.14).

Box 13.14: Partnership between IFC and C2FO Boosts Financing for African Enterprises

IFC, a World Bank Group member, has partnered with C_2FO, a global supply chain finance platform, to boost affordable finance access for African micro, small, and medium enterprises (MSMEs). This marks IFC's first dedicated supply chain finance facility for smaller businesses in Africa. MSMEs, representing up to 90% of businesses and 80% of jobs in Africa, often face challenges obtaining working capital through traditional means. This initiative aims to address these gaps by leveraging C2FO's patented technology and dynamic discounting model. The platform will connect MSME suppliers with anchor buyers and financial institutions, allowing MSMEs to convert sales receivables into immediate cash without collateral, thus improving access to affordable financing.The program will initially launch in Nigeria, with an estimated potential to unlock $25 billion annually for MSMEs. IFC Managing Director emphasized the importance of this partnership in addressing financing challenges and fostering economic growth. C_2FO CEO highlighted the impact of the collaboration, focusing on providing much-needed liquidity for MSMEs, starting with Nigeria's vibrant small business sector. This initiative aligns with broader efforts to strengthen food security and sustainable economic ecosystems across Africa.

Source World Bank (2024)

Limitations of Collaborative FinTech Models

The following are some of the challenges that confront the collaborative FinTech Models for enhancing financial inclusion.

1. **Regulatory Uncertainty and Fragmentation**

Collaborative FinTech models typically involve a range of stakeholders, including banks, FinTech companies, telecommunications providers, and other financial service actors. Each of these entities often operates under different regulatory frameworks and oversight bodies. This regulatory diversity can create significant challenges for collaboration, as there may be inconsistencies or gaps in legal obligations, compliance standards, and operational requirements. The absence of harmonised policies and clearly defined regulatory guidelines complicates the formation of effective partnerships, delays product development, and increases legal and operational risks. Consequently, this regulatory fragmentation can undermine the overall effectiveness of collaborative efforts aimed at enhancing financial inclusion (Fang & Wen, 2024).

2. **Infrastructure and Connectivity Constraints**

In some underserved and remote communities across Africa, the lack of reliable digital infrastructure significantly limits the potential of FinTech solutions, even when they are developed through strong collaborative efforts. Challenges such as limited internet connectivity, low mobile network coverage, irregular electricity supply, and insufficient access to affordable smartphones create barriers to accessing digital financial services (Adelaja et al., 2024). Without the foundational infrastructure, users are unable to fully engage with or benefit from these innovations. As a result, collaborative FinTech models may fall short of achieving their intended goals of inclusion and empowerment, particularly among the most marginalized populations.

3. **Data Privacy and Security Concerns**

In collaborative FinTech models, customer data is often shared among various stakeholders such as banks, FinTech firms, telecom companies, and regulators to enhance service delivery and financial inclusion (Ediagbonya & Tioluwani, 2023). However, this interconnectedness raises significant concerns about data privacy, protection, and cybersecurity. Inadequate or inconsistent data governance frameworks across partners may expose user information to misuse, unauthorized access, or breaches. The absence of strong, enforceable data protection policies not only increases security risks but also erodes user confidence in digital financial services. When users perceive their personal data to be unsafe, they are less likely to adopt or engage with these collaborative platforms.

4. **Unequal Bargaining Power**

Smaller FinTech companies often face significant challenges when entering into partnerships with larger, more established institutions such as banks or telecommunications firms (Harasim, 2021). These larger entities typically possess greater financial resources, regulatory influence, and market control, which can result in power imbalances during negotiations (Horváth et al., 2022). As a result, the terms of collaboration may disproportionately favour the larger partners, limiting the smaller

FinTech firms' ability to innovate or effectively contribute to inclusion-focused goals (Vasiljeva & Lukanova, 2016). This imbalance can stifle the intended impact of collaborative models, as the unique strengths of smaller FinTech such as agility, grassroots innovation, and local insights may be underutilized or overshadowed in the partnership.

5. **Competition vs. Collaboration Tension**

Traditional financial institutions and FinTech companies often operate with differing objectives, organizational cultures, and market strategies (Ha et al., 2025). While both parties may recognize the value of collaboration to enhance financial inclusion, aligning their interests can be difficult (Zubairu et al., 2025). Traditional institutions may be cautious about sharing customer data, technology, or market space, fearing loss of competitive advantage. Meanwhile, FinTechs may push for greater innovation and faster implementation. These conflicting priorities can create tension, limit transparency, and slow down decision-making processes. As a result, the effectiveness of partnerships intended to foster inclusive financial services may be compromised, reducing their impact on underserved populations (Tiony & Yin, 2024).

Key Considerations for Scaling FinTech Solutions

To attract partnerships and foster collaborations, FinTech solutions must prioritize affordable service delivery, enhance infrastructure development, embrace localization, safeguard data privacy, and promote digital literacy.

1. **Affordability in Service Provision**

To ensure that FinTech solutions are accessible to low-income users, companies must prioritize affordability by offering cost-effective services tailored to this demographic (McKinsey & Company, 2022a, b). This can be achieved through low transaction fees, flexible payment plans, or freemium models where basic services are free and advanced features come at a nominal cost. By leveraging technology such as mobile platforms and digital wallets, FinTech firms can reduce operational costs, passing those savings on to users. Additionally, collaborating with microfinance institutions and government programmes can provide subsidies or incentives, further reducing financial barriers. Making affordability a priority ensures financial inclusion and empowers underserved communities to access essential financial services.

2. **Enhancing Infrastructure Development**

Addressing challenges related to internet connectivity, electricity, and mobile network coverage is critical for ensuring the widespread adoption of FinTech solutions, particularly in underserved or rural areas (EIB, 2024). FinTech companies, in collaboration with governments and telecom providers, can invest in expanding digital infrastructure, including reliable internet and mobile networks, to reach more communities. Solar-powered solutions and off-grid energy systems can help mitigate unreliable electricity supply, enabling users to access financial services in remote locations. Additionally, designing offline-compatible services, such as USSD-based banking or low-data mobile apps, allows users to engage with financial platforms even in areas with limited connectivity, fostering greater inclusion and accessibility.

3. **Localization**

Tailoring FinTech solutions to meet the unique needs of different regions and populations is essential for maximizing impact and inclusivity (Iddrisu et al., 2025a, b). Each region or community has distinct economic conditions, cultural norms, and financial behaviours, requiring customized approaches to service delivery. By conducting in-depth market research and engaging with local stakeholders, FinTech companies can design products that address specific challenges, such as language barriers, varying income levels, and regulatory requirements. Solutions like micro-lending platforms, mobile banking apps, and digital wallets can be adapted to suit the preferences and needs of particular demographics, ensuring that FinTech services are relevant, accessible, and effective in promoting financial inclusion and economic empowerment.

4. **Ensuring Data Privacy**

Implementing robust data protection measures is essential for building consumer confidence in FinTech services (World Bank, 2022). With the increasing reliance on digital platforms for financial transactions, consumers need assurance that their personal and financial data is secure. FinTech companies must adopt stringent security protocols, including encryption, multi-factor authentication, and regular system audits, to safeguard sensitive information from cyber threats. Compliance with data privacy regulations, such as GDPR or other local frameworks, further enhances trust. Transparent communication about data usage, protection policies, and response plans in case of breaches is critical. By prioritizing data security, fintech firms can foster trust, encourage adoption, and enhance long-term user loyalty.

5. **Digital Literacy**

Investing in education and awareness campaigns is vital for building trust and driving adoption of FinTech solutions, particularly among underserved populations (Abdelghaffar et al., 2023). Many individuals are unfamiliar with digital financial services, and concerns about security, usability, or relevance may hinder their participation. FinTech companies can collaborate with governments, NGOs, and local organizations to develop educational programmes that explain the benefits of digital finance, such as mobile banking, digital payments, and online lending. These initiatives should focus on financial literacy, cybersecurity awareness, and practical demonstrations. By providing clear, accessible information and addressing common concerns, fintech firms can build trust, increase adoption, and empower communities to embrace innovative financial solution.

Conclusion

The evidence clearly demonstrates that financial inclusion plays a critical role in advancing the SDGs, particularly through the utilization of FinTech. Successful models, such as M-PESA, MMI, establishment of AFN, NIP and among others have significantly expanded financial access across Africa. However, the focus on remittances and payments must be broadened to include investment opportunities, savings, and other financial services. Therefore, the need to foster more collaborations and some development and NGOs are in the business of fostering collaborations. For instance, the chapter identified that some development and

NGOs enhance advocacy and policy support, capacity building and technical assistance, funding and investment, the creation of collaboration platforms, research and data collection, awareness and education and innovative pilots and prototypes. To attract partnerships and collaborations, FinTech solutions should focus on delivering affordable services, advancing infrastructure development, adopting localization strategies, ensuring data privacy, and promoting digital literacy.

The chapter provides some policy implications based on the discussions made. First, policymakers should support the development of diverse FinTech solutions that extend beyond remittances, promoting access to a wider range of financial services, including savings and investments, to foster financial inclusion. Second, Governments should continue to collaborate with private entities through PPP models, encouraging investment in financial infrastructure, capacity-building programmes, and technology platforms that enhance financial inclusion. Third, regulatory frameworks should be established or strengthened to promote FinTech innovation while ensuring consumer protection and maintaining financial stability. This includes enabling new business models like mobile banking and FinTech services that focus on underserved populations. Fourth, development organizations and NGOs should continue their efforts in providing technical assistance, capacity-building, and funding for FinTech startups, particularly those serving low-income or rural populations. Governments should collaborate with these entities to scale innovative pilots and prototypes aimed at achieving financial inclusion. Last, financial education initiatives, particularly those targeting rural and marginalized populations, should be expanded to raise awareness of the benefits of FinTech solutions and foster trust in digital financial services.

References

Abdelghaffar, R. A., Emam, H. A., & Samak, N. A. (2023). Financial inclusion and human development: Is there a nexus? *Journal of Humanities and Applied Social Sciences, 5*(3), 163–177. https://doi.org/10.1108/JHASS-11-2021-0178

Adelaja, A. O., Umeorah, S. C., Abikoye, B. E., & Nezianya, M. C. (2024). Advancing financial inclusion through fintech: Solutions for unbanked and underbanked populations. *World Journal of Advanced Research and Reviews, 23*(2), 427–438. https://doi.org/10.30574/wjarr.2024.23.2.2379

AfDB. (2013). *Regional Technical Assistance to support SME focused financial institutions benefiting under AfDB's Africa SME support Program*. https://www.afdb.org/sites/default/files/documents/projects-and-operations/multinational_-_multinational_-_technical_assistance_to_support_sme_focused_financial_institutions_benefiting_under_afdbs_africa_sme_support_program.pdf

AfDB. (2022a). *Africa Fintech Hub (The Hub)*. https://www.afdb.org/sites/default/files/documents/projects-and-operations/multinational_-_africa_fintech_hub_0.pdf

AfDB. (2022b). *Financial inclusion framework and implementation roadmap: An innovative financial inclusion framework to support artisanal and small-scale mining formalisation in Liberia*. https://www.afdb.org/sites/default/files/documents/publications/financial_inclusion_framework_and_implementation_roadmap_final_signed_version.pdf

AFI. (2018a). *Digital transformation of microfinance and digitization of micro-finance services to deepen financial inclusion in Africa*. https://www.afi-global.org/sites/default/files/publications/2018-08/AFI_AfPI_SpecialReport_AW_digital.pdf

AFI. (2018b, May 16). *Ghana's first Mobile Money Interoperability System deepens financial inclusion and promotes cashless agenda*. https://www.afi-global.org/news/ghanas-first-mobile-money-interoperability-system-deepens-financial-inclusion-and-promotes-cashless-agenda/

AFI. (2023). *The supervision of FinTech in the African Region*. https://www.afi-global.org/wp-content/uploads/2024/10/The-Supervision-of-Fintech-in-the-African-Region.pdf

AFN. (2024a). *Africa Fintech Hub: Online one-stop shop to strengthen FinTechs across Africa*. https://dev.africafintechnetwork.com/africa-fintech-hub/?_gl=1*1hse84t*_ga*MTEzNjcyMzc5OC4xNzQwOTQwMTk5*_ga_ZTS4VPY0BH*MTc0MDk0MDE5OC4xLjEuMTc0MDk0MDI3NS4wLjAuMA

AFN. (2024b). *With more than 40 member countries*. https://africafintechnetwork.com/about-us/

AfricaNenda. (2022). *The state of instant and inclusive payment systems in Africa: SIIPS 2022—Case study*. https://www.africanenda.org/uploads/files/22312_EN_SIIPS_Casestudy_NIP_HQ.pdf

Anane-Amponsah, M. (2024, February 19). *1,000 rural telephony sites completed*. Graphic Online. https://www.graphic.com.gh/news/general-news/ghana-news-1-000-rural-telephony-sites-completed.html

Baur-Yazbeck, S. (2021). *Development funders and inclusive Fintechs: Analyzing one decade of funding flows*.

Brac. (2025). *Kenya: The Africa Regional Office was set up in 2019 in Nairobi, Kenya as the hub which oversees programmatic operations of BRAC International in Uganda, Tanzania, Rwanda, Liberia, South Sudan, and Sierra Leone.* https://bracinternational.org/kenya/#our-story

Burkitt-Gray, A. (2023, February 9). *Rwanda to end 4G wholesale deal for KT partner.* https://www.capacitymedia.com/article/2b9bl3k0b92djbvw35iio/news/rwanda-to-end-4g-wholesale-deal-for-kt-partner

Business Today. (2023, January 24). *Konza technopolis kicks off access to affordable financing talks for its investors.*

Chimal, S., & Machado, A. (2022, March 18). *A path of opportunities in Mozambique: G2P digital payments and financial inclusion for social resilience.* https://blogs.worldbank.org/en/africacan/path-opportunities-mozambique-g2p-digital-payments-and-financial-inclusion-social

Cromwell, R. S., & Peprah, J. A. (2025). Banking business models and sustainable development: Challenges and opportunities. In I. N. Yakubu (Ed.), *Strategic approaches to banking business and sustainable development goals* (pp. 3–22). Springer. https://doi.org/10.1007/978-3-031-80744-2_1

Demirgüç-Kunt, A., Klapper, L., Singer, D., & Ansar, S. (2022). *The Global Findex Database 2021: Financial inclusion, digital payments, and resilience in the age of COVID-19.* World Bank Publications.

Doku, J. N., Iddrisu, K., Bortey, D. N. A. S., & Ladime, J. (2023). Impact of digital financial technology on financial inclusion in Sub- Saharan Africa: The moderation role of institutional quality. *African Finance Journal*, *25*(2).

Ediagbonya, V., & Tioluwani, C. (2023). The role of fintech in driving financial inclusion in developing and emerging markets: Issues, challenges and prospects. *Technological Sustainability, 2*(1), 100–119. https://doi.org/10.1108/TECHS-10-2021-0017

EIB. (2024). *Finance in Africa: Unlocking investment in an era of digital transformation and climate transition.*

Fang, Y., & Wen, G. (2024). Stability analysis of innovation collaboration between commercial banks and Fintech companies. *Mathematics, 12*(17), 2724. https://doi.org/10.3390/math12172724

FinTech Magazine Africa. (2025, February 18). *dLocal and AZA finance forge strategic partnership to enhance cross-border payments in Africa.*

FinTech News Network. (2025). *FinTech incubators and accelerators in Africa.* https://fintechnews.africa/fintech-incubators-and-accelerators-in-africa/

Fouejieu, A., Sahay, R., Cihak, M., & Chen, S. (2020). Financial inclusion and inequality: A cross-country analysis. *The Journal of International Trade & Economic Development, 29*(8), 1018–1048. https://doi.org/10.1080/09638199.2020.1785532

Ha, D., Le, P., & Nguyen, D. K. (2025). Financial inclusion and fintech: A state-of-the-art systematic literature review. *Financial Innovation, 11*(1), 69. https://doi.org/10.1186/s40854-024-00741-0

Harasim, J. (2021). FinTechs, BigTechs and Banks—When Cooperation and When Competition? *Journal of Risk and Financial Management, 14*(12), 614. https://doi.org/10.3390/jrfm14120614

Horváth, D., Kerényi, Á., & Szabó, R. Z. (2022). Intended benefits and challenges of cooperation between FinTechs and commercial banks. *Acta Oeconomica, 72*(3), 289–308. https://doi.org/10.1556/032.2022.00023

Hussain, S., Gul, R., & Ullah, S. (2023). Role of financial inclusion and ICT for sustainable economic development in developing countries. *Technological Forecasting and Social Change, 194*(September 2022), 122725. https://doi.org/10.1016/j.techfore.2023.122725

Iddrisu, K., Abor, J. Y., & Banyen, K. T. (2022). Fintech, foreign bank presence and inclusive finance in Africa: Using a quantile regression approach. *Cogent Economics & Finance, 10*(1). https://doi.org/10.1080/23322039.2022.2157120

Iddrisu, K., Doku, J. N., Abor, J. Y., & Dziwornu, R. (2023). Financial inclusion and inclusive growth in Africa: What is the moderation role of financial stability? *Cogent Economics & Finance, 11*(2). https://doi.org/10.1080/23322039.2023.2267857

Iddrisu, K., Ofoeda, I., Issah, O., & Iddrisu, M. (2025a). Gender equality and women's empowerment in banking. In I. Yakubu (Ed.), *Strategic approaches to banking business and sustainable development goals. Sustainable development goals series*(pp. 179–193). Springer. https://doi.org/10.1007/978-3-031-80744-2_11

Iddrisu, K., Yakubu, I. N., & Asongu, S. A. (2025b). FinTech innovations for sustainable banking. In *Strategic approaches to banking business and sustainable development goals. Sustainable development goals series* (pp. 63–86). Springer. https://doi.org/10.1007/978-3-031-80744-2_4

Interswitch. (2023). *Interswitch partners Central Bank of Nigeria (CBN) to sponsor the 2nd International Financial Inclusion Conference in Lagos*. https://interswitchgroup.com/interswitch-partners-central-bank-of-nigeria-cbn-to-sponsor-the-2nd/

Konza Technopolis. (2024, July 11). *Who manages Konza Technopolis?* https://konza.go.ke/knowledge-base/who-manages-konza-technopolis/?form=MG0AV3&form=MG0AV3

Kulu, E., & Bondzie, E. A. (2024). Mobile money, credit to deposit ratio and monetary policy: Empirics from Ghana. *Transnational Corporations Review, 16*(3), Article 200060. https://doi.org/10.1016/j.tncr.2024.200060

Mckinsey & Company. (2022a, June 29). *Driven by purpose: 15 years of M-Pesa's evolution*. Talking Business Matters. https://www.mckinsey.com/industries/financial-services/our-insights/driven-by-purpose-15-years-of-m-pesas-evolution

McKinsey & Company. (2022b). *Fintech in Africa: The end of the beginning*. https://www.mckinsey.com/industries/financial-services/our-insights/fintech-in-africa-the-end-of-the-beginning

Microsoft News Center. (2022, March 8). *Microsoft announces new initiatives to support 10,000 African start-ups over next five years*. https://news.microsoft.com/en-xm/2022/03/08/microsoft-announces-new-initiatives-to-support-10000-african-start-ups-over-next-five-years/

Ministry of Information. (2024). *Statement by the Minister for Communications and Digitalisation, Mrs. Ursula Owusu-Ekuful*. https://moc.gov.gh/wp-content/uploads/2023/03/FEB-2024-PRESS-BRIEFING_MOCD.pdf?form=MG0AV3&form=MG0AV3

Ndung'u, N. S. (2021). *A digital financial services revolution in Kenya: The M-Pesa case study*. https://aercafrica.org/old-website/wp-content/uploads/2021/03/AERC-MPesa-Case-Study.pdf

NIBSS. (2025). *Digital payment infrastructure to promote financial inclusion*. https://nibss-plc.com.ng/about-nibss/

Rattel, F. (2024). *The impact of mobile money interoperability on financial inclusion Evidence from five country case studies*.

Salampasis, D., & Mention, A.-L. (2018). FinTech: Harnessing innovation for financial inclusion. In *Handbook of blockchain, digital finance, and inclusion, Volume 2* (pp. 451–461). Elsevier. https://doi.org/10.1016/B978-0-12-812282-2.00018-8

Sanga, B., & Aziakpono, M. (2022). The impact of technological innovations on financial deepening: Implications for SME financing in Africa. *African Development Review, 34*(4), 429–442. https://doi.org/10.1111/1467-8268.12668

Sehloho, M. (2023, February 7). *Korea Telecom Rwanda Networks loses 4G infrastructure monopoly*. https://www.connectingafrica.com/4g-networks/korea-telecom-rwanda-networks-loses-4g-infrastructure-monopoly?form=MG0AV3&form=MG0AV3

Tech Culture Africa. (2025, January 18). *Top 10 Africa FinTech companies transforming finance in 2023*. https://techcultureafrica.com/african-fintechs?form=MG0AV3

Tiony, O. K., & Yin, Y. (2024). Financial technology and its role in promoting financial inclusion and economic growth in Kenya. *American Journal of Industrial and Business Management, 14*(07), 943–968. https://doi.org/10.4236/ajibm.2024.147049

UNDP Nigeria. (2025, January 12). *20 high impact fintech startups selected to advance to the acceleration phase of the Timbuktoo Fintech accelerator programme*. UNDP Nigeria.

UNEP FI. (2024). *About Us*. UNEP FI. https://www.unepfi.org/about/about-us/

Vasiljeva, T., & Lukanova, K. (2016). Commercial banks and fintech companies in the digital transformation: challenges for the future. *Journal of Business Management*, *11*.

Vodafone Group. (2025). *51 million: Customers are making over $314 billion in transactions per year through M-PESA*. https://www.vodafone.com/about-vodafone/what-we-do/m-pesa

Vota, W. (2022, August 1). *Apply Now: $120,000 for African financial technology startup companies*. https://www.ictworks.org/african-fintech-startup-companies/?form=MG0AV3&form=MG0AV3

World Bank. (2022). *Financial consumer protection and Fintech: An overview of new manifestations of consumer risks and emerging regulatory approaches*.

World Bank. (2024, October 28). *IFC and C2FO partner to enhance financing for local enterprises in Africa*. https://www.ifc.org/en/pressroom/2024/ifc-and-c2fo-partner-to-enhance-financing-for-local-enterprises-in-africa

Zubairu, I., Amanquah, B., Kwarteng, F., & Bortey, N. (2025). Examining the role of Financial Technology (FinTech) in financial inclusion in Ghana: An evaluation of the strategies, impacts, and challenges in practice. *International Journal of Economics, Finance and Management Sciences*, *13*(1), 1–19. https://doi.org/10.11648/j.ijefm.20251301.11

CHAPTER 14

The Future of Financial Inclusion in Africa: Policy and Strategic Innovations

Mohammed Ridwan Saani, Ibrahim Nandom Yakubu, Mubarik Salifu, and Abdul-Latif Mohammed

Introduction

Financial inclusion in Africa stands at a pivotal crossroads. Over the past two decades, the continent has witnessed significant progress, largely driven by the rapid spread of mobile money, agent banking, and digital financial services. These innovations have expanded access to millions

M. R. Saani · M. Salifu (✉)
School of Economics, University for Development Studies, Tamale, Ghana
e-mail: smubarik@uds.edu.gh

M. R. Saani
e-mail: msaani@uds.edu.gh

I. N. Yakubu
School of Business, University for Development Studies, Tamale, Ghana
e-mail: ibrahim.yakubu@uds.edu.gh

A.-L. Mohammed
Newcastle Business School, University of Newcastle, Callaghan, NSW, Australia
e-mail: AbdulLatif.Mohammed@uon.edu.au

I. N. Yakubu (ed.), *Banking on Inclusion*, Sustainable Development Goals Series, https://doi.org/10.1007/978-3-031-96716-0_14

of previously unbanked individuals, particularly in East and West Africa (Goodwell, 2025; World Bank, 2024). However, as Chapter 1 demonstrated, this progress has been uneven, and exclusion remains widespread. More than 350 million African adults remain outside the formal financial system, and even among those with accounts, many do not use them regularly or meaningfully (AfricaNenda, 2023).

As Africa's economies undergo structural transformation, fueled by urbanization, digitalization, and demographic shifts, the urgency to move beyond access toward meaningful financial empowerment has never been greater. The continent's youthful population, expanding digital infrastructure, and growing fintech sector present an unprecedented opportunity to leapfrog traditional financial models and build inclusive, people-centered systems (Klapper et al., 2025). At the same time, challenges related to inequality, informality, regulatory fragmentation, digital literacy, and trust continue to limit the impact of financial inclusion initiatives (Anakpo et al., 2023).

The COVID-19 pandemic further exposed and intensified these gaps. It catalyzed the digitization of government-to-person (G2P) transfers, merchant payments, and remittances, yet also highlighted structural weaknesses in identity systems, infrastructure, and ecosystem coordination (Global Partnership for Financial Inclusion, 2021; Ha & Nguyen, 2024). In the post-pandemic era, financial inclusion must be reimagined, not as a siloed development goal but as a foundational enabler of inclusive economic recovery, resilience, and long-term transformation.

This chapter explores the future of financial inclusion in Africa through the lens of strategic innovation and policy reform. It argues that the next phase of inclusion must go beyond account proliferation to focus on usage, relevance, empowerment, and impact. It also emphasizes the importance of inclusive ecosystems where regulation, infrastructure, product design, and consumer protection evolve in tandem to meet the needs of all, especially the underserved.

Drawing from emerging trends, global best practices, and local innovations, the chapter identifies strategic policy levers, technological enablers, and institutional pathways that can help build inclusive, resilient, and equitable financial systems across the continent. In doing so, it provides a roadmap for governments, central banks, development partners, and private sector actors committed to achieving universal, meaningful financial inclusion in Africa.

Rethinking Financial Inclusion in the Digital Age

In recent years, the concept of financial inclusion has evolved from a narrow focus on account ownership to a broader vision of economic participation, resilience, and empowerment. Nowhere is this shift more urgent than in Africa, where mobile technology has revolutionized access but has not yet translated into widespread financial capability or sustained economic uplift (European Investment Bank, 2024; Onyango, 2025). As the continent becomes increasingly digitized, it is imperative to rethink what financial inclusion should mean in this new context.

The digital era presents a unique opportunity for Africa to leapfrog legacy systems and build inclusive financial ecosystems tailored to its development realities. With over 650 million mobile phone users and a fast-growing fintech landscape, Africa is poised to harness digital infrastructure to serve populations historically excluded from formal banking (GSMA, 2024; Mahlangu, 2024). However, the rapid digitalization of financial services also presents new challenges, including the deepening of the digital divide, increased exposure to cyber vulnerabilities, and the marginalization of those without identification, literacy, or stable internet access (Natalucci et al., 2024; Weisman-Pitts, 2024).

Traditional definitions of inclusion, centered around access to a bank account, are no longer adequate. While account ownership is a necessary first step, it is not sufficient. Inclusion must now be measured by how people use financial tools, how those tools meet their needs, and how they translate into improved well-being and agency (Women's World Banking, 2023). An individual with a dormant account or limited ability to transact meaningfully is not truly included. Likewise, access to credit without transparency, security, or fair terms may do more harm than good.

This broader framing of financial inclusion in the digital age requires attention to three interrelated goals: access, usage, and impact. First, people must be able to easily and affordably access financial services through channels that reflect their realities, whether mobile money, agent networks, cooperatives, or digital banks. Second, they must use these services regularly and confidently, engaging in savings, payments, credit, and insurance in ways that support their livelihoods. Third, the services must have measurable impact, enhancing resilience to shocks, enabling investment in education or enterprise, and strengthening autonomy, especially for women and youth. Achieving this broader vision also depends on building inclusive digital public infrastructure (Batagoda,

2024; Özyilmaz, 2024). This includes interoperable payment systems, robust digital identity frameworks, credit and data-sharing platforms, and consumer protection systems adapted to digital contexts. As seen in countries like India, Brazil, and Rwanda, when public and private actors invest in shared rails, such as instant payment switches and national ID-linked wallets, new opportunities emerge to reach underserved users at scale and reduce costs for providers (see Box 14.1).

Rethinking inclusion also requires moving from vertical, product-specific approaches to ecosystem-level strategies (Tugendhat, 2024). This means aligning regulation, innovation, infrastructure, and demand-side capabilities. For example, digital financial services are most effective when they are embedded in broader systems such as agriculture value chains, health programs, social protection transfers, or e-commerce platforms. When users encounter finance not as an isolated product but as part of a relevant life solution, adoption is more likely and more impactful.

Lastly, the future of financial inclusion must be human-centered. Technology can expand reach, but meaningful inclusion will require trust, relevance, and safety (Nesbitt, 2022). This calls for design approaches that consider the needs of low-literacy users, women with limited decision-making power, or youth navigating informal economies. It also demands strong safeguards for data privacy, algorithmic fairness, and grievance redress.

In essence, the digital age requires a bold rethinking of financial inclusion, not as a one-size-fits-all target but as a dynamic process grounded in usage, empowerment, and resilience. This vision must inform the policies, platforms, and partnerships that shape the next generation of inclusive finance in Africa. The next section explores the key policy levers that can support this transformation.

Box 14.1 Leveraging Shared Digital Payment Rails for Scalable Financial Inclusion

Several countries illustrate how collaborative investments in shared digital infrastructure can advance financial inclusion and innovation. India's Unified Payments Interface (UPI), developed by the National Payments Corporation of India, is a prime example. It connects banks, fintechs, and digital wallets through an interoperable platform, enabling fast and low-cost mobile payments. Its success is attributed to joint efforts by government, banks, and technology firms, which supported its rapid adoption. Similarly, Brazil's PIX system, launched by the Central Bank, offers free and real-time payments for all, driving high transaction volumes and fostering financial innovation. In Rwanda, systems like R-Switch and the upcoming National Digital Payment System promote interoperability among banks, microfinance institutions, and mobile wallets, reducing costs and expanding access to digital financial services. These examples show that public and private cooperation in building inclusive digital infrastructure creates the foundation for scalable and accessible financial ecosystems.

Source D'Silva et al. (2019), Cracknell (2023)

Strategic Policy Levers for Inclusive Finance

As Africa's financial ecosystem evolves through digital transformation, policy and regulation must adapt to foster innovation while ensuring inclusion and protection. This section outlines key policy levers for advancing inclusive finance: regulatory innovation, national financial inclusion strategies, gender- and youth-responsive policies, and consumer protection with financial literacy.

Regulatory Innovation and Enabling Frameworks

Inclusive finance requires flexible, adaptive regulation that accommodates new digital actors and platforms (Mensah, 2025). Traditional banking laws often hinder low-margin, digital-first services. Tiered Know Your Customer (KYC) frameworks have proven effective in expanding access by easing identification requirements for low-value accounts, as seen in Kenya and Ghana. Regulatory sandboxes in countries like Nigeria, Rwanda, and South Africa allow safe experimentation with new financial products. Meanwhile, interoperability mandates, such as those introduced in Tanzania, help reduce transaction costs and expand access by enabling seamless transfers across mobile money providers. Without these reforms, digital financial services may remain fragmented and inaccessible to the underserved (Haider, 2025).

National Financial Inclusion Strategies and Central Bank Leadership

Government-led strategies are essential for sustained financial inclusion. Over 40 African countries have developed national financial inclusion strategies (NFIS) that set clear targets and outline stakeholder responsibilities (World Bank, 2022). Central banks play a vital leadership role in shaping regulatory frameworks, fostering innovation, and coordinating across sectors. Institutions like the Bank of Ghana and Central Bank of Kenya have pioneered digital finance reforms, often turning pilot initiatives into national programs. However, NFIS must include concrete implementation plans, measurable outcomes, and sustainable funding (Clancy et al., 2025). Alignment with broader development strategies enhances their relevance and impact.

Gender-Intentional and Youth-Inclusive Policy Design

Financial exclusion in Africa disproportionately affects women and youth. Women face systemic barriers to identification, credit, and ownership, while young people often lack the credentials required for formal financial access (Klapper et al., 2025; Yeboua & Cilliers, 2025). Addressing these gaps requires intentional policy design. Gender-focused strategies include legal reforms, financial education for women, and the development of tailored products such as privacy-protective savings accounts and informal-income-linked credit. Rwanda has led by integrating gender data into its financial sector planning.[1] For youth, school-linked savings programs, entrepreneurship finance, and integration of mobile wallets with educational IDs offer promising models for inclusion.[2]

Financial Consumer Protection and Literacy

As digital finance expands, users face increasing risks from fraud, hidden charges, and misinformation. Effective consumer protection frameworks must address these challenges with transparency standards, accessible

[1] Access to Finance Rwanda. (2021). FinScope Rwanda 2020: Gender Report. Retrieved from https://afr.rw/wp-content/uploads/2021/03/FinScope-Rwanda-2020-Gender-Report-Final.pdf.

[2] Innovations for Poverty Action. (2014). *The Impact of Youth Savings Accounts: Research Brief.* Retrieved from https://poverty-action.org/sites/default/files/publications/youthsavings_researchbrief_ipa_a4_141107.pdf.

complaints systems, and data privacy safeguards tailored to digital contexts (Rowena, 2025). Financial and digital literacy are equally critical. Public campaigns and school-based programs can equip users with the knowledge to navigate financial products confidently. In Kenya and Nigeria, telecom-led SMS tools and radio campaigns have successfully extended financial education to rural and underserved communities.[3]

Leveraging Technology and Innovation for Inclusion

Technology is a critical driver of Africa's financial inclusion journey. Innovations such as mobile money, digital credit, and fintech platforms have enabled millions to access financial services, often for the first time. These solutions have bypassed traditional banking constraints by offering convenient, low-cost, and accessible alternatives (Han, 2024; Helal & Versi, 2024). However, technology is not inherently inclusive. Without deliberate policy direction and user-centered design, digital tools may reinforce existing gaps or create new forms of exclusion (Aouinti, 2025). This section examines how Africa can strategically leverage existing and emerging technologies to build inclusive, scalable, and resilient financial systems, highlighting the opportunities and risks associated with these technologies.

Mobile Money: Africa's Financial Inclusion Flagship

Mobile money has revolutionized financial inclusion in Africa by providing accessible, low-cost financial services via mobile phones. Platforms such as M-Pesa, MTN Mobile Money, and Airtel Money have allowed millions to store, send, and receive money without needing a traditional bank account (Bwakira, 2024). They also support adjacent services like credit, savings, and bill payments. Governments have used mobile money to disburse social transfers, especially in remote areas (see Box 14.2). However, gaps remain in usage, rural access, and gender

[3] Faulu (2014). *Financial Literacy Opportunities for Rural Agripreneurs.* Retrieved from https://www.faulukenya.com/about-us/media/financial-literacy-opportunities-for-rural-agripreneurs/

Central Bank of Nigeria. (2016). *National Financial Literacy Framework.* Retrieved from https://www.cbn.gov.ng/out/2016/cfpd/financial%20literacy.pdf.

parity. Addressing challenges such as agent liquidity, transaction costs, and interoperability is essential. Tailored products that reflect local needs and improved infrastructure can further scale mobile money's transformative potential.

Box 14.2 Leveraging Mobile Money for Social Transfer Disbursement: Government Initiatives in Kenya, Niger, and Uganda

Governments have successfully utilized mobile money platforms to deliver social transfers, particularly in remote regions, thereby advancing financial inclusion and lowering transaction costs. In Kenya, for instance, the government used M-Pesa to distribute cash transfers to vulnerable groups, including during the COVID-19 pandemic, ensuring rapid, secure, and transparent fund delivery without requiring recipients to visit banks. In Niger, mobile money enabled the payment of government transfers, which not only saved recipients time but also contributed to improved household nutrition. In Uganda, expanding the network of mobile money agents in rural and low-income areas helped facilitate access to social transfers, though research indicates that agent availability must be supported by additional measures such as training and incentives to maximize impact. These examples demonstrate that integrating mobile money platforms with social protection initiatives can effectively extend services to underserved populations, enhance program efficiency, and empower recipients with more secure and flexible financial options.

Source Brooks et al. (2022) and Aker et al. (2016)

Agent Banking and Last-Mile Delivery

Agent banking extends financial access to underserved populations by using local businesses or individuals to provide services on behalf of formal institutions (Velmie, 2024). It reduces the need for costly brick-and-mortar branches while offering users personalized support, especially in rural and low-literacy communities. The agency banking model can bridge informal practices with formal systems.[4] However, ensuring agent liquidity, training, and trust is essential to success (Yazdanpanah, 2024). Governments can support scale-up through interoperable agent

[4] For further information on agency banking models and their impact on financial inclusion, see https://www.codebtech.com/shops-turned-banks-agency-banking-in-africa/

registries, fair compensation policies, and enabling regulation. Agent banking remains a crucial delivery model to achieve inclusive financial ecosystems across Africa's geographically and economically diverse settings (Msutwana, 2024).

Digital Identity and e-KYC

Digital identity is a foundational enabler of financial inclusion. Millions of Africans, especially women and rural dwellers, remain excluded from finance due to lack of formal ID (Pomerai, 2024). Digital identity systems such as the Ghana Card, Nigeria's NIN, and Kenya's Huduma Namba are beginning to address this barrier.[5] When integrated with mobile networks and e-KYC protocols, they enable cost-effective onboarding and remote account opening. However, challenges around data privacy, biometric errors, and exclusion risks persist. For impact, ID systems must be interoperable, accessible, and secure. Inclusive digital ID frameworks can greatly expand financial access, reduce fraud, and strengthen regulatory compliance across the continent (Venter, 2023).

Fintech and Inclusive Digital Platforms

Africa's fintech sector has grown rapidly, creating innovative solutions that enhance payments, savings, lending, and insurance (Fintech Africa, 2025). Companies like Flutterwave, Chipper Cash, and M-KOPA serve unbanked populations by using mobile platforms and alternative data. Pay-as-you-go solar financing, algorithmic microloans, and gamified savings apps are examples of inclusive fintech innovations.[6] While fintech offers immense promise, risks such as over-indebtedness, algorithmic discrimination, and weak consumer protection must be managed. Regulatory sandboxes, ethical design standards, and strategic partnerships are

[5] For further information on national digital identity initiatives, see Ghana's efforts to make the Ghana Card a multipurpose platform for seamless services (https://www.biometricupdate.com/202502/ghana-to-make-national-id-a-multipurpose-card-for-seamless-services) and Nigeria's launch of a multiuse biometric ID card to support economic and financial inclusion (https://www.biometricupdate.com/202501/nigeria-launching-multiuse-biometric-id-card-to-drive-economic-financial-inclusion).

[6] For more information on innovative funding approaches and FinTech innovations in emerging markets, see https://www.cgap.org/sites/default/files/publications/FN_Innovative%20Funding%20Approaches_final_0.pdf.

critical for scaling responsibly. With the right safeguards, fintech platforms can significantly reduce barriers to finance for women, youth, informal workers, and other underserved groups.

Emerging Technologies: Blockchain, AI, and Open Finance

Emerging technologies present new opportunities to transform Africa's financial systems. For instance, blockchain enables secure, low-cost, and transparent financial transactions.[7] Artificial intelligence is being used to create alternative credit scores, detect fraud, and personalize financial services (Wortmann, 2025). Open finance allows third-party providers to access financial data, fostering innovation and visibility for those with informal financial histories. However, inclusive data governance, algorithmic transparency, and institutional capacity are essential to avoid unintended exclusion. When designed with equity in mind, these technologies can advance financial inclusion and build more resilient digital economies.

Building Inclusive Ecosystems and Institutions

Achieving meaningful financial inclusion in Africa requires more than technology and regulation; it depends on functional ecosystems. A financial ecosystem consists of the infrastructure, institutions, and partnerships that support access to and effective use of financial services. These ecosystems must go beyond banks and fintechs to include government agencies, telecoms, civil society, educational systems, and regional bodies. This section explores how Africa can strengthen financial ecosystems through four strategic pathways: infrastructure and interoperability, integration with social and economic sectors, regional cooperation, and cross-sector partnerships. The goal is to align systems around inclusion so that financial services can contribute to development, equity, and economic resilience.

[7] For more information on recent advances in blockchain technology within Africa, see https://publication.aercafricalibrary.org/server/api/core/bitstreams/f79f78f1-59bb-436f-aaa6-50296bd7d112/content.

Infrastructure and Interoperability as Foundations

Robust digital infrastructure is the foundation of inclusive financial systems. This includes digital ID, instant payments, credit reference systems, and secure data-sharing frameworks. Interoperability ensures users can transact across providers, institutions, and platforms without friction. Investments in rural connectivity, such as mobile towers and solar-powered kiosks, are essential for reaching underserved areas. Governments must treat digital infrastructure as a public good, working with telecoms and development banks to extend access. Without shared rails and platforms, innovation remains fragmented, costs stay high, and excluded populations continue to face barriers.

Linking Finance to Social, Agricultural, and MSME Systems

Financial inclusion has the greatest impact when embedded into real-life systems. Digitized social protection schemes can introduce excluded populations, especially women, to formal financial services. Zambia's Social Cash Transfer Program, for instance, links mobile wallets with broader service offerings like insurance and savings.[8] In agriculture, platforms such as Tulaa and DigiFarm provide bundled financial tools that support farmers with input credit, insurance, and market access.[9] For MSMEs, digital payments, mobile POS systems, and inventory apps improve formalization and credit access (Arner et al., 2022). Linking financial services to productive sectors enhances adoption, builds resilience, and turns finance into a tool for empowerment and economic participation.

Regional Cooperation and Harmonization

Regional integration plays a crucial role in expanding financial inclusion. Initiatives like the African Continental Free Trade Area (AfCFTA) and the

[8] Read on the Zambia Social Cash Transfer (SCT) program at https://documents1.worldbank.org/curated/en/099534410262224257/pdf/IDU06413176f065c104eb30b8aa0193dffe6e272.pdf.

[9] To read more on Tulaa, DigiFarm, and other digital agricultural platform companies, see https://www.econstor.eu/bitstream/10419/246478/1/ZEF-Working-Paper-209.pdf.

Pan-African Payment and Settlement System (PAPSS) create opportunities for cross-border payments and financial connectivity. Regional blocs such as the Economic Community of West African States (ECOWAS) and Southern African Development Community (SADC) can harmonize regulations for mobile money, remittances, and digital identity systems. The West African Economic and Monetary Union (WAEMU)'s shared regulatory framework, for instance, enables mobile money services to scale across West Africa.[10] Regional cooperation also supports knowledge exchange and capacity building through platforms like the Alliance for Financial Inclusion. Harmonized frameworks reduce fragmentation, lower access barriers, and allow innovations to scale across multiple markets (Challapalli, 2023).

Multi-Stakeholder and Cross-Sectoral Partnerships

Inclusive financial systems require collaboration across sectors. Governments, private companies, civil society, and development partners each play distinct but complementary roles. Public–private partnerships can digitize services like school fee payments or social transfers, combining scale with accessibility. Civil society organizations support user education, monitor financial inclusion outcomes, and ensure underserved voices are heard. Development partners can invest in infrastructure, convene innovation labs, and support experimentation and evaluation. When coordinated effectively, multi-stakeholder partnerships reduce duplication, align incentives, and deliver financial solutions that are inclusive, sustainable, and demand-driven. Building trust and cooperation across stakeholders is essential for ecosystem-wide impact.

Pathways Forward and Recommendations

Strategic Priorities for Stakeholders

Accelerating financial inclusion in Africa requires collective action from governments, regulators, financial service providers, development partners, and civil society. Governments must prioritize financial inclusion

[10] See page 27 of The State of the Industry Report on Mobile Money 2024, available at https://www.gsma.com/sotir/wp-content/uploads/2024/03/GSMA-SOTIR-2024_Report.pdf.

as a development goal by investing in digital ID systems, interoperable payment platforms, and rural connectivity. Central banks should enable innovation through risk-based regulations that protect consumers and promote coordination. Financial providers must focus on user-centered products that reflect the realities of underserved populations. Development partners should shift from fragmented pilot funding to support scalable infrastructure and regulatory innovation. Civil society plays a vital role in literacy, advocacy, and bridging the gap between users and institutions. Through alignment and collaboration, financial ecosystems can become more equitable, inclusive, and sustainable across the continent.

Guiding Principles for Inclusive Financial Systems

To ensure impact, inclusive financial systems must be built on five core principles. First is inclusion by design. Services must intentionally address the needs of excluded groups such as women, youth, and rural populations. Second is interoperability and integration across providers, sectors, and data systems to improve accessibility and reduce fragmentation. Third, protection and empowerment are essential, with strong consumer safeguards, financial education, and ethical data governance. Fourth is ecosystem thinking, embedding finance within existing social, agricultural, and educational structures to increase adoption and relevance. Lastly, financial inclusion must be treated as a public good, warranting public investment in digital infrastructure and regulation. These principles offer a roadmap for inclusive, resilient financial systems.

A Continental Vision

Africa stands at a strategic inflection point where it can transform financial inclusion through a unified continental approach. The AfCFTA, along with digital innovations such as the Pan-African Payment and Settlement System (PAPSS), presents opportunities to facilitate cross-border financial access and reduce costs. Harmonizing identity systems and regulatory standards across countries will help break down jurisdictional barriers. Regional leaders like Kenya, Ghana, and Rwanda can guide peer countries through knowledge sharing. Institutions such as the African Union and regional economic communities must play coordinating roles. With the right leadership and equity-centered policies, Africa can set a global example in inclusive digital finance by building systems that prioritize people, drive shared prosperity, and advance economic justice.

Conclusion

Africa's financial inclusion landscape is undergoing rapid and transformative change. The continent has made remarkable progress, with millions of people gaining access to financial services through mobile money, agent networks, and innovative fintech solutions. Hitherto, as this chapter has demonstrated, access alone is no longer sufficient. The future of financial inclusion in Africa must be defined not by the number of accounts opened, but by how financial services are used, whether they deliver real value, and whether they empower people to participate fully and equitably in economic life.

The journey ahead demands a paradigm shift from fragmented, product-led approaches to coordinated, ecosystem-based strategies. It requires stakeholders to look beyond short-term access targets and embrace long-term system building. This includes regulatory frameworks that promote innovation while safeguarding users, digital public infrastructure that serves as a shared utility, and products designed with empathy for the realities of low-income, excluded populations.

Inclusion must be intentional. Women, youth, informal workers, and rural populations remain systematically underserved. Their financial needs must not only be recognized but prioritized in product design, policy formulation, and resource allocation. Inclusion must also be safe. As more Africans engage with digital financial tools, ensuring data protection, transparency, and recourse becomes imperative for building trust and avoiding harm.

The chapter has outlined a strategic vision: build inclusive infrastructure, foster enabling regulation, integrate financial services into real-world systems like agriculture and social protection, and ensure that innovation is accompanied by protection and empowerment. It has called on governments to lead, the private sector to innovate responsibly, civil society to advocate and educate, and development partners to support systems change.

Importantly, Africa need not follow the path of others. It can chart a uniquely African model of inclusive finance, one that harnesses mobile technology, community networks, local ingenuity, and regional cooperation to reach the furthest margins. The building blocks are already in place. What is needed now is ambition, alignment, and action. If achieved, inclusive finance will not only improve livelihoods. It will support entrepreneurship, reduce inequality, build resilience, and accelerate progress toward the Sustainable Development Goals. It will empower a generation to imagine, create, and thrive.

References

AfricaNenda. (2023). *What does it feel like to be unbanked?* https://www.africanenda.org/en/blog/2023/what-does-it-feel-like-to-be-unbanked

Aker, J. C., Boumnijel, R., McClelland, A., & Tierney, N. (2016). Payment mechanisms and antipoverty programs: Evidence from a mobile money cash transfer experiment in Niger. *Economic Development and Cultural Change, 65*(1), 1–37.

Anakpo, G., Xhate, Z., & Mishi, S. (2023). The policies, practices, and challenges of digital financial inclusion for sustainable development: The case of the developing economy. *FinTech, 2*(2), 327–343.

Aouinti, A. (2025). *Accelerating Action to Bridge the Financial Inclusion Gap.* https://www.africanenda.org/en/blog/2025/accelerating-action-to-bridge-the-financial-inclusion-gap

Arner, D. W., Animashaun, S., Charamba, K., & Cai, Y. (2022). MSME access to finance: The role of digital payments. *United Nations, Economic and Social Commission for Asia and the Pacific, MSME Financing Series*, (7).

Batagoda, U. (2024). *The intersection of digital identity and financial inclusion: New trends, opportunities, and challenges.* https://www.linkedin.com/pulse/intersection-digital-identity-financial-inclusion-new-upul-batagoda-51wtc

Brooks, W., Donovan, K., Johnson, T. R., & Oluoch-Aridi, J. (2022). Cash transfers as a response to COVID-19: Experimental evidence from Kenya. *Journal of Development Economics, 158*, Article 102929.

Bwakira, C. (2024). *Interoperability between mobile money and card is enabling Africa's access to the global financial system.* https://www.cnbcafrica.com/2024/interoperability-between-mobile-money-and-card-is-enabling-africas-access-to-the-global-financial-system/

Challapalli, S. (2023). Benefits and constraints associated with the harmonization of financial regulations: An overview. *Asian Journal of Economics, Business and Accounting, 23*(15), 49–56.

Clancy, M., Cain, R., & Thompson, S. (2025). *Central Bank Regulatory & Supervisory Outlook 2025: Banks, Payment and e-money firms, retail credit firms, investment firms and securities markets.* https://www.arthurcox.com/insights/central-bank-regulatory-supervisory-outlook-2025-banks-payment-and-e-money-firms-retail-credit-firms-investment-firms-and-securities-markets/

Cracknell, D. (2023). *Financial inclusion, interoperability and market development in the East African community*. https://publication.aercafricalibrary.org/items/879c66e7-6a38-4743-8c9e-902530266f3f

D'Silva, D., Filková, Z., Packer, F., & Tiwari, S. (2019). The design of digital financial infrastructure: Lessons from India. *BIS paper*. https://www.bis.org/publ/bppdf/bispap106.pdf

European Investment Bank. (2024). *Digital financial services in Africa*. https://www.eib.org/files/publications/20240033_finance_in_africa_chapter5_en.pdf

Fintech Africa. (2025). *A look at Africa's most valuable Fintech Unicorns of 2025*. https://fintechnews.africa/45050/fintechafrica/a-look-at-africas-most-valuable-fintech-unicorns-of-2025/

Global Partnership for Financial Inclusion (GPFI). (2021). *The impact of COVID-19 on digital financial inclusion*. https://www.gpfi.org/sites/gpfi/files/sites/default/files/5_WB%20Report_The%20impact%20of%20COVID-19%20on%20digital%20financial%20inclusion.pdf

Goodwell. (2025). *Financial inclusion: Driving economic growth for individuals and underserved communities across Africa*. https://goodwell.nl/news/financial-inclusion-driving-economic-growth-for-individuals-and-underserved-communities-across-africa/

GSMA. (2024). *The mobile economy Sub-Saharan Africa 2024*. https://www.gsma.com/solutions-and-impact/connectivity-for-good/mobile-economy/sub-saharan-africa/

Ha, D., & Nguyen, K. (2024). Unlocking financial access in a developing country amidst COVID-19: The impacts of financial literacy and fintech. *Journal of the Asia Pacific Economy*, 1–37.

Haider, A. (2025). *Key regulations shaping the Fintech Industry in 2025*. https://www.linkedin.com/pulse/key-regulations-shaping-fintech-industry-2025-azeem-haider-7vsee

Han, S. (2024). Digital finance and financial inclusion in Africa. *KIEP Research Paper, World Economy Brief (WEB)*, 24–15.

Helal, R., & Versi, A. (2024). *Going digital—Africa's path to growth and prosperity*. https://african.business/2024/07/african-banker/going-digital-africas-path-to-growth-and-prosperity

Klapper, L., Mbabazi, L. N., & Nsanzabaganwa, M. (2025). *Financial inclusion in Africa: Progress, challenges, and the road ahead*. https://blogs.worldbank.org/en/developmenttalk/financial-inclusion-in-africa--progress--challenges--and-the-roa0

Mahlangu, B. (2024). *Connecting a continent: The mobile revolution transforming Africa's digital landscape*. https://www.finextra.com/blogposting/27154/connecting-a-continent-the-mobile-revolution-transforming-africas-digital-landscape

Mensah, S. (2025). *The imperative for progressive regulations*. https://www.africanenda.org/en/blog/2025/the-imperative-for-progressive-regulations

Msutwana, M. (2024). *How agency banking expands access*. https://onafriq.com/insights/article/closing-the-financial-access-gap-in-developing-economies

Natalucci, F., Qureshi, M. S., & Suntheim, F. (2024). *Rising cyber threats pose serious concerns for financial stability*. https://www.imf.org/en/Blogs/Articles/2024/04/09/rising-cyber-threats-pose-serious-concerns-for-financial-stability

Nesbitt, P. (2022). *The future of finance is human-centered*. https://www.forbes.com/councils/forbesfinancecouncil/2022/06/23/the-future-of-finance-is-human-centered/

Onyango, A. O. (2025). *Mobile money is transforming financial inclusion in Sub-Saharan Africa*. https://www.techforgood.net/thoughtleadership/mobile-money-is-transforming-financial-inclusion-in-sub-saharan-africa

Özyilmaz, H. (2024). *How do instant interoperable payment systems transform modern economies?* https://poverty-action.org/sites/default/files/2024-11/2024-10_fit_in_initiative_how_iips_transform_modern_eco.pdf

Pomerai, M. (2024). Nature of rural women's financial exclusion in Zimbabwe. *International Journal of Research and Innovation in Social Science, 8*(4), 1770–1776.

Rowena, A. (2025). *Fraud prevention strategies for 2025 to combat emerging digital threats*. https://fintechnews.hk/32208/regtech/fraud-prevention-strategies-2025/

Tugendhat, E. (2024). *Inclusive growth: A strategy for 2025 that's both timely and timeless*. https://thepalladiumgroupusa.com/news/Inclusive-Growth-A-Strategy-for-2025-Thats-Both-Timely-and-Timeless

Velmie. (2024). *Agency banking in Africa: Trends to watch in 2025 and beyond*. https://www.velmie.com/post/agency-banking-in-africa-trends-to-watch-in-2025-and-beyond

Venter, D. (2023). *The role of digital identity in promoting financial access and inclusion in Africa*. https://www.finextra.com/blogposting/25115/the-role-of-digital-identity-in-promoting-financial-access-and-inclusion-in-africa

Weisman-Pitts, J. (2024). *Addressing the digital divide in access to banking and financial services*. https://www.globalbankingandfinance.com/addressing-the-digital-divide-in-access-to-banking-and-financial-services

Women's World Banking. (2023). *From exclusion to empowerment: The meaning of financial inclusion*. https://www.womensworldbanking.org/insights/from-exclusion-to-empowerment-the-meaning-of-financial-inclusion/

World Bank. (2022). *National financial inclusion strategies resource center*. https://www.worldbank.org/en/topic/financialinclusion/brief/financial-inclusion-strategies-resource-center

World Bank. (2024). *Data from the Global Findex 2021: The impact of mobile money in Sub-Saharan Africa*. https://www.worldbank.org/en/publication/globalfindex/brief/data-from-the-global-findex-2021-the-impact-of-mobile-money-in-sub-saharan-africa

Wortmann, K. (2025). *African payment trends for 2025: Transitioning to a touch-free economy*. https://africa.businessinsider.com/local/leaders/african-payment-trends-for-2025-transitioning-to-a-touch-free-economy/j8b3c8f

Yazdanpanah, A. (2024). *Agent of change: The rise of agency banking in Africa*. https://www.mobifin.com/blog/agent-of-change-the-rise-of-agency-banking-in-africa/

Yeboua, K., & Cilliers, J. (2025). *Gender economic participation*. https://futures.issafrica.org/thematic/guide.pdf?thematic=16-gender&topic=05-economic-participation

Index

I. N. Yakubu (ed.), *Banking on Inclusion*, Sustainable Development Goals Series, https://doi.org/10.1007/978-3-031-96716-0

GPSR Compliance

The European Union's (EU) General Product Safety Regulation (GPSR) is a set of rules that requires consumer products to be safe and our obligations to ensure this.

If you have any concerns about our products, you can contact us on ProductSafety@springernature.com

In case Publisher is established outside the EU, the EU authorized representative is:

Springer Nature Customer Service Center GmbH
Europaplatz 3
69115 Heidelberg, Germany

Batch number: 10755348

Printed by Printforce, the Netherlands